THE PROGRE[illegible] UNDERGROUND

KEV ROWLAND

Vol 2

Edited by Jonathan Downes
Typeset by Jonathan Downes, Kev Rowland
Cover by Martin Springett
This edition - layout by SPiderKaT for CFZ Communications
Using Microsoft Word 2000, Microsoft Publisher 2000, Adobe Photoshop CS.

First published by Gonzo Multimedia 2019

c/o Brooks City,
6th Floor New Baltic House,
65 Fenchurch Street,
London EC3M 4BE
Fax: +44 (0)191 5121104
Tel: +44 (0) 191 5849144
International Numbers:
Germany: Freephone 08000 825 699
USA: Freephone 18666 747 289

ISBN: 978-1-908728-88-3

Dedicated to my incredible wife Sara: without her support, Feedback would never have kept going for all the years it did. It is also dedicated to my amazing daughters Nicola, Elizabeth, Hannah and Amanda, who grew up thinking that having a dad stuck at a computer all the time, while playing strange and often unusual music very loudly, was the normal thing to do.

Foreword

I have been privileged to have lived with a copy of this book for a few months now, and to have known Kevin for a very long time.

I remember the first time I met him: his enthusiasm and knowledge of "the music" was addictive. I was trudging around the lower ends of the British Neo Prog scene at the time, my then band Casual Affair had been working hard for close to ten years, released a vinyl single, an album, even a long form VHS concert video, and generally whored our arses off trying to get an elusive major deal, disillusioned and exhausted by music, and my private life a "car crash" of epic proportions. We (The Band) played to the same fifty people wherever in the country we played, response was always great, but we could not break out of that circle. The British Prog scene was dying on its feet, and so were we.

Kev offered a personal and professional glimmer of light, a genuine, honest hard-working guy, whose love for music matched my own. His knowledge of the obscure bands rivalled mine and he instantly felt like a "brother from a different mother". Our relationship became more professional when he kindly agreed to represent my new band (following the demise of Casual Affair) Freewill, working on our newsletters and helping us with gigs.

That band folded quickly, but our friendship became stronger. I was a witness at his wedding to the ever-patient Sara, and when I eventually got married and had children, he was the obvious choice to be 'God Father' to one of my sons.

Credo were just about to start a bit of a trajectory at this point, and the pages you are about to read not only chronicle a period of my life with Casual Affair, Freewill and ultimately Credo, but more importantly the entire underground Neo Prog and Rock scene in the UK.

I remember many happy hours with Kev, at gigs I was playing, bands we were watching, family days, drunken nights (which I won't elaborate on here!). All fuelled by his encyclopaedic knowledge of the music scene, interest in the bands, and the people involved.

Sadly, for me, and I suspect for us both, Kev moved to the other side of the world just as Credo hit a run of great gigs and reviews around the world. We still have kept in touch, and my abiding wish is that one day I will look out into an audience and see him there again.

Until then, be like me, gorge yourself on the contents and memories in this book, relive those timeless moments, see if the predictions for world fame ever came true, and reflect on the reviewer's initial thoughts on albums that have since become classics.

All that is left for me as I enter my twenty-fifth year as vocalist with Credo is to say, thanks Kev for the memories, and then, even more thanks for putting those memories into a book we can all enjoy.

Hope you enjoy the book, buckle up tight, and, come on, let's party like it's 1992.........

Mark Colton, Credo

Introduction

Here is the second volume of my three-book series, documenting the progressive rock scene of 1991-2006, with all the progressive reviews and interviews I wrote during that period. I may no longer agree with the sentiments in some cases, but here they are as they originally appeared, warts and all. It doesn't profess to cover every important band and release during that period, but instead is a reflection of material I either purchased or was sent to review. If you already have the first volume in the series then you already know the story below, and if not why not? Where else can you find reviews like these? Read on, I hope you enjoy it.

At the end of the Sixties, musicians realised that they were no longer constrained by having to fit into defined musical forms and the three-minute single. Instead, the only limits were their musical ability and imagination: this led to an explosion of music as styles as diverse as jazz, blues and classical crashed headlong into electric and eclectic instrumentation. Progressive rock was born, and not only was it embraced by fans worldwide but also by critics (at least for a while) and bands as diverse as Jethro Tull, Genesis, Pink Floyd, King Crimson, ELP and Gentle Giant among many others found huge success and sales. However, 1976 was year zero for prog, with punk supposedly sweeping away the 'dinosaurs' of music.

As far as many critics (and it must be said many fans as well), this was the end for the prog scene, although some bands from the Seventies still found huge success in both albums and ticket sales. The only prog band recognised as such to gain major success within the UK was Marillion, but once Fish had parted ways, they also suffered the same fate. One wonders if anyone had been brave enough to tarnish Radiohead with the 'progressive' label if they would have had success.

After leaving university in 1984, I found myself working in London, and thought if I joined Mensa, I might be able to make new friends. Although I had little in common with many of the 35,000 members, I soon discovered there were sub-clubs called Special Interest Groups, and in 1988 saw an advert asking if there was anyone interested in rock music. Enough people replied, and there was soon a new group, RockSIG. I wanted to be involved and had the taste having written an article on Carmen for the Jethro Tull fanzine 'A New Day', so inundated the secretary with pieces. The first newsletter came out in October 1988 and at 28 pages was respectable enough but inside #5 (April 1990) the secretary announced her resignation. I had enjoyed writing and thought I would give it a shot. After all, it couldn't be much hassle, right? I produced #6 in Nov 1990 - it came in at 60 pages and I soon realised this length could not last. I was right. It got bigger!

I was with another Mensan one night, and he asked if I was aware of the underground progressive rock scene? This was 1991, when the music press refused to acknowledge that such a thing dared to exist and was pre-internet. He lent me some music by Galahad and Twelfth Night, and some copies of a fanzine called 'Blindsight'. I loved the music I heard and wrote to Galahad to buy their CD and cassette and was soon corresponding with Stu Nicholson. Shortly thereafter, a demo arrived, 'From The River To The Sea' by Big Big Train. I knew nothing of the band, but they were sending me music. What would happen if I used the addresses in Blindsight and wrote to bands to see if they wanted me to write about what they were doing? I could never have imagined what would happen.

A reader poll in #11 gave our newsletter a name and over the years 'Feedback' grew until it reached a peak with #50, which gave postal workers hernias in August 1998 and was some 284 pages long! I became very involved with some bands, trying to get gigs for both Freewill (and running their newsletter) and Credo, and writing the blurb for a Galahad compilation. In 2006, some sixteen years, 80+ issues and more than 11,000 pages of print later I stepped down, as we moved to New Zealand.

The support of my amazing wife and family over those sixteen years must be recognised, as I could not have done it without them. Sara became used to our bedroom being awash with CDs, photos, press releases etc., and by the end I was on my fifth computer, having started running the mag using an electronic typewriter with 1K of memory!!

Many of these bands are no longer in existence, while others are still going strong, but very few ever reached the wider success and acclaim they deserved. As Feedback was produced officially as a "newsletter" for a closed group, it did mean that those who were members were treated in my writing more as friends than public, and that they all knew something about the scene either through direct involvement or from reading what I had written previously. This book captures a time gone by, and one that now we have ready access to information can never exist again, but back then it was very special indeed.

Album Reviews

ICON

ICON

This album should capture the imagination of many fans who will not have heard of the name before, well it is a new band after all. But what makes this special is that this is the first time that John Wetton and Geoffrey Downes have worked together like this since John last left Asia. Sure, there are some important guests playing their part but Steve Christey (Jadis) and John Mitchell (Arena, Kino) are there as the full members together with Annie Haslam (Renaissance), Ian McDonald (Foreigner, King Crimson), Hugh McDowell (ELO) and Mike Stobbie (Pallas). Musically virtually any of these songs could have sat on the debut Asia album, and are all played with a lot of punch and drama. There certainly is not much in the way of fancy soloing, this is all about good honest rock music played in the definite fashion of Asia. I am not sure what John Payne will be thinking about all of this, as he is still the vocalist of Asia, and here he sees his bandmate going off and revisiting the glories of times past. It is just impossible to play this album without a huge smile on the face as it is just glorious. If you loved the band of twenty plus years ago then this is an album that you simply can't live without as anthem follows poptastic melodic anthem. Only two of the songs are over six minutes long, and "Meet Me At Midnight" is only just over two minutes thirty, but John and Geoffrey were always about great hooks and less of the epic, and in mixing acoustic guitars and solid riffs with great hooks and overbearing keyboards plus John's vocals means that this is music to savour. You may have guessed that I loved this from start to end, and if you are an Asia fan then you will as well.

#84, July 2005

IGZIT-NINE
IGZIT-NINE

This is the debut album by Igzit-Nine and again shows that there are plenty of strong jazz-fusion bands in Japan. Since the recording of the album the rhythm section has been replaced by the guys from Sixnorth – I do not know the reason why as the ones on the album seem to be doing a strong job to me. This album has much more of a progressive feel about it than the others reviewed in this issue, much more in the fusion vein than just avant garde jazz (I use the word 'just' very loosely of course). With each song about five minutes long, it allows the band to stretch out while not getting too far away from the theme. This is music that is structured and complex, with many layers so that the listener needs to pay attention to get the most out of it. It is music that both jazz fans and progheads will enjoy while those into fusion will have a blast. Not too far out of the norm, its' very listenable nature makes this an album to savour.

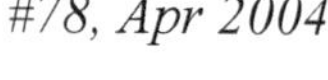
#78, Apr 2004

ILÚVATAR
ILÚVATAR

Ilúvatar are an American outfit who obviously love UK prog with a passion, as they take influences such as Genesis, Floyd and Marillion and mix them with others closer to home such as Kansas, Styx and Rush. The result is a hard-hitting yet extremely melodic album that would happily grace the collection of any lover of melodic or prog lover. Phew! Stop for breath. The reason I am so excited about this, is that until Larry sent me this CD, I had never heard of them, and he has a real gem here. "In The Eye" is literally blasting out of the speakers as I write this, and it shows that prog does not have to be sanitised and AOR-ised to death but can be played with a passion and conviction. If this band are half as good in a live environment as they are on this debut CD, then they must be superb. This starts off with the instrumental "Ilúvatar", which is lulling, dreamlike and full of keyboards but it is a plot to make the listener turn up the stereo. Next up is "In The Eye", which is in three parts. The first of these, "Look Us In The Eye", starts off gently enough (although the drumming gives some idea of what is going to happen) and then the guitar breaks free and Glenn McLaughlin's strong clear vocals rides over the maelstrom. I love this song! It reminds me of Kansas at their hardest rocking best, and that is just about the ultimate in American rock, believe me. "Eagle" shows another side of Ilúvatar, as Glenn is accompanied by gently picked guitar (similar in style to Rush's "Soliloquy"). Each song somehow seems better than the last – I have not been this excited about an American album in years. What do I have to do to make you go out and buy it now?! Kinesis Discs have a real discovery here, and I look forward to the next release by a band that could become huge! This is a band to look out for, and if you like American rock then you simply must have this CD as it is brilliance of the highest order.

#25, Oct 1994

ILÚVATAR
CHILDREN

A while ago I raved about Ilúvatar's debut CD, so I was extremely pleased to receive the follow-up. Since the debut, bassist Mick Trimble has been replaced by Dean Morekas, but apart from this the line-up is still the same. Vocalist Glenn McLaughlin sounds uncannily like Martin Wilson from GLD, but I am willing for forgive him for his sins. Ilúvatar's great strengths, as shown on the debut, is the ability to write great songs that are of interest to the prog fan while maintaining that hint of American rock/ AOR that will find them new fans. For the most part the guitarwork seems a little too subdued for my liking, but on "Cracker" it is rightly back where it belongs with Ilúvatar, namely centre stage. Overall this is an enjoyable album, and one that I expect I will be playing quite a lot, but I do not get that feeling of extreme brilliance that I felt with the first. Ilúvatar have a lot to offer but they do need to crank up that guitar a little more. I should make mention of the artwork, which on the inlay and on the CD itself is outstanding, and this time manages to impress more than the music,

#33, Feb 1996

ILÚVATAR
SIDESHOW

This is a mid-priced CD designed to satisfy the band's growing number of fans who are waiting impatiently for the follow-up to 'Children'. Their self-titled debut is one of my favourite American progressive releases, so I was looking forward to this one with interest as it contains four live cuts, with three remixes and a new song completing the album. These live songs are interesting as it sees the guitar much higher in the mix, proving that these guys do not wimp out when it comes to concerts, unlike some.

It is also interesting to hear the one cover version, namely "Sparks", an instrumental from 'Tommy', an unlikely source for a prog band but it works well. Ilúvatar are very much a Nineties band, taking the rock element and mixing it with IQ yet at the same time nodding towards AOR. Very American, but it works extremely well. The fretless bass on "All We Are" is very effective, as they even manage to capture a recent Yes sound. As a mid-price introduction then this is worth seeking, although if you have never heard of the band but are feeling brave then I urge you to discover their debut. Their next album (due later this year) will be the last release on Kinesis as Larry Kolota, label boss, has decided to have a private life back again as he no longer has the time to pursue his hobby. Personally, I would like to take this opportunity to thank Larry for all the great music he has given us over the years and wish him all the best for the future.

#50, Aug 1998

ILÚVATAR
A STORY TWO DAYS WIDE...

So, the last release ever from Kinesis. Larry Kolota has decided to call it a day and all those in the prog world will miss the releases from this high-quality label. He has managed to go out on a real high as well, as this album by Ilúvatar lives up to the promise of their superb debut album some years ago. I have been a bit disappointed with the intervening releases but with this one they have again struck that rich vein of tunes and musical excellence which will have all progheads up and dancing (or at least nodding appreciatively in time to the music). It captures all that is good about modern 'neo-prog': there are some rocky sections, some that sound as if they have been listening to classic Marillion, and others that come totally out of left field. "Better Days" is full of these, with some great keyboard sounds, but when it is back to the chorus it is all gentle and light with harmony vocals. Glenn has always had a great voice and here he can show it off. Only one song over ten minutes long ("Indian Rain" is a nearly impressive fifteen), but it is all about quality and not length. There is still plenty of time for interplay, musical jousting and switches of time signature and melody, along with everything else that will keep the proghead amused. A wonderful album that will be a great addition to the collection of those into progressive rock. I do not know which label will be releasing the next Ilúvatar album, but based on this record companies will be beating a path to their door.

#57, Mar 2000

ILUZJON
CITY ZEN

I know that I have said this many times, but there is some wonderful music coming out of Poland, and this is yet another band that I have discovered due to my great friend Artur Chachlowski. All the lyrics are in English, and these have been reproduced in English, but unfortunately their site is only available in Polish, so I do not have a great deal to go on. At the time of recording they were a trio, but since then they have lost their guitarist/bassist (bit careless), so instead of a photo of him on the site there is instead a large '?'. That all being put to one side, what we have here is very accessible, very enjoyable prog music. They are obviously hugely influenced by Pendragon, combined with a love of the gentler side of King Crimson and have melded these together in an album that is both light and layered. "If" is a wonderfully controlled ballad with a Floyd-like feel with good vocals and Crimson-style powerful guitar, but even although there is the feeling that the band can blast it out, they are much happier at the softer end of the spectrum.

#86, Feb 2006

IMAGIN'ARIA
PROGETTO T.I.'A.

This is the fourth album by Italian band Imagin'aria but is the first I have heard from them. According to what I have been reading on the web, the previous releases have been symphonic hard rock with some prog influences – but if that is the case then the band have totally turned that around as while there are some undoubted hard rock influences, especially with the guitars, this is now much more of a prog album that has been influenced by PFM, Eloy and Floyd. Apparently, this is a concept album, based on a science fiction story about constellations, planets and the close relationship between humans and artificial intelligence, but it is all sung in Italian, so I do not have any idea as to what is going on. The start of the booklet contains two pages of text, so I presume that this gives the background, but as that too is in Italian, I am none the wiser. Musically this album covers many bases, with gentle almost folky music giving way something that is more powerful. The vocals are very good, and it is strange to note that this is a standard rock line-up with singer, two guitarists, bass and drums with no keyboard player in sight (the sounds that are used are apparently triggered by the guitars). The more I have played it, the more I got out of it, and musically it is very good indeed. If this had been sung in English, then I am sure that we would be reading a lot more about it as this is a very positive work. If you enjoy your prog European and do not mind the language difficulty, then this is worth seeking out.
#89, Sep 2006

INCANDESCENT SKY
PATHS AND ANGLES

This is the second album from Incandescent Sky, and is an interesting atmospheric trawl through different styles of prog music. Sometimes there is the feeling that this is a band that has been very influenced by Ozric Tentacles, with dreamy passages and gentle meandering percussion yet there are other times when the band is right there in your face with a guitar driven attack and extremely accessible melodies. They also sometimes move gently into the New Age end of space rock, which is in direct comparison to other material. The band seem to be very much at home no matter what style they are playing, and for an instrumental album it is certainly extremely varied and, for the most part, interesting. It did take me a while to get into this, just because there are so many styles, but if you enjoy King Crimson, Porcupine Tree or want to find out about a band trying to bring together many styles then this could be for you.
#87, Apr 2006

INES PROJECT
SLIPPING INTO THE UNKNOWN

I remember reviewing this band's debut album 'Hunting The Fox' some eight years ago when they were just called Ines and were signed to Peter Wustmann's Music Is Intelligence label (which sadly collapsed in 1999). This is their second album for Tempus Fugit, following on from 'The Flow' which came out in 1999 and the band have been renamed to avoid any confusions with other acts featuring a singer called Ines. This album has been recorded using guest male vocalists for the most part, with Ines writing the music and her husband Hansi providing the lyrics. It is hard to describe this, as although there are definite progressive elements that have been influenced by Eastern and Asian styles, there are mainstream sounds which are combined into a melodic whole. The vocals are calm and gentle, well sung, and sometimes contrasting with what is going on underneath and at others in perfect harmony. It is not the most exciting rock album I have heard but it is one that invites the listener to play close attention and then play it again when it has finished. An album that deserves to be heard, at least. *#70, Oct 2002*

THE INHABITANTS OF YIP
A FISH IN THE SKY

Avalon Records, the label set up by Galahad, have now released the debut album by The Inhabitants of Yip, 'A Fish In The Sky', and it is a good solid slice of rock. But what type of rock? TIOY do not seem to be content to restrict themselves to any one style of music, which means that from opening with a Zeppelin style number ("The Mysteries") they move through prog and psychedelia with nods to the Sixties along the way. This may be great fun to them, and enjoyable to those who have wide ranging tastes, but what about those (who seem to be the clear majority) who only buy or listen to one style of music? Hopefully, the proghead will investigate further and discover that TIOY are attempting to progress through and master many differing sounds. But will the average punter who may enjoy the pop rock of "Flying In The Moonlight" also listen to the psychedelia of "Terrifically Amazing"? Overall, I found it a very enjoyable album and I look forward to the next one with interest.*#36, Aug 1996*

INKÁBB HOLNAP
TOMORROW INSTEAD

Melodic instrumental prog (apart from one song which features two female singers), this is extremely polished music from Hungary. It is an album that can be drifted into, as it lulls away at times or holds the listener spellbound as it drives long with some soaring guitar lines. Almost Camel-esque, this is music that progheads need to discover. There have been some great prog bands coming out of Hungary over recent years and this must be one of the finest. The guitar can be soothing a la Gary Chandler or cutting while the

rhythm section keeps it driving along. There is some interesting interplay with the keyboards, and the feeling that the band are going to fall into jazz territory, but although they do flirt with it at times, they never go the whole hog. This is an album that works on all levels.
#78, Apr 2004

INTERPOSE+
INTERPOSE+
Interpose+ first came together in 1986 when Tanaka Kenji (guitar) and Sato Katsu (drums), both from the band Libido, decided that they wanted to perform something that was musically different to what they had been doing before. They got a band together, but by 1990 they had broken up, then started over again in 1991 only for that line-up to fold the following year. Eventually Tanaka and Sato met in 2001 and decided to try it again, and although they still seem fraught with line-up problems (both the keyboard player and bassist have left since the album was recorded) they do at least now have an album to show for all their efforts over the last twenty years. Singer Sayuri Aruga has a wonderfully clear voice, and she certainly rises above all that is going on beneath her. It is also noticeable that a key part of the sound on the opening number "Aircon" is my favourite Japanese violinist, Akihisa Tsuboy of KBB who certainly adds an extra facet. But the band are more than capable of standing on their own and even though the vocals are in Japanese this in no way detracts from what is a very fine debut. Just five songs (with two of them instrumentals), spread over 47 minutes, the band have enough room to be able to spread out yet also stay focussed on the task in hand. Musically they are a classically based prog band, but also bringing in elements of RIO and even Renaissance. All the guys are strong musicians, with the bass particularly important in underpinning the whole sound, and Sayuri is a real find. This release is one of the best Japanese prog albums around
#86, Feb 2006

INTO ETERNITY
INTO ETERNITY
No press release, but I believe this album came out in the States two years ago and has now been released in Europe by Dutch label DVS Records. There are lots of keyboards and melodies, and the band at times manage to come across as a powerful prog metal act, yet at others they are much more into death metal territory. This is heightened using two distinctly different vocalists, and while lead singer Tim Roth has the pure sounds, it is the gruff growls that are set against him that takes this onto another level. Yes, they can be pleasant, witness the acoustic guitar and harmonies at the beginning of "Left Behind", but it is much more fun when they are blasting it out. Overall this is a well-controlled lesson in power and use of contrasts.
#62, May 2001

IONA
THE BOOK OF KELLS

Iona were formed in the summer of 1989, taking their inspiration from visits to the islands of Iona and Lindisfarne, and state that their aim is to create "spiritual, atmospheric music that will also inspire". The line-up is Dave Bainbridge (keyboards, guitar – Dave has also played with many top names including Buddy Guy, Jack Bruce and Paul Jones), Joanne Hogg (vocals, keyboards, acoustic guitar), Nick Beggs (Chapman Stick, bass – Nick has played with loads of top artists including Cliff Richard, Gary Numan and Toyah Wilcox, but will always be remembered as the man with the weird haircut in Kajagoogoo), Terl Bryant (drums, percussion – Cliff Richard, Steve Taylor (he can be seen playing with Some Band on the excellent 'Limelight' video recorded at Greenbelt) and Pete Murphy (Bauhaus) among others), and new recruit Mike Haughton (sax, flute, vocals – Mike was previously in the critically acclaimed Australian folkies Mara!). Mike replaced David Fitzgerald who played on the first two CDs. The first self-titled album was released in June 1990 in UK and Europe, with an October release in the USA, and up to the end of 1992 had sold a respectable 30,000 copies. The band have been featured on both national and local TV and radio and had a concert broadcast live in Holland in 1991. On the live front, they have supported bands such as Steeleye Span and Runrig and have played throughout Europe. 'The Book Of Kells' was released in July 1992 and is a musical interpretation of the priceless 8th Century illuminated manuscript of the same name, which is thought by many to be the pinnacle of Celtic art.

Right from the opening held-down keyboard chords, and the lulling voice, I found myself drawn in. Some music is designed to provoke a certain reaction, and in my case, I found myself relaxing and drifting on the music in a way that was both fulfilling and deeply enjoyable. My mind was filled with images of the Western Isles, one of my favourite places in the world, combined with religious elements. The feelings were so strong that I do not think it would be possible to disassociate the religious aspect from the music at all. While one can say that the music at times is reminiscent of Clannad, Camel or Enya, the only word that gives it justice is "beautiful": it is just so different to most of the music I hear, a real joy, and one that should be taken on board by all of you. The second track, "Revelation", is quite invigorating compared with many of the others and could be a single. Of course, if it were, then the computer-driven rubbish that plagues the airwaves would have to make way for some real music: powerful, yet for the most part restrained playing by all the band allows Joanne to command the scene and provides for a real modern classic. There are many sides to Iona, and I have yet to decide which I like the best. There is a distinct impression that if they wanted to, they could let rip and go hell for leather, but it is possible that restraint is their very strength. The instrumental passages, of which there are many, do not have room for self-indulgence, although technically there is a lot going on for most of the time. Sometimes the keyboards take over and lull you into a dreamlike state, only for the rhythm section to cut in along with a flute or rock guitar. I feel that the band could play for hours, improvising and developing along any given theme. I have not heard the first one, but this is brilliant. They have just finished recording their third album, 'Beyond These Shores', which is due out on November 1st. It features some guest musicians, the most notable of whom is Robert

Fripp of King Crimson. I urge you to make the effort to discover Iona; those who do will find themselves all the richer for it.
#20, Oct 1993

IONA
BEYOND THESE SHORES
Back in #20 I gave a full history of Iona, along with a review of their excellent second album, 'The Book Of Kells'. I'm glad to be in the happy position of being able to report that their new CD is along similar lines to the last and is also well worth investigating. There are also a few guest musicians involved this time, with the most noteworthy being Robert Fripp: which just goes to show how highly Iona are rated by others. As before, the band provide a backdrop of myriad styles for Joanne Hogg to put her pure clear vocals against. Some feature percussion to the fore (such as "Today"), while others start slow and then build such as "Bird of Heaven", which totally changes repeatedly. There is far more than one style at work here, and the songs are complex yet simple at the same time. It is obvious that each musician is a master of his craft, and they interweave and relate to each other with consummate skill. Restraint is the order of the day: but when music is as beautiful as this, it does not need pure energy and power to get the message across. This is very much an album for lovers of good high-quality music, which does not pander to fashion. Turn off the lights, draw the curtains and let the music of Iona carry you far beyond your wildest dreams.
#22, Mar 1994

IQ
LIVING PROOF
IQ are a band that at one time, in the very early days of this magazine, used to feature quite heavily. Although they released some great albums in the Eighties, they never achieved the popular support they deserved, although many bands of today cite them as important influences. This could all be set to change with original vocalist Peter Nicholls firmly back in the fold, and very good publicity concerning the new album, which should be out later in the year: they even warranted a six-page history in February's Record Collector. What we have here though, is not a new album but rather one that has been reissued on compact disc for the first time. Back in 1985 IQ were asked at very short notice to play a gig that could be filmed for the 'Live In London' series (this is the same series that spawned Twelfth Night's excellent 'Creepshow' video). Within three days they had organised and played a gig at Camden Palace. Because of requests by the producer, the set was a shortened one and concentrated mainly on material from 'The Wake'. The band split from their label, Irate, in the same year who then promptly issued 'Living Proof' as a joint album and video: the band attempted to get the album withdrawn, and it was eventually deleted in 1987. By the end of 1985 Peter had left IQ to form Niadem's Ghost, and because of this 'Living Proof' gained a lot of importance for

fans, who saw it as the closing of a chapter in the history of IQ. A decision was made by the band to release it on their own Giant Electric Pea label, and after being remastered and "tidied up" it came out at the end of last year. As well as Peter, it features Martin Orford on keyboards, Mike Holmes on guitar, Paul Cook on drums, and Tim Esau on bass. As a matter of interest, in the 1993 line-up only John Jowitt is different. With nine tracks at nearly an hour in length, it is a worthwhile effort, but should it have been re-released?

"Indubitably my dear Watson", as Holmes would have said if he was around today and into great music. It kicks off with "Awake and Nervous", and I defy anyone to stop themselves from jumping up and down as the band drive along behind Martin's keyboards. The song changes as Peter's distinctive voice takes control: why this band were never recognised as a major force by the public is beyond me. "Outer Limits", "It All Stops Here" and "Just Changing Hands" keep the momentum going with loads of time changes and anything and everything that a prog rock lover could possibly wish for. Then we are heralded with the far heavier, far more menacing, "The Wake". True, there is light and shade, but the shade is there in force. "The Magic Roundabout" opens with the soaring keyboards of Martin, but soon all hell breaks loose in a burst of prog mayhem as the band attempt to break the speed of light. Extremely complex and fluid playing finally calms down so that Peter can take charge and set the mood. "Widow's Peak", "The Thousand Days" and "Corners" are the final three on the album.

Although not recorded under perfect conditions, and with a set they wouldn't have necessarily chosen for themselves, the album is not only historically interesting but a great one to have in the collection. Anyone who is into IQ simply MUST get 'Living Proof' and to anyone who is remotely interested in the current wave of prog bands then this album is essential to find out where a lot of them are coming from.
#17, Mar 1993

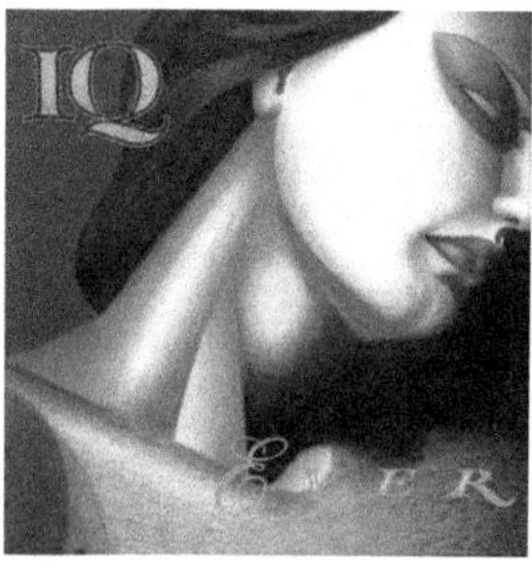

IQ
EVER

It is four years since the last IQ album 'Are You Sitting Comfortably', and with original singer Peter Nicholls very much back in the fold and ex-Ark bassist John Jowitt now an established member of the band, this was a CD that I and many others have been eagerly awaiting. Opener "The Darkest Hour" grabs your attention right from the off with John and Paul laying down the backbone for some frantic interplay between Martin and Mike. Having got your attention, they shift the song into a lighter mode and Peter's distinctive vocals take control of this commercial belter. The harmonies are spot on and there are enough mood and style changes to satisfy the progger, yet this is such a great song that it will interest even the casual onlooker. I knew the first time I played the CD that if all the songs were half as good as this then IQ would have a real winner on their hands. "Falling Senses" started with gentle acoustic guitars and sensitive keyboards that leaves plenty of room for Peter's voice. It is a beautiful ballad that is aided by the sound of an inspired fretless bass line. The song is divided in two, and the second part is a far more menacing instrumental.

"Out of Nowhere" is my favourite track on the album. Mike riffs the guitar, and IQ show how a prog band can rock with the best of them. If you like rock with great musicianship and outstanding vocals, then you will love this, it's great! "Further Away" is far more delicate and keyboard-based, showing off the emotional and sensitive sides of IQ. It delicately builds to a climax where suddenly the guitar and bass are riffing, providing a deep undertone for Martin to lay down some evocative keyboards. The song is transformed into a dynamic rock number and continues to change, meld and progress in a way that is both fluid and consistent, keeping the interest right to the end. "Leap of Faith' is more of a rocker again, but it is so easy to listen to and enjoy, even on first hearing. "Came Down" provides a fitting closer with an almost anthemic style. Loads of harmony vocals, but still plenty of room for almost hypnotic guitar.

So, there you have it, six tracks of sheer unadulterated brilliance. I'm glad I received this near the deadline as otherwise I would never have played anything else and would never have got this issue of Feedback finished! 'Ever' is a masterpiece, a wonderful collection of differing styles and moods but more importantly all the songs themselves are just great. I know that many of you will already have bought this, but if you have not then I cannot recommend it highly enough.
#19, Aug 1993

IQ
J'AI POLLETTE D'ARNU

This album was issued by GEP, a label set up by Mike Holmes, Martin Orford and Laurence Dyer to promote prog. This, the first release on the new label, saw a certain number of loose ends being tied up, with a collection of four "rare" singles tracks, and four live recordings. Of the eight, one featured original singer Peter Nicholls, and the others Paul Menel. Having played this a great deal over recent weeks, it is amazing just how strong it all is. There is always the danger with a compilation of this type that the songs, although scarce and therefore desirable for that fact alone, are not actually any good. But in this case, they are all winners, and would have happily graced any album. Opener "It All Stops Here" shows IQ at their rockin' proggin' best, as they go up and down the scales, interplaying as only IQ can. The bass and guitar are in perfect harmony, then the partnership turns and twists, yet it all comes together in the end. After a complex and complicated introduction, the song settles down for a while as Paul's clear and melodic vocals take control. Soon the rest of the guys take over and the music just gets far more intense and heavier as Mike and Martin vie for dominance: IQ at their very best. "Sera Sera" is a peaceful interlude with some gorgeous guitar from Mike. Paul's vocals are benefited with some harmony work from Tim and Martin, who as well as providing some delicious keyboards adds some delicate flute. "Intelligence Quotient" starts off acoustically, but changes into a Genesis feeling instrumental, with loads of menace and power. Vocals finally make an appearance in the third minute, delicate and gentle, contrasting with the staccato guitarwork. Gradually from here on the song builds and expands. A song of very many parts, at well over seven minutes in length, there is within it every aspect of what makes IQ such a great band. "Dans Le Parc Du Chateau Noir" shows the earlier side of the band, with Peter Nicholls. Loads of menace, with deep guitarwork which is very much the dominant force in this song, taking the melody for even longer than the vocals.

The second part of the CD was recorded on IQ's UK tour in 1989. The first song is a medley comprising "The Last Human Gateway", "Outer Limits", "It All Stops Here" (again) and "The Enemy Smacks". It is more than fourteen minutes long, but the songs are put together so well that it is not possible to hear the join, and Paul takes on the older material with confidence and passion. Obviously with a piece of this length there are many differing elements and high points, but for me it is the interplay between the keyboards of Martin and the guitar of Mike that makes this special. "Common Ground" is far more relaxed, with a mellow feel, relying far more on the vocals for the most part, gradually building to the guitar solo. "Promises" is one of my all-time favourite IQ songs, and here it is with a long keyboard introduction which gives way to wonderful harmony vocals: what a start to the song. I defy anyone who loves prog or melodic rock not to fall in love with it the first time they hear it. Truly outstanding. Last and certainly not least is "Wurensh", another of IQ's more commercial numbers which belts along as all good prog rock songs should.

There you have it, a compilation set that came out more than two years ago, but still sounding fresh today. For IQ fans this is an essential purchase, and if you have been wondering what all the fuss is about then I urge you to get this an introduction to the band.
#20, Oct 1993

IQ
TALES FROM THE LUSH ATTIC

IQ's debut vinyl album was released in 1983, initially only available through mail order or at gigs. At long last it has been released on CD in the UK (although it has previously been available as an import). Recorded in just five days, it remains one of the most important debut albums in progdom. It kicks off with "The Last Human Gateway", which scrapes in at just under twenty minutes in length. You can imagine reviewers everywhere fighting each other to get the chance to criticize a debut prog album starting with a cut of that length. What it does is give the band a real opportunity to shine in all departments, whether it is Martin Orford providing dazzling keyboard runs or swirling backdrops; Mike Holmes playing gently or searing the frets; Tim Esau and Paul Cook keeping the rhythm section nailed down, or Peter Nicholls providing some of the most emotive vocals around. IQ were bound to be compared with groups like Genesis, but it was not long before bands were compared to IQ, such was the importance of their music. "Through The Corridors" is driven by the guitar, and in direct comparison to the previous track, proves you can write good songs at under 2 ½ minutes in length. Now would be a good time to turn the vinyl album over, with the second side starting with "Awake and Nervous". This is one of my real IQ favourites, and the interplay between Mike and Martin is superb – a good bouncy up and down song! A piano solo based on the opening phrase of the final song "The Enemy Smacks" is next, with one of the finest song titles of all time – "My Baby Treats Me Right 'Cos I'm A Hard Lovin' Man All Night Long". The vinyl album closes with "The Enemy Smacks", a tried and tested number of the band, it shows them at full strength. At just under fourteen minutes it provides more evidence, if any were needed, that IQ are a melodic progressive rock band of real quality.

There is a bonus track on the CD of "Just Changing Hands", which was recorded in 1984 and appeared as the B side of the "Barbell Is In" single. A live version of this song is already available on 'Living Proof'. It is strange to think that this album is now twelve years old. Any band would be more than proud to be able to release music of this importance and relevance today!
#27, Feb 1995

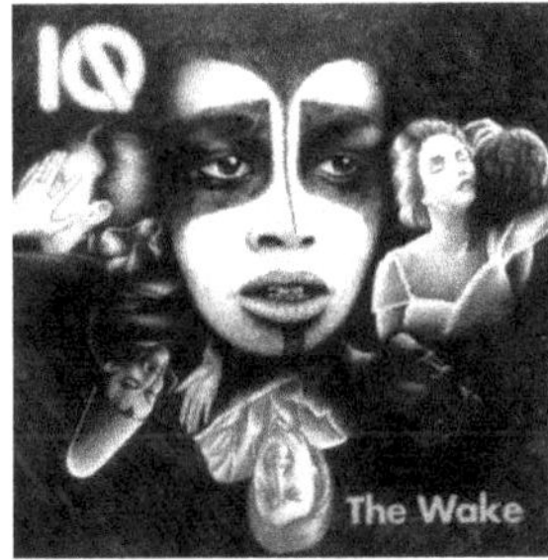

IQ
THE WAKE

So, onto the difficult second album. No sweat. 'The Wake" showed a harder, rawer edge to IQ as they developed their sound, becoming more majestic and dramatic. The album revolved around the theme of death and the possibility of an afterlife. "Outer Limits" encapsulates IQ as the time, emotional and mood changes stretch the very boundaries of progressive rock. It is listenable and commercial, yet at the same time it is challenging and diverse. Peter is at his most emotional and fraught self, and the overall effect is simply stunning. The title cut is next and threatens to blow the bass speakers as it proves that prog bands can be as heavy and menacing as they come. "The Magic Roundabout" starts with held-down keyboard chords, but as the listener is lulled into a false sense of security, suddenly Paul and Tim put in a sudden burst and we are off. The bass work on this is just superb. "Corners" is a total change of pace as a drum machine is used to provide the basis for a far more commercial approach (this song was used as a single). "Widow's Peak" was the oldest song on the album, being first played in January 1984, and again it is the ever-changing moods and melodies that capture the ear, from the gentle to the bombastic. "The Thousand Days" is a fun bouncing joyous number, in total contrast to what some see as IQ's finest song, "Headlong". The vocal passages have a minimum of backing, allowing Peter to shine through, while the instrumental passages, in direct contrast, are thundering and menacing. There are three bonus songs on the CD: "Dans Le Parc Du Chateau Noir" appeared on the B-side of the 12" version of "Barbell Is In" and can be found on the 'J'ai Pollette D'arnu' CD. The other two tracks are extremely interesting, as they are demos of songs that later appeared on the album itself, namely "The Thousand Days" and "The Magic Roundabout". A superb album. I am sure that many of you already have 'The Wake' in your collection, but it is worth getting on CD.
#27, Feb 1995

IQ
NINE IS A POND IS HERE

This is not a reissue on the band's own GEP label, but rather one that I have only just acquired. After Peter's shock departure from IQ he was replaced by Paul Menel: there was a tour coming up with Magnum, so obviously, some serious rehearsal was needed. While in a studio in Kingston it was suggested that these sessions were recorded to try and generate some much-needed revenue before the next album. It was decided to release a double album 'bootleg' of the proceedings, and with the pressing initially only supposed to be 1500 this album quickly gained some notoriety among fans. The first three sides were totally live in the studio (no overdubs at all) while the fourth was general weird stuff from over the years, and it is the first three sides that was later released on CD by the French label MSI. Obviously, most of the material comes from the two albums, although "Fascination" stems from IQ's debut cassette album 'Seven Stories Into Eight' as does "Intelligence Quotient" (here titled "IQ"). There is also a number that hasn't been released elsewhere, and it is understandable as to why, although it must be said that the "Glenn Miller Medley" is great fun. All in all, this is an interesting album showing the band at the very beginning of the second phase of their career and is one to get only after you have all the others.

#27, Feb 1995

IQ
NOMZAMO

This was the first 'proper' album with Paul Menel, and it heralded a new direction for the band. Paul's vocals were pure and clear, rather than emotive, and made the sound more commercial. This was a move that alienated some fans, but also made them many more. "No Love Lost" is rich in harmonies and although the bass line is solid rather than inventive, it did herald the shift in direction. "Promises (As The Years Go By)" is the one that got away and is probably the best example of the new sound of IQ as the band mixed pop and prog in a way that should have guaranteed them a hit single. The vocals soar, and I defy anyone who like melodic rock not to absolutely love this. "Nomzamo" uses a drum machine to great effect as the vocals shine, and when the guitars finally make an entrance the music swells and rises. "Still Life" is balladlike in its approach and features some emotive fretless bass and stark vocals; the use of sax is a departure for the band that works well. "Passing Strangers" is another overt attempt at a pop song that to my ears works very well indeed, as it bounces along (again with some great harmonies). "Human Nature" is more like old times, but it is to "Screaming" that I probably turn to most. Sequencers kick off what is again a pop/rock number with soaring vocals, but it is just plain FUN! Considering the song is about death, it is something of a strange contrast "When I take my dying breath, you'd better bet your life, I'm going out screaming, like I came in now, screaming". The final song is "Common Ground", a respectful number about the Battle of the Somme, sung mostly as a lament, the guitars eventually arrive to great effect. There are three bonus songs on the CD. The first is

"Colourflow", which was on the 12" of "Passing Strangers", which also contained the next track, a piano/vocal version of "No Love Lost". One of my most magical musical memories (alliteration rules) is seeing Martin perform this solo at Whitchurch a few years ago. I do like the full version, but to my ears this is just so far superior. The CD closes with a live version of "Common Ground". This album is a mix of old and new, that many felt did not work quite as well as it could (although I loved it, and still do).
 # 27, Feb 1995

IQ
ARE YOU SITTING COMFORTABLY...?
Here, finally, is the last re-release by IQ. Originally dating from 1989, this was the second album to feature Paul Menel on vocals, and the promise of what might be that was heralded on 'Nomzamo' comes to joyful fruition on 'Are You Sitting Comfortably...?' It is an album that by whatever standards you wish to use, just must be hailed as a classic. The band are as musically tight as one would expect from a hard-working outfit recording their fourth studio album with just a single change in band personnel. Paul was by now extremely happy in his role, and his vocals rise and shine with great melody, mixing well with the harmonies provided by Martin and Tim. Straight from the off, with the slowly rising and eventually dominating "War Heroes" we are deep in the musical melodious world of IQ. Next up is "Drive", the hit single that never was. Infectious in the extreme, it is indeed a sad indictment of the music charts in the UK that this was never a huge seller. The menace of "Nostalgia" moves us neatly into "Falling Apart At The Seams", which gradually builds up tempo, and rises on the bass to be a dramatic rocker. IQ are, and always have been, a rock band first and foremost and this album proves it again and again. The musical hooks in this song alone would put even the most hardened anti-progger in ecstasy (yes, I like this one). I have not the time to give a track by track, blow by blow résumé of the album, but I must just mention one more, "Wurensh". Great keyboards, great guitar, stunning vocals, loads of melody and time changes… I'm in heaven. In case you have not got the picture, all the IQ albums should be in any decent rock lover's collection and that includes 'Are You Sitting Comfortably...?'. Also, there is a bonus song, a live rendition of "Nothing At All".
#29, Jun 1995

IQ
FOREVER LIVE
On June 12th 1993, IQ played a gig at the Stadthalle, Kleve, to launch their new album 'Ever'. It was decided to film and record the gig to provide the definitive live video and CD, and nearly three years down the line all the technical problems have finally been solved and the boxed set is available. The price of £35 may put off the wary, but it is more than worth the money. Inside the sturdy box is a sixteen-page 12" square glossy book containing many photos of the gig and background information. But what to

play first, the video or the CD? I chose the video and could play some of it as it was my birthday, and this was one of my presents. What was immediately apparent was that a lot of time and effort had been put into this project and many cameras had been utilised, with the shots and images being moved around and placed over the top of each other: the result being possibly the best music video I have ever seen. It certainly puts many broadcast transmissions to shame! The crowd were going mad and all the guys seemed to be totally relaxed, managing to forget just how much it was all costing. This was a top-quality gig from IQ, proving yet again just why they are so popular and why they have managed to survive for so long playing music that is virtually hated by all the mass media. The only other IQ video I have is from the 'Living Proof' live set from 1985 and there is just no comparison: remember that one was recorded and broadcast on television! So, onto the double CD. The complete set is here, including "No Love Lost" which unfortunately did not make it onto the video. IQ revel in the live environment and I could play this all day, as it is just brilliant! So, is it worth paying out all that money? If you even remotely like progressive melodic rock then you have no option as this is essential, and no other band have managed to come up with such a complete package. You probably will not read reviews of this as the band are not supplying promo copies due to cost, and they have not advertised it because it is selling so well. Get out your chequebooks boys and girls, this is a boxed set you simply must have, as no music collection can be called complete without it.
#35, June 1996

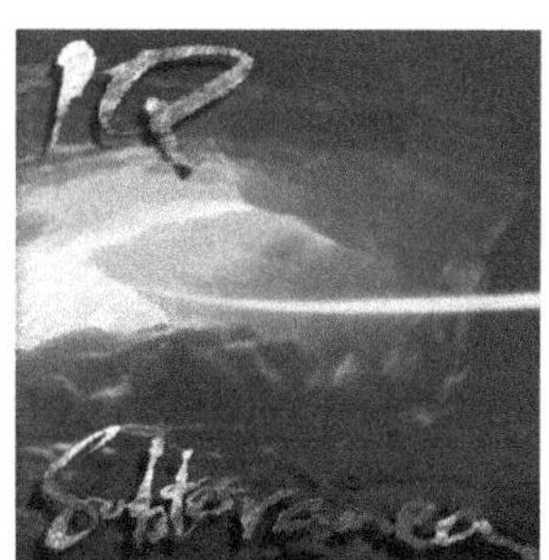

IQ
SUBTERRANEA
With this release, IQ have set themselves up to be shot down in flames. They know it, and everyone can imagine what the press are going to say. Not content with releasing a concept CD they have made it a double, and to compound these sins they have produced a stage show around the album (that has already been performed and I could not get to see it, damn). Go on, I dare any of you to say, 'The Lamb Lies Down On Broadway'. Oh, shit, I did it. Now that's out of the way I ought to also mention the artwork, which is inspiring throughout, with loads of different images. Musically this is instantly recognisable as IQ, although with some important changes. The first of these is that with virtually no time constraints on either song or total album length, they have allowed themselves the opportunity to expand, and Martin has even purchased a totally new keyboard set up that has provided him with even more sounds at his disposal than he had before. Peter is singing with more conviction than on 'Ever' (the only other studio album recorded with this line-up), possibly because he is more into it again. Cookie will always be the perfect drummer, nothing new there, while JJ's move into the Arena camp has given him more experience in working in different musical fields. Mike has also found room to move between styles of guitar, so an acoustic can be used in one area, a guitar synth in another, while it can all be turned up and cranked out somewhere else. They have also been playing close attention to the current prog scene. One of the major bands to explode out of the States recently is of course Spock's Beard whose trademark is blistering runs of intertwined playing which can blast off at a tangent and IQ have

brought some of these into their own music, showing that the old 'uns can hack it just as well as the new breed. This is a long album, more than 100 minutes, and it can take a lot of playing to get the best out of it. Someone who did not like it when I spoke to him about it, dropped me a line the following week telling me just how good it was. I fell in love with it the first time I heard it and have enjoyed it more and more ever since. This is the best thing IQ have done, and I just do not know how they will follow this up, but if you want to get hold of the pinnacle of British prog then this is the album to get. It just does not get any better than this. *#44, Sept 1997*

IQ

FOREVER LIVE

For those of you who did not purchase the brilliant, fantastic, wonderful video and CD boxed set it is now possible to buy the double CD on its' own. Released with much of the artwork and information that was in the boxed set, there is now no excuse not to hear one of the best British bands doing what they do best, strutting their stuff in front of a crowd. IQ has been at the top of the British prog tree for so long that it is impossible to say just how important they have been to the progressive scene. There are many bands around the world today, which either still imitate or started life trying to emulate their heroes. This is the only 'official' live album during the band's best part of twenty-year life span ('Living Proof' was originally a bootleg which IQ finally released having cleaned up the sound). Apart from John Jowitt on bass, these guys played on the first IQ album all those years ago. You do not need me to tell you that Cookie is a superb drummer, that John is known as 'Mr Bass', that Mike can still riff like a bastard (although his hair has improved since those early days), while in Martin Orford they have one of the truly great keyboard players of recent times. Then there is of course Peter Nicholls, who is recognised as one of the greatest frontmen ever to tread the boards. His break from the band only seems to have done him good, as promoting his first album with IQ for years, the album 'Ever', and the consequent live tour was extremely important. The fact that the band decided to hire a video crew to put together the ultimate live package shows the confidence they had in their own ability and the loyalty of their fans. Many of the fans view 'Ever' as not only a great comeback album but also the best they had ever done (up to that point). So, it was one night in Germany that all the cameras and tape decks started to roll. Fourteen songs later and it was all over. What can be said about it? If you like IQ then you know what I am saying, but if you have never heard them then you owe it to your ears to go out and discover what they are all about and this is as good a place to start as any. Mixing and blending songs from throughout their career, old numbers such as "The Wake" and "Widow's Peak" stand proudly against songs such as "Out of Nowhere" (my personal favourite from 'Ever', if any song deserves to be called a "bouncy up and down song" then this is it). This is a record of a band at the peak of their powers. The confidence that they showed here was such as that the next album they released was THE concept album of the Nineties, and one of the greatest ever released. If you have ever wondered what IQ album should be the one start with, I can say that this is the one to get. Just work your way backwards from here. Of course, the band still have the video and CD boxed set for sale, and that is really worth getting ….*#50, Aug 1998*

IQ

SEVEN STORIES INTO 98

Surely one of the most fabled debut releases is the 'Seven Stories Into Eight' cassette that was released in 1982 by the newly formed IQ. For many years, fans that came to the band later have been asking about this, and it has become something of a Holy Grail for some, as the band did not make it available after 1984. After the success of 'Subterranea', the decision was made to at long last make the early recordings again available to the fans, but after listening to the original masters IQ discovered that they had deteriorated so much as to be virtually unusable. It was obvious that the best that could be done was to digitally enhance a cassette copy, but they were loath to inflict this on the fan that may have only recently discovered them. The words "Rip Off" was to be avoided at all cost. So, the decision was taken to do the best that they could with a copy of the original recordings and make these available on CD. At the same time, they would go into a studio and within five days would re-record and mix all the songs (as well as a bonus) so the fan could have both the original and what they would sound like today. As Martin said, he expected the fan to play the original versions once just to hear exactly what they sounded like, and then concentrate on playing the newer versions. By having them as a double CD with copious sleeve notes and photos (including Martin with a beard!) then this seemed to be the best of both worlds, and it certainly seems to be the case. Even to fans that have never heard the original tape before (myself included) then some of the songs themselves ("Barbell Is In", "Intelligence Quotient", "Fascination", "It All Stops Here") are fairly well known. But, it still must have come as quite a shock to John Jowitt (the only IQ member not to play on the original) that he had just nine days to learn all the songs, but he did a good job. The result is an album that is worth listening to in its' own right, regardless of its' scarcity value. As this has been thought of with the fan in mind it is not generally available, and the pressing run is likely to be limited, although it is already selling better than the band thought possible. This may be basically a re-recording of an album that is now sixteen years old, but the songs and material is still more than viable (particularly the stunning version of "It All Stops Here", one of my favourite IQ numbers), which shows just how dynamic and musically important the band have been throughout their career, even back to their earliest days. While I would hesitate to recommend this as the perfect starting point for a non-IQ fan, there is a lot going for it, and with the two CDs, sixteen-page booklet, and history and photos this is worth laying your hands on. *#50, Aug 1998*

IQ

THE LOST ATTIC

It has been a busy couple of years for IQ. First off, they gave us 'Subterranea', followed by a double CD containing a totally re-recorded version of their first album 'Seven Stories Into Eight' and here they are back again with another CD subtitled 'A Collection of Rarities (1983-1999). Not content with just providing rarities, they have also included unreleased numbers as well as going back into the studio to re-record their rarest single

"Hollow Afternoon" which was originally given away free at gigs and only 500 were ever pressed. Two songs appear which originally appeared on SI compilations and have been unavailable since that company went bust: "N.T.O.C. (Resistance)" originally featured on the 'SI Compilation Too' album and saw the recording debut of ex-Ark bassist John Jowitt, while "Apathetic, And Here, I.." was taken from the Geoff Mann tribute album 'Mannerisms'. The first of these is probably my favourite song on the album, and one that I have been playing regularly over the last six years. Not only was it a great song, but it meant that after a period of uncertainty IQ were back and appeared to be even stronger than before. As with 'Seven Stories Into 98' there is a wonderful booklet containing history, lyrics and comments about each recording by the band, now all we must do is wait for the next one. How about "Flak", "Lost Horizon", "Robo 2", "Funk Is In My Brain", "Stomach of Animal", and "Beef In Box" lads?
#53, May 1999

IQ
SUBTERRANEA – THE CONCERT

IQ
SUBTERRANEA – THE CONCERT (VIDEO)

Ask any prog lover to name the most important concept album of the Nineties and they will come up with IQ's 'Subterranea'. When they took it on the road, they amazed audiences with the use of film and using a front projection screen where the band could be seen performing behind a screen on which images were shown. By also using an actor, with vocalist Peter Nicholls playing his part to the full, the story was brought to life and the complete double album was played in its' entirety. On 4th April 1999, the show was recorded at Tilburg in Holland and has now been released on double CD and on video. I have found it very difficult to review this. Why? Because it is just so good, and it is impossible to convey in words just what this package is like. There is an explanatory booklet in both CD and video, giving details of the story and containing many photos. The film and the live almost seems to merge, with the specially shot footage giving way to Peter sat on the stage. There is no talking between the individual songs, so there is no distraction from the story or effect. IQ has used dramatic camera angles and technology to add to the overall impression of what was going on. At times the stage seemed very small for all that was taking place, but with films sometimes behind the band, and sometimes in front, along with extremely dramatic lighting, it is no surprise. The viewer is taken along for the ride, and the result is one of the most powerful and invigorating concert videos I have ever seen. The music must be something very special indeed to be able to lift the band above all the effects and be more than bit players, but it is all here in a glorious cohesion of strength and beauty. The CD will be bought to play in the stereo, but I would urge all who enjoy progressive rock to get the video as it shows IQ at their best. It will be difficult for them to be able to surpass this, so I look forward to the next album with great interest indeed. If ever there was a 'must get' then these are it.
#60, Oct 2000

IQ

THE SEVENTH HOUSE

At the end of the first verse of "The Wrong Side Of Weird", a few bars capture for me what makes IQ the top progressive band in Europe. Up to then the band has been slowly building through the introduction and then the verse itself. The keyboards play a repeated motif, but the simple act of changing the bass line totally changes the mood and attack. Ask five IQ fans to pick the single most important member of the band and they could each well pick a different person. Peter Nicholls is without doubt not only a superb lyricist and vocalist, but also one of the best frontmen in the business. Widge not only is renowned for his keyboard playing but also for the fact that many bands would love to have him as a singer. Michael Holmes is a guitarist with control of so many different styles, while John Jowitt is Mr Bass. That only leaves Paul Cook. One of the times I played the album I concentrated solely on the drums, and his impact not only on what he plays but where he does not (if that makes sense) is superb. There is a long period on "Weird" where he does not play at all, but when he comes back in, the fills and patterns he plays totally switch the mood. It is hard yet to say if this is my favourite IQ album, ask me again in a year or so when it has sunk into my psyche. If you like prog, then you must have this. Yet again, IQ set the standard.

#62, May 2001

IQ

DARK MATTER

IQ are back with their new studio album, and it has been met with universal acclaim. IQ have been at the top of the UK prog tree for over twenty years and this release very much cements the position. This is class music produced by a class act. John and Paul revel in playing in complex time signatures and provide a solid backdrop for Martin and Mike to play against. Martin seems to have had a bigger than usual influence on the sound of this album, due partly to using different keyboards which has given the band a sound that seems to have rooted firmly in the Seventies while being stretched very firmly into the 21st century. IQ's music is always distinctively their own, there is no-one else in the scene who sounds like them, music that shifts and moves and can be short and sharp and long and complex. The closing number "Harvest Of Souls" is one of the longest pieces they have ever attempted at 25 minutes (not including 'Subterranea' of course), and opener "Sacred Sound" is also over 11 minutes long, yet in the middle there are three much shorter numbers which complement these.

As well as the music, there are the lyrics and distinctive vocals of Peter Nicholls. His lyrics can still be obscure, yet they are fascinating to read and listen to. There is no break between the songs, so that the music sweeps from one theme to another. The bombastic and complex opener gives way to the restrained "Red Dust Shadow" while "You Never Will" is full of menace and edge. "Born Brilliant" is almost 'Welcome To The Machine' style Floyd, but that soon gives way to something that is ethereal and simple, yet also with a promise of much more to come. The way it breaks into bass and guitar syncopated rhythm is almost a trademark, only IQ could carry this off. Of course, all of this is leading to the title cut which starts as a gentle number with Peter singing gently and clearly, with delicate guitar and keyboards behind. A couple of minutes in and it is acoustic guitar, and all is pleasant. Of course, it was never going to stay that way for too long.... Gradually the music builds, moving away from the tranquillity but so carefully that the listener is not sure where the journey is going to end. As the music moves on, the simple complexity and grandeur is almost breath-taking, yet this is also very much a rock number that drives and twists.

Yet another masterpiece from IQ, one that will hopefully find them many new fans as well as more than pleasing the faithful.
#80, Jul 2004

THE IRE
FIRST IMPRESSIONS

THE IRE
SWIMMING AGAINST THE TIDE
The Ire were formed in 1990 from various Norwich rock bands, including Terminus, Silas and The Law. The first demo came out in 1990 with Ian Futter on vocals, Chris Phillips on guitar, Paul Redden on bass, Leigh Storey on keyboards and Dave Sparrow on drums. The demo contains some very powerful rock, with keyboards being kept to a minimum, adding to instead of dominating the sound.

By the time the second demo came out in 1992, Steve Holmes had replaced Chris Phillips, who had left to work with Gods Acre and begin recording tracks for the Earthstone CD 'Seed'. The music had become heavier, although there was still a place for keyboards, very much as an extra to the prog rock sound. Although The Ire can still be perceived as being a prog band, they are a lot heavier than most of those around, while "Free Yourself" is far jazzier, and a light relief. By the middle of 1993, Steve Holmes left the band and although he was replaced for one gig by Daniel Storey, The Ire broke up. After Chris Phillips and Chris Bond had finished work on the Earthstone CD, they decided to work with Ian Futter and the band are reforming, although the music will be taking a more keyboard-based direction. I look forward to that with interest.
#22, Mar 1994

IRON CLOWNS
COLOUR OF DANGER

Iron Clowns were formed by John Duggan (vocals) in 1990. Inspired by artists such as Peter Gabriel, Rain Tree Crow, Blue Nile and Talking Heads they recorded their first demo 'Tidings' in 1991. This received much critical acclaim and interest from producers such as Steve Nye. This CD contains twelve tracks, and John (vocals, keyboards) is joined by Dave Bowner (guitar, stick, sitar), Nick Moorbath (keyboards), Bob Prowse (drums, keyboards), Rick Edwards (congas, percussion) and Jerry Soffe (bass, percussion, keyboards). These last two are also on the new The Guitar Orchestra CD. I have seen their music described as 'Passion' Peter Gabriel meeting Ozric Tentacles, and this is probably a good description. Swirling keyboards combined with intricate bass and guitar lines along with strong percussion and melodic vocals means that Iron Clowns provide high quality music with an almost ethereal dreamlike quality.

The Ozric tendency comes through clearest on the longest song, "Taking The Clouds Home", which has more than a touch of Hawkwind about it as well. At over fifteen minutes in length this was apparently heavily edited from a session where they bounced ideas off each other. Musical themes come and go, as first one and then another dominates proceedings with Jerry Soffe keeping the whole thing together. An interesting album which will be appreciated by those into Ozrics and more keyboard-oriented sounds. Certainly worth hearing.
#25, Oct 1994

IVANHOE
SYMBOLS OF TIME

Every so often I get a CD, put it on the player, and it immediately screams class at me and that is the case with 'Symbols of Time' by German outfit Ivanhoe. It is obvious that they have been listening to Queensrÿche and Dream Theater albums, and here they are crunching their way through melodic and technical hard rock in a brilliant fashion. They are very tight, and have produced some great songs, but do have one outstanding asset, namely Andy Franck, vocalist extraordinaire. The bloke's range is phenomenal, and the power in the voice is awesome. Whether it is on the slower, softer pieces such as the atmospheric "Raining Tears" or the powerful "Irrigate Poisoning" he is always in total control and adjusts his singing style so that he fits perfectly to what is required. In fact, there are passages of the latter where he sounds uncannily like Tony Mills of Shy during their classic "Break Down The Walls". This is an album that will be appreciated by those into good hard melodic rock or the very much heavier side of prog.
#32, Dec 1995

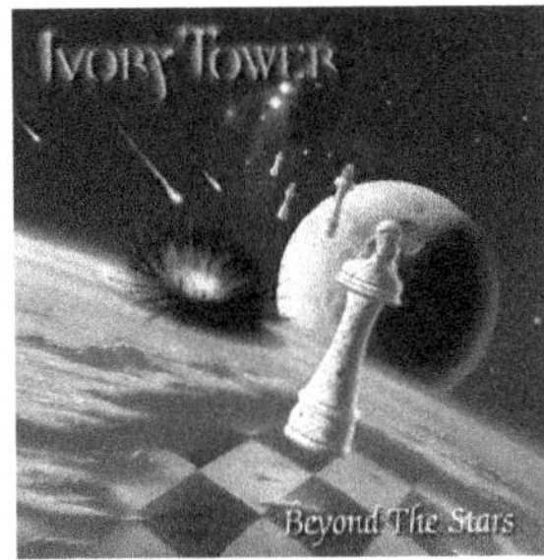

IVORY TOWER
BEYOND THE STARS

This is the second album from German band Ivory Tower, following on from their self-titled debut in 1998. It is certainly very powerful, firmly around prog metal, which appears to have many more followers on the continent than it does in the UK. At times, it is very heavy indeed, with the guitar of Sven Böge obviously being multi-tracked many times. The result is an album that may be too heavy for followers of prog who have ended up listening to this genre almost by accident. If, however, you are a hard rock fan who enjoys metal with melody then here is an album that you can get your ears into. With songs varying in length from under two minutes to nearly twelve, the band shows that they can concentrate on small themes or spread out and diversify. The production is also very good indeed, which is a plus as this is a relatively new band and it is mostly self-produced. The result is an album that is worth seeking out.
#58, May 2000

DANIEL J
LOSING TIME

Daniel J is the son of noted saxophonist Jaroslav Jakubovic and is such a talent that at the age of fifteen he arranged, produced and played keyboards, bass, guitar and drums on his father's solo saxophone album of famous commercials tunes. Leaving Israel for America he met and impressed Dream Theater keyboard player Jordan Rudess who had him play on his solo album, and here returns the favour. It is quite hard to describe the music that Daniel is producing as it is extremely heavy indeed and much rockier that one would normally expect from this label. The bottom end sound is quite extraordinary, and while he has a pleasant singing voice it is the sound emanating from his guitar and the bass that captures the imagination. It is as if King's X have joined forces with the slower more demonic aspects of Steve Vai and have combined to produce an album that is often pursued at doom speed while on others, such as "Xilted" are all out rock attack. This is an album that is probably not going to be appreciated by progheads, although it is on a label that is generally promotes that genre, as this is a song based, very hard rock album. It would be viewed as metal if it was not for the songs, which are far more melodic than one would expect given the heaviness. The result is something that is quite different, yet commercial and very appealing at the same time. Technically very clever with some fine touches, it is the guitar sound and superb musicianship that makes this a very interesting album indeed.
#85, Nov 2005

JADIS
MORE THAN MEETS THE EYE

Jadis have had a chequered career to date, being in many shapes and forms since their inception in the mid-Eighties. They became a full-time gigging outfit in 1987 when they

supported IQ on the 'Nomzamo' tour in Britain and Europe and supported Marillion on the 'Clutching At Straws' tour in 1988. After this they slogged through pubs and clubs in Britain, playing over 150 dates and building up a substantial following. They recorded a couple of demo tapes, produced by Steve Rothery, which sold well and in February 1989 they sold out their debut headline at The Marquee. There were severe line-up changes in the summer of that year, and Gary Chandler (guitar, vocals) was joined by Martin Orford from IQ on keyboards, and Steve Christey on drums. 1990 saw them playing more outside gigs and festivals and in the October, they headlined a major gig in Germany and in the summer of 1991 played the Rougemont Festival in France. The rest of the time was spent writing new material, and from December 1991 to February this year they recorded 'More Than Meets The Eye'.

It is hard to find a word that fully describes this album. Ones that spring readily to mind are "timeless", "brilliant", "amazing" and "wonderful", but I think I will just have to stick with "classic". Yes, this is a masterpiece: there are seven songs on this forty-six-minute-long album, and it is impossible to find a bad thing to say about it. The album starts with "Sleepwalk", and the guitar chords are answered by the keyboards as the drums and bass join in and swing the song into action (bass on the album and at gigs is provided by IQ bassist John Jowitt). The keyboards provide a swirling backdrop for Gary to put his guitar against, using it as a voice picking out the melody instead of just another interminable guitar solo. It takes three minutes for the harmony vocals to start, and it is only then that you realise that you have been listening to an instrumental passage. This typifies the album as there are long instrumental passages, but as the guitar plays the melody you just get lost in the majesty of the music and do not miss the singing at all. Strangely enough the songs still manage to sound accessible and (dare one say it?) commercial. There is wonderful interplay between Gary and Martin, with Steve and John pinning down the rhythm. "Hiding In The Corner" is the most commercial song on the album, with some great rock guitarwork and singing, yet always with the stamp of Jadis all over it.

Prog bands have always been accused of letting their musical skill and self-indulgence detract from the job at hand with long boring instrumental passages, but Jadis manage always to avoid the trap. Sure, the passages are long, but they are always extremely melodic and part of the songs. My favourite is "Wonderful World", which contains all their trademarks with great guitar lines, supported with brilliant keyboards and harmony vocals. After the second chorus Gary starts playing a guitar run, repeated in a rockier fashion, with the rest of the band in there playing for all their worth. I think I could listen to that ten seconds or so all day and not get tired of it. It heralds a change in the song, as it lightens up for a while, until the riffs start all over again. Fantastic. I know I keep saying this about various bands, but Jadis should be mega huge. Any A&R man worth his salt should grab them warmly by the throat and not let go until they have signed a five-album deal. Jadis is a name to look out for, and 'More Than Meets The Eye' is an essential purchase.
#14, Jul 1992

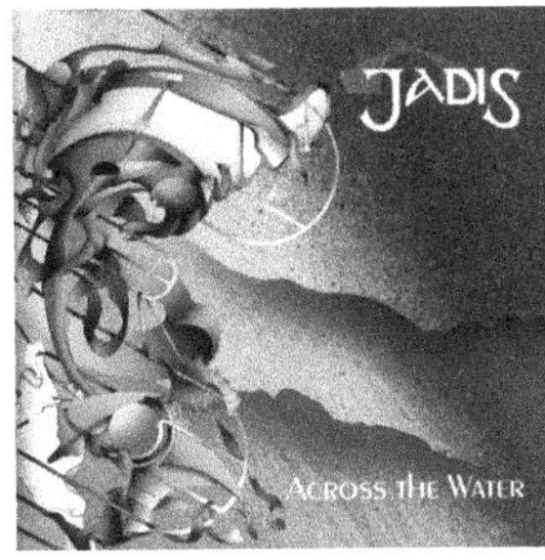

JADIS
ACROSS THE WATER

It seems ages since I was raving and enthusing over the debut CD by Jadis, 'More Than Meets The Eye', and some two years after its release it is still an extremely regular visitor to my CD player. I mean, it is just a phenomenal album and there are few who have heard it who would disagree with me. So, having released a stunning debut, of course the question would be when and how good would be the follow-up? Well, for one reason or another it has taken a long time to get the boys back into the studio, Whenever I saw Gary Chandler (vocals, guitar) I would be told a different time, but at long last it is here. The line-up is the same, with Gary being joined by Martin Orford (keyboards, backing vocals), John Jowitt (bass) and Steve Christey (drums). Both John and Martin are also full-time members of IQ, and since the release of 'Across The Water' John has left Jadis due to time commitments. Rob Aubrey was again in the production and engineering seat, and artwork was again by Geoff Chandler, so all was lined up for a sequel. But could it possibly be as good? Jadis have a very distinctive sound, which although many have tried to copy no-one else has managed to get quite right. It relies on Gary's subtle guitarwork combined with layers of keyboards, which conjure up moods and images almost without equal. Gary's vocal style fits the music perfectly, almost like an extra instrument, but for the most part it is the guitar that is the most important element. There are long instrumental passages, but the lack of vocals is not missed at all. However, when Martin joins with Gary in perfect harmony then it is the most glorious sound in the world. Steve and John provide the backdrop for the two main players to just expand and explore. You may have guessed by now that I am deeply in love with the CD, seven songs of sheer perfection. If I had to pick one out as being the best, then at a pinch it would probably be "Everywhere I Turn" as it takes all the best bits of Jadis and puts them all into one song. Listen to those soaring harmonies, that guitarwork. Oh, and there is a keyboard run of such speed that it takes the breath away. That passage only lasts a few seconds, but it transforms the mood of the song, as does the very short burst of double bass drumming. Then it is time for the guitar break. Heaven is mine. If you bought 'More Than Meets The Eye' then you must buy this. If you have not, then you should go out and get both today. Music as good as this should not be missed. You owe it to your ears.

#24, Jul 1994

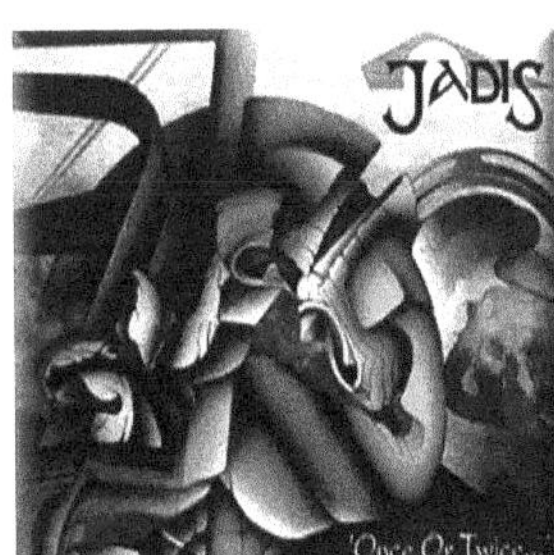

JADIS
ONCE OR TWICE

Like the 'Once Upon A Time' CD, this contains some songs that were written between 1986 and 1989. "Your Changing Face" is one of the band's most loved songs but has only appeared on CD on the 'SI Compilation Disc Too' set, and like the other two studio numbers marks the first appearance of the new line-up as Gary Chandler (guitar, vocals) and Steve Christey (drums) have been joined by Steve Hunt (bass) and Mike Torr (keyboards). They have taken a slightly different track to the previous version, but the result is the same, a truly classic song. Gary's guitar sound is extremely distinctive, with his mellow

vocals always taking second place and it is wonderful to hear this being made more widely available again. "In The Dark" and "Taking Your Time" are the other two studio numbers, with the fourth being a blinding live version of "Hiding In The Corner" (recorded when Martin Orford was still in the band). This shows Jadis at their very best, melodic yet dramatic and powerful at the same time. If you are a Jadis fan, then this falls under the "must have" category.
#38, Nov 1996

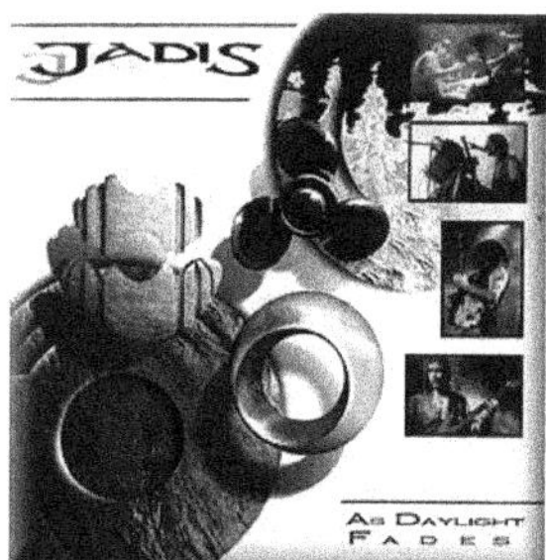

JADIS
AS DAYLIGHT FADES

South coast proggers Jadis have been around for quite a while, and I have long been a fan. Their debut CD 'More Than Meets The Eye' is one of the best albums released in the Nineties, and if you are a fan of great melodic progressive rock and have not heard it yet then you need to do so, now, today! This album is a live recording, mostly from the '96 New Forest gig. Keyboard player Mike Torr was under pressure as this was his first tour replacing IQ stalwart Martin Orford, but he and relatively new bassist Steve Hunt (who replaced IQ and Arena bassist John Jowitt) gelled in well with drummer Steve Christey and guitarist/vocalist Gary Chandler. Gary is the focus of attention as it is his melodic singing and fluent guitar style that is very much the sound of Jadis. It is of little surprise that the album opens with a number from 'More Than...', namely "Sleepwalk", and although it is perfect in many ways, it pales when compared with the mighty "Wonderful World" which comes later, which was also originally from the debut. Here it is treated more as a rock number, from which it benefits, and probably comes out as being superior to the original version, which is no mean feat, I can assure you. Whether it is the vocals, or the lengthy instrumental passages that hold the attention, there is no doubt that while this is in no way a hard rock album, it is very much indeed a rock album, and deserves to be played at maximum volume (although I must confess that my kids tell me that I play all my music way too loud). This is a great album from a great band.
#49, May 1998

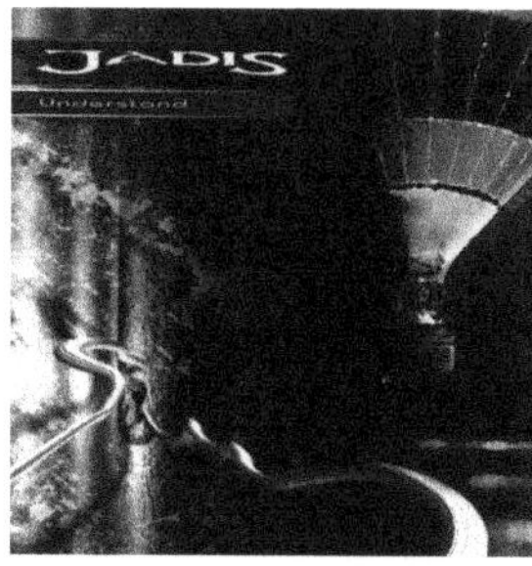

JADIS
UNDERSTAND

And, lo, it came to pass, that the classic Jadis line-up reformed and recorded an album together. Then they rested. And it was good. Well, after some time away IQ-ing and Arena-ing, Martin Orford (keyboards, vocals) and John Jowitt (bass) are now back in the Jadis camp. While both are of course still key players in IQ, John has now left Arena, which has given him some more time and he has returned to the fold. With Steve Christey on drums and Gary Chandler on vocals and guitar, the line-up which gave us the classic, timeless 'More Than Meets The Eye' are back together once again. From opener "Where In The World" it is apparent that they are immediately back on top form. Gary has a distinctive vocal style, added to his melodic guitar playing which also

has a unique sound, which gives Jadis a musical melody all their own. There are soaring vocals, guitar leads to die for, and the music is all held together in a way that many bands can never achieve, however much they strive. It is hard to pick out a favourite, as I enjoyed all eight songs immensely, and only time will tell if I feel this to be better than 'More...', which is still very much a regular on my player. It is the best release since their debut full-length CD, many moons ago, and who knows, given a year or two I may even say that it is better. If you have never heard Jadis and you enjoy melodic progressive rock, then you are missing a treat.
#58, May 2000

JADIS
MEDIUM RARE

Still one of the few prog bands who have a definitive sound of their own, Jadis has been for many years the showcase for the vocals and guitar of Gary Chandler (and long may it continue to do so). This album brings together the two CD EP's of rare material they released some time ago, along with lots of extra stuff to bring it up to more than seventy minutes in length. The songs are from various sources, and there are comments about each along with who played on it – just a shame that for some reason the CD plays in the order of the back of the booklet, but this is a slightly different order to the listing inside. But this is just nit picking as the album is strong enough to stand as a standard release. Personal favourites are the acoustic medley (don't like the naff fade out though) and "This Changing Face" which both feature just Gary and Widge. Please can we have a complete album of this some time? As well as these, some demoes, unreleased material and live cuts make this an album that any Jadis fan will be proud to own.
#62, May 2001

JADIS
ALIVE OUTSIDE

While Gary Chandler is of course the main man, and drummer Stephen Christey has been there for many a moon, there are many fans (myself included) that felt that Jadis without Martin Orford were not really Jadis at all. With John Jowitt also back in the fold, then the classic line-up was back together once again and while 'As Daylight Fades' was only released three years ago, it is fitting that another live album has been released featuring these guys. Three songs feature on both, but when they are as good as "Wonderful World" or "Batstein" who cares? Jadis have one of the most instantly recognisable sounds in the prog world, due mostly to Gary's laid-back vocals and guitar work. With JJ and Steve in perfect harmony, and Gary and Widge having one of the most understanding of partnerships, then it is no surprise that they sound like they are having a great time. Songs such as "Where in The World" are uplifting and powerful, while "Racing Sideways" is just clean plain fun. When Gary tells the crowd how long they are planning to play, Widge also joins in. What do you want from an album: Great songs, musical ability, and harmony vocals? There is all this and much, much more. They even throw in a couple of covers for good measures ("Comfortably Numb" is awesome). They may never have fully been appreciated in the UK, but this is one of our great prog bands. *#65, Dec 2001*

JADIS
FANATIC

Look at my CD collection and the one that looks the most battered is probably Jadis' debut album, 'More Than Meets The Eye'. It is a classic, and one that still is regularly played in my house, very loudly. Jadis are a prog band that simply do not sound like anybody else: while the music can be very complex, it is also often very simple, with the main components often being the two lead instruments of Gary's guitar and his voice. They are both instantly recognisable, solid yet fluid, gentle but hard when required. While Jadis will only ever be recognised as such while Gary is in the band, the others are key. Martin and Gary have built up an understanding over the years that very few guitarists and keyboard players have, as anybody who has seen their sets as a duo will attest to. This means that either can provide lead knowing exactly what the other will be doing, and this interaction also comes through in their studio work.

The album starts with "The Great Outside", and the cinematic view of a guitarist gently picking some strings while sat outside a house in the Deep South, late in the night. That gives way to Jadis opening proceedings with a crunching start. This is a prog band that has never been afraid to rock, but always within certain constraints. They are not a hard rock outfit, but one that brings melody and harmony together in a way envied by many but perfected by no others. The title cut is the shortest number, at just over four minutes, but none of these are exceptionally long, with "What Kind Of Reason" being just over double that. What Jadis manage to do is to capture a place that is timeless, a world that the listener can just drop into and feel that it is a place of safety and tranquillity and one that can be enjoyed forever. Is this a better album than their debut? Pass, ask again in another ten years and I might be able to tell you – but I do know that it is certainly one of the most enjoyable albums I have ever had the pleasure to listen to.*#74, Jun 2003*

JADIS
PHOTOPLAY

So Jadis are back with their new studio album, and it appears that this will be the last with the reformed 'classic' line-up, as Martin Orford (keyboards, vocals) has again left to pursue both solo and matters IQ. Steve Thorne has come in to help on the harmony vocals, with the rest of the line-up being of course Steve Christey (drums), John Jowitt (bass) and some bloke called Gary Chandler on vocals and guitars. Jadis have one of the most distinctive sounds around, with both Gary's vocals and his guitar sound immediately recognisable.

This album seems to place a higher focus on both, with Martin primarily providing a backdrop for Gary to play against. For me this album has seen Gary move the band even further away from the prog scene so that it is much more into melodic rock. Hell, let's get away from labels and little boxes and instead of trying to say that this is neo-prog or prog or melodic rock or something else altogether let's instead say that this is melodic guitar based classic rock that very few bands can deliver. Jadis ooze class in the way that other bands perspire, there are never any rough edges as the music is highly honed and polished so that the listener is drawn in from the first note to the end and the only thing to do when it has finished is to put it on again. And again. And again. It is really hard to describe this if you have not come across Jadis before, as their sound is so different to everyone else, but this is a superb album which again shows that it may now be fifteen years since their killer debut CD 'More Than Meets The Eye' (what do you mean you have not got it – consider yourself a musical numbskull and go and get the remaster immediately, if not sooner) but they are still producing music of the very highest quality. But if you have come across Jadis before then rest assured this is an album that is even more in your face than 'Fanatic' and is one that I very highly recommend.
#86, Feb 2006

JAÉN KIEF
LAS HADAS NO VUELAN MÁS I. VAGAS NUBES
Jaén Kief is not the name of a person, but that of an eight-person line-up from Colombia. They took the name from two words, "Jaén" which is a grape variety that grows in Spain and "Kief", which means absolute rest. The idea was to create a name that when plugged into a search engine would only bring back details of the band. That it does, but unfortunately the majority of them are in languages I can't read! The album was originally released in 2003 but it has just been picked up by Musea who have reissued it. All the lyrics are in Spanish, so again I do not know what is going on, but musically this is quite interesting with a strong use of acoustic guitar among the rock epics. There is a feeling of space within the music and the vocals are very clear, with the use of two singers, male and female. There is very strong musicianship, and if this was in English then I am sure that it is something that I would find even more interesting. As it is, this is a strong release from Musea with lots of different progressive styles going on, but here I feel that I need to know the words to fully appreciate it. Solemn, with a feeling of reverence, there are times when it is reminiscent of early Seventies Floyd with strong symphonic passages.
#88, Jun 2006

JANISON EDGE
THE SERVICES OF MARY GOODE
I have been waiting for this album for quite a while, knowing most of those involved. When it arrived, I was impressed with the artwork, but a little surprised to see that it was on their own label, as all those involved apart from singer Sue Element are in signed bands. Keyboard player Mike Varty is in Credo and Shadowland, drummer Dave Wagstaffe is in Landmarq, guitarist Ian Salmon is in Shadowland and bassist Paul Brown

is in Medicine Man. Although not a concept album in its truest sense, there are a lot of threads running through this album, linked back to the central character Mary Goode. Sue has a lovely voice, while musically the band appear to be very much rooted in Seventies Genesis. At times, it is like Gabriel, while at others it is more like 'Wind & Wuthering' but musically the band never seem to veer too far away from that as a basis. That is not to say that they sound like Genesis, far from it, but rather that there is a feel about the whole proceedings. Some of Ian's guitarwork is much more like Gary Chandler than Steve Hackett, and with Sue's melodic voice laid over the musical backdrop it is very pleasant. Ah, that might be the problem here. It is pleasant but not exciting or invigorating or exploring new areas. It is late evening relaxing music, but not something that is going to set the world alight.

Halfway through "Beneath The Boy" the song takes on a far more Legend-like slant, and Mike provides some blistering keyboard runs, but it never takes off in the way that Legend would. Possibly I'm being unfair, but this is a good as opposed to a great prog album.
#51, Jan 1999

THE JELLY JAM
2
The problem with a band that is a side-project is that each review always states which bands the musicians are in for their 'day job' and this will be no different. Formed out of Platypus (in itself a side project) this is the second album from Ty Tabor (King's X), John Myung (Dream Theater) and Rod Morgenstein (Dixie Dregs). But it does not seem fair to call this a side project as these guys are deadly serious about what they are doing and have created music to be proud of that is complex yet simple, dark yet full of lightness, heavy as hell yet with a deftness of touch that moves it away from being overpowering. When I first started listening to it, I felt that the band it reminded me most of was Dan Reed Network, although not quite as funky. The band themselves see the music as an amalgam of Black Sabbath and Jane's Addiction with The Beatles riding shotgun over proceedings.

It is always melodic yet sometimes is almost threatening with a bleak passion. They are as happy with a laid-back attitude as they are on riff-hungry numbers such as the powering "Runaway". It is the fact that they are such good musicians that even small drum solos are taken with good humour, as this is a band that has nothing to prove so are out to have a blast and take the listener along for the ride. There are so many good things on this album that just to listen to it makes me smile: this is fun melodic rock with loads of good influences brought together by some guys having a good time.
#81, Dec 2004

JEREMY MORRIS
OPEN YOUR HEART

JEREMY
SOLID ROCK

JEREMY
PILGRIM'S JOURNEY

To call Jeremy Morris prolific is something of an understatement. 'Pilgrim's Journey', his 1995 release on Kinesis, was his fifteenth album! When you bear in mind that he also has five children (I have enough problems with four!) then I can only be amazed at his energy and management of time.

All his albums, apart from 'Pilgrim', have been released on his own JAM label and recorded at his own studio, which gives him the artistic freedom he requires. Although a consummate multi-instrumentalist he has steered away from the dangers of programming and instead employed the services of Dave Dietrich on drums. 'Open Your Heart' and 'Solid Rock' are both song-based, lightweight AOR, Prog, Pomp albums that are very enjoyable indeed. His vocal style is like Nick Barrett's, and the albums remind me of 80's US rock. They are very easy albums to get into, and he has a very fluid guitar style that adds to the overall effect.

'Pilgrim's Journey' is a far more 'serious' affair. This is a totally solo, instrumental progressive rock album which starts life as a gentle multi-layered keyboard piece, with some lovely deft touches, just to gradually let the album wash around and over you. However, this is far more than some self-indulgent keyboard meanderings as acoustic guitar lets itself be known, making way for the fluid electric leads so dominant on the other albums. It is at times reminiscent of Anthony Phillips, at others Steve Hackett, while fans of Mike Oldfield and Gordon Giltrap will also find much on here to enjoy. Instrumental one-man progressive rock CDs seem to fall into one of two categories, either "look how clever I am but forget all sense of melody or tunes" or ones that fully warrant further investigation. I am happy to report that this falls into the latter.
#41, Apr 1997

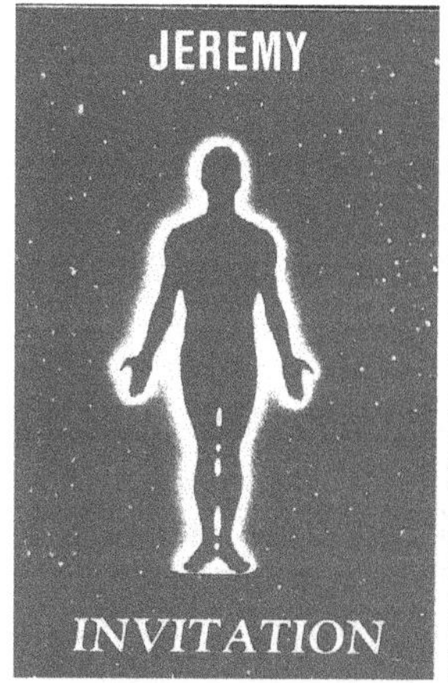

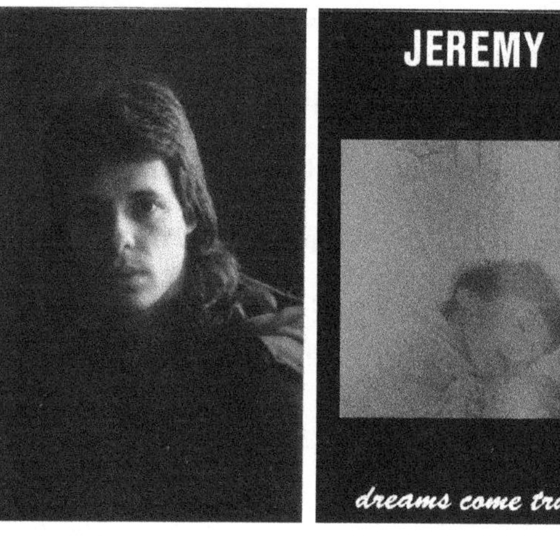

JEREMY
INVITATION

JEREMY
GREEN

JEREMY
SOUL SAVER

JEREMY
DREAMS COME TRUE

Since the last issue of Feedback, I have again heard from Jeremy Morris who, not content with having three CDs reviewed in the last issue, has now sent me four cassettes to review in this one! Having listened to them, I know now that not only is Jeremy extremely prolific but also that he has a wide range of tastes and styles.

'Invitation' is a collection of demos from the mid Seventies and Jeremy himself says that these are for completists only. He does himself something of an injustice here, as although they are whimsical and very Beatles oriented (with Jeremy sounding less like Nick Barrett and more like John Lennon) they are certainly very enjoyable, although lightweight. This was his first release, recorded between 1975 and 1978 and his guitar work is fluid and interesting although here he is concentrating more on acoustic instrumentation. 'Green' was recorded between 1978 and 1980 and is very similar in fashion, and I am sure that it is by design that the artwork for each complements the other. 'Soul Saver' is again marked down as being demos for the diehard, and was recorded between 1978 and 1979, and is the first to feature a band, and Jeremy is very much electric again. It is an album of tunes that will appeal to those into soft rock and as the title suggests it is a Christian album and certainly stands up well against the 'White Metal' albums that I have heard from that period. 'Dreams Come True' is an instrumental progressive album from 1993 and is the only one of these four to feature solely Jeremy and drummer Dave Dietrich, the pairing that also featured on the albums I reviewed last time. The difference between these and the other recordings shows just why Jeremy views the others as just demos, as this release is far more mature in every way. Not content with "just" being a good guitarist, Jeremy displays some wonderful pianowork as well as good keyboard control. The use of a 'real' drummer again lifts Jeremy away from many of the other sole multi-instrumentalists. He is certainly not short of ideas and tunes, and where he finds the time, I just do not know.
#42, July 1997

JEREMY
CELESTIAL CITY

I have reviewed quite a few of Jeremy's albums over the last few years, and it still surprises me that he can be so prolific. This is his second album for Kinesis and continues the story and themes of his last album, 'Pilgrim's Progress'. For those who have not heard of him before, Jeremy is a multi-instrumentalist who delights in bringing music of the highest order, reminiscent of bands such as Camel and artists such as Steve Hackett and Anthony Phillips. 'Celestial City'; contains thirteen songs, some very short while others stretch, and my favourite at present is the fifteen-minute plus "The Door" which has some very Genesis-like guitarwork. Even though this is music without words, the impression is that Jeremy always knows exactly where to go and how to get there; this is not meaningless meanderings. Although he may not be as well-known over here as he should be, even in the progressive field, that does not mean his talent or music is any less. If you enjoy progressive music that is gentle and lilting without becoming New Age then this is very much the album for you. *#50, Aug 1998*

JEREMY
KINGDOM COME

JEREMY
LOST AND FOUND

JEREMY
STILL WATERS

JEREMY
FIND THE WAY TO BE HAPPY

JEREMY
ONLY LOVE REMAINS

JEREMY
HOME IN THE SKY

JEREMY + PROGRESSOR
THE PEARL OF GREAT PRICE

You may recall from my darXtar review that I had gone into the roof to sort out my cassettes. One artist that I kept coming across was Jeremy Morris, who at one point many years ago I had been in contact with regularly. We had lost touch, and the tapes reminded me that I used to enjoy his music, so I wondered what he was now doing and if he was still in the music business. The answer to that, simply, is 'yes'. He has now released more than thirty albums, and these are not CD-R's with a photocopied insert, but proper productions with full artwork and booklets. I now have seven of his more recent albums to review, covering a multitude of styles and genres (the last CD I reviewed was 'Salt The Planet', aeons ago). First into the player was the (I suppose that should be 'a') 2002 release, 'Kingdom Come'. This is the third in a trilogy of instrumental progressive albums that started with 'Pilgrim's Journey' and carried through with 'Celestial City'. Only seven songs, it still clocks in at a very respectable seventy plus minutes, which is helped in no small way by the title song which is nearly half the album's total length. I had forgotten quite how pleasant it is to listen Jeremy's material, he has the confidence of the multi-instrumentalist combined with a strong knowledge of arrangements, so he knows whether a song calls for an acoustic guitar at this part, or what synth sound to use or what effects to employ. There is quite a heavy use of keyboards, which creates almost a Tangerine Dream feel at times, while others are more reminiscent of Camel and even Mike Oldfield. For me this was an enjoyable start to looking again at his catalogue.

'Lost and Found' from 2004 is such a different release from the previous one that it is hard to realise that it is the same person at the heart of it all. It is about now that thoughts start to turn to Todd Rundgren, as this album (27 songs on a single CD) is packed full of songs that are power pop to the max. This is not a solo album, as he has brought in many guests to assist him in producing an album that absolutely screams psychedelia at the top of its voice. So many songs could be lifted as singles, especially in the American market, that it is an embarrassment that they have not been. It is not surprising that there is a Byrds cover included, as well as one from The Who, and even Anthony Phillip's "Silver Song". This music is layered, with harmony vocals abounding that it brings back a time long gone yet is all so refreshing and vibrant. This was his 30th release and although the man is a total workaholic, one must wonder how a major hasn't picked this up. If you think that The Magic Numbers are the band to be looking for then you ought to search this out.

Also from 2004 is 'Still Waters', which is again a totally solo instrumental album, but this time Jeremy is just using acoustic six and twelve-string guitars. Among the people he has dedicated this to can be found Gordon Giltrap, Anthony Phillips and Steve Hackett, all of whom have a track performed as a tribute. This is an album to be listened to at the end of the day when you want to be in a reflective mood, as it is stunningly beautiful. It is delicate and very emotional, containing a lot of passion in these gently strummed or picked notes. When playing in this medium one must be dedicated to get the best out of his instrument and in many ways, this does remind me more of Giltrap than of the others, although mostly his dreamier and gentle side than when he is blasting away at high speed. So, three albums in, and three totally different styles and types of music, which in some ways shows why it can be so difficult to get a handle on an artist so prolific as Jeremy as he seems to be so strong at whatever it is he wants to achieve, yet at the same time he can be producing albums that bear no musical relationship to each other which may in turn mean that fans of his pop style may not want to listen to gentle acoustic guitar!

'Find the Way To Be Happy' is one of four Jeremy CDs that I have here from 2005 and is a solid return to the power pop psych of 'Lost and Found'. The harmonies are lush, and even though this was recorded with only three other musicians, the feeling is yet again of

many people involved with arrangements that are both layered and immediate. There is even a Sweet cover on here, but not one that I had come across before, "Are You Coming Up To See Me?", which is certainly different to the usual "Blockbuster". Again, this album is just packed full of hooks and riffs, and after playing do not be surprised to go around singing the chorus to "What God Wants" which also features some wonderfully distorted guitar and even a sitar! 22 songs on this single CD, and it closes with Jeremy's distorted rocked out version of "Star Spangled Banner". I think I may have heard this done before somewhere, yet in some ways it is totally in keeping with the rest of the album, but also very much off the wall so is quite fun.

'Only Love Remains' is in many ways a direct continuation of 'Happy' as again it is a band playing wonderful power pop but here the guitar seems to be that much further forward and a bit less of the psych, at least on some. Only fourteen songs on this album, as there are fewer short ones, and he even allows himself to stretch out with one, "The Actor (Part 2)" which is over six minutes long. My favourite is probably "This Is War" which starts off rocky and the guitar stays a constant throughout, and there is even some distortion laid over the top, and a double-tracked distorted guitar solo which seems perfect for the number itself. That is one of the joys of Jeremy's music in that he can keep it simple, or be intricate, which means that it is always a surprise when putting on a CD as one never knows quite what is going to jump out of the speakers.

So far within these albums we have had instrumental prog, acoustic guitar, and a few of power pop, so of course it is about time for Jeremy to produce yet another style. Here is another instrumental album but this time Jeremy is playing just a grand piano. This is again a very delicate album, with stacks of emotion, and has a lot in common with 'Still Waters' in that this is reflective, and something to create an atmosphere in which to think. He has a nice touch on the keyboards, and while there is a certain simplicity about what he is doing, this is not grandiose in the manner of Wakeman or Emerson: it certainly captures the attention and again is one that is to be played at the end of the day. It is strange to think that the person playing this has also written and produced two power pop albums in the same year. And if that was not enough…

'The Pearl Of Great Price' was a project which saw Jeremy joining forces with Russian musician Progressor (Vitaly Menshikov) and Brian Hirsch to create an album that is quite different to those that he has been producing himself. Here the keyboard sounds are far more spacey and clinical, and to these he has added some dynamic guitar solos so that even though there are three people playing keyboards it is often his guitar that is the driving force, giving it a quite Gilmore-esque feel. Of all the ones I have played, this is probably the one that I have enjoyed least, as it does not always seem to quite gel and there is the feeling somehow that the music was being forced out whereas on his own albums it seems to flow very naturally. The synth drums do absolutely nothing for me either, but this is the one album where Jeremy can provide electric guitar with long drawn out solos.

So, there you have it, seven albums from a fascinating musician who is a great talent. It is wonderful to be back in touch with him again after all this time and the realisation that I still have a lot of catching up to do with his material is both a daunting prospect and one that I look forward to.
#86, Feb 2006

JEREMY
POP DREAMS

JEREMY
FRUIT TREE

JEREMY
KING OF KINGS

JEREMY
LORD OF LORDS

GUILLERMO CAZENAVE
DÚPLEX

GUILL & JEM
TWO SUNS

When I got back in touch with Jeremy a few months ago, I told him that I hadn't heard anything since 'Salt The Planet'. With this set of CDs, plus the ones I reviewed in #86 I think that I am now back up to date! The title of this 2003 release gives the game away as to what the style is that one will find inside the covers. This is Sixties style psych pop at its finest – he has obviously been paying very close attention to what was happening in the UK and there is that naïve joy that can only be found in recordings of that period. The backing vocals are lush, and not at all self-conscious in a way not normally found these days. Pick any of the fifteen songs and you are onto a winner, as I can guarantee that whichever one you are playing will be the favourite. Even the sound of the instruments makes the listener think that this is a long-lost classic as opposed to something that is only a few years old. Go on, I dare you to listen to this without smiling and humming along...

'Fruit Tree', also from 2003, shows another side to Jeremy as here he is seated at a grand piano. There are no vocals, no studio trickery, and just one man creating beautiful modern classical music. This is music that can be played gently in the background or listened to intently and works extremely well on both levels. This is all about music that is accessible, with the emphasis on beauty as opposed to showing how quickly and cleverly he can play. There are many little fills that demonstrate the skill that he has; it is just that the music he is developing does not need it. I can 'see' him in my mind playing the piano with his eyes closed as he loses himself.

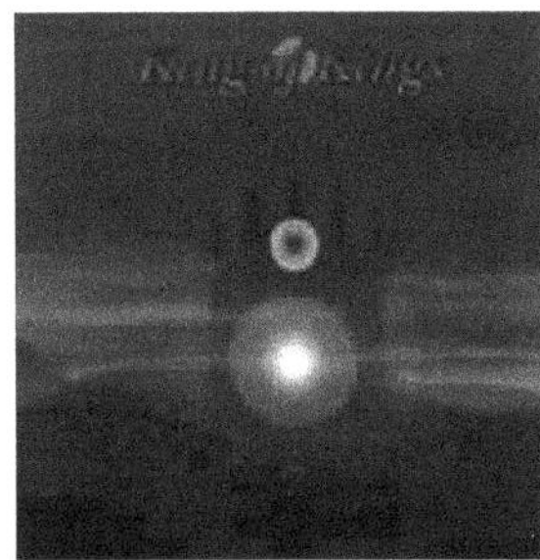

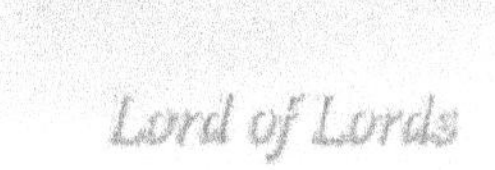

'Kings Of Kings' is from 2004 and is the first in a series of Praise and Worship recordings. This is again just Jeremy but here he has opened his box of tricks and is revelling in his role as multi-instrumentalist. It is again softly sung but here we have 32 songs with nothing more than 3½ minutes long, and many under two. This style of worship to my ears is something that is very Pentecostal and even within the Church in this country I would have thought that this would have limited appeal. But Jeremy has again put all his talents against it so that although this is a more restricted style, he has still put his psych pop layerings all over it. 'Lord Of Lords' came out the following year and is in a similar style to 'King Of Kings', although here Jeremy has moved even more firmly into his normal style and away from some of the more Pentecostal stylings of the first one. There are also some longer songs here that allows him to spread out a bit more with a couple of numbers five minutes long. The harmonies and melodies are still here, but of the two I would argue that this is the more mature album and the one that is easier to listen to and to enjoy. Even the shorter songs have more presence and are away from the more gospel style of the previous.

Unfortunately, I have very little information on Cazenave's album, as the booklet is in Spanish as is the label site. However, this appears to be a collection of recordings covering a period of twenty-one years, where Guillermo has been collaborating with other musicians. Those involved are: Quique Berro, Steven Halpern, Juan Puñet, Arden Wilken, Andrés Gil, Anthony Phillips, Jeremy and many others. This is a very diverse album, so much so that I doubt if any one person would enjoy listening to it all the way through. He is trying to portray a vast amount of styles, and while this works the result is somewhat overpowering. The song with Anthony Phillips is quite unlike anything I have heard from Anthony before and I am not sure that it works. The best number is the closing "Truth" which is over twelve minutes long and features Jeremy on vocals. This is much more laid back and slowly progresses and meanders along in a very pleasant fashion indeed.

I do not know anything about the last release either, and there is nothing in the booklet saying who played here, but one presumes that it is just Guill Cazenave and Jeremy. Interestingly this also includes the song that Jeremy performed on the previous album, "Truth", and as this is by far the better album, I know which one I would buy to get this. There are two singer songwriters bouncing off each other, and while there is other instrumentation, they are at their best when it is just acoustic guitars. There is one cover on here, that of Anthony Phillips' "Silver Song" which will obviously be of interest to Genesis fans, and overall this double CD works very well indeed.

So, there you have it – progressive multi-instrumentalist, pianist, psychedelic pop muso, singer-songwriter. Whatever way you look at it, Jeremy is an incredible talent.
#87, Apr 2006

JEREMY
FAITHFUL AND TRUE

'Faithful and True' is the third in Jeremy's Praise and Worship recordings, containing twenty songs which are his "true love songs to God". According to the website "Fans of classic Byrds, Beatles, Hollies, Simon and Garfunkel, and happy spiritual sounds are sure to dig the ultra-positive good vibrations of 'Faithful and True'. It's all about peace, love, and understanding." Those who might be expecting a series of short hymn-like pieces are going to be surprised as there are two numbers stretching to ten minutes. Jeremy has a wonderful talent for moving through whatever genre he wants to investigate so here there are large elements of prog as well as some of his more melodic pop, all swathed with an evangelical feel that will be easily recognisable to anyone who has regularly attended that style of church. This will not be of interest to everyone, but this is an album that Christians will get a lot out of. Do not forget, it is also possible to get the rest of his albums on the site as well – many of which have been reviewed in Feedback at one time or another.
#88, Jun 2006

JERONIMO ROAD
LIVE AT THE ORANGE

Jeronimo Road was a band put together by Adam Wakeman, along with guitarist Fraser T. Smith. Fraser had previously been in the band La Salle (now there is an awesome album that needs to see the light of day, I love it!) and he soon brought on-board the singer from that band, Damian Wilson (also ex-Landmarq and ex-Threshold), and the line-up on this live recording was completed by Phil Williams on bass and Mark Heaney on drums. The idea was that this would be a showcase for record companies, but the gig on 27th July 1996 was one of only a few that the band completed, and they soon folded to each go onto other things. With musicians such as these, it is no surprise that the band are cooking, with the rhythm section keeping it rocking with Adam and Fraser trading licks.

The result is an album that is full of power, sometimes being driven by keyboards and at others by guitar, and this is a technical rock album with plenty going for it. I have long been a fan of Damian's vocals and yet again he here proves that he has one of the finest voices in UK rock. Often quick and intricate, this is music that shows off the talents of those involved without ever losing the feeling that this is very much a song-based outfit. This also includes the only surviving studio tracks of the band plus a multi-media section. This includes a biography, a mixing desk so that you can have fun with one of their songs, along with histories, what are they doing now and some more unreleased material. Overall this is well worth investigating.
#87, Apr 2006

STEVE JOLIFFE
INVITATION
This album takes pieces from eleven of Steve's solo albums recorded between 1979 and 1996. He is probably best known for his work with Tangerine Dream, although he has also recently been working with Eat Static. I enjoy keyboard and atmospheric music but for the most part this is just plain boring. Be warned.
#56, Jan 2000

JONES, EVANS, TURNER
LIVE
The full title of this album is 'Mazlyn Jones and Guy Evans with Nik Turner and friends - Live' and is taken from three separate gigs: one had the three of them plus Angus Lamond, Joe Shields and Dave Starky, one with just Mazlyn and Guy, and one with the two of them plus Angus and Dan Miles. Although not totally an instrumental album, the vocals are few and far between. Mazlyn is known as an acoustic singer-songwriter, while Guy is of course from VDGG as well as Peter Hamill's K Group and Mother Gong, while Nik was a founder of Hawkwind and Inner City Unit. It is of little surprise that the main element of the music is jazz mixing with prog, but the added use of Indian instrumentation in the form of a santor and the use of a didgeridoo has added a far more 'world' feel to proceedings. Guy has often been interested in producing percussive elements from other than drums, he did just that with Echo City of course, and this in turn also adds a distinctive air to proceedings.

It is an album with no overdubs whatsoever and obviously has a very 'live' feel. Whether it will be if interest outside of the jazz or world music field I doubt, but it is an enjoyable album nonetheless and one for the free festival attendees.
#43, Aug 1997

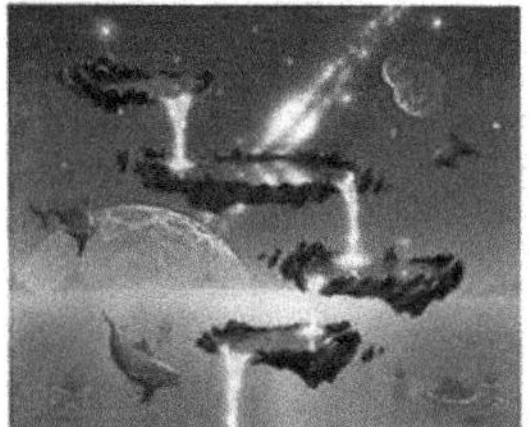

MAZLYN JONES
ANGELS OVER WATER

'Angels Over Water' is a collection of instrumentals from Mazyln's previous six albums, plus twenty-three minutes of new compositions featuring didgeridoo and violin. Some of you may have seen Mazlyn on tour either supporting bands such as BJH, Renaissance, Bob Geldof, Judie Tzuke etc. or in his own right. He sometimes performs as a solo artist, and at others is joined by Guy Evans on percussion and Nik Turner (ex-Hawkwind among others) on sax. Mazlyn manages to create a real collage of sound, and he has been described by German radio as a one-man Pink Floyd and although much of his music is acoustic or electric, it is certainly easy to find where they get this description from. Each song has very much a distinct style, and I have discovered that it greatly benefits from being played on headphones as there are so many nuances and deft touches that can easily be missed when playing through speakers. A darkened room with this playing and time to let the mind drift along on the winds of thought created by his music is sheer heaven. For anyone interested in music that mixes folk with New Age then here is an album for you. On the sleeve, Mazlyn explains some of the reasoning behind the CD, which makes interesting reading. I must also mention the fantastic sleeve by Steven Johannesson (very much in the style of Roger Dean) which is available as a print. If you feel intrigued enough to discover this wonderful CD then it is available from Isle of Light Records.

#21, Jan 1994

NIGEL MAZLYN JONES
BEHIND THE STONE

It has been far too long since I last had an album by Nigel to review. I remember when Rog Patterson sent me 'Angels Over Water', and the way that I knew that the album had to be something very special to live up to the superb artwork, and I was not wrong. This album shows Nigel playing songs accompanying himself on six or twelve-string guitars and using the skills of guests such as Phil Beer (Show Of Hands), Steve Joliffe (Tangerine Dream), Guy Evans (VDGG) and Rog Patterson. This is an album of atmosphere, what the listener would hear if he was at a gig. In fact, many of these songs are concert favourites that for one reason or another have never made it onto an album, while some others were written for the BBC. The songs are very powerful, with Nigel showing that there is no need for amplification turned to the max to convey strong emotions and feelings. The deeply thoughtful and provocative "In The Mystery" which sounds as if it belongs in a monastery, offsets songs such as the raucous "Unconditional Love". Nigel uses lyrics to show his strong ecological beliefs and they make the listener think, as they are very much part of the musical whole and belong to the man behind the song. When Nigel says what is happening to the world, and why, and what our own role is in this, then the passion is there to be felt. A superb album, by a singer-songwriter who has been concentrating on issues other than musical in recent years, but he is back with an album to be proud of.

#60, Oct 2000

JUMP
THE WINDS OF CHANGE

JUMP
WORLD OF WONDER

Jump were formed in 1990 and comprise guitarist Pete Davies (ex-The Big Rain), Hugh Gascoyne (bass), John Dexter Jones (vocals, ex-Rutterkin and ex-Thief), Mo (keyboards), Steve Hayes (guitars) and Andy Barker (drums and occasional vocals). Some of you may have seen the name Jump in Kerrang! because the mass media have been so impressed with them to grant them positive reviews. For those of you who have not seen Jump on one of their 200 plus gigs they have played around the country, or heard either of these two CDs, then you are missing out on a real treat. Jump are a classic English rock band that will be loved by the prog fan and the hardened rocker as well, as influences such as Tull and Marillion can be heard while at the same time there are definite nods to acts such as Grace or Red Jasper. Interested? Read on.

After their first year together, Jump went into MARS studio in Bucks to record their debut CD 'The Winds Of Change'. On listening to the debut, it is hard to realise that it was recorded and mixed in only 25 hours! Basically, it is a live album, with just the vocals being recorded separately. Jump's strength lies in the fact that they write strong songs and are not afraid to have them last under three minutes! Opening song is "The Lightbox" and the sharp staccato guitar works with the drawn-out keyboard chords to provide perfect backing for the vocals. Here is a rock band, different to the norm, using two guitarists but all too soon it is over, and the harmony vocals lead us into "A Picture In Gold". Already one is deep into the work of Jump. There are twelve tracks on this CD, none of them more than six minutes in length, which is rather different from the normal prog bands these days, but there again the music is as well so it should be expected. One of my favourites is "The Mystic", with some riffing guitars providing a dark image during the verse then turn for the chorus, great stuff: just proves that songs can be effective when only 3 ½ minutes long – not many prog bands seem to realise this. There is still room for changes of moods and styles, great lyrics, and loads of enjoyment. There are just so many different types of songs on this album, from the dirty and funky "Shelter Me", the beautiful and gentle ballad that is "A New World", the acoustic "Working For A Living" or the commercial belter "You Will Be Queen", Anyone who likes good rock, well played, cannot fail to fall head over heels in love with this album. It is not surprising that Jump managed to continue to build on their success as a live draw and sell respectable quantities of the CD, mainly at gigs. The revenue from this meant that the band had more time and money to go back into the studio and record the follow-up, 'World Of Wonder', which was released in March this year. the album is a step forward in terms of production and the songs are still of the very highest quality.

"A Northern Man" commences proceedings, as John seemingly forces the words "Believe me son, we can't fail". Gentle acoustic verses contrast with the hard rock of the chorus. Really, this song typifies what Jump are all about, as there are contrasting styles put together with great singing to provide a desired effect. As on the first album, when Jump feels that a song should finish it does, there are not any long-drawn-out goodbyes. It can be heard that Jump are very much a live act as these songs have been designed to transfer to the stage, and it is difficult to pick any that wouldn't work. I heard 'World of Wonder' prior to 'The Winds Of Change' (I'm the world's expert at being awkward, just ask Sara) and I was playing it and talking about it to anyone who would listen: it is just so good. There are ten tracks and by the end all you can do is let it play all over again. Other real highlights are the title track, which somehow manages to sound commercial although at times there are so many things going on it is amazing that it holds together, such as on "Where Silver Calls", where Mo's keyboards provide a swirling curtain for the guitars to be laid against, but it is the final number on the CD that is my real favourite. "Whip-Hand Jack" begins with John dedicating it to all the lowlife, with just Mo providing backing. As the song takes shape all the others join in, albeit reservedly and the song climaxes as it builds to the chorus where it is riffed out. 'World of Wonder' is probably the stronger of the two CDs, but they are both worth obtaining.

Jump have taken a whole host of influences and have put them together in a way that is interesting to anyone into good rock music, who does not feel the necessity to have it labelled one form or another to be able to enjoy it. I am convinced that given the right breaks Jump could find themselves being major players, but whether the fickle music press is ready for a talent as different as this remains to be seen. They are currently working on their third album and expect to have it ready for the beginning of 1994.
#19, Aug 1993

JUMP
...AND ALL THE KING'S MEN
Back in #19 I raved over the first two CDs by Jump. They have now returned with their third and in my opinion it is their best to date, and I loved the others! Jump are a six-piece based in High Wycombe, and they bring together a myriad of styles that makes them friends in both the heavy rock and progressive rock fields. Twin guitars provide the backbone to one of the best vocalists in the business, John Dexter Jones. Having played literally hundreds of gigs together, the band are obviously tight, and this well-crafted album shows a band at the height of their powers. Opener "All The King's Horses" gradually builds up and up onto the chorus where the song becomes a real hard rock number with John forcing the lyrics out. They sound nothing like Marillion, yet at the same time this song made me think of a harder better version of "Market Square Heroes" (although in reality it is nothing like it). It is quickly apparent that the songs are more commercial and accessible than the first two albums, and this is very much in their favour. Chrissie Hammond (ex-Cheetah, and currently with Rick Wakeman) is guest vocalist on some tracks and this provides an extra edge to the band. Her voice fits in very well with John's and on tracks such as "Share The Shame", a hard-edged ballad, it adds to what is already a great song. Songs are very much the order of the day; there is no time for incessant rambling solos but rather short direct hard punches. The twelve tracks on here prove that Jump have

what it takes to impress: styles may change throughout, but always interest is maintained. Take "Judgement Day" for example, in under four minutes, there is hard harmony vocals from John and Chrissie with minor accompaniment from Mo, but there is also room for power chords, slide guitar and a song that develops and changes many times. Yet it grooves along, and it is almost impossible to listen to without moving one part of your body or another. Jump have produced the goods yet again. Even better than 'The Winds of Change' or 'World of Wonder', '...And All The King's Men' shows a band of real substance. What do they have to do to be recognised as one of the best bands around? Do your ears a favour and get this album now.
#23, May 1994

JUMP
MYTH OF INDEPENDENCE

As promised in #30, here is a 'proper' review of Jump's fourth, and easily best, album to date. Now, I enjoyed the other three immensely but having lived with these songs for a while, it just must be the strongest set they have delivered. On top of that, Mark Kelly (he of Marillion) has done a top-notch job on the production, and no matter how loud you play it, it still sounds brilliant. In fact, the louder you play it the better it gets! It is of little surprise that a band that has played more than 500 gigs with an unchanged line-up is tighter than a duck's ass, but what puts Jump head and shoulders above the rest is their refusal to conform. To get anywhere in the music business these days you should fit in a pigeonhole but Jump steadfastly refuse to accept that and cross musical boundaries with ease and disdain. Jump are a rock band and that is the only way to describe them. "Tower Of Babel" starts with some atmospheric guitar and keyboards which leads into a funky number; then as John starts to spit venom the whole band moves up a gear and the song takes on a far more menacing stance as befits a song complaining about not being able to express yourself exactly as you want to as it may upset someone. In total contrast, "Princess Of The People" is a tongue in cheek look at Lady Di. It is when listening to this that one realises just how many little deft touches are being added into the song by the two guitarists, Pete and Steve. "Keep The Blues" is based around some great guitarwork, but of the eleven songs on the album the one that best stands as a typical Jump number is "Blind Birds". It begins life acoustically but comes to life with some great guitar and some wonderful nuances by Mo on keyboards. There is room for some power chords, time changes and mood swings as it goes to a fair while the lyrics are dark.

In my humble opinion Jump are one of the top live bands in the UK and with this superb album have managed to capture the essence of what they are about. Sooner or later the clear majority of the record buying public will cotton onto Jump. Now is the time to be ahead of the pack. Go on, set a trend, get 'The Myth Of Independence' today. You can thank me later...
#31, Oct 1995

JUMP

LIVING IN A PROMISED LAND

There can be very few bands in the world that can say that they have made it to their fifth album with the same line-up that recorded the debut. This band have not changed since their inception, and the music they are producing now is the best of their career. Although they have always been a heavily gigging band, it is over the last year or so that they have gained more public prominence, touring with both Marillion and Fish. The last album was produced by Marillion keyboard maestro Mark Kelly, while for this it is a return to MARS, and for some reason they are all the better for it. I have long been a fan of Jump, both in the studio and in the live environment where they are a breath-taking act and have always found their music to be of the highest quality, with great songs. So why is it then that I find this album so much better than those that have gone before? There is no doubt that this is easily their finest work to date, but is it because Mo seems to have been given a more prominent role on keyboards, is it because Pete and Steve are playing their guitars better than ever before? It can't be because the rhythm section is tighter, because they have always been red hot, or is it because frontman John Dexter Jones is singing with more confidence? Confidence, I think that may well be the key word. Jump has always had a strong and loyal fanbase, but they have now proved to themselves that by touring with two well-known acts they can play to large unfamiliar crowds and win them over. There is a market for their music, and although I am sure they always believed it, now they know it.

From the beginning of the opening track, where one of the guitars and the keyboards were joined in a melody lead, giving way to a Grace-style song, I found myself thinking there was something different. Everything seems to have moved up a notch in terms of quality, and when you think that what they released previously was good, that is something indeed. This is a rock album, which hits a lot of the bases covered by that term. There is prog, yes, but if I had to describe this in a few words I would say that it is a melodic rock album influenced as much by folk and bands like Tull as by bands like Marillion. The guitars leads are very crisp and clear, with "The Pressed Man" sounding as if Martin Lancelot Barre was present. Best track? No competition to these ears. "Promised Land Blues" is halfway through the album and start heavily enough although soon becomes gentle. John sings clearly and softly while there are some Tull-style leads over the top but gradually, ever so gradually, as John sings a damning indictment of the state of our country the music picks up the rawness and roughness of the words and becomes a kicking bouncing rock number. I must admit that this is very Fish in overall style, and it possible that they have picked up the influence without ever being aware of it. There is even a singalong near the end! This is sheer brilliance and is already my favourite all-time Jump number.

To sum up, if you have enjoyed Jump previously then you will have no hesitation in running out and getting this as soon as it is available, but if you have yet to buy a Jump album but were lucky enough to see them on tour recently then you must get this. However, if you have missed out on them over the last eight years then BUY THIS NOW!*#47, Feb 1998*

JUMP
THE FREEDOM TRAIN

JUMP
MATTHEW

After nine years with the same line-up, and five studio albums behind them, the time was right to release a live album. What was also special about this night was that it was to be the last gig with Hugh Gascoyne on bass, who had decided to leave. The booklet is a tribute to Hugh, which I have not seen from a band to a departing member before. The front cover shows the five remaining members of the band waiting at a train station, with a poster of Hugh on the station wall. The photo on the rear shows the five all staring at the photo with new bassist Andy Faulkner (Walking On Ice) just walking into shot. The photo on the rear of the tray card shows the six of them walking off to catch 'The Freedom Train'. The words in the booklet also show just how much Hugh was admired and respected by the rest of the band, but also how they knew that they would continue without him. Jump seem to virtually live on the road at times, I have lost count of how many times I have seen them (favourite gig was probably at The Marquee when they completely outshone GLD, although some of the gigs with Credo were also superb) and have met and talked with them many times.

John Dexter Jones is renowned as being one of the finest frontmen in the business, as well as being a great singer; twin guitarists Pete Davies and Steve Hayes have an intimate understanding of each other, Mo fills in the missing pieces with gentle keyboards while Hugh and Andy Barker were totally solid. Jump are one of the 'oddities' of the progressive scene, in that they have been embraced by that crowd but in reality, they have little musical affinity with much of the prog crowd. Firstly, they are very much guitar based, with keyboards just used for melodic effect as opposed to being a lead instrument, and they are also very much a songs outfit. They play English Rock, and while they have been likened to both Marillion and Fish at times, with whom they have both completed UK tours, they are very much their own band with their own sound. This album has provided the opportunity to have almost a 'Best Of' package, while at the same time the versions on offer are superior to those which were recorded in the studio as John reacts to the crowd and the passion is there for all to hear. Personal favourites are probably "The Pressed Man" and "Shed No Tears" but there is not a duff song to be heard.

The new album, 'Matthew', shows the band at probably their most confident ever, and is a major step forward from their last album 'Living In A Promised Land'. The songs are very strong, and the production is top quality. There is so much on here to enjoy, but the highlights are the way that they encompass slightly different musical ideas to give reach song a very strong identity. The slide guitar on "Alone Ahead" is not overpowering but is integral. Probably my favourite part is the lazy introduction to "The Highway Man": it's only a few bars but it proves that anything Wishbone Ash can do, then Jump can do at least as well. Two superb albums from one of the UK's best bands. *#59, July 2000*

JUMP
ON IMPULSE

What can be said about Jump that hasn't been already? Surely there can be few discerning rock lovers out there who have not seen this band on one of their many treks around the country, and hopefully I will again have the chance to catch up with them when they headline the Friday night at Whitchurch on 2nd August. This is their eighth album, in which time they have had only one change of line-up, and even new boy Andy Faulkner has been with them for more than three years. While they often find themselves placed in with the prog crowd, the band have musically little in common with the many bands basing their whole career on the collected works of Genesis or Pink Floyd. This is a rock band, first and foremost, and while the foundations are a strong rhythm section with some added keyboards, the band are driven by the twin guitars of Steve Hayes and Pete Davies. They have complementary styles and can play harmonies, riffs, or add gentle touches and musical lines to give songs depth and presence. Talking of presence, at the front of all of this is the towering figure of one John Dexter Jones who not only provides a fair set of pipes but strides the stage and the music like a Welshman on a mission. 'On Impulse' takes a little while to get going, and while I enjoyed the first few songs, I felt that the edge was not quite there, but "Bethesda" marked a turning point. The delicacy of the music belies the power and emotion of the words and the band have come alive. "Right Winger" is strong on slide guitar, while "Thom's New Clothes" is a lesson in building to a crescendo and sounds like classic Horslips. Having started to crank it up, the highlight of the album is next in "Like A Drum". The guitars are powerful, and the emotion and passion are physical beasts, just waiting to be unleashed as they are on the bridge. This must be awesome live. To follow that up is a delicate number, John and an acoustic guitar, while "Doctor Spin" again shows the band rocking along. Overall it may not be a truly great album, but it does contain some truly great songs and I am sure that with more plays I will appreciate the whole even more. *#69, Aug 2002*

JUMP
HOME SONGS

There surely can't be much left to say about these guys – for years they have been one of the hardest gigging bands in the UK and they have released the odd album or two, all the same high quality. In fact, apart from the extremely amicable parting from their original bassist a few years ago they still have the same line -up as when they started (although for this album they have now added a backing singer). This is British rock; I would hesitate at using the word 'English' as that may just upset the rather tall and very vocal front man John Dexter Jones. Jump never fail to produce the goods, and 'Home Songs' is another case in point, although I did find that this album took a bit more perseverance than its predecessor 'On Impulse'. It is songs such as "The Better Part Of Valour" that show this band at their best (is that a mandolin I hear?): it is strong and powerful yet at the same time with plenty of room for John to take centre stage. These guys may never be fashionable, but they know what they want to produce, and do not worry if the record buying masses never see things their way. This is quality and they know it. They do sometimes step almost into the prog field, with "Never Too Far" having some Marillion-esque tendencies, but then they also put on some slide guitar just to ensure that no-one thinks that they are clones of anyone. Jump often get lumped in with prog bands, as they seem to share a similar audience, but they have more in common with class acts of old than they do with neo-prog pretenders of today. It is another album by Jump, therefore it is good: a mathematical certainty. *#73, Apr 2003*

JUMP
A MAN WAS MADE

JUMP
FAITHFUL FAITHLESS

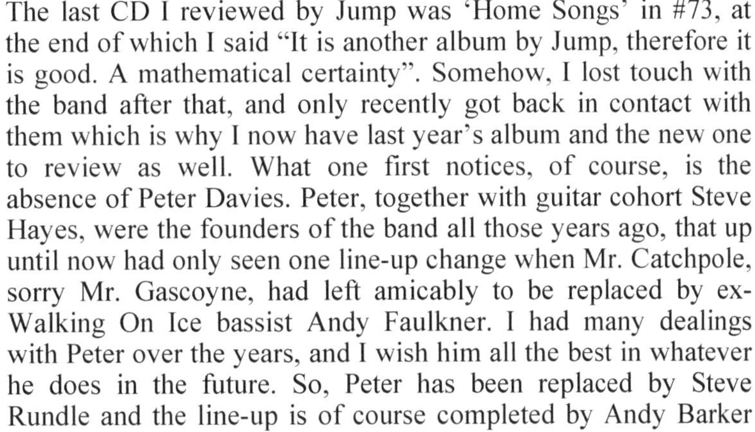

The last CD I reviewed by Jump was 'Home Songs' in #73, at the end of which I said "It is another album by Jump, therefore it is good. A mathematical certainty". Somehow, I lost touch with the band after that, and only recently got back in contact with them which is why I now have last year's album and the new one to review as well. What one first notices, of course, is the absence of Peter Davies. Peter, together with guitar cohort Steve Hayes, were the founders of the band all those years ago, that up until now had only seen one line-up change when Mr. Catchpole, sorry Mr. Gascoyne, had left amicably to be replaced by ex-Walking On Ice bassist Andy Faulkner. I had many dealings with Peter over the years, and I wish him all the best in whatever he does in the future. So, Peter has been replaced by Steve Rundle and the line-up is of course completed by Andy Barker on drums, Mo on keyboards, and the unique and amazing John Dexter Jones on vocals. If you have not yet experienced the wonder that is Jump onstage, then a) you have no excuse if you live in the UK as they always seem to be on the road and b) you do not know what you are missing. Of course, if you have seen Jump live you will know that the musicians must work damn hard to get themselves noticed, due to the stage presence of the rather excitable Welshman.

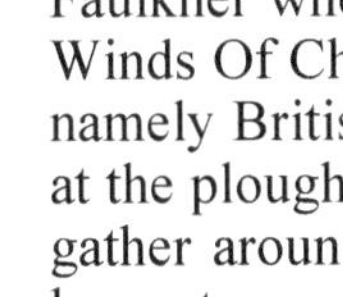

But these are not live albums, but new studio works and if my maths is correct then 2004's 'A Man Was Made' was their ninth studio album, their fourth with new boy Andy Faulkner who must be rather pleased to be able to drop that tag now. Since 1991's 'The Winds Of Change' Jump have forged a furrow in what is a pretty empty and barren field, namely British song-based rock with progressive overtones. For a while they were joined at the plough by Grace but again they seem to be working alone and while the crows may gather around, these guys (sorry Mo) just keep producing the goods and there is a rich harvest every season. Okay, enough analogies, but whatever you could possibly want from song-based rock is here. There is passion, melody, music to rock to and music to think to. You can find yourself singing along to "Such Sweet Sorrow" or listening intently to the piano-based "Drinking In The Darkness". Peter may have left but again the band are mining the deep vein of their musical heritage.

Another year and yet another studio album, the second with the new line-up so of course Ronnie is an old hand by now. It opens with "Shoulder To The Wheel" which is gentle and delicate yet also has a very Wishbone Ash sound to the guitars. In many ways, this is a rockier album that its predecessor, but there is also the space and thoughtfulness that make Jump stand out so much from the rest of the crowd. This is rock music of the old school that asks for respect and expects the audience to be moved by songs that can be both simple and complex, yet always containing a straightforward dignity and power missing from most. Jump are a band that have always worked hard on the live circuit and produce consistently strong albums that reward repeated plays time and again, and these are no different. Jump have been going for fifteen years now and I for one hope that they will still be striving and producing wonderful songs for many years yet. I believe that the next release will be a live album, which I am looking forward to hearing – it is far too long since I last saw them in concert – but with these albums they have again reawakened my interest in a wonderful band. *#85, Nov 2005*

KADA
OHOÁÉ,B

Kada were formed in 1995 by guitarist Laszlo Valik who wanted to play a complex and complicated form of jazz. He describes the music as "free-structural-progressive-avantgarde-rock-jazz-noise -core", and this their third album was recorded live with a basic structure being extended with improvisations. Although Laszlo is the bandleader, he does not feel the need to dominate proceedings, so it is not unusual for the brass section to be taking control of the music and leading it through with the rest providing support. This is music that to the unwary may just seem like a lot of noise, but it does not take very long for the listener to be aware of just what these guys are trying to achieve, and from there on in this all makes wonderful musical sense. They may be Hungarian but as all the music is instrumental, there are no vocals to contend with, and the impression is that these guys have been listening to Miles and are more influenced by what has been happening on the other side of the pond as opposed to bringing in many influences from their own country. The booklet and packaging have all been completed in a simplistic childlike style and the result works very well. I was very impressed with this and I am sure that other jazz lovers will feel the same. *#88, Jun 2006*

MARIUS KAHAN
TOMORROW'S MEMORIES

Not my usual cup of tea, but I found that I warmed up very quickly to this violin-led instrumental release. Mostly a jazz album, Marius is more than willing to share the musical leads with the rest of the guys which means that his own sound is fresh and has something to bounce off. I particularly enjoyed the use of acoustic bass on "Desert Orchid", which displays a very languid feel, with Marius often not playing for bars at a time, which means that his presence is amplified when he again takes over from the guitarists. If jazz is your thing, then this debut album is well worth investigating as Marius does things with a fiddle that I found at times very reminiscent of Courtney Pine. *#56, Jan 2000*

KAIPA
KEYHOLDER

Kaipa were one of the top Swedish bands of the Seventies but split in 1982. Eventually, guitarist Roine Stolt burst back onto the scene with the album 'The Flower King', formed a band to promote the album, and the rest is history. In 2002 he re-joined forces with keyboard player Hans Lundin plus new members, drummer Morgan Ågren (Zappa), bassist Jonas Reingold (Flower Kings) and singer Patrik Lundström (Ritual). They released 'Notes From The Past' and have now been joined by additional singer Aleena for their new work, 'Keyholder'. Given the history between Roine and Hans, it is probably not surprising that this album looks backwards far more than many other modern progressive bands. Yes, there are sections which come across as Flower Kings, but that is not surprising given that Roine writes for both, but this album has a much more Seventies feel to it. It is as if someone has taken bands such as Yes and Gentle Giant from that period and then thrown them straight into the modern arena and told them to get on with it. This album can be extremely intense or even light hearted – Jonas has an extremely important part to play, as he must switch between lead melody to background many times within certain songs, providing the bedrock for Roine and Hans. The use of Aleena as an additional lead vocalist has also given the band another melodic style, as her pure clear vocals contrast well with Patrik. On "A Complex Work Of Art" she shines, lifting the music to even greater heights. I have been a critic of recent Flower Kings albums in that they can come across as just too long, with the impression of filler material, but even though this album comes in at nearly eighty minutes (eight songs) that accusation just cannot be made this time. All progheads with half an ear to the classic period will find this a joy from start to end.
#78, Apr 2004

KAIPA
MINDREVOLUTIONS

It is now thirty years since the first Kaipa album, although many of their fans will only be aware of the music that has been created since the 'reformation' in 2002 when original members Hans Lundin and Roine Stolt put together a band working together under that banner. All the music on this album is by Hans, with Roine assisting on the lyrics – given his other projects it is probably not surprising that he does not have time to write for Kaipa as well. However, one of the main influences from The Flower Kings is apparent, in that this is again an eighty-minute-long album and one wonders if judicious editing would have improved the overall feel. But, when it works, such as on the hugely impressive "Electric Leaves" with Aleena and Patrik trading vocals, it is an album to

enjoy. Hans concentrates very much on Seventies-style sounds on the keyboards while yet again Roine shows what a fine guitarist he is either in a supportive role or taking on the lead with some very solid solos. There are going to be some who find the title track hugely inspiring and a classic piece of art, while others are going to say that at twenty-five minutes long it does not hold the attention as it should during the three sections, although it does contain some fine passages. Overall, I do not think that this can be viewed as a classic Kaipa album, but it does stand up against much of the other progressive albums that are being released and this view could well just be down to personal taste on my part. By the way, love the artwork.
#84, July 2005

KALO
SPIRAL DREAM
This mostly instrumental Japanese album kicks off with some dominant guitar with swirling keyboards behind – then it is straight into a guitar-led waltz through some glorious prog, with more than one eye on IQ, but probably in a rockier fashion such as Uli Jon Roth. But this does not last too long, and soon it is into the realm of dreams and gentleness, which then seem to last for a lot of the album. The band have decided on their musical style, but it does mean that soon this album is nothing more than background. That is a shame as if there had been more music like the first number "Dhavrani" then this would have been an album to cherish.
#79, May 2004

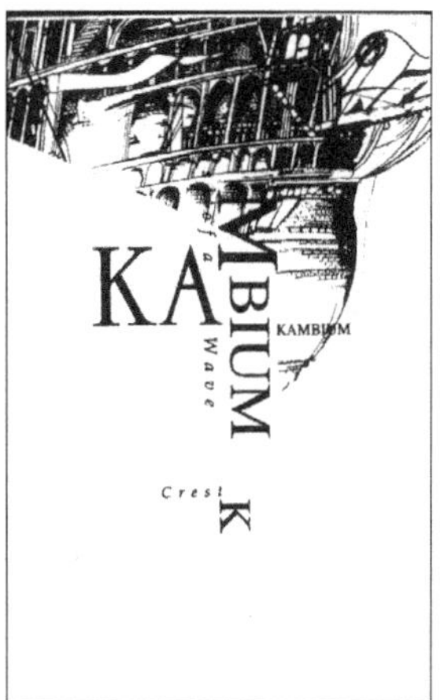

KAMBIUM
CREST OF A WAVE

KAMBIUM
WELCOME TO THE BOOMTOWN
At long last here is a band that is local to me who are worth discovering, which makes a pleasant change. What is also different is that here is one that can truly be said to be "progressing", mixing together so many different influences and styles that they end up with one all their own. Taking different songs, you could say that they sound a bit like Tull, The Cult, Fairport, Led Zep, The Waterboys and loads of others, mixing folk and indie rock with nonchalance. Interested? Kambium are Simon Hall (vocals, acoustic guitar), Michael Upjohn (guitars, backing vocals), Chris Vallis (bass, backing vocals) and Matt Dowden (percussion, backing vocals). On top of that they have a guest mandolin player in Az, and a guest violinist in Jak. They have been together for more than two years now and have managed to play more than 100 gigs even though their drummer is a lighting engineer and keeps disappearing to Europe on tour. They have released two tapes, 'Crest of A Wave' and 'Welcome To The Boomtown', both of which I found very refreshing.

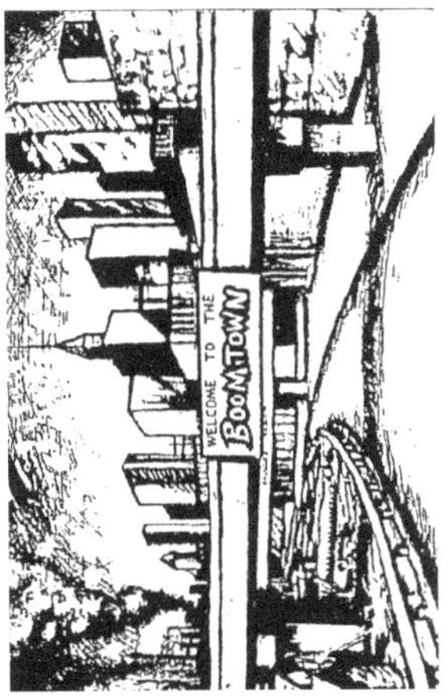

The former contains six songs, and was even played by Tommy Vance, not bad for a first demo. Standout is the wonderful "Kingsborough Green", which is dominated by powerful acoustic guitar and good harmony vocals. 'Welcome To The Boomtown' contains five songs, and all the lyrics are printed on the insert. Starter "Not What I Need" shows a real urgency to the band, yet at the same time a more definite move into the acoustic arena. This is not pure folk, but rather a complex rock song played virtually totally acoustically, with loads of energy and enthusiasm. Just to show the diversity of the band, that is followed by the belter "Hurry Hurry". Kambium are a band that are musically diverse, and to my ears exciting just because they are so different to much of the current prog scene. They are a band that would be at home supporting Jump, Red Jasper or Grace, but they are very much their own. They are recording new songs (the tapes are about eighteen months old) and hope to have a CD EP out sometime in the future.
#20, Oct 1993

KAMELOT
THE BLACK HALO
One of the best quotes I saw about this album was when one reviewer said, "imagine if Magnum played power metal". Somehow, I can't ever see that happening, and personally I am not sure where he got the idea from, but it is a great quote nonetheless – it just shows what weird thoughts go through our minds when we are trying to describe music to people. Personally, I would rather think of this of an extremely heavy power metal band playing melodic rock with some prog tendencies. As if Threshold or Dream Theater were playing something just a little less complex than their normal prog metal. However you try and judge this album, it comes up trumps all the way, whether it is in the songs, the musicianship or the production it is just impossible to pick fault. This is music that is exciting and powerful, yet there is also enough light with the shade to show off the dynamics. This is their eighth album in ten years, but the quantity certainly does not seem to have an impact in the quality: maybe the reverse is true as they are gelling into one of the top power metal acts around. In some ways, this is a continuation of the Faustus themes from their last album, 'Epica', but it can be enjoyed even if that album has not been heard.

Many reviewers have already been giving this album top marks and hailing it as one of the albums of 2005 and this time it would only be churlish of me to disagree with them. This is a quality album; power metal just can't get any better than this – if you want intensity and melody combined with plenty of riffs and great songs then this should be investigated further.
#83, Mar 2005

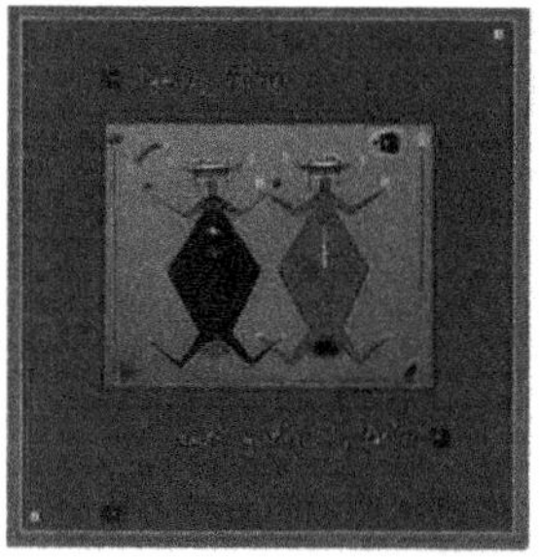

KAMPEC DOLORES
EARTH MOTHER SKY FATHER
It does not take a lot to get me confused I know, but this is an album by a Hungarian band released on a Japanese label, and now being sent to me in England to review. The band have been together in one shape or another since 1984, and the name means "the end of pains" but strangely neither of the words are Hungarian: 'Kampec' is Yiddish, while 'Dolores' is Latin. Add to that the musical style which is a strange mixture of folk and avant garde jazz and vocals which owe as much to Poly Styrene as it does to Björk or Indian-style singing, and I think I can safely say that this is one of the more unusual albums that I have been sent to listen to. The sound is very good but overall the result is something that I can never imagine me listening to again, which is a shame as they obviously know what they are doing and there is some great bass work but maybe my eclectic tastes are not as eclectic as I thought. *#86, Feb 2006*

KANSAS
SOMEWHERE TO ELSEWHERE
There cannot be many bands from America who were as important in the Seventies as Kansas. Sadly, known by many in the UK only for "Carry On Wayward Son", they released a host of magnificent albums. It is their 1975 album 'Masque' that I am now looking at, while listening to the new CD. Why? Firstly, THE line-up is back together for the first time in far too long. Phil Ehart, Steve Walsh, Dave Hope, Rich Williams, Kerry Livgren and Robbie Steinhardt are in full flow, along with Billy Greer who also provides bass guitar (as well as Dave) and some lead vocals. Secondly, the opening cut is a sequel to one of their classic numbers, "Icarus – Borne On Wings Of Steel", which first appeared on 'Masque'. With Kerry Livgren providing all the songs, Kansas are a band re-born. When I first listened to this, I knew that it was going to be a problem, solely because it was going to be difficult to get anything else on the player. If anyone has never heard Kansas (musical education sadly lacking), they mixed distinctively different lead vocalists with strong use of piano and violin in a melodic rock setting and are one of the few American bands that have an instantly recognisable sound and style. They have released many classic numbers, but in an extensive compilation, some of the songs contained on the new CD would have to be included. Please, please can Kansas tour to promote this: their double live album 'Two For The Show' is often a visitor to my record player, and to see them in concert playing their classics along with songs from here would be a gig made in heaven. *#59, July 2000*

KANSAS
DEVICE-VOICE-DRUM
There are few, if any, modern bands that can match the pedigree of the mighty Kansas. The fact they have even managed to have a hit single over here (back when that meant something) shows their appeal. They may no longer have their main songwriter Kerry

Livgren on board, and original bassist Dave Hope is also missing, but long-time member Billy Greer has taken his place and the others are all original. Phil Ehart (drums), Robby Steinhardt (vocals, violin), Richard Williams (guitar) and Steve Walsh (vocals, keyboards) were all there some thirty years ago and while they produce a sound that is timeless, they certainly do not sound old. This double CD live set was recorded at Earthlink Live! in 2002 and they were even joined at times by a 60-voice choir. This is a compilation of many of their finest moments and while fans will always moan that there is a song missing that they would have liked, no-one can argue that these songs are not representative of one of America's greatest bands. They span their career from the debut up to 'Somewhere From Elsewhere' from 2000. Both "Icarus II" and "Icarus" are here, as well as numbers such as "Journey From Mariabronn", "Point Of Know Return", "Dust In The Wind" and "Play The Game Tonight". Only seventeen audio tracks, it just does not seem enough somehow. It ends with a gentle acoustic introduction and Steve singing, "Once I rose above the noise and confusion…" The shout goes up "Are you ready??" and the three-part harmonies kick off the mighty "Carry On Wayward Son".

This double disc is being released in conjunction with a DVD and as a taster the CD has been enhanced with a video of the band performing "Distant Vision", as well as screensavers, photos and links to the website. This is a great collection of superb melodic progressive rock, and a must have for any fan of the genre.
#72, Feb 2003

KARA
KARA

Kara are a three piece, and this is their debut release. Colin Mold provides guitars, keyboards and vocals, Kirsta Johnson takes care of lead vocals, recorders, flute and keyboards while Steve Barfoot provides drums and vocals. They have played with Magenta in the past, but the only similarity between the two bands is that they have female singers who approach music in a melodic and clearly defined manner, because while Magenta are far more bombastic and overtly proggy due to the influences of Rob Reed, here the music is being approached from a far more simplistic and even folky arena. It is interesting to note that the one 'cover', is an arrangement of the traditional song "She Moves Through The Fair". The music is far more minimalist; evoking atmosphere and emotion, and the first part of "Eye Of The Great God" always makes me think of a clifftop looking over the sea and islands. But it is not all laid back and whimsical, there is some serious Gilmore style guitar and while Kara could never overtly be called a rock band this is an album that is certainly interesting. They may find themselves a bit split between two camps, as there are times when they are not proggy enough for that crowd, and too rocky for the folk crowd, but if you appreciate both styles or even just good music then you ought to find out more.
#86, Feb 2006

KARCIUS
SPHERE

Karcius are an instrumental quartet from Canada who have just signed to Unicorn. As part of that deal their 2003 debut 'Sphere' has been remastered and will be reissued by the label in March with a new album to follow later this year. But for now, I have the original release to listen to, and very good it is too. There seem to be quite a few instrumental acts coming out of Canada who love to mix fusion with prog and try to create something that is a whole new game, and Karcius are a case in point. With only the drummer seemingly happy to sit at the back and do what he does best, it is left to the others to take up the lead roles, with even the bass getting on the act. Simon L'Espérance has a fine touch on guitar and he is not afraid to move away from clean lines to something more distorted or rocky when the need arises while keyboard player Mingan Sauriol also has a delicate touch, and with his strong use of piano among his repertoire he seems to keep the music well grounded. There are plenty of jazzy breaks and interludes, but this is mostly music with a purpose and is the more enjoyable for that.
#86, Feb 2006

KARCIUS
KALEIDOSCOPE

Three years after the release of their debut album independently, the Canadian quartet are back with their second album, and now that they are signed to Unicorn (who have also reissued the debut) hopefully they will be getting far more attention. This is progressive music with a jazz influence, played by people who care deeply about both styles and consequently the fusion works very well indeed. There are times when they side more with one than the other, such as on "Maintenant" where the melody is carried by piano with guitar interludes, but the most important instrument on the track is the wonderfully delicate fretless bass which is slid to great effect carrying plenty of emotion and almost desperation in its notes. Although they can do gentle jazz, they can also blast it out and on "Destination" Simon L'Espérance leads the way with some great guitar but there is never the thought that this will become a straightforward guitar workout, as there is just so much going on. This album is stunning from start to end, both in terms of the musicianship being displayed but also by the maturity and consistency of the music that they are providing. The songs never meander but display direction and focus which in turn keeps the listener very interested indeed. Karcius are one of the top instrumental progressive rock/fusion bands around and this album is one to savour. *#88, Jun 2006*

KARDA ESTRA
EVE

I am not sure how many years I have been writing about Richard Wileman, but it is more than either he or I would like to admit. From Lives & Times to Karda Estra I have always felt an affinity with his work, and this album is no different. As Karda Estra he has

brought in much more classical styles and haunting visual imagery, using Ileesha Bailey's vocals as another musical instrument. The use of woodwind and violins as lead players is a powerful tool when placed against a sparse background, and while the music can never be said to be over the top, he does manage to convey some real menace during "The Pale Ray". Seven songs yet again prove to my mind that Richard is one of our finest prog musicians who has now moved over to 'the other side' and should be thought of as a classical composer who just happens to use electric instruments from time to time. A haunting powerful album, that is gentle and background yet also hard and dynamic. *#65, Dec 2001*

KARDA ESTRA
VOIVODE DRACULA

With this release Richard Wileman has moved even further away from the musical conventions that would normally be given the term progressive rock, and even deeper into the world of modern classical music. Richard has a skill for bringing to life images and thoughts through music, which is always interesting and intriguing, and in this case blessed with a gothic darkness. Ileesha Bailey again uses her voice more as an ethereal musical instrument, but the main melody is often carried by woodwind, in particular the oboe. This CD is broken into five parts and is Richard's interpretation of the legend of Dracula. It is a haunting dramatic piece of music, with Richard bringing into play little tonal colours that add greatly as they move in and out of the whole. This is incredibly powerful, with Richard using his guests wisely, and the result is a towering piece of music. This deserves to be taken out of the progressive field and used by those looking for exciting film music, or just listened to intently by those who want their music to be vibrant and intriguing, if more than a little dark. *#80, Jul 2004*

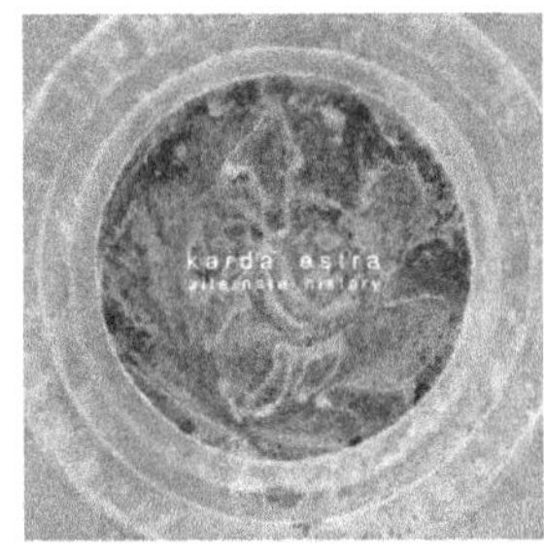

KARDA ESTRA
ALTERNATE HISTORY

I have been singing the praises of Richard Wileman for more years than I care to remember, and now those who have wondered what I have been harping on about can find out for themselves at the ridiculously low price of just £3.99 including p&p! This is a compilation that contains pieces from Richard's albums, plus some songs that were previously unavailable. Richard creates music is far more classical than just prog, and the music is visual in a way that is hard to describe. He uses female vocals as an instrument, and the result is something that is haunting and beautiful – quite unlike anything else within the progressive scene, and much more in keeping with contemporary classical music. Always powerful and inspiring, this may not be the sort of music that you normally listen to, but I do highly recommend it. *#82, Jan 2005*

KARDA ESTRA
THE AGE OF SCIENCE AND ENLIGHTENMENT

When it comes to music of beauty and elegance then there are few that can match Richard Wileman and Karda Estra. Although Richard is often still viewed as a progressive artist, that is probably due more to his past and the labels to which he has signed (SI and Cyclops) as opposed to the music that he is producing, as this is far more in keeping with modern classical as opposed to rock. Of the entire progressive scene, it is fair to say that he has more in common with Steve Hackett than anyone else, yet this music is more accessible and enjoyable. There is a grace and beauty that transcends idioms and styles, with Ileesha providing wonderful choral style vocals when required. Richard continues to produce music of the highest quality, and I feel that with this album he has moved away from the more cinematic and visual soundscapes of the last few albums into something that that should be listened to with respect. Just lie back and let the music take you to places in your mind that you rarely visit – you will be well rewarded for it.
#88, Jun 2006

KARFAGEN
CONTINIUM

Karfagen is the name of the project that was first started in 1997 by Antony Kalugin whilst studying at architectural college in the Ukraine. He formed a band that played a few gigs, but they soon fell apart with only Sergei Kovalev remaining with Antony. In 2002, Antony released a solo album and over the new few years either composed or performed on more than 40 albums which gave him the impetus to get back into the studio himself and the result is 'Continium'. This is mostly instrumental, with both Antony and Ikeg Polyanskiy providing keyboards and Koysta Shepelenko on drums, Sergei on accordion and then various guests providing bass, guitars etc. This is a very dynamic album, obviously very keyboard oriented, which as well as hints of Camel also contains many folk influences. There are strange woodwind sounds to be heard, and the music is very heavily arranged with instruments moving in and out of the melody. If one was to guess which country the music originated from one would probably guess Eastern Europe, just from some of the nuances and touches, but that certainly is not overpowering, and the result is a well-constructed instrumental album that at times has more than a hint of Karda Estra about it as well as some strong brass. *#89, Sep 2006*

KAVA KAVA
YOU CAN LIVE HERE

Kava Kava was formed in 1991 as a four-piece, although they have just added another two members. They have been mainly a live act, building on a style of music that is a "unique blend of rock, psychedelic improvisation, funk and jazz, which is at once groove oriented, melodic, free form, head-bending and surprisingly dance friendly". In the first two years of their existence the band released three tapes, then in 1993 released the

'Dither' EP CD on their own Chocolate Fireguard label and following a gig at The Marquee in 1994 they were signed up by Delerium Records and 'You Can Live Here' is the first album to come from that association, released last year. Also in 1995 they released a 12" single, "Swivel EP", which was produced by ex-Tull sticksman Barriemore Barlow, who will also be producing the next album when they start recording later this month. Kava Kava certainly are progressive in the sense that they are taking many different styles of music and melding it in a unique form, but they have little or nothing in common with many of the bands in the Progressive Rock Directory. At times frantic and frenetic, while at others more restful, this is a superb album. Focus on any instrument and you will find a lot going on: there is some brilliant fretwork but right up there is some stunning bass. This is an album that will appeal to those not worried about labels, but just want to listen to some great music.*#33, Feb 1996*

KBB
FOUR CORNER'S SKY

This is the second album from Japan's KBB and one that I was looking forward to. I have not heard KBB's debut album but have heard some of their songs and I still play Akihisa's album that he recorded with Natsuki Kido. Akihisa plays violin and guitar (and wrote six of the seven songs); Toshimitsu Takahashi is on keyboards, Dani on bass and guitar and Shirou Sugano on drums. So quite an unusual line-up, and in many ways, an unusual album: this is jazz-rock with very strong progressive tendencies. Curved Air is probably the closest comparison, but even that does not cover it. It is instrumental, but that is primarily because there is just no room for vocals. In "Kraken's Brain Is Blasting" there is a passage where all the band take off in a tumultuous run with Akihisa just managing to keep in front. At times the guys play a concerted piece which is at odds to the main melody, yet at others they are very much locked together. On "Slave Nature" there is a much more prog feel to proceedings with some great fretless bass just behind the lead instrument, whether it is violin, keyboard or electric guitar. For those who enjoy complex instrumental music at its' very best.
#76, Oct 2003

KBB
LIVE 2004

When I received some CDs from my good friend Hiroshi Masuda in Japan, there was no doubt at all as to the first one to get into my player. I am a huge fan of KBB in general and of Akihisa Tsuboy in particular. He is an incredible violinist, and while he has guested on other Japanese albums, and has released an incredible CD with Natsuki Kido which should be in all good music lover's collections, it is with KBB he really belongs. The line-up is Toshimitsu Takahashi on keyboards, Dani on bass and

Shirou Sugano on drums and these guys really kick. With a strong rhythm section, but no guitar, it is up to Akihisa and Toshimitsu to back each other up all the time so if the lead role is a keyboard freak out as on "Inner Flames" then Akihisa has to keep himself in check and play in support and bide his time before he can again take the pivotal role. Recorded over two nights at Silver Elephant in Tokyo, this shows a band that has total confidence in their own musical ability, combined with an innate understanding of what each other is going to be doing at any moment in time. The result is an album of instrumental progressive music with hints of jazz and even folk that is incredibly tight and extremely well performed. I hope that one day this band will release a DVD as I would love to see them in concert if this is anything to go by. Easily one of the best bands coming out of Japan, this is a great album.
#86, Feb 2006

KENZINER
THE PROPHECIES

This is the second album by Finnish symphonic prog metallers Kenziner, following on from 1998's 'Timescape'. It has been produced by workaholic David T. Chastain (who has also worked with frontman Stephen Fredrick and drummer Brian Harris), but he has not played guitar himself on this release: mind you, with Jarno Keskinen on board he was never going to be missed. Keyboard player Mikko Harkin completes the line-up. Kenziner concentrate on intricate melodies, which are played ferociously quickly and with lots of power, and the result is an album that has incredible note density, but melody and tunes had not been forsaken in the pursuit of speed. It is almost what early Megadeth would have been playing it if they had been weaned on prog; certainly, fans of Malmsteen will listen to this and wonder what he can do to compete with these songs. This truly impressive album must be heard to be believed. If technical metal played at a rate of knots is your thing, then go no further.
#56, Jan 2000

KING BATHMAT
FANTASTIC FREAK SHOW CARNIVAL

King Bathmat is now a trio of John Bassett (vocals, bass), Lee Sulsh (guitar) and Bernie Smirnoff (drums) but originally it was just multi-instrumentalist John Bassett who writes all the material, produces, mixes and masters it etc. This certainly sounds like a band recording, and I am glad that the music is as good as I hoped that it might be, as for some reason I feel that the band name is one of the best that I have heard in a long time. I was worried that the music could not live up to the image and I certainly needn't have been concerned as this songs-based album has just about everything going for it. What do you want? Psychedelia, lush harmonies, strong hooks, influences from bands as diverse as REM and Seahorses while at the same time very much maintaining its' own destiny? John states that the title track was supposed to be

'Magical Mystery Tour' meets Black Sabbath, while others are even more bizarre. What is so blindingly obvious throughout the album that here is something that is going to appeal to those who revel in the fact that their musical tastes are out of the ordinary as well as appealing to the mainstream. The only thing holding these guys back are publicity as it is not down to strength of material, as this is an album that I fell in love with the very first time I played it, and each time I hear it I get something else from it. This is a class album from a British band that deserves your support.
#84, July 2005

KING'S X
BLACK LIKE SUNDAY
This album features songs that the trio originally wrote some twenty years ago when they were not even known as King's X, and they have been resurrected due to fan requests. Unfortunately, the promo only features seven of the fourteen songs (missing out a number called "Johnny" which is over eleven minutes long). But even on only being able to listen to half an album it is possible to gain some idea of just how good this is. Doug Pinnick (vocals, bass), Ty Tabor (vocals, guitar) and Jerry Gaskill (vocals, drums) have brought together all their melodic and pop influences with their rock ambitions in a way that all fans of classic melodic rock will want to have. Most of the fourteen numbers are under four minutes long, but on the ones I have heard, this is plenty long enough for the band to move around inside the tunes. The album starts slowly with the title cut, but with "Rock Pile" the energy levels are pushed up and the height of the bar is raised. With all three singing, the harmony vocals are spot on, yet the music is still hard and quite heavy. There are lots of Beatles' influences in this album, which is fine with me. I would like to have heard more of the album to be able to make a call but what I have heard has been very strong if you like melodic rock.
#74, Jun 2003

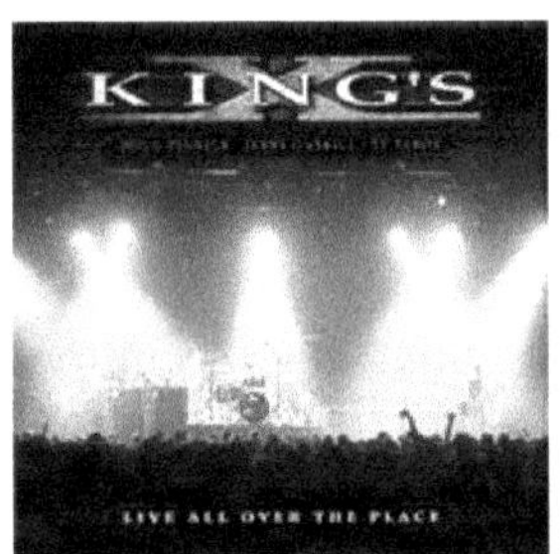

KING'S X
LIVE ALL OVER THE PLACE
King's X burst onto the scene with 1988's 'Out Of The Silent Planet', and since then they have released numerous albums as well as finding time to work on plenty of side-projects. But it is as King's X that the trio of Jerry Gaskill, Doug Pinnick and Ty Tabor are best-known. For this release, they chose recordings that to them had the best vibe, and then did nothing to them so if you were in the crowd at the night of the recording then this is exactly what you would have heard. There is even a rousing version of "Manic Depression" which features Jeff Ament (Pearl Jam) guesting on bass. There is also a section of the CD which features the acoustic element of their 2003 tour, with seven songs being performed in this format. But those who want to hear "Dogman" or "Cigarettes" fully cranked up need not worry, as they are available in full on rock outs. King's X may not be in the popular music press as much as they used to be, but they still

have a loyal fanbase and if you have not been able to catch them on tour and see what all the fuss is about then this double CD appears to be a true and honest representation of one of the best rock trios around, mixing straight ahead rock with loads of other influences including psychedelia to create a rich fat sound.
#82, Jan 2005

KING'S X
OGRE TONES
I have not always 'got' what King's X are about, although I have always enjoyed their respective solo projects, but for me this album shines through with what Doug Pinnick (vocals, bass), Jerry Gaskill (drums) and Ty Tabor (guitars) have been doing all these years. This is easily the best King's X album I have heard and one that has been spending a lot of time on my player. It is heavy, oh boy is it heavy, with a bottom end that just wants to kill the speakers: try to imagine a stoner rock band with a groove combined with The Beatles and then you may just get some idea of what this is about. I put on the first song and was blown away by "Alone" which I felt just had to be the best number on the album. By the time I had reached third song "Hurricane" I decided that the wisest course of action was to wait until I had heard the whole album before making that call. It finished and I felt that this was not possible, so of course had to play it again. And again.

This is an album that just drags the listener in, with the combination of styles and heaviness meaning that they are so different to much else that is around yet is commercial and totally approachable all at the same time. This review does not do this justice. If you enjoy good rock, whatever the genre, then this is something that you should investigate. You owe it to your ears.
#85, Nov 2005

KINO
PICTURE
Guitarist and singer John Mitchell (Arena, The Urbane) was approached by Inside Out boss Thomas Weber and asked if he would mind doing something like The Urbane but with a stronger prog attitude. He asked whom he might involve in the project, and John thought of keyboard player John Beck (It Bites) who he had met on a tour in Japan with John Wetton. Pete Trewavas approached Thomas independently talking about how Neal Morse had left Transatlantic, and that he would like to work with John Beck at some point and was then told about the Mitchell/Beck project. Pete was enthusiastic about this and brought in drummer Chris Maitland, who he knew from when Porcupine Tree supported Marillion. So, we have four very different musicians from four very different British progressive rock bands, so there was no doubt that they were going to produce an album that contains elements of all four plus lots more besides. The result is one that is

already pushing for the accolade progressive debut of the year. Each time I play this I get more from it, as the band throw caution to the wind and just play whatever they want.

How about releasing an edit of "Telling Me To Tell You" as a single and watching it rise to the top of the charts with its' infectious chorus and melodies? Or how about a nine-minute opening track ("Losers Day Parade") that just rips through loads of different styles, and captures the listener straight from the off? In fact, the only thing wrong with this album is the way that it took up so much time in my player.

This is BRITISH progressive rock at its' finest, with great musicianship and songs that really are that and just not exercises in complexity. Yes, this album can be extremely complicated at times, but it can also be very simple, and is full of twists and turns that cannot fail to impress any proghead. This is a debut that is worth seeking out immediately, if not sooner.
#83, Mar 2005

KITARO
THINKING OF YOU
Kitaro has sold over 15 million albums since leaving Far East Family Band in 1979, and it is not hard to see why. He performs most of the music himself, but whereas other solo multi-instrumentalists tend to concentrate either on keyboards or on guitars, he uses a wide variety of sounds to bring his music to life. It is very evocative, powerful and visual, while managing to bring in much of his Japanese heritage. It is music that is relaxing, but not New Age, is often quite different in approach to Western music, while always being accessible. There is some delicate woodwind on the album, conveying a beauty and innocence not often heard in today's music scene. The album is a delight.
#57, Mar 2000

KNITTING BY TWILIGHT
SOMEONE TO BREAK THE SILENCE
Knitting By Twilight is a musical collective that started in 1994 when John Orsi and Michael Watson wanted a place where they could release music that they considered unsuitable for their normal bands. This is not actually a full-length album, but a taster for their next album 'An Evening Out Of Time' along with some otherwise unavailable material. It is certainly hard to categorise what they are trying to do, as in many ways this is music that is more about creating an atmosphere than it is about the songs themselves. Musically the band seem to be all over the place from gentle almost New Age pieces to others that are far more dramatic and strident. It is something that one would almost expect to be purely instrumental in nature, but that is not the case with this as there are songs as well.
#87, Apr 2006

NELKO KOLAROV
DAY OF WRATH

I am not sent much in the way of Bulgarian progressive music. Okay, that probably is the understatement of the year as prior to this release I had hardly heard any at all. Kolarov is not a name that many in the West will have heard of, but if you read the small print on Nikolo Kotzsev's 'Nostradamus' project you will find that Nelko was conductor. Seeing that the cover and all the booklet was in Bulgarian I was not surprised to find that the album is also sung in that language, but what did surprise me was just how good this is. No meandering along in a half-hearted fashion, this is prog album with a solid dose of AOR-style rock and if it was not for the lyrics one would swear that this was from some unknown top American band. I first played this on the way to Scotland, loved it so much that I played it again and the next day emailed my friend Artur in Poland to tell him that he had to get this CD onto his radio show. It is bright, it is clean, and Nelko certainly knows his way around the keyboards. But this is not the sort of album that one would expect from a band led by a keyboard player, as although they are obviously important this is all about the songs and the band being very much a band and not hanging onto their leaders' apron strings. This probably will not be the easiest album in the country to get hold of, but it is just so good that if it were on a more well-known Western label then I am sure that many of the prog sites would have picked this up. Totally accessible, I can keep this on all night, even though I have not a clue what they are singing about!
#84, July 2005

KOOCH
ZEMZEME (WHISPER)

Dave Wagstaffe recently sent me this album, which I do not think is currently available. The web site does not appear to have been updated for a few years, and this is not a band I had heard of previously. Kooch are, or were, formed by vocalist/guitarist Cyrus Khajavi who between 1981 and 1987 was playing in Quasar. The recording line-up of Kooch also features Dave (drums), bassist Keith Turner and guitarist Uwe D'Rose as well as Claire Lindley on violin and Brian Mullan on cello/keyboards. Of course, Keith was a founder member of Quasar, and both Dave and Uwe were in that band prior to leaving to form Landmarq. But this is not a prog album in any sense of the word as Cyrus has gone back to his roots, namely North Eastern Iran, to bring together an album that tries to meld together Eastern and Western music. I have played this quite a lot now, and initially I found the vocals very grating: that is not because Cyrus does not have a good voice, it is just that I am not used to listening to this type of singing for any length of time, as it is quite different to 'normal' Western styles. Add to that he is singing in a language that I cannot comprehend so it must be treated as an instrument in its' own right. This is an intriguing album, and while I can understand possibly why it may not appeal to many, I am a bit surprised that it did not receive more publicity on its' release than it did. It was recorded at Thin Ice by Karl Groom, and mastered by Rob Aubrey (IQ etc.) so why did it not feature within the prog scene? But maybe that is the problem. People normally

associated with prog recorded it, but this is most definitely not a prog album. What it is, is an album that provides an insight into a very different form of music that is strangely compelling and at other times is intensely beautiful with some delicate guitar and forms. Interesting.
#74, Jun 2003

KOPECKY
KOPECKY
I hear a great deal of progressive rock, much more than the normal punter, and while I may get excited from time to time it is rare that anything new, or 'progressive', ever reaches my ears. So, when I first started listening to this instrumental CD, which had arrived from the States, I found that I was intrigued, which in turn made way for me to being totally focussed on what I was hearing. Kopecky are a trio of brothers with Joe on guitar, Paul on percussion and William on bass, sitar and keyboards. Any of these instruments can take on the lead role, with the fretless bass being especially effective. But while on some numbers they are almost traditional, with rock themes being the basis for the melody (which moves and melds in glorious ways), on others they sound as if they have come straight out of the East. The use of sitar combined with complementary percussion gives the music an otherworldly exotic feel. Apparently, William's teacher, Veena Chandra, is a grand-disciple of Ravi Shankar, and here the sitar is an integral part of a rock band, not Indian-style music in its' own right. On "Sukha", while William plays a melody Joe is hard at work either emulating it or taking the music in a different direction altogether. For an instrumental album to fully hold the attention of the listener throughout its length it must be something special indeed, and I for one feel that my musical experience has been broadened by listening to this album.
#58, May 2000

KOPECKY
SERPENTINE KALEIDOSCOPE
It is always gratifying when I rave over an album to discover that I am not the only one with the same views. Having still not yet recovered from the delights of their debut album which I reviewed last issue, I am now listening to the second album for which they have signed to Cyclops in the UK. Of course, this means that it is readily available, so you should all rush out and buy it immediately, if not sooner! Kopecky are still the brothers Joe, Paul and William although they do have a couple of guest vocalists. Still, that is not to say that this is a songs-based album as such, as it is still mostly instrumental: what compositions these are. William manages to produce some very strange sounds and textures from his fretless bass, while Joe either leads the melody or pins the sound together on guitar while drummer Paul refuses to be left behind in the skill stakes. This is not background prog, it is music that can never be classified as neo-prog and will appeal to all those who like their music extremely complex, diverse, yet never too challenging. It

may be hard work, but it is always a pleasure. Surely, this is one of the best albums ever to come out of Tolworth: anyone who enjoys prog is missing out if this is not in their collection.
#59, July 2000

KOPECKY
BLOOD

There are not too many full instrumental trios out there that do not use keyboards, and even fewer where the musicians are all brothers. It is a while since I last heard any music from Kopecky and this album has reinvigorated my interest in them. Now signed to Canadian label Unicorn Records, I hope that having been on UK's Cyclops, Italy's Mellow Records and France's Musea they have now found their spiritual home which will allow them to be more prolific, and I believe that they have. Unicorn releases a lot of material that is jazz-oriented, and while Kopecky do not fit into that mould they do have the same inventiveness and musical complexity of many of that genre. This is music that is uncompromising, always looking forwards, as the brothers keep bouncing off each other and letting each take the lead as is appropriate. That this is challenging music is never in doubt, that many people will find it too complex and labyrinthine for their understanding is apparent.

Here is a rock band that are like no other, and five albums in they are still driving forward whatever perceived boundaries there may be. No keyboards, no vocals, and just three guys hitting those strings and drums to make a glorious togetherness that is like no other. It is hard to categorise exactly what style of music they are performing as by its very nature there is so much going on, they ignore genre categorisations altogether. By definition they are 'progressive', but musically this is much more in the hard rock almost shredder arena, but that is also not correct. Think of it as rock music played by three musicians linked by 'blood' and performing some of the most complex music around. It will take you a while to get into it, but once you do.... Superb.
#89, Sep 2006

KOSTAREV GROUP
LIVE @ INPROG 2003

According to the press release, the band put together by Alexander Kostarev is the leading progressive band in Moscow. I have no way of knowing if that is right or wrong, but I do know that this album is a mix and meld of so many different progressive styles as to be totally overpowering. The one thing that lets it down totally for me is the violin sound of Gennady Lavrentiev – to my ears it grates terribly, so much so that this music is endured rather than enjoyed. He can play well, but it sounds as if he is killing a cat. Add to the mix a keyboard player who also provides bass synth, a live wire drummer, a flautist who also plays sax and Alexander himself who

normally plays guitar but could also be on harmonica, then the instrumental mix is weird enough in itself. Added to that are the musical ideals of the band who include prog, jazz, fusion, avant-garde and anything else that one could imagine that might just about make this unlistenable and it is there somewhere. In many ways, it is an incredible album, one where the band seemingly are keeping it together and not jamming aimlessly, but even within prog circles this will have very limited appeal.
#85, Nov 2005

KREL
AD ASTRA

There are arguably far too few bands trying to emulate the mighty Hawkwind, so when I saw that this CD was by a band that had completed a full tour with them as long ago as 1992, I knew I was in for a treat. Then I read that Andy G had been inspired to set up the Dead Ernest label just to release this album and I was quite intrigued. What could this album contain to be so powerful? The answer is one of the most powerful space rock albums that I have heard in many an aeon. Krel are pretty much a one-man band these days with Martin M being joined by a guest on only a couple of the songs. This contains all that a space rock fan could want, with long held down keyboard chords a la Hawkwind, Floyd, or Gong. On top of that are the insistent repeated melodies, with a strong bass line, as well as vocals coming in and out of the mix. The album is now four years old and it is very much my loss that I have only just heard it. Let it not be yours and discover the space rock of Krel.
#65, Dec 2001

KREL
OUT OF SPACE

This is an unusual album, as although it is not stated in the rather sparse four-page booklet, the recordings themselves have been taken from different sources and then put together in a fashion that sounds like brand new music. Some of it is taken from material recorded on the 1992 ‘Electric Tepee’ tour where they supported Hawkwind, as well as old studio recordings and newer music recorded by the current line-up. It has been mooted that the holders of the true space rock crown are no longer Hawkwind, but Krel, and one can certainly hear where that argument has some justification. Songs like “Star Of Last” combine both delicate guitar solos and pounding space rhythms with the vocalists vying for attention as it pounds through and into the brain. There are times when it does not come through exactly as it should, but there are others where it works perfectly, and the result is a fine album indeed for those who enjoy this style of music. There are plenty of synths as well as a full-on rock band, and while some of the jams may not always be as powerful as they could be, the overall result is well worth investigation.
#87, Apr 2006

SONJA KRISTINA
HARMONICS OF LOVE

This is the follow-up to Sonja's wonderful 'Songs From The Acid Folk' and should be a lot easier to find. It took me ages to get the earlier CD, even though it had been reviewed in 'Q', but this time this has been released through HTD, so it should be far more straightforward. Only violinist Paul Sax has survived, as Sonja again tries to build a vehicle worthy of her vocal talents. This has a more electric sound than the last album but is still combining ambience and atmosphere as opposed to being a blasting straightforward rock band: it is all about mixing a myriad of influences and styles to create something that is more than about commercial success. This is music either to wake up to, or drift away on, music that needs to be listened to and not just put on as some background muzak. It is an album of depths and layers, and as you let the music flow over and around you, one realises that there is far more to it than initially thought possible. And at the very heart and soul of it are the glorious vocals of Sonja. It has been a long time since "Back Street Luv" found itself on Radio 1, but she still has a commanding presence and vocal talent. If you like your music laid back and enjoyable then there is much here for you: music to relax to.

#42, July 1997

K^2
BOOK OF THE DEAD

K^2 is the brainchild of Atlantis bassist and songwriter Ken Jacquess who decided that he wanted to write a concept album based on the Egyptian Book Of The Dead, and that he needed a brand-new group to be able to perform it. That group is certainly an eclectic mix, but any band involving Allan Holdsworth on guitar is always going to get noticed, and with drummer Doug Sanborn and keyboardist Ryo Okomuto (Spock's Beard) also on board there is no doubting the musical skills at Ken's disposal. To complete the line-up, he brought in Yvette Devereaux on violin and Shaun Guerin on vocals. Shaun is probably best known for his talents in the Peter Gabriel-era Genesis tribute band Cinema Show, and the vocals on this album are his last recorded work as he passed away shortly after completion. With Shaun's vocals, there is an early Genesis feel to some of what is going on, but the use of violin and Allan's guitar does lift this into a new dimension. Yes, there are times on the 23-minute-long opener "Infinite Voyage" where it is reminiscent of times past, but there are many others where the music is moving in a very different direction. The rhythm section at the back keeps it very tight while Ryo often also stays in the background to add colour, and this just gives rooms for some incredible violin and guitar duels. Allan has one of the most fluid styles around and he blends in extremely well. Overall the result is an album that will appeal to all progheads, being both extremely easy to get into on first hearing but also involving wonderful complexity and musical ability while never losing the musical thread of the songs themselves.

#84, July 2005

JAMES LABRIE
ELEMENTS OF PERSUASION

James LaBrie surely needs no introduction, as frontman of Dream Theater for the last fifteen years he is probably the most recognisable and influential prog metal vocalist in the world. Now he is back with his third solo album, and as previously he has been joined by keyboardist Matt Guillory, Mike Mangini (formerly Extreme) on drums, and bassist Bryan Beller, although he does have a new guitarist in Marco Sfogli, who is making his presence felt. What is apparent throughout the whole album is the sheer intensity of the emotions and the way the band is ripping through the different styles. This is music that is complex, music that is simple, music that moves and changes from song to song, but it is never too far away from strong hard melodic rock and it takes an extremely powerful singer to be able to keep in track with the band: needless to say, James is always in full control.

The only way to play and appreciate this album is as a full-on onslaught – this is not music which has been designed to be played gently in the background as an appetiser to a main event, but rather this needs to be appreciated and devoured and when the album has finished the experience should be repeated. Yes, there are gentle sections, yes, there are loops and programming, but these add to the diversity of the album and just makes it seem that much heavier when it kicks back in again. "Freak" has a decidedly strange beginning, with music swirling around and deliberately muffled until it is time for the verse proper to start and then James himself takes on an affected vocal style. There are times when it could almost be Marilyn Manson! It is this feel of not being restricted by any genre that makes this such a joy to listen to, but as I said earlier it is extremely intense so expect to be drained by the end of it. Although Dream Theater fans will want to get this, a much wider audience should also enjoy the experience. *#83, Mar 2005*

LANDBERK
ONE MAN TELL'S ANOTHER

Landberk are without doubt one of the most popular progressive bands to come out of Scandinavia in the Nineties. Mixing influences from bands such as King Crimson and Pink Floyd along with folk gives their music a class and edge missing from much of the current scene. All the lyrics are in English, and like the music, are not happy to be ploughing the same furrow all the time. Musical diversity is obviously important as opener "Time" has some folky guitar while the next, "Kontiki", has a totally different feel and uses a repeated keyboard riff (sounds like a Hammond to me) combined with some electric lead guitar lines: Robert Fripp would certainly be at home here. My favourite is probably "You Are", which starts with some wonderful vocals, accompanied only with gentle electric guitar: totally moody and atmospheric, which stays with the song even after the rest of the band have joined in. Vocalist Patrick Helje and the rest of the guys manage to produce a song and performance not unlike U2. A grower, Landberk have produced an album of great depth. *#31, Oct 1995*

LANDBERK
UNAFFECTED

Landberk are one of Scandinavia's hottest bands, and 'Unaffected' was recorded live in Italy and Germany at the beginning of last year. Of the eight songs, seven are originals, but it is probably the cover version that shows where Landberk are coming from as the song that opens proceedings is Peter Hammill's "Afterwards", and for the most part 'Unaffected' is dreamy and laid back. Landberk say that they are pure, literally "unaffected" by outside influences and they are certainly very different to what is happening in much of the prog scene today, but that is not to say that they have not been influenced by other bands and artists, with VDGG springing to mind. Having a keyboard player who professes to only playing Hammond Organ and Mellotron also puts a dated feel on proceedings. "Pray For Me Now" has an upbeat jazzy feel to it, but for the most part Landberk are content to stay in a dream world of their own making. With it being live it is a little rough at times around the edges, but overall this is an excellent album, one to savour. *#34, Apr 1996*

LANDMARQ
SOLITARY WITNESS

Landmarq were formed in 1990 by keyboard player Steve Leigh (ex-Tamarisk) after he left Quasar, although the name of the band did not become officially recognized until February 1991 when Steve Gee (bass, ex-Artemis) came up with it when he attempted to summarize the band in its musical context. After some early line-up changes the band settled down with Steve, Pete, Uwe D'Rose (guitar, ex-Relay) and Dave Wagstaffe (drums, also ex-Quasar). Vocalist at the time was Bob Daisley, and it was this line-up that went into the studio in Spring 1991 to record a three-track demo containing "Suite St. Helens", "Foxing The Fox" and "Here's To The Soldier". The demo was sent to SI Music in Amsterdam, who decided that they wanted to feature "Suite St. Helens" on a compilation they were putting together to celebrate ten years in the business, but they needed Landmarq to record a shortened version so that it could be used. However, the band found themselves without a singer as Bob Daisley left, but they managed to find a suitable replacement in Rob Lewis Jones who was appearing in a West End musical. The recording was finished in the summer, and there were so many favourable reports about the track that SI decided to sign the band to record an album. After the contract had been signed, Rob decided that he was going to leave the band to pursue his acting career, which meant that for the second time the band found themselves without a vocalist and with a recording contract to fulfill. Luckily for them they managed to recruit Damian Wilson (previously with Orphic Soup), and recording went ahead with Clive Nolan (Pendragon, Shadowland etc.) at the production helm, and he helped with lyrics for some of the songs.

'Solitary Witness' was released by SI on April 1st this year and is a really accessible album. Landmarq have been likened to a heavy version of Marillion, but that is not fair on either band. They are certainly heavier than acts like Galahad, but not as over the top as Freewill or Mentaur. The guitars tend to rock out with great power, but the keyboards of Steve keep the band firmly within the prog mould, although they must be one of the heaviest bands around within the genre. The album kicks off with "Killing Fields" which features some guitar/bass/keyboard runs almost reminiscent of classic Uriah Heep. Damian is a great vocalist, and is obviously extremely confident in his own ability, so much so that he "slides" from one note to another as an effect, as well as singing with real clarity. The song speeds up and slows down with great finesse, and there is a real air of accessibility about it. When I first played the album, I was hooked halfway through this song, and knew that if the rest of the album was as good as this then it would be a monster, and I was not disappointed. Gently picked guitar leads the way for the riffs that open "Forever Young" and the song bounces along on Uwe's guitar with Steve adding synthesizer runs to great effect. It does slow down to allow Steve to play some atmospheric keyboards and give Uwe the opportunity to shine with some Andy Latimer/ Steve Hackett style soaring guitar. Eventually Steve Gee's bass brings the song back to the original theme, and Damian continues to impress, ending with a powerful scream Steve Hogarth would be proud of. "April First" is an instrumental, and what is strange is that the main theme is played on piano. This is then repeated throughout the piece, while the other musicians join in to repeat and extend the original, variations on a theme.

"Foxing The Fox" tells the story of a fox hunt from the viewpoints of both the hunter and the prey, with the bass driving it along as the chase takes place. The song switches as the fox takes up the tale and tries to get away: Damian provides great vocal characterization as he switches from one to the other. Uwe's riffing takes us back to the huntsmen, but to tell you how the song ends would spoil the fun. Other tracks of real note are "Tippi Hedren" (which is about Hitchcock films, and starts with music from THAT shower scene) and the powerful ballad "After I Died Somewhere", which for the most part features some emotive vocals and great pianowork, but the guitar break forces the feelings home. The longest song is "Suite: St. Helens", which at more than ten minutes, comes across a lot stronger than it does on the SI compilation. The extended introduction shows just how powerful drumming can be employed to add a real edge to proceedings, as the rest of the instruments follow the guitar lead. A striking chord heralds the change into a gentle ballad, which becomes more emotive, then allows the song to return to the opening theme, only this time it is far harder. Great songs, well played, in fact a consummate album and it should appeal to all those who like good music as there is enough contrast within to satisfy all tastes.
#15, Oct 1992

LANDMARQ
INFINITY PARADE

Well, here is Landmarq's second album. I raved about their first album, 'Solitary Witness' back in #15, but for those of you have yet to come across them, Landmarq are a band of great talent who produce wonderful music. The line-up is the same as the debut, namely Steve Leigh (keyboards), Damian Wilson (vocals), Uwe D'Rose (guitar), Steve Gee (bass) and Dave

Wagstaffe (drums). So, the second album is often viewed as the "difficult" album, so could it live up to my expectations? YES! I loved the first album, but this is far better. The band have matured and here is a real 'band' album that possibly the first one was not. The Thin Ice production team are very much in evidence again, and I know through talking with Clive that he was extremely pleased with the way this came out, and I can see why. From the opener "Solitary Witness" to the closer "Embrace" we are taken on a tour of every aspect of good melodic prog rock. There are commercial belters, ballads, instrumentals, and the obligatory epic ("Ta Jiang" is nearly seventeen minutes long). Steve's keyboards are soaring and majestic, Uwe's guitar is spot on being melodic or hard as the mood requires, Dave and Steve pin it to the floor and then there is Damian. It is interesting to play this one and the Threshold album back to back as the only thing in common is Damian singing like a dream, and I still can't work out how he can so sound so much at home with two totally different kinds of music. There are seven songs on this fifty-five-minute-long album, and I love them all. Landmarq have created their own identity, and with this CD behind them can only move onto bigger and greater things. My favourite must be "The More You Seek The More You Lose" which is one of the rockier numbers and is up to date lyrically "Tell me who is Jesus Christ, Now isn't he a Texan, Who holds shootouts from a mansion, and is promising eternal life, To everyone's who there?" A wonderfully commercial pacey number with some great guitar from Uwe and very restrained keyboards from Steve. Against that, the ballad "Embrace" is astounding in its beauty. Landmarq have recently been touring Europe with bands such as Now, Wings of Steel and Timelock in support (all featured recently in Feedback). I hear the album is already selling well, and rightly so, it is brilliant!
#18, May 1993

LANDMARQ
THE VISION PIT

'Solitary Witness' and 'Infinity Parade' were both very popular albums, but it has taken a long time for the third to arrive, as there have been numerous problems with vocalists. After the release of the last album singer Damian Wilson left to join LaSalle (he was also shortlisted as the replacement for Bruce in Iron Maiden and to my mind the boys made the wrong choice in Blaze, but c'est la vie). It was never going to be easy to find another singer in anything like the same league, although Ian 'Moon' Gould did manage to stick the course for a while. However, disillusionment has meant that Landmarq are complete once more as Damian is again at the vocal helm. Landmarq are a top-class act, but Damian is just so good that he lifts them into another league altogether. Again, recorded and produced at Thin Ice, Clive and Karl have lovingly polished the sound and done a great job. Landmarq are on the softer side of prog rock and combine a good rhythm section and layers of keyboards with Uwe's distinctive guitar sound as the notes extend into each other. Add to that those vocals and you have a winning team. As with the other albums, this is very much a grower as there is so much in here to be appreciated and enjoyed. It may not set the rock charts buzzing, as there will be nary a mite of dandruff distributed, but again Landmarq have produced a prog album of the highest order. *#32, Dec 1995*

LANDMARQ
SCIENCE OF COINCIDENCE

Time for a history lesson. Many moons ago there was a band called Quasar who released a couple of albums, the second of which, 'The Loreli', was damn fine. Due to various reasons the personnel changed, and ex-members of Quasar found themselves a bassist and called themselves Landmarq. A recording deal was duly struck, but the record company boss made them change vocalists, and in came Damian Wilson. It is only recently, with the departure (for the second time) of Damian that the original line-up is back together, and Tracy Hitchings finds herself fronting a band again. For those of you who have only started getting Feedback recently, Tracy is in my opinion one of the finest female vocalists in the land, recording a wonderful solo album 'From Ignorance To Ecstasy', but one of many to suffer with the demise of SI Music. With Tracy on board the band appear to have been revitalised, as this is easily their strongest album to date, a joy to review. More Floydian in places that it has been before, the music seems to fit Tracy's vocals like the proverbial hand in glove. That is not to say that there are not heavy moments, such as the introduction to "Summer Madness", but this is not hard rock but progressive at its' finest.

Hopefully, this means that we are going to be seeing a very active Landmarq on the gigging front, as with Tracy back this is a band worth catching. By the way, those with extremely long memories may remember guitarist Uwe doing some covers for Feedback some years ago – a real all-rounder.

#49, May 1998

LANDMARQ
THUNDERSTRUCK

For some reason, Landmarq have never been one of the most fashionable of UK prog bands and I have never understood why that is. They have some great songs, and certainly can play well enough. Their debut album, 'Solitary Witness' was one of the best albums ever to come out on the Dutch SI label, and apart from Damian Wilson joining, leaving, joining and then leaving again, the line-up has been the same since inception. I first saw Tracy Hitchings sing with the band at The Standard some years ago, when she and Clive Nolan joined them on-stage for the encore (the sight of Clive having to read the lyrics he had written from a CD booklet will always be with me), and now she is back permanently and gives the music a different edge to when either Damian or Moon were at the front. I firmly believe that Tracy is one of the best female rock vocalists to come out of the UK (check out her solo album 'From Ignorance To Ecstasy'), and she gives the music just the right amount of lightness and balance. The result is that whether there is a full out barrage, or just gentle keyboards, the vocals are perfectly matched. This is a great live album, one that showcases the bands' many talents and I am sure that it will win them a lot of new friends, as well as satisfying lots of old ones

#57, Mar 2000

LANDMARQ
AFTERSHOCK

This is the follow-up album to 'Thunderstruck' as it is the second part of that live album and marks the end of an era for the band as it will be the last album to feature keyboard player Steve Leigh. Although the band have been a little careless with vocalists over the years (with Damian Wilson doing the hokey cokey, Moon never recording, and now Tracey who was the person they originally wanted to front the band years ago), this is the first time that they have had a change of 'musician'. So, the future is now with Spanish keyboardist Gonzalo Carrera (ex Galadriel etc.), but this album looks back with five of the six numbers taken from the three Damian albums. Tracy has long been one of my favourite female singers, and she gives the songs a different edge to that from Damian who was a very hard act to follow indeed. The fact that the guys had been playing together for many years certainly show as they have a total understanding of what they are about and with Tracy giving it her all, this captures one of the UK's most under-rated prog bands at their best. There is an instrumental version of the mighty "Ta Jiang" (here combined with "Narovlya") that is only half its' original length but it still shows what close understanding between a rhythm section and twin melodic lead instruments can provide. Uwe is never an over the top guitarist, but he has enough of an edge to give the music bite when it needs it while Steve's keyboards can be simple and almost understand or total pompous grandeur when the need arises. Yet again this is a solid testament to the band, and an album that all progheads will surely enjoy, but instead of just listening to the album why not get out and see them! They are playing some dates around the country soon – go out there and give the much-maligned prog scene some support.
#73, Apr 2003

LANDS END
TERRA SERRANUM

Lands End are an American band who signed to Cyclops after the success of their independently released debut CD 'Pacific Coast Highway'. It became one of the top ten releases of the year as judged by American prog magazines, but somehow, I never got to grips with it: it was all very clever but not my scene. However, I am all for giving a band another chance so here I am listening to the follow-up. Yet again Lands End mix together late Seventies Genesis with Barclay James Harvest and Camel and come up with an album that displays brilliant musicianship. But, to my mind I am afraid this is the best that could be said about it. It is dreamy and enjoyable in a similar way to Jadis, but with none of their emotion and dynamism, as the album is all pretty much played at the same level. I keep wishing that the guitarist would smother the keyboard player and turn up his amp, but to no avail: it is pleasant, but no more than that. If you are going to buy a Cyclops release this month then pass this one smartly by and grab Jump with both hands and listen to some great music.
#31, Oct 1995

LANDS END
AN OLDER LAND

This is the second Lands End album to be released on Cyclops, and the third I have heard. I know that Malcolm Parker (supremo head boss man) rates them extremely highly, and I know that they are clever at what they do, but so far, I have not been able to get to grips with it. This album appears to be a collection of older material, as opposed to a brand-new album, as it were. They have songs that contain interesting ideas, such as the almost tribal drums utilised on "Wind Across The Water", which also has some good guitarwork, but at times it is let down by the vocals. I think that this is the problem. The songs never sound quite right to me, for one reason or another. I can't put my hand on my heart and say that this is a bad album, there are too many good points to it for that, but neither could I say that it was essential.
#37, Oct 1996

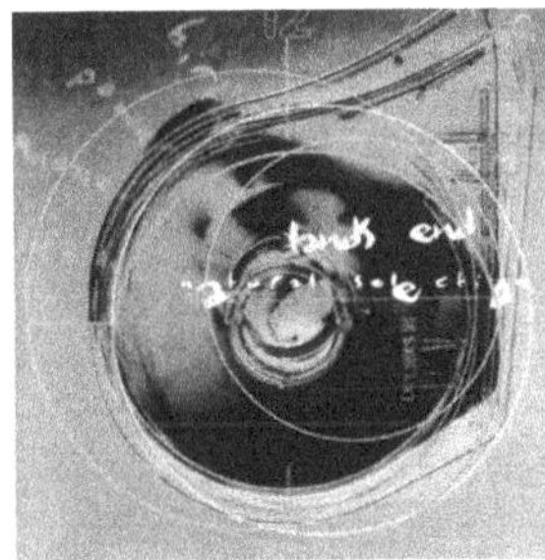

LANDS END
NATURAL SELECTION

This is a band that Malcolm Parker and I have discussed many times as he has always rated them extremely highly while I have begged to differ. However, at long last we concur, as I must say this is a glorious album with good melodies and well thought out structures. There is something here for nearly everyone with songs with some of the most interesting titles I have seen for a long time. How about opener "Strictly Speaking in Geographical Terms" which is followed by "From The Ruins Of A Fallen Empire", "Love Through The Winter and Blood in The Spring" and "An Emptiness That's Never Filled". This is not blasting rock as can be found in DGM or the power of Black Jester, and neither is it overtly complicated or classical like Sinkadus, but at times it is the sheer simplicity that is its' beauty. The first five songs, which are all good in their own way, contain some Floydian and high acoustic and light elements and add up to nearly forty-five minutes of music. But it is to closer "Natural Selection" that most proggers will turn to, which is some thirty minutes long. It starts off very gently indeed, and the band show their strength as they do not feel the need to fill the air with complexity but rather let the music live and breathe, and at times they use space and tranquillity as another instrument. So, Kev and Malcolm agree. Trumpets sound and people cry with joy. Well, not totally, because the CD booklet is truly naff, and the cover is awful so 10/10 for the music guys but 0/10 for the artwork. Sorry.
#47, Feb 1998

LANDS END
THE LOWER DEPTHS

It appears that Lands End have been through the mill, as this album finds them reduced to two original members, with the statement that the last time the four of them were together was February 1998. This has been released as a double disc, but I only have the primary

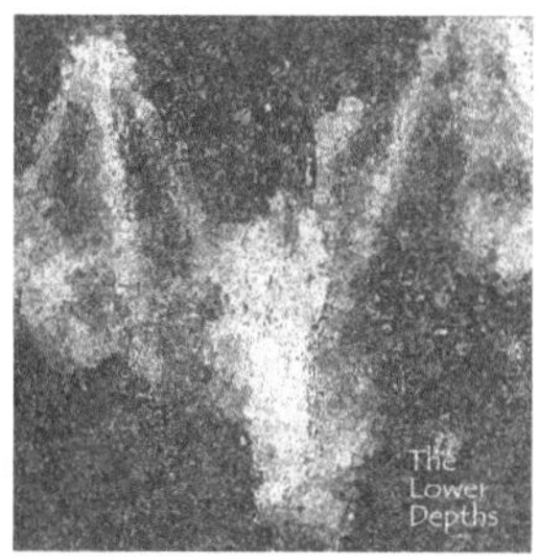

to review and the bonus contains mostly tracks including the original four members, including one piece that is 53 minutes long! With Mark Lavallee providing drums and Fred Hunter keyboards, bass, Taurus pedals and guitars they needed to get in some guests to fill out the sound. Original singer Jeff McFarland does sing on two numbers, but they obviously needed some more vocalists. Bruce Soord (The Pineapple Thief) sings on one and provides guitars on a couple of songs while Steve Anderson (Sphere³, GLD) also provides some extra muscle in the guitar department but the highlight is undoubtedly the vocals of Cathy Alexander (The Morrigan). It has been years since I last saw that band in concert, but she always came over well in that folk-rock environment but here in a prog band she appears to have really found her forte. Her vocals on the two epics really make them stand out. "Digital Signatures" is fourteen plus minutes of prog of the highest order while the 24 minutes of "A New World Order" is just superb. I sincerely hope that this is not the last that we hear of Cathy singing with Lands End as the songs of Fred Hunter are being taken to a new level and hopefully now that they have reached the depths, they will be able to get back up to the light. Extremely polished throughout, with good songs, this is prog that is both laid back and expansive, delicate but with an edge. Highly recommended.
#86, Feb 2006

LANA LANE
LOVE IS AN ILLUSION

LANA LANE
CURIOUS GOODS

LANA LANE
GARDEN OF THE MOON

LANA LANE
ECHOES FROM THE GARDEN

LANA LANE
LIVE IN JAPAN
One of the real benefits of running a magazine like Feedback is that sometimes, just sometimes, you are sent an album of such brilliance and magnitude that it literally leaves you scratching your head and thinking "How come I have never come across this artist before?" Such was the case when I was sent the most recent Lana Lane release. I then contacted Erik Norlander, who kindly sent me another three albums, along with one from Stefan Kost in Germany. That album 'Garden of the Moon', is amazingly enough the only one that is available in Europe, with the rest being Japanese releases. It surely can only be a matter of time until they are available over here, because these albums are wonderful. Lana has a tremendous voice, and by liaising with the brilliant Rocket Scientists has produced some incredible work. Of course, Rocket Scientists are a great band, and here they provide the basis of a group that includes three guitarists! Erik

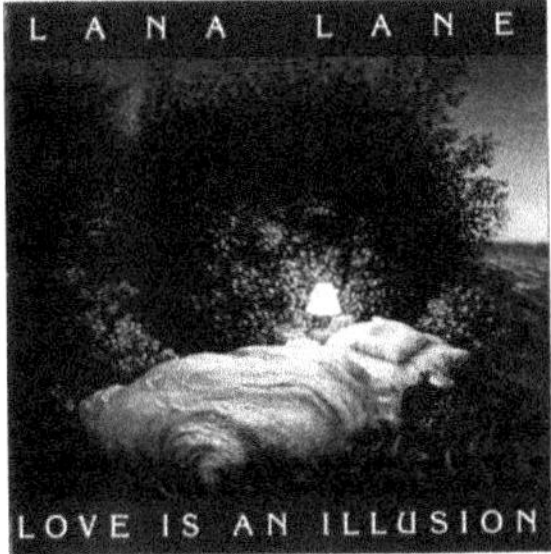

Norlander (keyboards, vocals), Tommy Amato (drums), Mark McCrite (guitar, vocals) and Don Schiff (stick, bass) of the Scientists are joined by Neil Citron (guitar, vocals) and Danelle Kern (rhythm guitar). First up is 'Love Is An Illusion', and thanks to the "Producer's Notes" by Erik which appears in the back of the CD I know a little of the background as although this is her first album, it is also very recent indeed. Originally released in 1995 when it was recorded on a shoestring budget, her subsequent success (mostly in Japan) let them go back and record both new songs, and new parts to original recordings. In one case, "Through The Fire", the drum and rhythm guitar parts were damaged on the original tapes, so they just went in and recorded totally new ones to fit in with the original keyboard and vocal tracks. Spot the join! In fact, the album was only completed in July so is both her oldest and newest recording. With both the lyrics and who played what, when, and what was altered, this is a very interesting booklet (by the way, the cover artwork for each album is by the same artist, Jacek Yerka, which gives them a very strong group identity), but at the end of the day it is the music that counts. With three guitarists, it would be expected that this would be very heavy indeed, but that is not the case. While it will always be seen as being a rock album, there are many more progressive elements than hard rock. Lana has a very strong, melodic, voice with a good range and the power she sometimes needs to get above the band. There is far much more going on in a musical sense that is normally found on one album. Is this down to the guitar interplay? Having an excellent keyboard player with many sounds at his disposal? Or a bassist who is far, far more than that, playing an instrument was developed by Emmett Chapman and Ned Steinberger. It is hard to pick a favourite, but I would probably plump for the title cut which is a straight in your face pounding melodic rock song, with Lana rising majestically above the music.

'Curious Goods' saw a change in the band, with Tony Franklin (who had played on one song on the previous album) coming in on bass and Neil the only guitarist. This is more progressive than the debut, and contains two covers, namely "Do It Again" and "Clouds". I should say that at times, there is too much space between the instruments, which means that of all the albums this is the one I enjoyed least (but is still brilliant in comparison to most). The major saving grace is the appearance of one of my favourites, "Symphony Of Angels (Arias and Fables)", although it does not have the same attack and thrust of the live version.

And so, onto the first of her albums that was released this year (including the re-worked debut there have been four), and the only one readily available in Europe as it has been released on the German label Angular Records (who, like Inside Out, are now distributed by SPV). With Lana's backing band again Rocket Scientists plus Neil and Danelle, the music really jumps. Having essentially produced two very different albums, the idea behind this release was to combine the two, which is done extremely effectively indeed. Lana sounds most at home here, and after a short instrumental is it into the driving commercial rock number "Destination Roswell". I would have thought that this would have been perfect for AOR Radio in the States as it is a great song, with a wonderful chorus, and the subject matter is very en vogue at present. With Danelle concentrating on providing a very heavy rhythm guitar, Mark working on acoustic and harmony, and Neil on harmony and leads, there is very little in the way of crossover. This is a symphonic rock album that works on all levels. If you want hard rock then it is there (just listen to "Evolution Revolution"), but never do the guitars manage to swamp the rest. Overall, and considering this is the easiest to get as well, this would be the studio album I would use as an introduction to Lana.

'Echoes From The Garden' was originated because of an idea by Naohiro Yamazaki, who has been guiding Lana's career since 1995. It was decided to release an album after the February release of 'Garden Of The Moon' but prior to her Japanese tour in April. The result is a mini-album containing three remixes, a longer version of "Evolution Revolution" and two new songs. The remixed "Seasons" works particularly well, as there is more space than on the original. The longer "Evolution Revolution" is also a winner, as is the atmospheric interpretation of "This Is Not America", which was originally written by David Bowie along with Pat Metheny and his keyboard player Lyle Mays. As a taster for Lana this works very well as an introduction, although the other new song "Leaving Standard" is not representative of her normal work, with a Hammond Organ taking the musical lead.

And then finally onto the album that started it all off for me, 'Live In Japan'. The band was Rocket Scientists plus Neil Citron, and the opening instrumental "Garden Of The Moon" did not let me know what to expect. This starts with a very atmospheric guitar from Neil, until it becomes more of a drum driven rock number. You can hear the crowd cheer as Lana makes her way onto the stage during the gentle introduction to "Coloured Life", and even in this very first song (the album was recorded at the first gig of the tour) her vocals have that edge of vitality that is not always captured in the studio. Mark McCrite's vocals appear higher in the mix as well, as more emphasis is placed on his ability to harmonise with Lana (as of course in this environment she can't sing backing as well). Mark is lead singer with Rocket Scientists and this gives the performance even more bite. Rocket Scientists are one of those bands who shine on stage and with an extra guitarist in Neil they put together a great show. "Coloured Life" is followed by "Destination Roswell" where Lana hits and holds the high notes while the guys provide low harmonies. Wonderful. There are eleven songs on this album, and really, every single one of them is a winner. But if I had to take just one version of one song with me of Lana's to that desert island then it would have to be "Symphony Of Angels". Starting with pneumatic drill-style riffing from Mark, with a lead line placed over the top by Neil, the first verse becomes a laid-back affair being led mostly by the bass, but it all changes going into the chorus, when it becomes a rock song in full flight, majestic, soaring, wonderful, brilliant. I have not been this excited about a new (to me, anyway) act since I first came across Spock's Beard. I urge you, nay beg you, to try and sample some of this wonderful box of delights that has been put on offer here for you. *#51, Jan 1999*

LANA LANE
SECRETS OF ASTROLOGY

This is the first I have heard of Lana since her live album in 1998, although she has released more material in the intervening time. The first things that I noticed was that firstly she was not using Jacek Yerka to provide her artwork, and secondly that apart from Erik Norlander, The Rocket Scientists are no longer the core of her backing band. Lana has made a definite break with her past, and the music reflects this. A lot of the music is much more rock based, with Lana taking a step away from the prog camp and into the mainstream AOR market. That is not to say that this is an overly commercial release, just that the edge has changed. In some ways, it is a much more polished release than I have heard from her before, with favourite "Raining" proving yet again what a superb voice she has. It is a very complete album and kicks off in a fine manner with a powering rock instrumental. If you have never heard Lana before then this is a very good album to begin with, although to hear her at her best I would still point to the superb 'Live In Japan' with the awesome "Symphony Of Angels".
#58, May 2000

LANA LANE
WINTER SESSIONS

LANA LANE
LADY MACBETH

When I was recovering from my motorbike accident back in 1998, one of the albums I played a great deal during that period was Lana's 'Live In Japan' which to me captured so many good things about music all in one place. The band were incredible, and then on top of that was Lana's wonderful vocals but somehow over the years I lost track of what she was doing. Now I have two Lana Lane albums to listen to, and it is a treat. First into the player was 'Winter Sessions' from 2003, and again I marvelled at the sheer musicality of what was being played. At the helm is her husband and keyboard player/producer Erik Norlander as well as the 'usual suspects' of Mark McCrite, Don Schiff and Neil Citron among others. The music has been arranged so that it is often layered like a fine orchestra, then on top of all that there are Lana's vocals. She has a wonderfully emotional high clear voice that contains a lot of passion and she rules the roost whether it is a full band playing or just some delicate piano lines. There are some wonderful ballads contained within this collection of songs, as well as some more powerful numbers and even some covers. I am not too sure of "A Whiter Shade Of Pale" as the music is often too close to the original, but there is more passion here than in the version created by Annie Lennox. "California Dreamin'" works far better, with the harmony vocals working particularly well, but the stand out number probably has to be "Spirit Of Glory" which brings together loads of different styles and really showcases her voice. The more I played that album the more I enjoyed it, but it was a grower, and that was not the case with 'Lady Macbeth' from 2005 as that grabs the attention with opener "The Dream That Never Ends" which is just totally over the top bombastic prog right through to last song "Dunsinane Walls". This is a concept album and it captures the power of Lana with some wonderful music. As well as Don Schiff playing N/S Stick they also used touring bassist Kristoffer Gildenlöw (Pain Of Salvation). This has given the music a more solid rock-oriented bottom line for the rest of the guys to build upon, and when they are all crunching away and Lana soars over the top as in "Someone To Believe" I feel that I have died and gone to heaven. It is a perfect combination of music and vocals, with the arrangement spot on. There is even a Quick Time video of that song on the disc. It is not all over the top of course, there are also slower numbers, where Lana relies on her voice to carry the more basic backing but of course she always does this with style and aplomb.

If you have never heard Lana before and you enjoy good strong female singers combined with great music and arrangements, then 'Lady Macbeth' is a wonderful place to start and is an album that I very highly recommend indeed. *#87, Apr 2006*

LANFEAR
TOWERS

Lanfear describe their music as power metal combined with classical instruments and epic progressive tracks and look to non -metal artists such as Mike Oldfield and early Genesis for inspiration. Stefan Zoerner (vocals, keyboards), Markus Ullrich (guitars), Alexander Palma (bass) and Jürgen Schrank (drums) are certainly very proficient and from "Hate-full Pride" to the epic (fifteen minutes plus) "The Towers of February" they kick up a technical metallic noise that is very pleasing to the ear. The music is more complex than Threshold, but even with only just one guitarist they manage to retain a real ferocity. This is prog metal at its best, although some prog fans will find the guitar just too intimidating for their tastes. There is a lot of very good music coming out of Germany right now, and Lanfear are up there with them.*#36, Aug 1996*

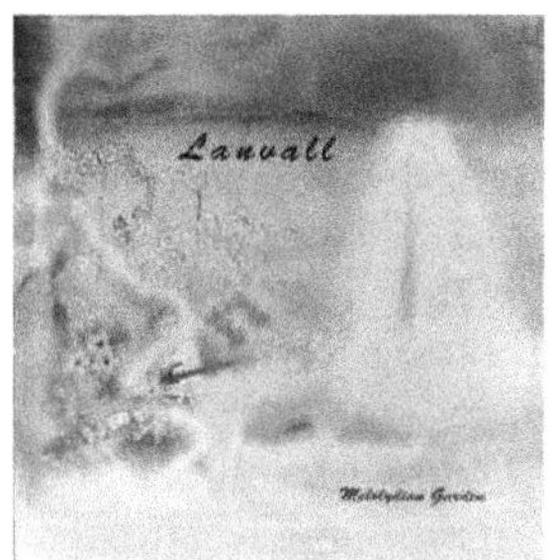

LANVALL
MELODYIAN GARDEN

A long time ago I received a demo tape from Arne Stockhamer in Austria. I enjoyed the guitarwork and am pleased to see that he has now released an instrumental CD (and changed his name to boot). A few of the tracks that were on the tape have resurfaced, but Arne now only supplies guitar, keyboards and flute as he is joined by Ulbi Ulbrecht (bass) and Thomas Schaufler (drums). The result is a dreamy album reminiscent at times of both Camel

and BJH, although some of the harder tracks like "Euphoria" are more Jadis in style, and 'Melodyian Garden' is an album to relax to. The guitars are not drowned in a sea of keyboards, but rather the emphasis is placed more on emotion and restraint than on blasting power chords. Arne (or Lanvall as I should call him), is an extremely adept guitarist and he has put together an instrumental album that is a real joy to listen to.
#32, Dec 1995

LAST TRIBE
WITCH DANCE

Last Tribe are back with a new line-up and a more complex sound. Although the music is still firmly steeped in melodic rock, this has a much more progressive sound. Technically very complex, this is more into the realms of Pain Of Salvation or possibly Stratovarius, yet at the same time there are some great hooks. There are sections of songs that are extremely commercial, such as in "Behind Your Eyes", yet there are also sections that are much more complicated which takes the song into new directions. The vocals soar, and the music crashes likes waves on a beach at night: this is much more than just melodic rock. The title cut blasts out with overlaid keyboard and guitars combining to give a feeling of depth and presence, then the hounds are unleashed, and the band have taken the challenge and are running with it. Driven along by the new rhythm section of Jaime Salazar (ex The Flower Kings) and Dick Löwgren, guitarist and keyboard player Magnus Karlsson and singer Rickard Bengtsson have taken Last Tribe to heights only dreamed of after the release of their debut. Yet again Frontiers have come up with another great release. *#68, Jun 2002*

LAST TURION
SEDUCTION OVERDOSE

This is progressive technical hard rock, bringing in influences such as Threshold and Dream Theater. It starts off innocently enough, with keyboards and guitar but something does not sound quite right, as if the production was a little off and you are listening to the sound through a filter. However, it's not the first time I have been sent an album with bad production, so I turned it up a bit. Mistake. A voice announces, "This album should be played at loud volume, preferably in a residential area" then the 'filter' is removed and the band crank into the title track. Wakes you up a bit, I can tell you. Instead of being naff, the production is quite superb, but it is the quality of the songs and musicianship that needs to be admired. I know nothing about the band themselves, but they must have been together for a while because the material is high class and these guys kick it. There is not a duff moment among the ten songs on show, and it is difficult to pick out a highlight: I would love to see them playing a gig with Threshold because that would be one to die for. If you like your hard rock melodic and are not afraid of keyboards in a hard rock setting then this is an album you simply must have.
#41, Apr 1997

LAST WARNING
FROM THE FLOOR OF THE WELL

Last Warning is an Italian band that has been going since 1987, although this line-up has only been together since 1992. This, their debut CD, clearly shows that they have been listening to a lot of Queensrÿche and Dream Theater as well as our own Threshold, and although prog is the order of the day it is delivered via rock keyboards and two dominating guitars turned up to ten. Campanotti Diego has a very powerful voice and he needs it to provide the control needed with a rock band at full throttle. Bands such as Last Warning blur the boundaries between what is regarded as hard rock and prog rock, and the question is then whether those who feel obliged to be pigeonholed in their likes will seek out a band not so easily categorised. I am convinced that this is the only reason why Threshold are not the major players in the UK rock scene that they should be, and I wonder whether the same fate will befall Last Warning. Still, they have played many gigs with bands as diverse as Carcass and Doctor & The Medics, so hopefully the fanbase is growing. If you like hard melodic rock, then there is much here for you. Take a risk and try a hard rock band that you will not read about in Metal Hammer.

#32, Dec 1995

LEGEND
LIGHT IN EXTENSION

Legend were formed in August 1988 by keyboard player Stephen Paine, and after an initial period of instability the line-up settled down with Debbie Chapman (vocals), Paul Thomson (guitar), Ian Lees (bass), Chris Haskayne (drums) and Steve. Throughout 1989 and 1990 the band gigged extensively in the North West, gradually building up a good following and a strong reputation for a great live show. Not content with relying solely on the music they also use pyrotechnics, laser and strobe effects, coupled with a forty-lantern light show. If that was not enough, they also use costumes, and have a 2.4 KW PA system to ensure that their music comes across loud and clear: quite a package to be putting into small clubs and venues. In 1990 they signed a management and sponsorship deal with Pagan Media Ltd, which culminated with the recording of their debut album. 'Light In Extension'. Graham raved over this in the last issue of Blindsight, and I can see why. This album is as prog as it comes, but unlike virtually all the other prog bands around they are not relying on Genesis for their influence, but from a rather different source, that of Steeleye Span. That is not to say that they sound like them, but rather it is an influence that they have incorporated into their own very distinct sound.

Kicking off with the title song, it opens with soaring keyboards and frenetic drumming which leaves you quite unprepared for the clarity and style of Debbie's singing. Debbie sounds and sings like Maddy Prior, and to say that the use of a clear, soaring voice singing effortlessly over the top of a powerful rock track is effective is just a minor understatement. However, the band are far more than just a backing group with a female lead, as they more than ably demonstrate throughout the album. They are tight, really tight, and great musicians to boot. As the song builds to its close the twin bass drums kick in and the keyboards provide a choral backdrop that soar above the menace and power of the blistering rock to great effect. "Hold The Flame" is a totally different track, being far lighter in mood; Paul plays a lead line throughout most of the song, mimicking the vocals. This brighter song provides the way for "Nightshade", which starts in a very Steeleye manner, but the chorus dispels all thought of folk rock. "Windsong" starts with a bass line that could have been lifted straight from Dave Pegg and the whole song has a folky element to it, again being of a far lighter nature; that is until the instrumental passage where Paul and Steve swap leads to great effect. I can imagine this being an extensive workout live, then quite suddenly the mood changes as a madrigal is played that then leads back into the song itself. It ends with Paul demonstrating some great axework and is a song to be proud of with many different elements, combining and adding instead of detracting from the whole. "The Pipes of Pan" is the rockiest track on the album and has great musicianship throughout. Again, it is a faster song, but Legend slow it down in the middle and break it up before speeding off again. More than anything else Legend are a band of contrast and use this to great advantage. "The Chase" gives the lads the opportunity to demonstrate their instrumental prowess, and Paul and Steve again take turns to provide the lead role. The combined effect is one of menace and terror, and the chase is on. "Lament" is a slow ballad that leads into the closer "Evidence of Autumn" where the gentle piano-based verse does not prepare you for the rock chorus.

The lyrics are Arthurian and paganistic and are well written. The CD has a colour cover and contains all the lyrics. The only moan I have about the album is that Chris loves to power around the kit, and it eventually detracts. However, since the album was recorded both Chris and Ian have left the band, to be replaced by John Macklin and Shaun McGowan respectively and that element has been removed from the music. This is a great album, and to promote it they also have a free three-track flexi available.
#12, May 1992

LEGEND
SECOND SIGHT

I've been waiting eagerly for this: I loved Legend's first album, and having seen them live and their excellent video, I was hoping that the new album would live up to my expectations. It has done far more than that, easily surpassing my highest hopes. The new rhythm section has put loads of life and vitality in to the band, and boy does it show. Opener "Dance" is a driving rock song, far heavier than anything on the debut. "New Horizons" continues in a similar vein, with riffing guitars, interspersed with atmospheric keyboards. Legend are totally unlike any of the other prog bands around, coming from the Steeleye and folk area, but this album has seen them move into heavier territory. Even with just an advance tape at my disposal, the dynamics are superb, and Jon and Steve have done an excellent job with the production. Debbie's pure clear vocals work extremely well with the new sound. "The Healer" starts off with just Debbie and piano, but gradually builds up into a very atmospheric ballad with restrained yet effective guitar.

The use of fretless bass on this album is also a bonus. "The Wild Hunt" starts off with unaccompanied vocals, but soon switches into folk-rock mode, which in turn becomes an acoustic number that turns and twists time and again. This song shows all the many different sides and strengths of Legend, as they move from one style to another. Steve seems to have rediscovered his keyboards as he produces more dynamic and interesting sounds than were on the debut. "The Legend" is one of the tracks that feature on the video, a restrained atmospheric rocker with a menacing middle section, where a repeated keyboard riff is gradually joined by the rest of the band; the vocals come in and suddenly the band are off the leash and up and running with the keyboards and guitar in perfect harmony. The last two songs, "I Close My Eyes" and "Mordred" are also of exceptionally high standard. Legend's first album was enjoyed by many (more than 11,000), but reservations were expressed about the rhythm section, but these have now been swept away as Legend has produced a follow-up that is truly magnificent. I always enjoyed 'Light In Extension', but 'Second Sight' is so much better. Confident in the direction that they want to take, this is an album that will be enjoyed by all lovers of good music. In many ways, it defies description as it is melodic, folky, rocky, with a mix of so many different styles and moods. I know that many of you enjoyed the flexi given away with Feedback last year, and if you enjoyed that then you will love this. Steve has sent me a full-colour mock-up of the CD cover and it is quite stunning. Full release details have yet to be finalised but if problems can be resolved with the Japanese distributors then it should be available after October 31st.

#20, Oct 1993

LEGEND

TRIPLE ASPECT

At long last here is the new opus from everybody's favourite pagan proggers. It has been a long time since 'Second Sight', not helped by bassist problems, which has now been resolved by guitarist Paul Thomson taking on the duties. Legend is first and foremost a rock band, although they are quite unlike any other group around. I am convinced that if I were played two bars of music by Legend I would recognise them easily, and that would be without Debbie's distinctive vocals. There are very few bands in the 'progressive' sphere that different. Musically Legend appear at times to be coming from the folk side, as there are definite touches of madrigals, however the mayhem that is also present is far more hard rock. Many would argue that it is Debbie's high clear vocals (like Maddy Prior) that make the band what it is, but the answer lies in the relationship between Paul and keyboard player Steve Paine. John Macklin's solid drumming should not be ignored, but it is Paul and Steve who are in firm control; Paul is happy to riff or play lead, as the role demands, while Steve is content to solo or utilise held down chords. All the time they are working off each other so that twin harmony leads a la Wishbone Ash (with Steve taking on one of the guitar roles) occur, as do the trading of runs a la Uriah Heep. With Paul also taking on the extra bass role this time, it means that the band seems tighter, and the music definitely benefits. The confidence comes through in the title song, which clocks in at just less than thirty minutes. The music turns, twists, dives and soars and can be frantic and dynamic, or soft and gentle. At times, it is peaceful and

reflective while at others it is energetic and rocking at full blast. Debbie's clear vocals ride clear of the maelstrom, with the clarity of polished glass. If you like the other two Legend albums you will surely love this one, and if you have not heard them then now is the time to start.
#36, Aug 1996

LEGER DE MAIN
THE CONCEPT OF OUR REALITY

It has been a long time since I reviewed the demo tapes that had been sent to me by American band Drama. Sadly, they are no more, but Chris Rodler (guitar, bass, keyboards) and Brett Rodler (drums) have joined forces with vocalist Melissa Blair to bring into being a dynamic new band, Leger de Main. Like Drama before them, Leger de Main has a heavy Rush influence, but it has been taken to new heights. Having stated their starting point, they have then taken off and developed a very technical form of prog rock, unlike virtually anything that is around (including Rush). Opener "To Live The Truth" is like a wild stallion running for its' life. It twists, changes, bucks and dives with tremendous speed and skill, and the power that is unleashed is almost frightening in its intensity. This is rock primarily, but not for the unwary. Highlight of the album must be the twenty-minute long "Enter Quietly" which starts with gentle classical guitar interplay that gradually brings in repeated themes. This is crashed into touch as the theme is taken on by the keyboards with the force of the rest of the band behind it. Back to classical guitar to accompany the delicate vocals, but again these do not last for long. Leger de Main have produced a piece de resistance. One to get, definitely.
#32, Dec 1995

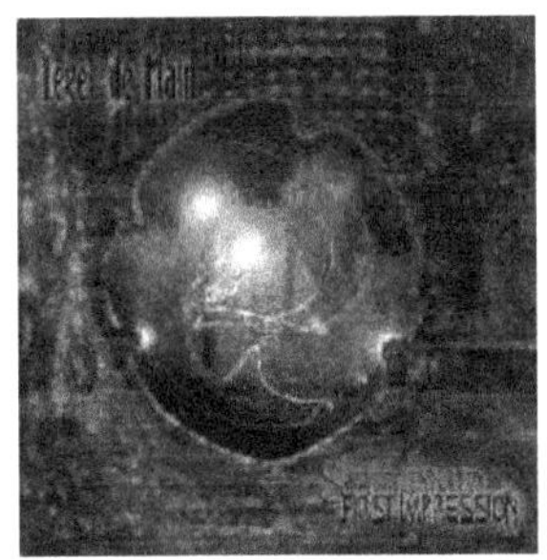

LEGER DE MAIN
SECOND FIRST IMPRESSION

It seems to have been a long time since Leger De Main's debut album 'The Concept Of Our Reality', but at long last they are back with the second. It is the same line-up of Chris Rodler (guitars, keyboards), Melissa Blair (vocals), Brett Rodler (drums) plus a few guest musicians, most notably bassist Kevin Hultberg. LDM's trademark is music that at times is extremely complex but laid over the top are the pure clear vocals of Melissa. Chris certainly is not afraid to lay down the law, either with strong keyboard sounds or with plain good old-fashioned riffs. He has certainly put the Rush ghost to rest, which was highly prevalent in his previous band Drama and carried over somewhat diluted into LDM's debut, but here it is gone for good. What has taken its' place is jazz fusion combined with prog rock in a way that is very powerful indeed. The first part of the twelve-minute "Some Shall Search" is a good example of this, with some quite complicated guitarwork driven on by Brett's powerhouse drumming. But after this hard introduction a classical guitar leads the way into Mellissa's vocals, only for the menace to return. I found myself thinking of Legend, not because they are musically the

same (Melissa sings in a lower register than Debbie), but in each case the vocalists are singing clear and seemingly without a care in the world while musically beneath them all hell can be breaking lose. I do not think that this is as good a release as the debut, but certainly it is still of great interest to the proghead.
#47, Feb 1998

LEGER DE MAIN
A LASTING IMPRESSION

It has been ten long years since Leger de Main released their debut 'The Concept Of Our Reality', and now it has again been made available for the first time in five years. It has been remastered and Chris and Melissa have recorded two acoustic versions as bonus cuts and if that was not enough there is a second disc, which contains the whole of their follow-up album 'Second First Impression'. Although there were some extra guests these albums were primarily the work of just two musicians, brothers Brett Rodler (drums) and Chris (everything else!), combining with the vocal talents of Melissa Blair (although I note on the reissue that she is Melissa Rodler). I have been a fan of these guys, from their early times in Drama right through to their current work in Razor Wire Shrine and their other projects, just because technically they are so skilled. Their music is always complex, often invigorating, and always exciting. In Melissa, they had a great singer who did rise above what they were doing. Chris can shred when he wants to, but the acoustic bonus songs show him in a different light and it also allows Melissa to be more reflective. Hey guys, this could be a different career direction, why not do a whole album like this, as these are great!! There will be quite a few progheads who will be interested in this release, which in the past has been described as what Rush would sound like if they were a prog band! It is strong complicated and complex rock that is technically superb and wonderful to listen to with Melissa's vocals soaring over the top of it all. *#85, Nov 2005*

LEMUR VOICE
DIVIDED

This is a complex album from Holland, which for many years was such a hotbed of progressive music but appears to be in decline over recent times. However, if this album is anything to go by, then they are back with a vengeance. I do not have any blurb on these guys, but it is hard to believe that it is a first album. This has a lot going for it, with strong tunes and melodies, interplay between the instruments, great vocals, and some long songs (but no real epics). The other thing that struck me immensely about this album is that it is very intense, much more upfront than many albums of this style. The result is an album that has enough facets on it to please the proghead, while probably giving enough emphasis on the guitars to bring in those who are more partial to technical rock. Either way, the proghead should investigate this album.
#56, Jan 2000

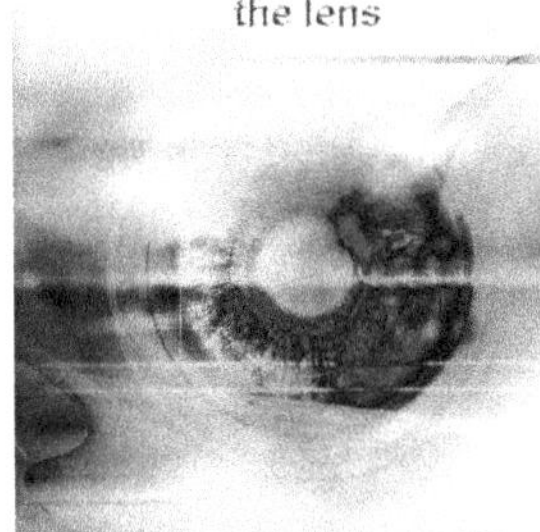

THE LENS
A WORD IN YOUR EYE

This album has been a long time coming, over twenty years in fact. The Lens was the band where Mike Holmes and Martin Orford (and sometimes Peter Nicholls) first played together. Mike formed the band in 1976, with Martin joining in 1977. The band never recorded and broke up in 1981, with Mike and Martin forming a new band, called IQ. Many IQ fans, myself included, have wondered what The Lens sounded like, as I was down in Devon when they were playing in London so never had the opportunity to hear them. This album is an attempt to put things right, although this is a new version with Mike providing bass as well as guitar, Martin keyboards, flute and the few vocals, and they are joined by Paul Cook on drums, with Tony Wright also providing the odd sax. Given that three of them are full-time members of IQ, and the other is often a guest for IQ, it is no surprise that at times they sound similar. What must be remembered though is that IQ grew out of The Lens, not the other way around. "Choosing A Farmer" is my favourite, with some great guitar and interplay between the main protagonists while Cookie shows what a superb drummer he is.

The album is mostly instrumental, although Martin does sing on "Childhood's End". It is one that will be a huge hit with all IQ fans, but will also appeal to all those who enjoy progressive rock. The songs all have purpose and although instrumental do not just meander through without meaning. A short history is provided in the booklet, and this is a release worth getting.
#66, Feb 2002

LEST
3937

Lest say that they are influenced by bands such as IQ and Pendragon, yet they seem to have moved away from that, as although this is a prog album the music has certainly also taken on some themes from hard rock. The vocals are strong, and the music shifts and flows well and I found that I kept being reminded of Salem Hill, and I would think that this release would be very much at home on Cyclops, although Inside Out would probably be interested as well. Although Lest started life in France in 1995 and did support quite a few well-known bands, by 1998 only Didier Kopp was left, and he decided to recruit new musicians and try a new style. The result is the album that I am listening to and they are again a gigging unit as well. Given that this is a demo, it is certainly very enjoyable, and I would have thought that many progheads would be interested in this band who on this evidence have a lot to offer.
#80, Jul 2004

LIGHT

LIGHT

Light have been going in one form or another since 1986, but the current four-man line-up came into being in 1992, and the flying Dutchmen have managed to produce the goods with this their debut CD. Unlike many of the Dutch prog bands that are around, Light have managed to create their own identity as they are not clones, but instead follow their own musical direction. This is extremely melodic, with great harmony vocals, while always maintaining a rock presence. This is not wimpish widdly-widdly prog, but rather a melodic rock band at the very top of their profession. It would be possible to cite Kansas as a starting point, or even IQ, but the very diversity of the music played by those two bands shows the reviewer's nightmare in trying to define the wonderful music produced by Light. From extremely short acoustic pieces to twenty minute plus grand epics, they are totally at home with what they are doing, whether that is playing with pace and venom or moving rapidly from one time change to another, or maybe dropping in that touch of jazz rock, Light are masters of all. Quite possibly, they have produced, with their debut album, the best prog I have heard come out of Holland.

#32, Dec 1995

THE LIGHT

ON A NEW HORIZON

Distributed in the UK by Escape Music, this American quintet have produced an American AOR, Prog crossover album that will surely be on every good music lover's Christmas list this year. Imagine '90125' period Yes mixed with 'Audio Visions' period Kansas with just a dash of 'Cornerstone' Styx and you will get close to some idea of what this band is about. I am amazed that I have not heard about this album through the prog scene as it is just brilliant. Vocalist David Downum has a style very like Steve Walsh and when those harmonies kick in, I am transported to heaven. I know that in this issue of Feedback I have raved over a few albums but it's not my fault that so much good music has come to my ears at once. 'On A New Horizon' is one of the best American albums of the year: Spock's Beard may well be more experimental in what they are doing, more progressive, but The Light are certainly giving them a run for their money. There is so much in here to enjoy, and it is totally immediate with ten songs and I love it. I am so glad that I have been sent this close to the deadline instead of a long time before because I would never have got anything else on the player. Ken Balagna (bass, vocals) has written all of the songs and he has this to say "The Light is all about getting back to basics. It's about the refinement and perfection of musical ideas. It's about music. Combined with the music are lyrics that reveal simple truths, concepts and perspectives often shrouded in symbology." The next album will be 'The Willing Suspension Of Disbelief' (carrying on an idea portrayed at the beginning of the final song, "Journey Home"). Meanwhile, this is an album that you just cannot live without.

#38, Nov 1996

LIGHTSPEED
WAVES

This is the third album from Canadian band Lightspeed and was released in 2004 but has only just come to my attention. The band have been going in various guises since the late Seventies, but the line-up here was John Persichini (vocals), Gene Murray (guitars), Gary Chappell (keyboards, vocals), Terry Crawford (drums, vocals) and Rod Chappell (bass, vocals). I do not know what the other albums are like, but if they are as polished as this one then I need to do some seeking out, as this is quite superb. Imagine Styx and Kansas having a party and inviting Saga along as special guests and you will have some idea as to what this band sounds like. This is very melodic AOR driven prog that contains great harmonies and hooks and is a delight from the start to end. They do not wimp out too much but maintain a fine balance between the guitars and keyboards with the vocals always taking centre stage.

It is hard to believe that music that has this much shine and sheer professionalism hasn't been heard by a wider audience, as if you like any of the mega million selling bands that I mentioned then you are going to love this – it is that simple. The band are not mimics; it is just that they are in a similar field and the harmony vocals are wonderful. From ballads through to rockier numbers this is a joy throughout and is very highly recommended. Let's just hope that they start getting more prolific!
#89, Sep 2006

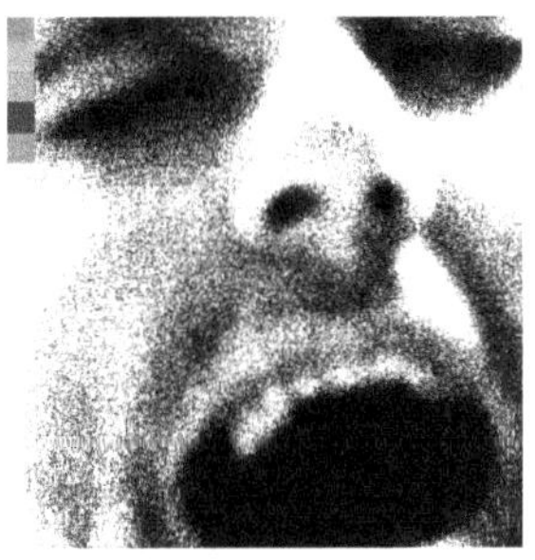

LIKE WENDY
ENDGAME

This 2004 album was the sixth release for Like Wendy, although up until this release it had been the work of just one man, Bert Heinen. He brought Mark-Jeroen Heek to assist on vocals for his fourth album, went back solo for his fifth, but the sixth finds him working fully with Mark-Jeroen so much so that the solo project is now a duo. Having not heard the other albums I can't say if the sound has changed much, but here we get Moody Blues mixed in Barclay James Harvest with plenty of analogue and early Seventies feel to produce an album that is not dramatically powerful but does have a great deal going for it. As one would expect from the two bands I have mentioned, this is quite a laid-back album with plenty of emotion and concentration on song structure and style as opposed to rocking out in your face, but there are some lovely John Lees/Steve Hackett style leads that brighten up the proceedings.

All the lyrics are in English and the result is an album that is very accessible and enjoyable to listen to. There are times when it can be a little too sedate, but if you enjoy your music at the softer end then this contains strong songs and good vocals and is well worth hearing
#87, Apr 2006

PAR LINDH PROJECT
GOTHIC IMPRESSIONS

Par Lindh has had a long musical career, most of it in the classical field. In 1980 he went to France to study the harpsichord and organ and used this as a base for concert tours in Europe. He also played with the Royal Swedish Chamber Orchestra for four years, and it was on his return to Sweden in 1988 that he decided to return to the progressive rock that he had first started playing in the Seventies. Having built his own studio, the first release was 'Gothic Impressions' and for this he used top Swedish musicians for each track as he saw fit. The most well-known of these to me is Roine Stolt (in an engineering role) who used to be in Kaipa and who released the brilliant 'The Flower King' last year. Par states that the music was mostly written in the Seventies and has attempted to use instruments from that period. True, the album does have a very Seventies feel to it, moving from ballads to instrumentals very easily. The instrumental sections are reminiscent of Rick Wakeman while the songs are a combination of ELP and The Moody Blues. The album works very well and will be enjoyed by those with a bent to the more classical forms.

#31, Oct 1995

PAR LINDH PROJECT
MUNDUS INCOMPETUS

It has been a long time since I last reviewed anything from Par Lindh; indeed, looking back at the index I see it was #31! They say that absence makes the heart grow fonder and that it is the case with 'Mundus Incompetus' as this is an album that many proggers will find enjoyable. This is far more orchestral and baroque in flavour than most, as there are long passages where Par takes the lead on a church organ. However, this is not church music, as Par aptly demonstrates when driving the music along with a Hammond in a very Keith Emerson-like style. It is not solely an instrumental album, as he utilises the talents of Magdalena Hagberg who has a very clear and choral voice. Quite a short album, at only forty-two minutes, but it is quality and not quantity. In fact, the third of the three songs is nearly twenty-seven minutes in length, which gives ample time for the band to display the versatility of their music. This is not easy listening prog, and those expecting them to sound quite like anybody else is going to be disappointed although as I said there are passages where they come across as like ELP and it is fans of that band who I would have thought would get the most out of this. However, if you enjoy that style of prog then there is much on here to enjoy.

#52, Feb 1999

LIQUID SCARLET
II

No prizes for working out that this is the band's second album, I hadn't heard the debut so was not quite sure what to expect from this Swedish quintet. But the first number,

Liquid Scarlet
II

"Lines Are Drawn Again" just totally blew me away. It commences life with some very delicate piano chords, and then Markus Fagervall joins in with delicate vocals. It is melancholic; it is haunting, yet at the same time simplistically beautiful. The lyrics fall out almost like a flow of consciousness and gradually the other instruments come in. Only ninety seconds into the album I was absolutely entranced and captivated as the song just kept building, but slowly, ever so slowly: imagine Coldplay with more passion and you might just get an idea of what was keeping me spellbound. At three minutes twenty seconds, the song takes a complete shift so although the gentle piano melody is still there underneath it is swamped by everything else that is going on. The song eventually finished at just over five minutes long and by now, I was determined to give this album my very closest attention, and I was richly rewarded. The main point of similarity with what they are trying to achieve is probably King Crimson, with complex guitar patterns and time signatures, combined with a knowledge of music far outside the prog mainstream to create something that is compelling, at times frenetic, at times beautiful, and at times simple and at others extremely complicated. This is not prog music that is going to fit merrily into one style or another as they are definitely trying to create their own sound, and, in some ways, they do come across as a 70's group, but very much mixing it up to date. "Killer Couple Strikes Again" is much more of a straightforward rock song, and it is probably not surprising that this has been released as the lead song on a twenty-one-minute-long EP, which apart from that one song contains four others not on the album. This is an exciting young band that I am sure are going to be creating quite a few waves within the prog world.
#86, Feb 2006

LITTLE ATLAS
WANDERLUST

This is the third album from Miami based quartet Little Atlas (who do have guests on violin and cuatro), but it is the first that I have heard, and I am now starting to wonder what the other two albums sound like as this is mighty fine. What they have done is taken some of the less bombastic elements of some great prog bands such as Spock's Beard and Genesis and mixed these with Rush and possibly even classic Styx (although not nearly so bland) to produce a sound that is immediately engaging and interesting while also being complex and complicated enough to certainly involve any proghead. The emphasis is very much on songs and although the seven on this album do manage to clock in at nearly an hour it never feels that there is an epic involved as the whole album is just so enjoyable. Steve Katsikas has a very clear voice, with a style not too far removed from Neal Morse, and within "Weariness Rides" he does have his vocals double tracked so that he can produce an a capella section so beloved of the Beard, but these guys are nothing like SB except for the small fact that they can involve the listener. This is prog that is more mature than many, no flashiness just for its' own sake but rather an album that has been well structured and is quite different to much that is currently around on the scene. This CD does also come with enhanced content. *#84, July 2005*

LITTLE TRAGEDIES
NEW FAUST

LITTLE TRAGEDIES
THE SIXTH SENSE

'New Faust' is the fourth (I think) album from Russian band Little Tragedies, the first on the Mals label, and are led by keyboard player and vocalist Gennady Ilyin. The band that many will think of when first hearing this is Emerson, Lake & Palmer, but there is a distinct Russian flavour – assisted of course by the lyrics, none of which are in English. But this is the lighter side of ELP, where Keith is reining in his bombast. There are times when Gennady lets the others have a larger part in proceedings, and the sax can be very effective indeed, but this is very much his band and he is always at the forefront of the music. There are some strong elements within this double CD, but they are few and far between. There are other Russian bands around that have impressed me more, so I probably will not be giving this the time that it deserves to be fully appreciated, although I have seen some very positive reviews about this indeed.

Not long after receiving 'New Faust' I was sent another Little Tragedies CD by Mals, 'Sixth Sense', so these guys are keeping up the pace. Again, all the lyrics are in Russian, but while the band still have ELP tendencies they have also now included some elements of Pink Floyd within their music and the feeling overall is much more reflective. This is more laid back and thoughtful, and the album is better because of it. In fact, it has caused me to rethink my views on 'New Faust' so much so that although I stand by my original review, I am going to go back to it when I have completed working on my pieces for #89 and listen to it a few times more. There is a polish and a substance to this album that progheads will enjoy even if they can't understand what Gennady is singing about – it is reflective and emotional with some very Gilmour like overtones.
#89, Sep 2006

LIVES AND TIMES
RATTLEBONES

LIVES AND TIMES
THE PULL OF A TIDE

LIVES AND TIMES
WAITING FOR THE PARADE

Lives and Times were formed in 1989 by Richard Wileman (guitars, keyboards, percussion) and Lorna Cumberland (vocals). For the next three years, they recorded demos, wrote songs and played gigs with various line-ups but never succeeded in getting a record deal, and in 1991 they split in frustration. Later the same year, Richard formed the No Image label with musician friend Nick Weaver, and their first release was a

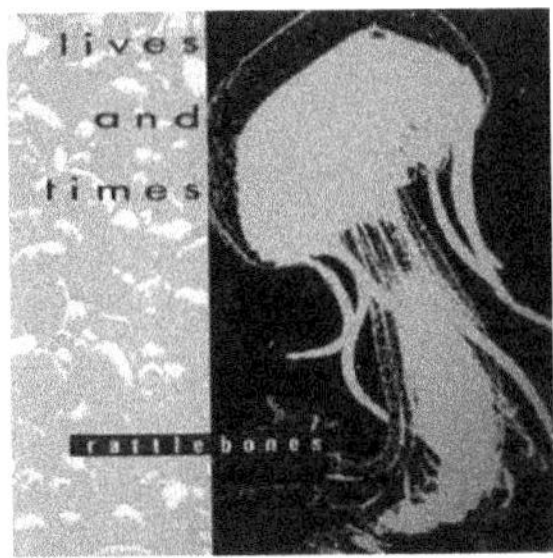

compilation of material. Richard then contacted Lorna, and they recorded four old Lives and Times numbers. As it all went so well, Nick decided to start a new project, Eternal Energy, and Richard and Lorna resurrected L&T.

'Rattlebones' was released in 1992, with Teresa Griffin on bass, and Richard providing the rest of the instrumentation. Lorna's voice is pure and clear, immediately bringing thoughts of Kate Bush or Maryen Cairns and the music is not prog, but varies between straight pop, classical, and even New Age! The vocals and music combine perfectly, but it is to the voice that the ears are drawn. Of the three CDs, this is probably the weakest with all the tracks being good, but none really standing out.

'The Pull Of A Tide' came out with 1993, with Chris Brown now resident bassist (although Teresa did play on a few of the tracks). The songwriting had improved and broadened into new directions. "Who Do You Live For?" starts with classical guitar, but then turns very nearly into a rock song and strong guitarwork and harmony vocals work well to create a standout track. "Kicking Against Nothing" is another example of the harder edge of L&T, with a strong riff and chorus. This CD is just as experimental as the first, but numbers such as these serve to emphasise that point. There are eighteen songs, and while they will not be to everyone's cup of tea on first listen, they are worth persevering with as they all grow on you.

'Waiting For The Parade' is the latest release, which this time is on the SI label. Phil Legende (of Lorien) is the only external musician, providing acoustic percussion on five of the nine tracks, with bass also now provided by Richard. Right from the off the hallmarks of the earlier albums are there, but for some reason they appear more accessible. The 'live' drumming helps as well, as it adds something to the songs. However, the most beautiful song on the album is "Deadline" where Richard provides the perfect backdrop for Lorna's haunting voice with classical acoustic guitar. "Divide" comes a very close second, as it gradually builds and builds.

Lives and Times are a group worth investigating for anyone who likes good singing and does not want crashing guitars or complicated prog. What L&T provide are well structured songs that show Lorna's voice off to best effect and take many shapes and forms, but it is on the latest CD that this comes off best. If you like good effective female vocals, then you are in for a treat.
#22, Mar 1994

LIVES AND TIMES
THE GREAT SAD HAPPY ENDING

Lives and Times are back with their fourth CD. Some of you may remember me reviewing the other three in #22, where I was impressed with the songs and singing, not to mention their musicianship. Lorna Cumberland again graces proceedings with her wonderful vocals; Richard Wileman plays everything except bass, which this time is provided by Andy Skittrall. Lorna's vocals are reminiscent of Kate Bush and Maryen Cairns, and the music is the perfect foil as moods and atmosphere are created with seeming ease. This atmospheric interpretation is the basis of the music of Lives and Times; there is no room here for crashing guitars or pounding drums, but instead well thought out material that is of extremely high quality. Every track is a winner, and the album will appeal to anyone who loves good music and is not afraid to sit and listen to it. I said that their last album 'Waiting For The Parade' was their best I was wrong. This one is. *#27, Feb 1995*

LIVES AND TIMES
THERE AND BACK AGAIN LANE

This is L&T's fifth album and is probably their most complete to date. I have long been a fan of Lorna Cumberland's beautiful clear vocals, and Richard Wileman and Andy Skittral have again pooled their resources to provide the perfect accompaniment. Although L&T will be seen by many as a prog band, they have little to do with the current underground as musically they follow their own path, not imitating others. The album opens with an air of menace on "Why Do I Watch?" which leads into a characteristically atmospheric number. The tempo is increased along with the volume and menace, but Lorna's voice still rises like a soaring angel above it all. Classical guitar plays an important part in this song, adding little touches here and there that manage to emphasise the electric riffing guitar. The music is often complex but never wanders into the realms of self-indulgence. "Darker" shows a totally different side to their music, with overlaid vocals and a musical background that switches themes and style, yet with the same melody underpinning it all. If you have had the good fortune to hear any of L&T's other albums then you will already be a fan, but if you have not and want to hear some interesting music combined with great vocals then you must get this. *#31 Oct 1995*

LIVES AND TIMES
HOARSE

After two CDs on their own No Image label, two more on SI and another on Cyclops, Lives And Times are back on their own again. Richard Wileman is still there of course; along with Andy Skittrall (for his third album with the band) and Phil Legende (who guested on the third CD 'Waiting For The Parade') but the most important aspect is that vocalist Lorna Cumberland is no longer in the band! Ileesha Bailey, who is a real find, has taken her place and this has heralded a slight shift in musical direction for the band. This is now a more forthright songs-based outfit producing numbers that wouldn't sound out of place either in the charts or any singer-songwriter connoisseur's playlist. There is far more emphasis on guitars and much less on keyboards. Some of the songs such as "Let The Clouds All Melt Away" are commercial with only a few (such as the preceding song, "Landmarks") sounding rocky and more challenging. The result is the most immediate album yet to come for the Swindon swingers and it is one that will appeal not only to the die-hard fan but also so many others who like good female vocals and most importantly of all, damn good songs. *#46, Dec 1997*

KERRY LIVGREN
WHEN THINGS GET ELECTRIC

Kerry Livgren should need no introduction whatsoever; as for many years, he was the chief songwriter, as well as providing guitar and keyboards, within the brilliant Kansas. 'When Things Get Electric' is his latest solo album, where he plays guitars, keyboards, some drums, and proceeds to engineer and produce it. Kerry has written some of the most popular songs of the last twenty years or so (for an example, how about "Carry On Wayward Son"?) so the fact that his album is jammed full of great tunes is of no surprise at all. Memories of Kansas are brought in, as Kerry has used their current violinist, David Ragsdale, to play against and licks and solos are traded to great effect. Kerry has used two vocalists, Darren Rogers and Jason Beddoe, and at times it could be Kansas that you are listening to, but this is a Kansas for 1996 with Kerry firmly at the helm. "Turn On The Lights" also brings back memories of Styx at their best. It is an album that I could rave about all day, as it is just wonderful, and we can all thank Escape Music for making it available in this country. If you have ever liked Kansas then this is an album you simply must get. *#35, June 1996*

LIZARD
W GALERII CZASU

Lizard is a band that I have come across before, receiving their demo from another Polish contact quite some time ago. This is the debut CD and is yet another good example of what CDs should be about. Even before putting it on the player one is impressed by the quality of artwork throughout the booklet, which also contains a good photo of the band and all the lyrics. The CD itself is also a high-quality picture disc, and rests in a clear tray, underneath which is another photo of the band. Ars Mundi put many Western labels to shame with their presentation. Putting that to one side, what about the music? This complex and complicated prog has a timeless quality about it. Less is more with this album, as at times it is only delicate piano and gentle vocals, but there are also times when the pace is quite frenetic. There is plenty of light and shade, and loads of feeling and expression, and is a joy to listen to with the music transcending the language barrier. *#40, Mar 1997*

LIZARD
PSYCHOPULS

This is one of those CDs that are almost impossible to describe, yet if the prog fan could get to hear this, they would undoubtedly enjoy it. It is not prog metal, but there are elements of it that are very heavy indeed. Sometimes this is almost straight ahead rock, then sometimes IQ style prog then there are others where it goes off into something that is very strange indeed. This is probably because one of the instruments in their musical arsenal is the violin, which is used sparingly but to great effect. It is not unusual for all the instruments to be following the same melody line, a la Uriah Heep, but it is the combination of these different elements that makes this such an intriguing album. Of course, the fact that all the lyrics are in Polish means that the concept itself is something of an enigma (the title track is subdivided into four 'Psychopuls' which in turn are further divided, giving a total of nine), but that just gives the music even more of an alien feel. Bringing together not only prog but hard rock and jazz means that this is an album that progheads should be seeking out.
#80, Jul 2004

HUW LLOYD LANGTON
ON THE MOVE…PLUS

Even though Huw left the band a long time ago, he will probably always be associated with Hawkwind. He originally joined when he was only seventeen, then left (playing with Widowmaker among others), before returning for another ten years. This was released in Sweden in 1997 where Huw recorded the album with the studio house band, Wayne Dexter. This is the first time that it has been released in the UK and contains three extra tracks. Not surprisingly, this is very much a guitar-based songs album that is full of class yet seems to be lost in a time warp. It is music that belongs in the Seventies, not the Nineties, yet there is just something in the way that he handles the guitar that makes me think of Gary Moore. While not as blues based there are some definite tinges there, and "No Participation" is a song that Gary would be proud to record. It will probably only appeal to ageing old gits like me and will never feature in Kerrang! But this is very solid indeed. *#64, Oct 2001*

LLYN Y MORYNION
LLYN Y MORYNION

Someone is having a laugh, someone in Germany. My good friend Artur Chachlowski recently sent me this CD from Poland, and as you can see the name of the band is Welsh! Strange, I thought. All the lyrics are in English so that was a good start, but what was most unusual was the music! Here is a German band with a Welsh name sounding 100% English! And not very modern English at that! Llyn Y Morynion (hereafter called Llyn)

are a progressive band mixing loads of influences, most of them English. Listen to the delicate ballad of "Poor Man's Child", with some wonderful classical guitar and haunting keyboards, and be stunned by the sheer beauty and majesty of the music. Conversely, be taken aback by the riffing power of "Drowned Day". Having played this a great deal, the band that I think that are most similar in the current scene is probably Legend, and even that link is tenuous. This album belongs more in the Seventies than the Nineties, but it also has a timeless quality, a feeling of being a classic. Unless they have an enormous stroke of luck, Llyn are going to release one of the best albums of the year (with some great packaging as well) and sell bugger all. If you like Legend, or Tull, or acoustic mixed with rock, oh hell, if you just like GREAT MUSIC then you owe it to yourself to get this.
#38, Nov 1996

LLYN Y MORYNION
ART Y SHOCK
I wrote to Llyn Y Morynion after I reviewed the brilliant debut album in the last issue, so imagine my delight when I received in the post this their new CD. If anything, this is better than the debut! Llyn mix so many different styles and mould them into something that is old, yet at the same time is refreshingly new. English folk seems to be taking a larger part this time, and there is even more use of acoustic guitar, but this provides the light to what can be heavy darkness. It is the darkness that seems to be most rooted in 1972, taking all the best bits of the prog, rock, folk boom of the late Sixties and coming up with a real gem. Matthias Jungkunz has a wonderfully clear voice, and this shows on "Grows An Oak", where it is the vocals that carry the song. Delicate use of a flute helps to build a classic ambience of almost Horslips proportions. I cannot stress too highly just what a wonderful band this is.
#39, Jan 1997

LLYN Y MORYNION
ANNIVERSARY
This is an album that you only ought to buy if you have got the first two, as it is very much a rarity's compilation for fans and is not up to the same standard as the two 'proper' albums which I have reviewed in the past. These, 'Llyn Y Morynion' and 'Art Y Shock' are just superb, and the debut is still a very regular visitor to my deck. They take many influences and manage to put these together into rock-based music, which anyone will half an ear will enjoy. The album is destined only for their home German market, as the entire booklet is printed in German, apart from the two reviews from a certain English fanzine that are printed in full! This is a great band that played a mini tour here last year, and I have just heard back from Lars who tells me that they will be back again later this year. They deserve more support.
#56, Jan 2000

'EMANUEL'

LOERMEL
EMANUEL

Loermel are a relatively new band who seem to be set on making big waves in the prog field. Graham Younger first wrote to me raving about them, mega reviews have appeared in all the prog fanzines so who are they and where are they from? In the beginning three music lovers, Vicky Horobin, Julie and Tansy decided that they wanted to be in a band and practised like mad. Gary White worked on his guitar, and Earth Terminus practiced in Blackpool. Julie decided that she was not going to stay in the band forever, so after Gary and Vicky met at Coventry Polytechnic he was asked to go along and practise with Vicky and Tansy. Tansy was the sister of Piers, drummer with Earth Terminus, and that band went to Coventry for a jam, which led to Nick Roach (bass) and Eric Porter (drums) joining Loermel. After a few gigs in Coventry the band moved to Manchester where they lived and wrote together. Eric moved to keyboards and new drummer Nigel Gregory was found, and with Vicky, Gary and Nick the line-up was complete.

Loermel went into the studio in November 1991 and recorded three songs, "Buried", "Hold Me Down" and "Emanuel". It was decided to release them all on a tape and they were approached by a young artist, Mark Kelly, who asked if he could design for them. The result is a cover far more complex than many other demos around and gives a good indication of what is to be found inside. This is complex and mature music, different to most of the other prog bands around today. This is prog through and through, not keyboard-oriented rock. Vicky's voice fits perfectly, sounding at times like Kate Bush, never strained but always with great power and emotion: the rest of the band providing the perfect foil for her voice. Loermel refrain from extended solos of long instrumental passages but prefer to make their statements as a group as opposed to a collection of individual musicians. The sound is definitely one of their own making, but possible musical references could be early IQ or All About Eve. There is a feeling of menace with all the songs, waiting to capture you as you fall deeper and deeper into the whirlpool of Loermel. I am fortunate to be able to review so many different and exciting bands, and if you also want to discover classic stunning prog then this is a band you cannot afford to miss. *#13, May 1992.*

BERTRAND LOREAU
PASSÉ COMPOSÉ

Bertrand has released four other albums on Musea and this is a collection of pieces from these plus some others, making up a tapestry of songs recorded over the last four years. Bertrand is a keyboard player, and on this release Olivier Briand (synths) and Lionel Palierne (guitar) join him. It is an instrumental album that is pleasant enough for the most part, meandering along gently touching on the banks of Tangerine Dream and Vangelis. The main issue is that when it is very good then it just about manages to become interesting,

but for much of the time is just boring. It is background, atmospheric music that could never possibly be regarded as anything else and if taken on that level it works quite well. If on the other hand you wanted to listen to something to be able to enjoy it for its' own sake, then this is not the album to have.
#69, Aug 2002

LORIEN
CHILDREN'S GAMES
Lorien started to come together in June 1989, when Mark McLeod (keyboards) and Darren Newitt (guitar) started writing material in the vein of Yes, Rush and Marillion. In February 1993, the duo advertised in Melody Maker for a vocalist and after auditions, the job was given to Sean Filkins, who had previously sung in space rock band Soma. Sean brought with him drummer Phil Legende, who had also been in Soma, while Phil in turn suggested Geoff Curtis (ex-Grim Reaper) on bass and Lorien were formed. When I put on the CD I was amazed by what I was hearing, as I pride myself on knowing most of what is going on within the UK prog scene yet here was a band of which I knew nothing, and they had produced a wonderful debut. The songs are commercial and very enjoyable; the vocals are spot on, and the musicianship top quality. If they have only been together a year, what are they going to be like in five years' time? "Hold The Key" commences proceedings and starts with unaccompanied harmony vocals, one sure way of grabbing my attention. So, turn up the volume a bit, settle back, then suddenly the song becomes a commercial rocker. The band are tight, and the use of harmony vocals within the song certainly adds to the overall effect.

Next up is "Lost For Words", a poignant song about a tender subject. Somehow, the music builds from just piano to more of a rocker, but at no time does it take away from the lyrics. "An old man looks out of the window, In his favourite chair he sits and stares, At the world outside as the people pass by, And looks back on his life, His fingers flick through the telephone book, He's trying to search for old friends, I'm sorry to say they've just passed away, Another ending to a lonely day". Songs such as the third part of "Losing It" show the band rocking at full pelt, with Phil Legende driving them on and on with some powerful drumming. However, the band are not content to sit in one style for too long and it gets slowed right down again. The title cut clocks in at over nineteen minutes (divided into nine separate sections) and shows off well the many strengths of the band with strong lyrics and differing musical styles. There is even room for an almost ballad in "Children's Games" itself, which contrasts greatly with the powerful "Children At Night" which just rocks along at great pace and intensity.

This is a wonderful debut, containing enough to interest anyone who likes good rock. We are going to be hearing a lot more from Lorien who are set to become major players with the UK prog scene.
#22, Mar 1994

LOST WORLD
TRAJECTORIES

There are times when I hear an album that really surprises me, not only because of what I am hearing but also my own reaction to it, and that is the case with 'Trajectories'. This is the first album from three Moscow Conservatory students (so it is a given that they can play, right?) Vassily Soloviev (flute, guitar), Alexander Akimov (keyboard, percussion, sound engineering) and Andrii Didorenko (guitar, bass guitar, electric violin). They have been joined by Alexei Rybakov on vocals for some of the songs, but it is the instrumentals that shine. They are mixing classical music with jazz and a lot of prog to create music that can be gentle and delicate or in your face: they know what they are doing musically and are not afraid to show it. Very much like King Crimson at times, while at others creating their own niche, this is extremely powerful stuff. The opening three numbers combine to form a suite that I would love to hear extended even more, as it sweeps and drives with some incredibly quick playing that gives way to some delicacy before backing out again. Apparently, this has also been scored and arranged for a symphony orchestra, which would be worth hearing. But that is one of the joys of this album – they are coming to it from a classical area and then bringing in other forms as they see fit – listen to "Birds" and one really is, but there are also some menacing chords and bass lines. The web site is available to view in English and their own guide to this album is well worth reading. This will not be to everyone's taste but is for those who feel musically adventurous.
#85, Nov 2005

LUCAS, WHITE & EDSEY
L.W.E.

Formed in 2000, this instrumental trio comprises keyboardist Frank Lucas (Neil Zaza, Michael Angelo), drummer Chuck White (Michael Angelo, Ion Vein) and bassist Steve Edsey (Dave Uhrich, Jeff Vincent). Frank has been studying with Jordan Rudess of Dream Theater and it was he who brought the band to the attention of ProgRock Records president Shawn Gordon who was impressed enough to sign them even though he himself is not usually excited by instrumental music. Given the line-up one is immediately going to compare these guys to ELP, and that is not too far away from the truth; they may be less bombastic, but while Chuck and Steve are great musicians this band is based around the keyboard playing of Frank Lucas. There is a high use of piano within the keyboard sound, and while the technical skills and ability cannot be doubted, this is all about the music as opposed to just showing off. This is very focussed and controlled, so that although each player has the chance to show off, it is all done within the context of the piece, which makes for a very enjoyable album indeed. Frank does let his hair down from time to time and one result is the tribute to his mentor "A Note To Jordan". They somehow always manage to keep the music very light-hearted and approachable with some Wakeman style flourishes at times, and the result is an instrumental album that is extremely enjoyable on first hearing. *#89, Sep 2006*

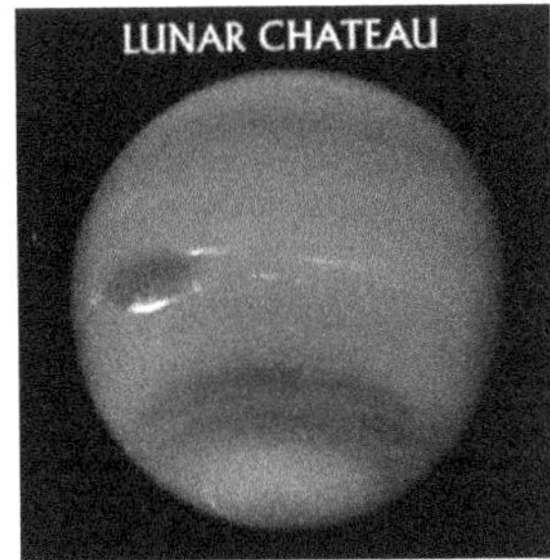

LUNAR CHATEAU
LUNAR CHATEAU

Lunar Chateau are an American outfit comprising Novak Sekulovich (keyboards, vocals), Paul Sekulovich (lead vocals, bass) and Milo Sekulovich (drums). Obvious comparisons with this set-up will be made with ELP, and the opening instrumental "The Thrust' does absolutely nothing to dispel this. However, Lunar Chateau combine their obvious technical abilities with a more direct and pop-oriented outlook. Only one track on the album is of any length (the closing "Aurora Borealis" at eight minutes) and the melodic vocals and pop sensibilities mean that the band are less ELP and more Tears For Fears and Alan Parsons Project. "The Eyes Of A Child" is probably the best example of their pop/prog outlook, with delicate vocals and keyboards combining to provide a simply beautiful haunting song. At times, I do wish that they would rock out a bit more, but with no guitar in evidence they are content to provide good music with no thoughts to what other people feel that they should be doing. Very much for those into the softer side of rock.*#26, Dec 1994*

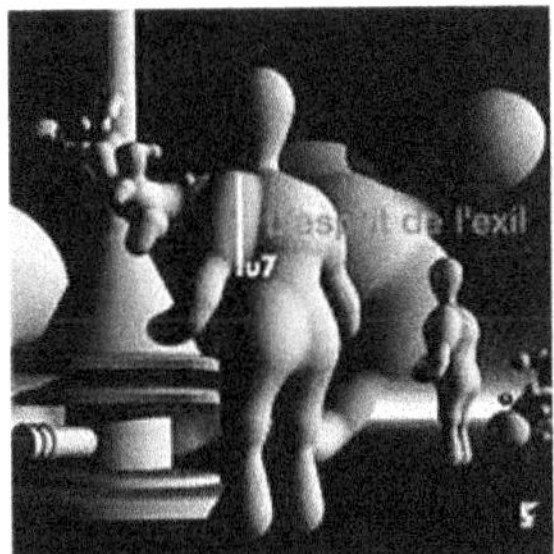

LU7
L'ESPRIT DE L'EXIL

Lu7 are a Japanese duo, and this is their second album. They may be a duo, but they bring in many guests to make what is a very listenable and enjoyable jazz-fusion album of all instrumentals, bar one song, which contains vocals. The one thing that may surprise listeners, and it certainly amazed me, is the choice of bagpipes on the first two songs! I may not listen to as much fusion as some, but I can be quite honest and say that I have never heard this instrument used within this genre before. In addition, I have no idea why a Japanese duo, using all Japanese musicians (except for the bagpipe player, who is of course Scottish), recording an album in Japan have released it with a French title. Putting this to one side, they have put a strong group of people together and the keyboards work well, providing extra support to the very lyrical style of guitarist Tsutomu Kurihara. The result is something that is worth hearing if you can lay your hands on it. *#86, Feb 2006*

LU7
EFFLORESCENCE

I previously reviewed Lu7's second album, but Musea have now also made this, the debut, available again. The biggest moan I have with this album, and to me it spoils it, is the use of a drum machine. Here it sounds even more dated and irrelevant than normal, and I kept asking myself what a real drummer could have done with this, as the rest is very good indeed. Lu7 are a duo comprising Tsutomu Kurihara on guitar and Luna Umegaki on keyboards, along with two guest bassists. This is gentle jazz rock which at times slips into lounge core, but for the most part this is gentle music that is designed to take the listener into a world of their own making. It is great to drift along to, and both musicians have good sounds – it feels quite uplifting. It may not be innovative, but it is certainly pleasant enough and I feel that I enjoyed this more than the follow-up. *#89, Sep 2006*

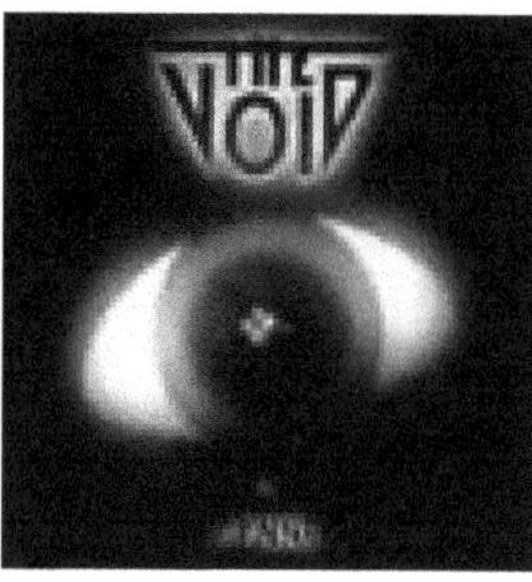

LYNNE

THE VOID

Bjørn Lynne is a Norwegian, currently residing in the UK, who I met a few years ago when Ken Senior of Evolution introduced us to each other. I already knew of him at that time, as he is one of the people behind the Norwegian fanzine Prognetik, but what I was not aware of was that he is also a recording artist in his own right, with 'The Void' being his newest release. I have since been informed that his other albums are electronic music, and he only has a few left, while this album sees a move into prog territory. The album is instrumental (with Bjørn providing keyboards, guitar and bass), and tells the story of a man in the 23rd Century going through space at many times the speed of light, totally out of control. Unlike many instrumental albums, it is never boring, as while there are dreamy passages there are also rocky elements that combine to make it always interesting and enjoyable. Bjørn recommends playing this at night with all the lights off, and I totally agree with him. This an instrumental album that should not be taken as background noise but listened to properly so that it can be enjoyed to the full.
#40, Mar 1997

BJØRN LYNNE

WIZARD OF THE WINDS

This is quite a different release for Cyclops, although they have released an album by Bjørn before. Firstly, it is being released under two titles, either 'Wizard of the Winds' or 'When The Gods Slept' and the reason for this is that this is a concept album based on the book written by Allan Cole. Now why that may not be unusual, what makes it so is that Allan Cole has written a short story for each of the songs on the album, which are effectively read out by Chris Blyth at the beginning of each. This makes for quite a different album, as the music (again this is instrumental) attempts to capture the power and vividness of the words. Musically it is at times quite orchestral, folky at others, while dark and menacing when the mood suits. It is an album that musically captures much of Rick Wakeman although the fact that Bjørn is as much a master of the guitar as the keyboard means that passages such as in "The Battle of Two Stones" is much rockier than Rick ever attempted. This is album that needs to be sat and listened to but rewards the patience. If you are a fan of Allan Cole or enjoy the genre of fantasy novels then the combination of the words with Bjørn's music makes this a compelling album. This is yet another winner following on from his superb 'The Void'
#49, May 1998

BJØRN LYNNE
WOLVES OF THE GODS

Following on from last year's 'Wizard of the Winds', which was based on a book by Allan Cole and featured spoken narrative between songs, Bjørn has this time again worked with Allan, but this time the narrative is only printed in the booklet and not spoken. Although the album is again based on a book by Allan, the author himself has this time written the accompanying narrative. This gives the album the opportunity to work on two levels, as it can be taken as a literal rendition or just music for its' own sake. I personally thought that 'Wizard' worked extremely well, but I can imagine that for a non-fantasy reader then the words may have been a bit much for repeated listening. In this instance, it is just a matter of closing the booklet and letting the music ride over you. Bjørn seems to have moved much more into the use of guitar in recent years, and he has enlisted the assistance of Rory McLeish to help with solo work on four numbers. Bjørn supplies everything else and even the wretched drum programming is almost listenable. This is a very enjoyable album, with majestic highs and lows, and in many ways, could be thought of as being perfect film music and as that is the idea behind it then it must be considered a success. It is an album that will appeal to all lovers of instrumental or neo prog as it is quite dynamic and even rocky in places. If you have not heard anything by Bjørn before them this is a good place to start. *#53, May 1999*

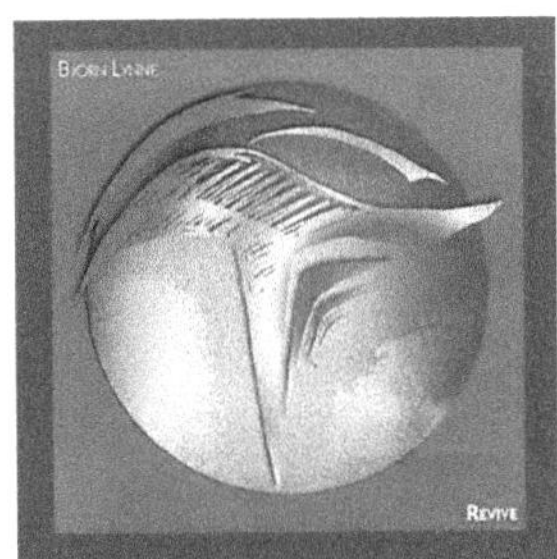

BJØRN LYNNE
REVIVE

'Revive' sees Bjørn move away from his recent epic albums to an album that appears much more influenced by bands such as Kraftwerk and Tangerine Dream. Some of the songs, such as "Himalayan Summit (Hightop)", sound as if they could have been edited down and released as a single, albeit nearly twenty years ago. It is quite a shift away from his more recent albums, and one that may well ostracise some of his fans as he has moved away from the progressive feel into an area that is much more in the vein of Krautrock. There are places, such as in "Moongazer", when the guitar makes an appearance but for the most part this is very highly keyboard dominated. I would much rather listen to 'Wolves Of The Gods' than this, sorry. *#59, July 2000*

BJØRN LYNNE
COLONY

Bjørn has certainly been prolific since he moved to the UK from his native Norway in 1995. This is his twelfth album, which puts the work rate of some bands that I could mention very much to shame. He is a multi-instrumentalist and he has very differing styles, per the theme that he has chosen for the album. This music is quite different to that which can be found on 'Wizard Of The Winds' and 'Wolves Of The Gods' for example and is totally instrumental. Bjørn has used two guests (one being Ken Senior), but they have each only played a small part on one song – the rest is all by Bjørn himself. This is great music to be either playing in the background, or when concentrating on something else. It is very space-like, and there are many repeated themes on the keyboards but Bjørn is also a strong guitarist and he moves the styles around while never rocking out too much. This is music that the listener can get lost in, creating its own world and I am sure that fans of electronic or progressive are going to love this. There are even sections of songs such as on "Endless Possibilities" that I can envisage being lifted to be used on dance numbers. Bjørn is currently recording music for the animated sci-fi series 'Animation', which is due to hit prime time national television next year. *#70, Oct 2002*

MADRIGAL
WAITING...

Madrigal were originally formed in 1977 by David Cebert (keyboards) and Kevin Dodson (vocals, drums), since when they have undergone numerous personnel changes. In 1982, there was a change in direction and a change in name, as they became a covers band called UVU to earn some money. This lasted until 1985 when the band broke up, which featured the end of the writing partnership of Cebert and Dodson. Kevin then decided to start work on an album with Michael Dornbirer on guitar and backing vocals, which became 'Waiting...'. At the time of the release Madrigal was still only the duo plus some guest musicians, including keyboard player Don Canon and original keyboard player Cebert. The songs were all original, except for "Five Gifts For Third Child" which came from a ballet written by Don Canon and performed by the Spokane Ballet in 1987. It is great to have an American prog album that sounds as if it should be British: and early Seventies British at that! The source is early Gabriel Genesis, and the result is interesting and entertaining. "Sister Happy" commences proceedings in a lazy laid-back Sixties mood that just makes you smile and get into the groove as it collects together a myriad of styles (including quite noticeably The Kinks) and produces something of joy. Songs such as "Next Wave" are quite different in style but have the link that they all make you want to move with the flow of the music. One thing I discovered is that whichever one I am listening to is most definitely my favourite, a very strange phenomenon. Overall, 'Waiting...' is a refreshing and enjoyable album. *#22, Mar 1994*

MAESTOSO
ONE DROP IN A DRY WORLD

This is Woolly Wolstenholme's first full-blown studio album for some twenty years, and surely an event that will have all self-respecting Barclay James Harvest fans reaching for their credit cards. Woolly was one of the founding members of that band, leaving in 1979 and not returning to the fold until 1998 when he was convinced to come out of retirement to work with John Lees in one of the two versions of the band (the other featuring Les Holroyd and Mel Pritchard). Working with John again obviously got his interest going and he formed a band, taking the name from the solo album that he was working on in 1980. Having played this album a great deal there is no doubt that the fact that he stayed out of the business for twenty years means that although farming had a good deal, music lovers had very much a raw deal. There are some wonderful songs here, "It's U" and the menacing Floydian "Blood & Bones" being strong examples. Woolly's vocals are clear and pure, as they were when he sang "Mockingbird" and as well as providing keyboards on the album, he also plays guitars. One of the joys of this album is the very different styles that are within it; although it should be of no surprise that one of these are BJH given that he was a key member for so long. "Souk" is a bringing together of rock and eastern styles, that has plenty of guitar and more menace and is strangely compelling, while "The Starving People Of The World All Thank You For Your Time" is a repetitive Manics number that is almost hypnotic. The final song of the album is "Carpet" which appears to me to be having quite a pop at someone, (I imagine Les Holroyd but I could well be wrong) where he sings "It was a magic carpet ride, But all your deeds were fratricide, You're like a train stuck on the track, You can't go forward, Will not go back, Was it the money, Was it the fame, That made you play a different game?". For any fan of BJH this is an album that should be purchased not just because it is by Woolly but because it is so damned good! *#80, Jul 2004*

MAGELLAN
HOUR OF RESTORATION

Now, I am not quite sure how this has happened, but I ended up with a vinyl Magellan album to review. What is even more unusual is that this is a Korean version of an American album that I got from an English PR company (who also could not explain it to me). This is a shame as someone has gone to a great deal of trouble to write a history of the band that I do not have a hope in hell of understanding! This album is from 1991, and I can remember it making a huge impact when it came out, which does not surprise me at all as it is quite brilliant. Magellan have a Yes fixation, in relation to the tight harmony vocals, but they are still very much their own band. Any Yes lover who likes the rockier aspect of that band's music, Seventies styles as opposed to Eighties, ought to discover this superb piece of work. From the fifteen-minute opener "Magna Carta" to the one-minute "Turning Circle" this is a joy. The only thing wrong with this album is that it came out six years ago and I have only just heard it! *#40, Mar 1997*

MAGELLAN
TEST OF WILLS

Magellan are now a trio, comprising Trent Gardner (vocals, keyboards, trombone), Wayne Gardner (guitar, bass, backing vocals) and Brad Kaiser (drums). The production is far better than on the vinyl debut I reviewed a few issues ago, and the music is tighter and far heavier. While undoubtedly progressive, Magellan are at the heavier end of the spectrum without going into the area occupied by Threshold and Queensrÿche. The very strong Yes-style vocal harmonies are very much in evidence but while that band appear to be on yet another decline (Rick Wakeman has left again), Magellan is very much on the up. Instead of being a parody, they are producing high quality prog that should be in everybody's collection. Turn it up and let the speakers approach meltdown as the guys attempt to dominate each other by sheer force of will and powering playing, yet at the same listen to the subtleties and melodies. They can rock like bastards when they want to, but at the same time there is the impression of the horse that is Magellan being under tight control, yet at full gallop instead of bolting to who knows where. We have been blessed with superb prog albums coming out of the States over the last two years, and Magellan have added to the ever-growing but still extremely select list. *#42, July 1997*

MAGELLAN
IMPOSSIBLE FIGURES

Now on their fifth album, it is often hard when listening to Magellan to realise that apart from a guest drummer, this is a two -man band. Trent Gardner provides the vocals and keyboards while his brother Wayne provides all the guitars. The music they create will be extremely familiar to all fans of Kansas, and it is of no surprise that Trent has worked with Steve Walsh in the past. The album starts with a small instrumental interlude, quaintly titled "Gorilla With A Pitchfork"; the keyboards build, and the music takes on a more dramatic, driving edge. This fades out to be replaced with "Killer Of Edge" – treated vocals give way to the guitar and gradually the song builds more and more, becoming a progressive rocker. This is the longest song on the album, at just over ten minutes and is succeeded by a piano/organ piece, "Bach 16" which in some ways sounds out of place yet also very much at home. Dramatic and frantic drumming heralds the start of "Late For Church", which is again followed by another instrumental. This move from instrumental to song then back again provides a deal of emphasis, and the highly vocal "Hymn For A Heathen" is a joy with great harmonies. Overall there are nine songs, and at no time can the listener even contemplate moving away or playing something else instead. This is a prog album that has its' roots very much in a similar vein to Kansas while trying to do something new, and any fans of one will enjoy very much the music of the other. Yet another extremely solid album from the Gardner brothers. *#78, Apr 2004*

MAGELLAN
SYMPHONY FOR A MISANTHROPE

Trent and Wayne Gardner are back with their sixth album in fifteen years, not a large output, but there are only two of them to provide vocals, guitar, bass, keyboards and trombone, although a quick look at the guests does show some well-known names such as Steve Walsh and Robert Berry among others. Magellan sound like a band as opposed to a project, have always produced consistently high-quality progressive rock music, and this album is no exception. Yes, they can play very prettily when they want

to, with some delicate pianowork, but it is when they are blasting through with the guitars and keyboards that the rock element of their music comes to prominence. This album contains many classical nuances as well as rock, but it is also quite dark in many ways. Trent explains this by saying "I'm always in a condition of evaluation, and I'm trying not to hide my head in the sand but on an unconscious level there certainly were some influence coming from the outside which is also responsible for the dark mood," and the seven songs all deal with the theme of the "miserable performance end result of humanity in almost all areas". It may be dark, and complex, but there is more than enough light against the shade and Trent and Wayne have produced an album that many will say is their finest and most complete to date.
#84, July 2005

MAGENTA
SEVEN
This is the second album from Magenta (the 'Seven' refers to the seven deadly sins) and it is a real shame that I missed the first as this is a delight. Rob Reed provides a great deal of the instruments, although the band does perform on this album (apparently, Rob provided all the instruments on the debut). Those with long memories may remember me reviewing his albums released under the name of Cyan many, many years ago. Rob is only providing backing vocals on this release, letting Christina take centre stage, and she is some singer following on in the steps of Annie Haslam although in a slightly lower (and warmer) register. This is not an album that is breaking any dynamic new ground musically, but they have taken the best bits of many bands (Yes, Genesis, Pink Floyd, Renaissance etc.) and created a style that is their own. One soon stops trying to play 'spot the band' and instead listen to a prog album that is full of melody and wonderful songs. The music is complex, but at the same time is straightforward yet full of twists and hooks that keep the listener intrigued as to what is going to happen next. Little tricks moving from full band to just voice and piano and then back again work well and the electric guitars provide a strong counterpoint to the keyboards. Lots of different things going on, this album is superb and one that I have been playing repeatedly.
#80, Jul 2004

MAGENTA
ANOTHER TIME… ANOTHER PLACE
Having just been voted top live band of the year (as well as having the top female vocalist) by the CRS, now is probably the best time they could think of for releasing an album capturing them in the concert environment. I missed seeing them recently (fancy having a support band on at 7.00!) and if this double CD is anything to go by, I missed a treat. One thing that makes this band stand out is that there is such strong musicianship throughout. At the heart of the band is Rob Reed, who I first came across years ago when he was recording as Cyan (nostalgia time – I used the artwork of one of his albums as

part of the cover for #18, back in May 1993!) who is an outstanding keyboard player, but Magenta are very much a band, with a rhythm section of Allan Mason-Jones and Matthew Cohen (who plays a six string bass) who control the bottom end and two guitarists in Martin Rosser and Chris Fry who are seemingly as happy to crank out some riffs as they are to play widdly-widdly. Then on top of it all are the vocals of Christina, who has a wonderful clear voice and is more than capable of staying on top of whatever the band throw at her – some task. This band is a melting pot, so that the only term that could be used to describe them would be 'progressive', but there is some hard rock, flamenco, pop, virtually all styles of music thrown in, but it all makes sense. The band can go from onslaught to gentle vocals and piano and off on yet another tangent just as quickly. No-one could ever get bored listening to this music, there is just so much going on either with whichever instrument is currently taking the lead role or the rest that are bubbling away under the surface. Magenta have been making quite a name for themselves within the progressive scene in the UK and rightly so, this is a very enjoyable release. They are planning a live DVD later this year and I for one am looking forward to it.
#82, Jan 2005

MAGENTA
HOME

If you act quickly, you will be able to buy both 'Home' and 'New York Suite' as a slip sleeved set. Given that the latter directly complements the former and will not be available in its' own right until September you are probably best going straight off to the website now. Given that the set is £15 and 'Home' on its own is £10 you may as well get the set. But, why should you? Magenta have been building a firm reputation over recent years as one of the finest symphonic prog rock bands in the UK and here they have taken a step change in their approach. In Christina, they have one of the finest singers around and while that has always been an important facet of their music, here they have thrust her firmly into centre stage. On this album, the band has become the vehicle to transport her voice with it much more to the fore. Musically the band are taking elements of Pink Floyd and Genesis (the lighter parts), and then mixing it up with material that could almost be said to be singer-songwriter. It is the mixing of all the elements that make this music 'progressive', but someone not knowing the label that we stick on bands probably wouldn't use that term. The music feels far more arranged and scored than before, multi-layered and orchestrated. This is a very mature album, one where the biggest problem will be getting it in front of the large audience, which music of this quality deserves. The more I have played this, the more I have been impressed with what they have produced. Complex fills, Hackett-like guitars and strong piano and keyboards have combined to produce one of the strongest albums of the year, whatever the genre. This album crosses musical boundaries, and totally blows away the myth that progressive rock is not accessible and should only be listened to by a small minority. If you enjoy good music, then you need to buy this. Period.
#88, Jun 2006

MAGIC MOMENTS AT TWILIGHT TIME
CREAVOLUTION

At long last, here is the latest album by MMATT. There is not enough time or space to be able to describe what Mick has gone through to get this out on CD, but let's just say that it has been problematic, so let's get down to the music. MMATT is a three-piece, with Mick Magic providing the keyboards, guitars and some vocals, Leonie Jackson (vocals) and Sammi Taylor (some backing vocals). On top of that Mick has utilised the talents of Damien Page (lead guitar on three songs), and three other lead vocalists (Inga Leru, Brian John Doran and Gary St. John). MMATT have been likened in the past to Hawkwind, but the music is not always as intense or heavy as that, although it does have its moments. Not out and out space rock then, but music that has been heavily influenced. Trippy keyboards, along with special effects, make this a wonderful album to enjoy and the use of different singers with different styles adds to the overall effect of a very well thought out album. Mick has managed to create something that will be enjoyed by a whole cross section, whether they are space rockers, proggers, EM freaks, or just those into plain good songs and performances. Write away and order it today! As well as running MMATT Mick also runs Music & Elsewhere, an extremely important tape label operating in the underground. So far, they have released about 350 albums by a multitude of bands. To keep everyone up to date on what is happening they also run a newsletter which is packed full of information about what good music is about, and how to make more contacts. On top of that, it is a non-profit making organisation!

#36, Aug 1996

MAGIC PIE
MOTIONS OF DESIRE

Sometimes an album is sent to me and I fall head over heels with it on first hearing, and find the more I listen to it the more I enjoy it. Of course, the problem then is getting it off the player so that I can get on with listening some of the other stuff that I need to review: this album is one of those. It does not have the most inspiring artwork in the world yet put on this album and any prog fan will immediately fall in love with it. It is quite difficult to describe as there are many classic 70's influences, as well as Flower Kings, Spock's Beard and The Beatles but the result is something that should surely just be described as 'classic'. There are great harmonies when needed, acoustic guitar when required, slabs of Hammond Organs and Moogs at times, so that when the former is in play it is almost as if Heep have gone back in time. But by bringing in modern influences this is not an album that can be considered as retro, rather that they have taken the best of different eras of progressive music and have put it together into something that is extremely accessible and easy to listen to yet also has a great deal going on within it. This album just reinforces my opinion that there is so much great music out there that is demanding to be heard which is just not getting the publicity it deserves. There is a section during "Motions Of Desire" where the acoustic guitars are riffing away and there is some great bass being slapped around. They can bring it down, in quite a jazz fashion, yet they can

be there right in the face instead. They play gently and slowly, or quickly and passionately but even though musically they are jumping all over the place it all seems to make perfect sense. This is a great prog album, so you all need to buy it to so that these guys will be able to make another, and I can hear that as well!!
#85, Nov 2005

MAGNESIS
L'IMMORTEL OPÉRA

This is the sixth album by French progressive act Magnesis, a concept album that includes fantasy, a pact with the devil and even Mozart. All the lyrics are in French, but while there are some who may appreciate this extremely laid back and theatrical style, it does little or nothing for me. This album appears to meander along on its own way, but not taking the listener with it. Possibly if I could understand the words, then I would feel differently about it but somehow, I do not think so. There are two keyboard players in the band, but there is very little drama, and even less to engage the listener and make it exciting. There is a very theatrical feel about the whole thing, but it does tend wash over and one bland and uninspired musical setting soon gives away to another. There will be some I am sure who will herald this as a return to the great progressive rock of the Seventies, but if this is great music, then this is why punk came along.
#86, Feb 2006

MAGNITUDE 9
CHAOS TO CONTROL

According to the blurb, Magnitude 9 are a "Progressive Power Metal Band" – always nice to be able to pin a category on a band I suppose. In some ways, they are heavier than Threshold, and they certainly seem to have more intensity, but at the same time it gets a bit overpowering and they appear to be just a little too clever for their own good. There is a real necessity to learn that less can be more, and Magnitude 9 appear to have a long way to go before they reach that point. For example, there is no doubting that they are very fine musicians, but is there any need for guitarist Rob Johnson to put in blistering speed runs all over the place? Yes, it is all very clever; but it does not do anything for the music and becomes a distraction. What it makes me think of is Yngwie Malmsteen, and I am sure that if you are a fan of his then you will find much in here to enjoy, but instead if you want music that has passion and not just speed that you are better off giving this a miss.

That is not to say that this is a bad album, but just one that does not have enough imagination or melodies to make me want to play it again. Maybe the next one will be better…
#51, Jan 1999

MAGNITUDE NINE
DECODING THE SOUL

Progressive melodic metal band Magnitude Nine are back with their third album, and guitarist Rob Johnson shows no sign of slowing down his band. In fact, they have got heavier, although ex-Psycho Drama frontman Corey Brown is more than up to the task. This album has been co-produced by Michael Vescera who has sung in various bands, including Yngwie Malmsteen's Rising Force. I am sure that this last connection has helped as there are times when Rob's solo work is just as fluid and rapid but the difference between this and Rising Force is that here the guitars make sense within the song and do not overpower what is going on. The result is an album that needs to be played at top volume to get the most of it, with melodic rock songs and great harmony vocals vying for place with some shredding guitar. He is fast, but while that is often his main form of attack, within solos he can play with restraint when required. In "Walk Through The Fire" they even have a song that could find itself played on rock radio, a heavier darker style of rock that is also extremely melodic, as if Europe had cranked the guitars up even more. Solid, enjoyable with some great guitar work, this gives prog metal a good name. *#78, Apr 2004*

NICK MAGNUS
STRAIGHT ON TILL MORNING

Nick Magnus has played with many of the top names, including Steve Hackett, Chris Rea and Brian May. He has also had success with the Project D 'Synthesiser' albums as well as writing film and television soundtracks, writing on current keyboard technology, and demonstrating for a major musical company: 'Straight On Till Morning' is his first solo album, and damn fine it is too. I always find it difficult to describe solo keyboard albums as many of them seem to fall into the dreaded category 'New Age', but I am glad to say that this one does not. Of course, there are dreamscapes, but with a heavy use of piano there is far more emotion portrayed. Nick manages to build layers of sound into proper songs without words, a rare thing indeed. At times, it is relaxing, yet at others almost overpowering and at the end, there is a real sense of wanting to play it again. Songs like "Campus Fugit" just belt along with a real sense of purpose. This keyboard album is better than many, and one that I will often be returning to. *#23, May 2004*

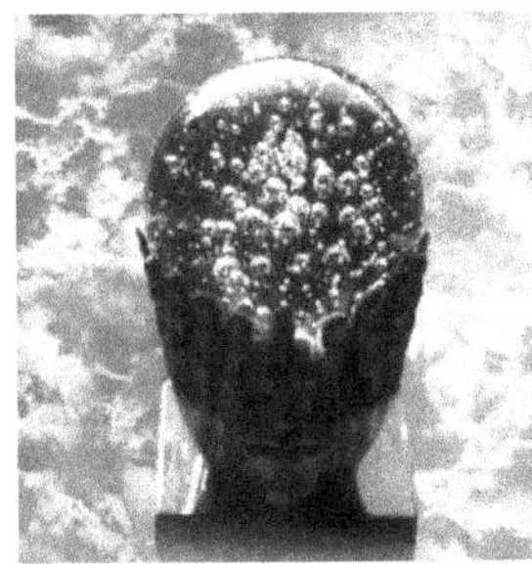

MAGUS
ECHOES FROM THE DAWN OF THE MILLENIUM 1987 - 1999

Virtually none of the songs on this CD have been available before, as they are either remixes, demoes or just previously unreleased in any format. Magus is for the most part Andrew Robinson, although others do make valuable contributions. He appears now to again have a band around him, so the future looks bright. I have always enjoyed his albums, and this

collection gives the opportunity to look over the length of his recording career. While most of it is instrumental, it manages to maintain interest throughout, sometimes using samples or tactile ideas. The guitars and keyboards work in perfect harmony, and it is possible to just close the eyes and drift into this surreal world and become part of it.
#61, Feb 2001

MARTIN MAHEUX
CIRCLE SIBYLLE
Martin Maheux is drummer with Spaced Out and this is his second solo album, following on from 2002's 'Physics Of Light'. Here he has been joined by a string quartet, plus brass and a piano with himself on drums. The result is music that is very jazz focussed, with the strings adding an extra element to proceedings. Totally instrumental, it is perhaps surprising that Martin sees himself here more as an arranger and composer than performer and often takes a back seat, or does not play at all, allowing more space into the overall sound. It is when the guys move away from standard jazz and into other areas using the strings as the main force as opposed to the piano, that this album gets interesting as here the music is fusing together jazz and classical forms in a way that is both interesting and inspired, creating a beauty all its own. This is one for jazz lovers, and while purists may not be too fond of this, those who enjoy their music to have variety and still be accessible while being challenging will find much here to enjoy.
#87, Apr 2006

MALOMBRA
OUR LADY OF THE BONES
This is my first contact with Italian label Black Widow and know nothing at all about Malombra except for the fact that they are Italian, and this is their second album. What is clear is that they do not sound like anyone else and the music is not very accessible and seems to be coming from very many musical directions. One track features violin, another harpsichord, while Goth style organ chords also make appearances. It makes me think of a prog band involved with Hammer House of Horror! Little things such as commercial considerations do not seem to matter (like re-recording places where vocalist Mercy goes off key during a long note) so the music is, um, challenging.

Well, that is all the bad things out of the way. This is an interesting album precisely because of what I have already said. On top of that, Matteo Ricci is a phenomenal guitarist. True, his solos do tend to go on a bit, and wander all over the place, but it is all in good fun. If you are fed up with standard prog, then give Malombra a try.
#34, Apr 1996

MALOMBRA
THE DISSOLUTION AGE

I love this album, it is grating and crashing, progressive rock that is truly striving to be that. It brings together Poisoned Electrick Head with Fields Of The Nephilim and Ultravox in an unholy union that works brilliantly well. It is intense and needs to be played loudly to be fully appreciated, and as it swirls in and out of the mind, it takes with it more than a few brain cells. It is not all hard and fast, as there is a very reflective and emotional number in "The Duncan Browne Song" which is a fetching tribute to the musician and composer probably best known for his part in Metro, who died of cancer in 1993. This is not prog that sits in the neatly compartmentalised section of wannabes, but music that is trying to create something new and dark. It is driven along by pounding drums and bass, while the guitars and keyboards do their best to stop the powerful vocals, but to no avail. This is an album that many progheads will shy away from for being too intense, but that is their loss as this is one I will be playing a great deal. *#69, Aug 2002*

MANGALA VALLIS
LYCANTHROPE

'Lycanthrope' is the new album from Mangala Vallis and it is sure to excite quite a few progheads before they even listen to it, as not only does it feature as guest on a few tracks David Jackson from VDGG, but also has on lead vocals Bernardo Lanzetti who is probably best known in this country for being lead singer with PFM, the wonderful Italian prog band that were signed to Manticore in the Seventies. It is the Seventies that this band are looking back to with this concept album, as there is nothing neo-prog about this – it is the real deal. With all the lyrics in English this is wonderfully fresh, inviting, yet extremely regressive all at the same time. Great tunes, melodies, complex interplay, dated keyboards, wonderful vocals, who could possibly wish for more? Bernardo is quite like Roger Chapman in his vocal style, so some may not find this quite to their taste, but many will, and they must seek this out. It is a majestic album that sounds nothing like Genesis at their peak but has the same power and presence. Powerful and passionate this is a prog album that all progheads who enjoy the music from thirty years ago definitely need to seek out straight away. *#86, Feb 2006*

MANITOU
LOOKING FOR THE LOST

Manitou were formed in 1986 when Harry Skinner (guitar, vocals), Peter Hibbit (drums) and Nick Simon (bass) added Dave Thomas on keyboards. It is interesting to note that both Peter and Nick were involved in the early days of Galahad. They did not manage to get a record deal, but did get sponsorship from National Panasonic and Yamaha, and this, along with extensive radio play, led to a successful tour of Japan. Following this they struck a deal with a London-based record company to start work on the first album, but this was aborted after the producer disappeared with the master tapes. Nick was very disillusioned with the whole thing so left the band, who decided to keep going and recruited Sean Carter as replacement. Manitou went into 'Room With A View' (used by Galahad among others) and came out with their first CD, 'Looking For The Lost', which has been released on their own label, Mojo Records.

This is something to be proud of, and if I was pushed to describe it then I would call it "classic" English rock. It is not HR or HM, but at the same time it is not really prog. Sure, the keyboards are an important part of it but then so are the guitars. What comes across is a tremendous sense of maturity: the songs have been well thought out, are all accessible at first listen, and are all totally enjoyable. Harry has a great voice, deep and melodic, which is used to great effect. There is real power in his voice, and he is no mean guitarist either (by the way this is the only CD I have that features the singer playing didgeridoo, check out the beginning of "Medicine Man"). The band gel together and are very tight indeed. From the first song "My Time" to the last, "Satellite Girl", here is an album that exceed expectation and delivers. It will appeal to the HR fan who is looking for melody, and the prog fan who is looking for some real guitarwork. Tracks like "When The Wind Blows" have a real energy and dynamism, and that is followed by "Swimming Upstream" which I found reminiscent of Chris Rea. I have found it difficult to pick out a favourite as I like all of them, but I think it would probably be "Last Night Jericho" which has a powerful chorus. There again the instrumental "Alaska" is damn good as well. An album worth discovering, it is also available on cassette.
#19, Aug 1993

GEOFF MANN
SECOND CHANTS

This album was the follow-up to Geoff's 'Chants Would Be A Fine Thing' and was recorded during what was a very busy period as he was still working with Eh! Geoff Mann Band, and had also released an instrumental album with Marc Catley ('The Off The End of the Pier Show'). In fact, this album was recorded and mixed in less than a week but somehow, he managed to provide fifteen songs of outstanding quality, with a total running time of more than sixty-one minutes. There is a comprehensive lyric and art booklet with the album, the cover recalling Twelfth Night's 'Fact and Fiction', with its stark drawing of a figure. The album features several guests, but only Peter Nicholls of IQ gets the chance to shine. The album itself is full of differing musical ideas, with a very heavy use of sound effects. It is musically very difficult to describe, as it is quite unlike any other album I have heard. As always with Geoff, his lyrics stand up to very close examination, and this time they seem to be concerned with darker aspects "Stropping the razor of greed, Against sensitive plant skin, Shaving off our atmosphere, Shaving off fauna and flora, Sharp in judgement over every facet of our behaviour except stupidity". Special mention must be made of the comic song "Yes", which is used to brighten up the album. It features rent-a-crowd and was obviously recorded "live". The concept is that of a TV studio, with various guests wandering in and out. As well as taking the piss, Geoff and

Peter sing a duet, virtually unaccompanied. It does not matter that it is not always quite right, what does matter is the genuineness and honesty. I love it. This is the sort of album which is loved or hated, there is no middle ground. Geoff's voice may not be to everyone's taste, but this is an album worth investigating.
#17, Mar 1993

GEOFF MANN
IN ONE ERA
In 1990 Geoff had the idea of releasing 'I May Sing Grace' and 'Psalm Enchanted Evening', his second and third solo albums after leaving Twelfth Night (originally only on vinyl), as one CD. He felt that 'In One Era' would be the right title, explaining it as follows "In One Era, a pun of course. I do not know if you use the phrase 'In one ear and out of the other', it refers to a statement that no-one listens to!". This did not happen in Geoff's lifetime, but Malcolm Parker has worked with Andy Labrow to produce a CD as close to Geoff's original concept as possible. Tapes have been 'cleaned up', but not remixed at Jane Mann's request. Lyrics, together with photos from the period, complete the package. Geoff had a unique vocal style and managed to pull together a lot of different styles in a way totally his own. Certainly, he is the most off the wall Christian artist to promote his faith through music. He was still developing his solo styles at this time, and elements can be seen that came through in his later works. Far more immediate than albums such as 'Second Chants', there is no doubting the Mann's talent. Geoff recorded albums incredibly quickly, with the two on here taking less than two weeks in total! There was never a sense of rush, but rather that he knew his own mind very much and what he wanted to achieve. For any lover or Geoff Mann or Twelfth Night, this CD is an essential purchase as it is making available at long last music long deleted. However, if you are a Christian or just a lover of music that can be challenging at times, yet always brilliant, then this is one for you. Geoff's life was cut tragically short by cancer, but he managed to cram more into a few years than anybody had a right to expect. His recording legacy is tremendously important, and this release shows all his many strengths.
#23, May 2004

GEOFF MANN WITH THE BOND
PEACE OFFERING
After leaving Twelfth Night, Geoff recorded three solo albums before linking up with Dave Mortimer (guitar), Steve Ridley (keyboards) and Andy Mason (drums) as The Bond (note: as The Bond, not as Geoff Mann with The Bond). Two demo tracks were recorded, but soon afterwards Andy left to be replaced by a drum machine. More demos were recorded, which resulted in an album deal, and 'Won By One' was released in 1987 with all new recordings. This sold well enough for the band to be offered another, and 'Prints of Peace' came out in 1989. 'Peace Offering' contains the second album in its entirety, plus five demos of songs that later appeared on the debut. Long-time Geoff supporter and

close friend Andy Labrow has put this package together, which includes a brief biography as well as lyrics and photos.

These two albums saw Geoff concentrating very much on his Christian faith, and lyrically the songs are very much in that domain. Although they're not as progressive as his time with Twelfth Night, these are never straight-ahead rock numbers. Geoff has a singular distinctive voice, capable of portraying tremendous emotion, and it is his vocals that are very much to the fore. Songs such as "Seriously Siblings" has so much power contained in the vocals that it quite takes the breath away, but my favourite is probably "Sob Stories" which was covered so well by Eh! on Geoff's tribute album. I still wonder why Geoff was taken away from us so early in his life, but in that time, he still packed in far more than many of us will ever achieve. If you have ever loved his work with Twelfth Night, Mark Catley, Eh, A Geoff Mann Band or his solo works then now is the time to discover the joys of The Bond.
#38, Nov 1996

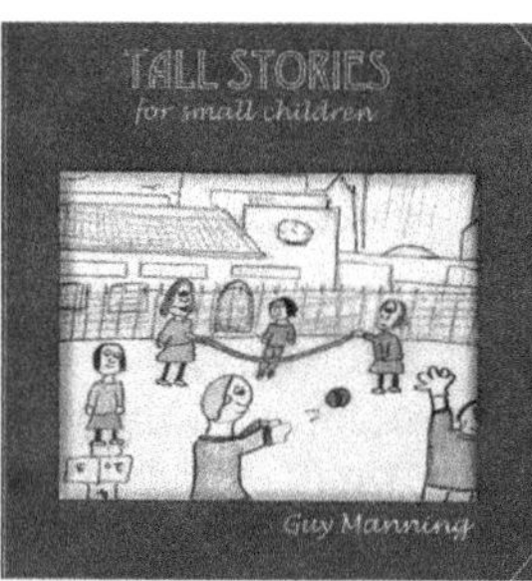

GUY MANNING
TALL STORIES FOR SMALL CHILDREN

MANNING
THE CURE

Guy is guitarist with Parallel Or Ninety Degrees, and on his debut album he was joined by PO90 keyboard player Andy Tillison, as well as bassist Jonathan Barrett, Simon Baskind on drums, Pav Chana on tablas and Jon Burr on harmonica. The album is very impressive, mature in outlook, and while there are many pieces that would not sound out of place on a Pink Floyd album, there are also others which are far more reflective and Roy Harper in style. Three of the songs are epics, sub-divided into smaller songs that can be accessed separately. The vocals and music work so well together that the listener can concentrate heavily on the lyrics. The album was so well received that Guy Manning became Manning the band, and Guy, Andy, Jonathan and Simon went back into the studio, this time with Laura Fowles on sax, and Ian Tothill and Iain Fairbairn on violin. In many ways, this album is much deeper than the debut, and is far more intense. Again, they are hearkening back to Floyd, but also Genesis and VDGG. There are long instrumental passages with some great guitar and keyboard interplay, and while it is not as immediate as the debut, given time it is the more rewarding. Both albums show that it is still possible to discover artists who are not afraid to provide strong songs and musicianship, and do not need to use volume and effects. Both are worth investigation if you enjoy any of the aforementioned bands, but in my mind, the second is the better.
#59, July 2000

MANNING
CASCADE
This is the third album by Guy Manning and is easily his best to date. Any Tull lover will immediately warm to songs such as "Tears In The Rain" where Guy accompanies himself on acoustic guitar and there is just a little background keyboards to add texture. I kept thinking that it would fit quite well on 'Minstrel In The Gallery', on side two just after "Baker St. Muse". Although Guy provides many of the instruments, he has brought in a couple of guests to add some extra colours such as saxophone. Cyclops boss Malcolm Parker feels that the title cut could be a contender for prog song of the year and while I am not prepared to go that far, there are some very pleasant Floydian nuances that make it a great introduction to the album. He even manages to bring in some VDGG as well as some quite commercial pop touches to the same song. Of course, the follow-up, "By The Book" could only start by having a multi-tracked sax jazz introduction. The album would have made sense otherwise, even if it did not come across as Gary Numan playing acoustic jazz prog!! There are some wonderful songs on here, and I am sure that many progheads will enjoy this album that is a slice out of time. It certainly does not belong in this century.
#65, Dec 2001

MANNING
THE RAGGED CURTAIN
This is the fourth album from Manning (as this is a full-blown band now, and not just Guy Manning solo) and sees the songwriting take on a more mature angle, moving away from the progressive scene into one that is far more British in outlook, almost as if Richard Thompson has been involved with Grace. There are also small passages where people are talking about relationships, which gives the album something of a 'Dark Side Of the Moon' feeling. Although the album does contain strong musicianship, it is geared towards providing a strong backdrop for the emotive vocals, and it is these that drive the music ever onwards. Of the musicians, special mention must be made of Laura Fowles, whose sax playing takes the songs into another area. It is the album closer that shows Guy at his most inventive: at twenty-five minutes long, "Ragged Curtains" allows him to bring together styles from the early Seventies up to the present day. It starts gently with keyboards and woodwind, vocals murmuring gently over the top, and then it becomes a vehicle for sax and guitar interplay before going off again onto another tack. All the way through is the impression that this is a 'grown up' album, and although Guy has temporarily lost some of the band, they are still playing some dates soon. Guy will always be associated with Parallel Or Ninety Degrees, and with Andy Tillison-Diskdrive guesting on this and temporarily covering live keyboards that association looks set to continue. An album that is much more than 'just' prog.
#73, Apr 2003

MANNING
THE VIEW FROM MY WINDOW

So, Guy is back with his fifth album, and yet again I am amazed at just how powerful his songs can be. If ever there was a modern songwriter and performer who was trying to pick up on the electric side of Richard Thompson then it must be him, and opening song "Phase (The Open & The Widening Sky)" reinforces that idea. It is powerful and commercial, yet has a strong guitar line throughout, just behind the vocals, or sometimes replacing them. But this album appears to be deeper, with more influences, more darkness, than before. Play the introduction to the title number and you could be forgiven for wondering what on earth you were listening to, as many musical styles come together in a bazaar. But the guitar cuts through everything like a shining ray of light, before giving way to acoustic strumming and the feeling that Guy has turned his attention to one of our great eccentrics, Roy Harper. The keyboards are much more delicate at this point, with the focus very much on the vocals. The major opus of the album is called simply "Suite: Dreams", and is over twenty minutes long, which allows Guy to run through many emotions and styles. Possibly the most powerful is when he is just accompanied by piano and some sweeping keyboards in the background: it may be simple but is effective. This gives way to some lounge style noodlings before again being moved into something more dramatic and moving, almost as if the listener is bursting into the sunlight. In some ways Guy is the least progressive act on Malcolm's label, yet in others he is the most as he crosses boundaries and performs music that wouldn't normally have that tag. Again, this is a wonderful piece of work that I recommend whole heartedly.
#78, Apr 2004

MANNING
A MATTER OF LIFE AND DEATH

MANNING
ONE SMALL STEP…

Guy's sixth album saw him make the move away from Cyclops to ProgRock Records, and while this was Malcolm's loss, Shawn must have welcomed Guy warmly as this concept album sees him at his strongest so far. He has brought with him the band that he has used previously, and Andy Tillison even joins in on a couple of songs. Guy has a style that can only be described as 'English', bringing in the influences he grew up with and mixing it up with his own ideas to create music that at times is evocative of Ian Anderson, at others Peter Hammill and others Roy Harper. The full title of the album is 'A Matter Of Life And Death (The Journal Of Abel Mann)', a character he introduced on his debut album, and is exactly what the title describes, a journey through his journal. It is a very paced album, full of layers that is meant to be savoured. This is not over the top bombastic prog, but something that is meant to be listened to many times and enjoyed.

There are not any overtly long songs on the sixth album, not something that could be said

of Guy's seventh, 'One Small Step...', which contains a suite as the title song, which is over thirty minutes long. But, before we get to that there are four other numbers, and again he has fleshed out the sound with the band and mention must again be made of Laura Fowles who on "In Swingtime" excels herself, with her sax tying the whole thing together. As on all his other works Guy has brought together his influences and has created an album that is full of thought and passion, whether it is in the strong lyrics or in the carefully constructed music. "Night Voices" could almost be considered as a single, with the arrangement complementing the vocals perfectly, and with Laura joining him on singing the chorus it gives the whole song a lift. Even young (ish) Mr Orford helps with some flute on the album but of course what progheads want to know, is what is the long track like? I am not sure why progheads like their music long, probably because it gives the opportunity for complex ideas to be fully expressed – this is not punk after all! What is unusual compared with other modern long prog numbers, is that Guy has based this around an acoustic guitar, and although other instruments are used, these are sparing. There is a passion and urgency in what he is doing, so that at times he comes across like Harry Chapin, but a Harry that grew up on prog instead of singer-songwriters. Hopefully, you will be encouraged to find out more about Guy and his music: I have never heard a poor album from Guy, they are all worth investing in – there are so few prog bands making music of this class and quality these days. He is quite different to what else is out there.

#86, Feb 2006

MAN ON FIRE

HABITAT

This is the third album from Man On Fire, but the first one to see Adrian Belew firmly ensconced in the guitarist role, while David Ragsdale (Kansas, Salem Hill) is back repeating his guest role that he undertook on the second album. This is a concept as 'Habitat' details many different lives existing within the confines of a single urban city block. Each song then tries to paint a musical portrait of one or more of the individuals living in this area. The band are unusual in that Steve Carroll is a member of the band even though he has no performing part to play as he is the lyricist – it shows just how highly they regard that section of the work. Although Jeff Hodges has a wonderfully melodic voice this is an album that can take quite a lot of time to get into, at least it did with me. I think that is because when the band decided that they want to do bleak, they really can, and Adrian definitely fits into this role with ease. One thing that is a definite plus is the use of fretless bass by Eric Sands – being able to slide notes into each other gives the music a very interesting feel that just cannot be achieved when using a fretted. Although some will feel duty bound to find this out just because Adrian is involved, that is a shame as this complex album does have a great deal going for it – just take the time and persevere and eventually it will all become clear.

#84, July 2005

MARILLION
THIS STRANGE ENGINE

For some reason, this is an album that has been creating quite a stir among fans, as it is either hated or loved in approximately equal measures. I was curious to hear it as I hadn't purchased a Marillion album since 'Season's End' and felt that it was about time to rediscover a band that was very important to me in my younger days. The line-up has been surprisingly resilient, as apart from the departure of Fish and Mick Pointer, this is still the same band that set the prog world alight more than fifteen years ago. Pete Trewavas and Ian Mosley provide the dynamic rhythm section while Mark Kelly proves that being bald does not diminish from his keyboard prowess. Steve Rothery has always been a favoured guitarist of mine (especially since the day I read an interview where he told the story of recording so loudly that he knocked himself out in the studio playing power chords) while Steve Hogarth is a truly great singer. Coming to this album having none of the recent material, I was relieved to hear a band still sounding fresh and enjoyable after such a long time. Steve's vocals are pushed very much to the fore (especially on the delicate introduction to "Memory Of Water"), and there is also a heavy use of acoustic guitar. The album commences (as did the live show I saw recently) with "Man Of A Thousand Faces", a strong acoustic number that has rapidly become one of my favourite Marillion songs. If I had to pick a fault with the album it would be that there is a lot going on at a fairly quiet acoustic level. That is not to say that there are no rock elements in place, but that I would rather that there had been a lot more. "Hope For The Future" almost has a calypso beat, which is not quite what I expected from the angry band that cranked out "Forgotten Sons". It is a very enjoyable album, but if I had to choose between this and 'Sunsets On Empire' then I am afraid that the latter would win rather easily.

#42, July 1997

MARILLION
MARBLES

I grew up on Marillion. I have all of their early singles on 12", and when I finally saw them on the 'Misplaced Childhood' tour I was in heaven. Of course, the tall Scottish person left to be replaced by Steve Hogarth and musically the band changed. I have seen them in concert twice since then and have enjoyed what I have seen, but still it is the earliest material that gets the loudest roars. This is all very unfair to a band that were at the vanguard of the progressive rock boom in the early Eighties and the only one that ever reached the commercial heights that they deserved. Now of course they are a cottage industry and with this release achieved two top twenty singles from mobilising their fanbase and managed to get some fans to pay for this album before it was written, let alone recorded. It is still possible to buy this as a double CD through their site, together with a 128-page book, but the album I am listening to is the single album that most would have seen in the shops. But what is it like? Well, it is okay, but little more than that. Of all the guys involved in the band the one that has been heard most of over the years is Pete Trewavas, but one does wonder what outlets Steve Rothery has to blast

away his guitar. However, if you can get through this album to "Drilling Holes" be prepared to be amazed as this is a song that captures all the passion of old as it builds and changes. It is dramatic and powerful, in a way that the rest of the album is not. This is the first album I have heard since 'This Strange Engine', which was the first that I had heard since 'Season's End', and as I said before it is okay. Nothing more than that.
#84, July 2005

MK II
BURNING DAYLIGHT
When Geoff Mann died early last year, his band were obviously left with some difficult decisions. They could break up, find another vocalist, or become an instrumental trio. They chose the last, and Eh! Geoff Mann Band became Mk II. Having worked together for several years, and recorded two albums for Music For Nations ('Loud Symbols' and 'Ministry of The Interior'), as well as touring all over Britain and Europe it is obvious that John Maycraft (guitars, mandolin, MIDI), Paul Keeble (bass, acoustic guitar, whistle, MIDI) and Gary Mitchell (drums) have a good understanding of each other. This is more than evident in their debut album, as the ideas bounce from each other in a constant stream of differing melodies, counter melodies and great musicianship. The band that everyone seems to be comparing them with is Pink Floyd, and while there are similarities, there is a harder edge apparent in some songs (for example "The Cube") which provides the contrast for softer moments ("Expansion I"). It is an album that does need listening to, as there is more going on than meets the ear on first attempt, whether it is the distorted guitar solo on one song or the simple use of acoustic guitar as backing on another, this album grows as the listener gets more out of each time. This must have been extremely difficult for Mk II to record, if only for emotional reasons, but they have proved that they are far more than just the guys left behind and have a great deal to offer.
#25, Oct 1994

MASQUE
FLESH THAT UNDERSTANDS
This Swedish band is comprised of Magnus Berggren (bass), Johan Engstrom (guitars), Stefan Kalin (vocals), Lars Kallfelt (drums) and Jerker Rellmark (keyboards, vocals). All the lyrics are in English, and the nine song fifty-five-minute-long CD is very accessible indeed. They have already found themselves compared with All About Eve, Violet Hour and Happy The Man, and although elements of all these can be found, Masque still manage to create their own sound. The guitar is more to the fore than with many of the current prog scene, but it is never overpowering. Indeed, it is only on careful listening that the most important instrument can be discerned to be the bass, as behind the melody line there is at times some tremendously fast and intricate playing, yet always this adds to, instead of detracting from, the music. Masque are not afraid to switch from electric to acoustic and return (as on the wonderfully commercial sounding

"Feeding Her") yet remain totally accessible. It was an album I enjoyed on first listen and at times I found myself thinking of Big Big Train, especially on "A Confident Dance" which could have been cut by the Dorset proggers. I know many importers have this CD available, and I can see why. With their feet firmly in the commercial prog rock setting, they have produced an album that is enjoyable, packed full of good songs and musicianship without being pretentious. This is worth looking out for.
#19, Aug 1993

MASQUE
TEN WAYS
Many moons ago I reviewed the debut album by Swedish band Masque, 'Flesh That Understands', and I have just been sent the follow-up by vocalist Jerker Rellmark who informs me that guitarist Johan Engstrom has moved to another part of Sweden, and that the band are now rehearsing and working under the name Grape. So, what does the final recording of Masque sound like? It is very good as the band have moved on quite a lot since the debut and have taken on board many differing influences. While the songs are not necessarily those that you would sing in the bath, they are very melodic and enjoyable on first hearing. For the most part Masque inhabit the same area of prog as Camel or Happy The Man, being gentle and laid back yet at the same time being very sophisticated with a lot going on. There are some very deft touches with the guitar, and the use of African drum in places, along with some brass instruments, expands the sound and appeal. "The Scent" is the most up-tempo number, with some glorious bass lines at the beginning and almost develops into funk. Jerker has a good clear voice and is reminiscent at times of Peter Nicholls. Overall, the album works extremely well and although I enjoyed the debut, this shows progression and is worth investigating.
#32, Dec 1995

MASTERMIND
III – TRAGIC SYMPHONY
This is the third album by American outfit Mastermind. The group comprises Rich Berends (vocals) and Bill Berends (everything else), although Phil Antolino joins them on bass when they play live. Quite how Bill provides keyboards and guitar at the same time I do not know, but this is their first release for Cyclops, the other albums now deleted. It is an album very much of two parts, with the first comprising three songs and the second being "Tragic Symphony", which is in three movements. They are an extremely intense outfit, and although they are not as heavy as Dream Theater or Threshold, Bill still crunches out the power chords. There is a symphonic sound, and it is of no surprise that as well as ELP they have also been compared with Mahler: it is this classical element to their prog that makes them stand out from the rest. It is unusual for an American band to be making music of this depth, and the final movement of "Tragic Symphony" is just superb. The two albums released by

American bands on the Cyclops label this month could not be further apart in terms of style and execution, but they will both be labelled prog. Of the two I would probably turn to the brilliant Echolyn, but this also has a lot going for it.
#30, Aug 1995

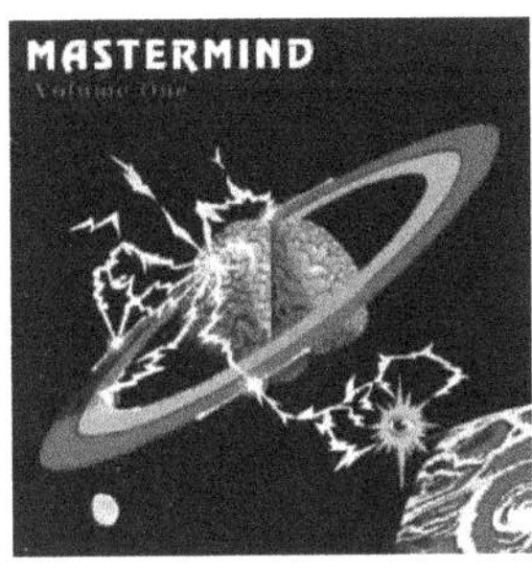

MASTERMIND
VOLUME ONE

Following on from the third Mastermind album, which came out on Cyclops a while ago, we now have a reissue of their first with some bonus tracks. Bill Berends provided all the instrumentation apart from percussion, which is provided by Rich Berends. Mastermind specialise in, for the most part, a bombastic style of progressive rock, although there are some songs that are far more pop and keyboard oriented such as "Long Distance Love Affair", while "Eye of the Storm" also works as a heavier pomp AOR affair. Although at times they seem to be striving for an almost hard rock approach, the songs are mostly keyboard led: the pomp and bombast sound very American, and overall the album works very well. Bill is a very good musician and manages to make Mastermind sound more like a band than they actually are.
#36, Aug 1996

MASTERMIND
IV – UNTIL ETERNITY

Mastermind is still Rich Berends (drums) and Bill Berends (everything else) with a live bassist (Phil Antolino). Musically the band seem to have moved in leaps and bounds since 'III', as although the orchestral elements are still playing a large part, they have turned up the guitars and moved more into a complex rock field: I am sure that this is going to make them many more converts, including me. Although I have enjoyed what has gone before, it all pales when compared with this as there seems to be so much more depth and power to the proceedings. Bill is an amazing guitarist and has balanced the use of musical skill against pointless meanderings. The result is an album that is enjoyable from first song "Under The Wheels", which is a well thought out tirade against the decline in standards and the increase in fear and the power of the gun, to the closing instrumental "Until Eternity". "The Tempest" is almost ELP-like at times, with complex keyboards runs, but they never rocked like this. The sound is firmly rooted in what has gone before but melded perfectly into American stadium rock for the nineties. Full of pomp and prog, this is an album to savour and enjoy.
#37, Oct 1996

MASTERMIND
EXCELSIOR!

This is the first album by Mastermind since leaving Cyclops and one that has also seen a change in line-up and approach. Bill Berends (guitars) and his brother Rich (drums) have been joined by Jens Johansson on keyboards, whereas Bill used to provide these as well. Along with many others, I was simply stunned when I saw them play The Orange a few years ago, with Rich being one of the most exciting and dynamic drummers I have ever had the pleasure to experience, and Bill switching between guitar and MIDI throughout with great skill. Of course, there he was also providing vocals, but 'Excelsior!' is an instrumental album. Gaining a top keyboard player has squeezed the sound so that there is not any room for vocals; with so much going on, they are never missed. This is very high standard instrumental music with focus, no meaningless meanderings or ego boosts. The guys are very relaxed in their skill and it is as much about what they do not play as it is about what they do. Rich is content to provide a simple shuffle, or forceful powerful rolls around the kit, whatever the music dictates while both Bill and Jens happily swap leads which may involve incredibly quick playing or just the few notes here and there to carry the mood. If you have previously liked Mastermind then you will love this, and if you are a proghead then do not be put off by the word "instrumental". This is excellent.

#54, July 1999

MASTERMIND
ANGELS OF THE APOCALYPSE

Mastermind is certainly not a band content to sit on their previous achievements and is yet again moving off into pastures new. Last year they brought in keyboard wizard Jens Johansson (Stratovarius) and recorded an instrumental album. This year the Berends brothers have managed to retain Jens but have also brought in a female vocalist, Lisa Bouchelle. Considering that up to last year Rich Berends provided drums and Bill everything else (with a bassist added for live work), it is quite a move to take. When I saw them at The Orange a few years ago I was amazed by their virtuosity and they seem to have taken on a new life since then. Opener "The End Of The World" (over ten minutes) moves from driving rock track to a jam, where Bill lets loose on the guitar. Rich shows why he is one of the top drummers in the world with some amazing fills, and Jens fits in well without being overpowering. Each of the ten tracks is a gem, and they even cover a number from ELP, "The Endless Enigma". Mastermind is progressing, and this is an album that all progheads should rush and get straight away. Just superb.

#57, Mar 2000

MATTER OF TASTE
CHATEAU OBSCURE

MATTER OF TASTE
JACK OF SPADES

There do not appear to be that many progressive rock bands hailing from Austria, but here are the first two albums from one of them. I notice that the first is on their own label while the second is on Peter Wustmann's Music is Intelligence, so he must think that they will sell well in Germany. With three different lead singers singing two songs, and another singing the last, it is sometimes difficult to get a grip on the band's identity. The first album seems very laid back as well and although they describe themselves as progressive this is a million miles removed from Rocket Scientists. I am not sure either of "Resurrection Song" which sees them ripping apart from Beethoven and overall, this is just far too laid back. A drop in vocalists from four to two, and a higher concentration on guitars and more up-tempo numbers means that 'Jack Of Spades' is a far superior album to the debut, although they do tend to lose it a little in the slower numbers. Franz's guitar is much more important, almost as if he is trying to turn the band into much more of a hard rock outfit. This he does not quite manage, but whereas the first album was just interesting this has some bloody good moments on it.
#51, Jan 1999

McGILL, MANRING, STEVENS
ADDITION BY SUBTRACTION

This album is by Scott McGill, Michael Manring and Vic Stevens, and has been released on Free Electric Sound, a new label set up by prog outfit The Laser's Edge. I have been a fan of other releases by the label, but I have not enjoyed this as much, which may be due more to my own personal musical tastes than the quality of the music. It is a fine jazz-rock instrumental album, and while lovers of that genre may get something from this, I do not believe the press release, which states that it is "surely designed to become a classic for fans of heavy progressive rock, metal, and fusion". There is no doubt that the guys can play, but I prefer my music with more tunes and feel.
#63, Jul 2001

McGILL, MANRING, STEVENS
WHAT WE DO

Take three extrovert extremely talented musicians and set them on the world of jazz, and the result is something like MMS. When they started thinking of ideas for their third instrumental album the concept started to form of taking modern jazz standards and deconstructing then reconstructing the material, and 'What We Do' is the result. Whether

it is Miles Davis, Sonny Rollins, Herbie Hancock or Coltrane, no one is safe, and the result is an album that needs to be listened to very carefully indeed. This is not jazz lite or background noise, this is music for the jazz fan to listen to and dissect. The use of both fretless bass and fretless guitars within their musical canon adds an extra sound to what they are doing, and the result is something that those into jazz certainly need to hear at least. Even the label states that "It's a mutated soundscape that will make the trio villains to some and hopefully heroes to many". It is something that needs to be taken very seriously indeed. *#89, Sep 2006*

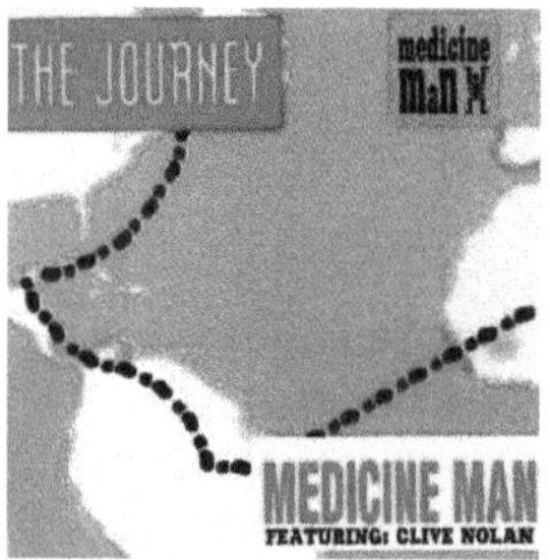

MEDICINE MAN
THE JOURNEY

Medicine Man is the name of a project that has been put together by songwriter and drummer John Bowman and features Clive Nolan (keyboards, Arena, Shadowland, Pendragon), Karl Groom (guitar, Threshold, Shadowland), Peter Gee (bass, Pendragon, Mercy Train) and Ian 'Moon' Gould (vocals, Landmarq). Recorded at Thin Ice, the album is of the high quality that one would expect from those involved, yet at the same time this is quite different from their other work. This is probably because John does not come from the same prog background, and the whole approach is far more pop rock. The songs are fairly verse/chorus oriented, but lyrically they are very strong, and the result is an album that is immensely enjoyable and extremely easy to listen to. I found that even on first hearing the songs were like old friends. This is the first time I have heard Ian sing in the studio (although I have seen him play live with Landmarq) and was impressed with the depth and range, as well as the emotional qualities of his voice. Although all the songs are good, there is one real standout for me, "Two Sides". Musically it starts with just Ian (whose voice has been 'treated' as in "Video Killed The Radio Star") and a repeated keyboard sequence. Bass joins this gradually, and then the drums herald the arrival of the guitar. This mix of pop and rough-edged rock is used to emphasise the hard-hitting lyrics about how wonderful modern technology is, then comparing it with all the people dying in the world today. I know that since recording, Ian has left Medicine Man, but hopefully this is not the last we have heard of John Bowman and his project. *#32, Dec 1995*

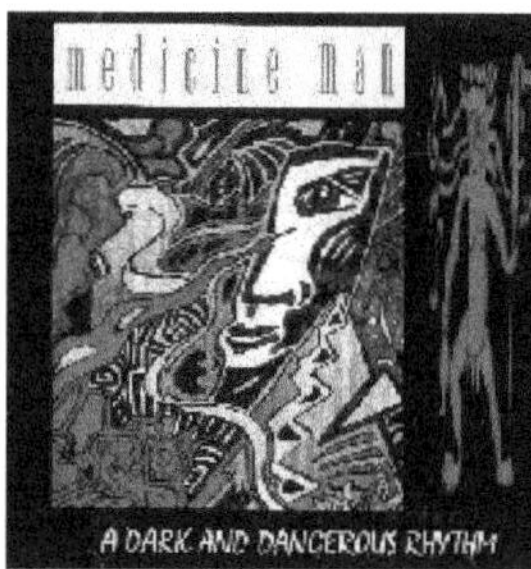

MEDICINE MAN
A DARK AND DANGEROUS RHYTHM

This is the follow-up to the 1995 debut 'The Journey'. Although drummer John Bowman had written all the songs, that ended up with Clive Nolan (Arena, Shadowland, Pendragon etc.) on keyboards, Karl Groom (Threshold, Shadowland) on guitar, Peter Gee (Pendragon) on bass and Moon Gould (Landmarq) on vocals. This time, although Clive and Karl have again produced this at Thin Ice Studios they are musically only involved in a small way, as this is now more of a band and not a project. But what about the album itself? I enjoyed the last one, although it was far more 'poppy' than I would have expected at times. This is again more commercial than a lot of music I listen to, yet at the same time is more progressive than the last one. Although John has again written the lyrics, this time the music is credited to the band. The album title is taken from "Fatal Cure", which is my favourite song and is a light-hearted good commercial rock number with a sing-along chorus. I do not think that nearly as many people picked up on the previous album as they should have done, but hopefully they will this time. Paul Wilson has a great voice, and combined with some good commercial rock tunes, assist in making this an album to discover. *#42, July 1997*

MELBOURNE
NIGHT STAR

This is the second album from Carrie Melbourne and her husband Doug, and Jamie Fisher from Sphere[3] has now joined them on drums. Carrie is best known for being in Babylon Zoo when they hit No.1 with "Spaceman" but has also been performing with Tricky and most recently with Mike Oldfield while Doug is best known for his work with ReGenesis. This is not the sort of record that you are going to play to get rid of the cobwebs, as it is dreamy and reflective. That the label is already saying that it is going to be used as library music shows that they do not imagine that it will top the hit parade. It is very much New Age, and as the band has the strap line under their name of "Beautiful songs influenced by world music and electronica" it is a safe bet that Slayer fans will not be beating down any doors to purchase this. It is very good at what it does but is not something to which I will be returning to often.
#70, Oct 2002

MEN OF LAKE
OUT OF THE WATER

'Out Of The Water' is the third album by this Italian outfit, and on first hearing it is difficult to believe that this is a brand-new release, and not one from the early Seventies. It is at times like these that the word "progressive" becomes truly redundant, as the music is actually "regressive". Still, does that imply that the CD is not any good? I hope not as the more I played this the more I liked it. Band leader Maurizio Poli (vocals etc.) stamps his sound all over this recording with a heavy use of Hammond Organ and Moog. Opening tracks "Vipers (In The Bottom Of The Well)" belts along quite nicely with vocals being slightly distorted and the bass deep and rumbling, even more so than the sound used by Chris Squire. To follow this with a ballad just shows off the strength of the band and the songs. Italy has a growing prog scene and Men Of Lake manage to be big players within it. Last issue I praised Asgard to the heavens, and while Men of Lake are totally different, it shows that the Italian scene needs closer investigation. Steve Paine of Legend was singing the praises of this album to me recently and I must agree with him as this is very enjoyable, if a little dated. *#24, Jul 1994*

MENTAUR
TRY YOUR BRAKES

MENTAUR
VERDICT

MENTAUR
TIME BEING

Mentaur have just released their third tape, 'Time Being', so now is probably a good time to tell you about a band described by The Organ as "the best prog band to emerge this year, total Prog and proud of it".

The nucleus of the band came together at Marlborough College, Wiltshire, in January 1989. Keyboard player and songwriter Tim Ridley, drummer Ed Lepper and bassist Jim Gross put together a band called Mordred, with guitarist Rob Barter joining in April of the same year, and the first gig taking place just a month later. Because of an American funk-thrash outfit called Mordred they decided a name change was in order, and so became Mordrydd UK. A seven-track cassette album was released in the November, titled 'No Mortal Man. I have not heard this, although three of the songs were re-recorded for 'Verdict', but the consensus appears to be that although the music was fine, the singing left a little to be desired, as the vocals were being carried out by bassist Jim Gross. Because of this the decision was made to find a vocalist and first up was Steve Cochrane, who joined the band in February 1990. The band celebrated by changing their name to Mentaur and had Steve re-record all the vocals on the initial tape. However, after a relatively short time they decided that he was not the man for the job and replaced him with Dan Hart.

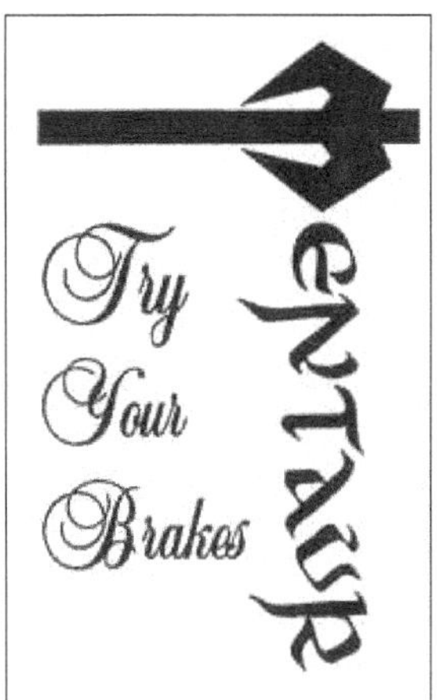

Dan joined in time for the band to bail him out of jail so that he could front them at the Bristol Bierkeller in September. Dan's powerful voice complimented finally the soundscapes created by the band, and they started to step up a gear. The same month saw them in the studio recording a three-track demo for record companies. However, due to demand from fans they instead recorded four songs and made 'Try Your Brakes' available to their growing contingent of fans (current sales more than two thousand). The tape kicks off with "Silver Snakes", which is a wonderfully commercial rock number with lots of contrasting passages. Strangely, for what is a rock song, there is a lot of piano, which is replaced by soaring keyboards as the guitars kick in. "Distant Ways" is a sensitive ballad dominated by the pianowork of Tim who is quite in demand as a session musician, and it is not difficult to see why. More in the rock vein is "Red Seas", where guitar and keyboards combine in unison in a manner that is at times reminiscent of Uriah Heep. Highlight of the tape is the epic "Day of Wrath", which takes up the whole of the second side. Apparently, the song is "based on the Dies Irae with references to the Latin text and the Gregorian Plainchant". Well, that's what Tim says, and he should know. To my ears it is wonderful prog-out, with ballad sections and at times, rocking guitar.

In August 1991 founder member Jim Gross left the band due to "musical differences", and Tim's brother Nick replaced him. The guys quickly recorded 'Verdict' live in the studio, with three of the songs ("The Questing Beast", "Oracles" and "Imperatrix") all having previously appeared on the 'No Mortal Man' demo. 'Verdict' shows the band stretching their creative wings further, yet at the same time not "selling out". The two opening numbers, "Child On Trial" and "Towers of Silence" show a much quieter side, with Dan not sounding totally confident when singing in a sustained lower style. "The Questing Beast" shows a harder yet controlled side to Mentaur's music, with the keyboards and guitar combining in a very commercial sound. Indeed, Rob is considerably restrained, in great contrast to the live sound. This side finishes with my favourite Mentaur song, "Passive Resistance". Starting with repeated keyboard riffs and gentle singing, the bass gradually joins in and the pace slowly increases. The first chorus finds Dan singing accompanied only by riffing guitar and drums, "What makes me think you have no right, I am free and free to choose, no self-control, no self-respect, well mate I'm playing to lose". This is repeated with the rest of the band and leads into a quiet passage, with Tim very much in control. Dan's repeat of the chorus is virtually unaccompanied and shows his voice off well. The only fault with this song is that every time I play it I compare it with the version they play at gigs, which is a real killer with loads of guitar and audience participation. Side Two commences with "Imperatrix", where Rob proves he can riff with the best of them, yet at the same time making way for Tim so that the song has plenty of contrast. Soaring keyboards even provide opportunity for a Floyd-style guitar solo until Tim lets rip with a wonderfully quick keyboard passages, driven along by the bass. This leads the way for a guitar and keyboard duel (to my ears Tim sneaks it by a whisker). When I reviewed Mentaur supporting Casual Affair back in #12, I said that "Summermoonsong" was one of the highlights, and here it is in full glory with Dan singing the ballad accompanied only by piano-dominated keyboards. "Chasing Time" is a great contrast, as the guys rock along giving a better indication of their live sound. "Oracles" has a very definite Sabbath feel to it, strange for a prog band. An example of how Mentaur make their own musical rules, as the leaden riff trades places with the gentle keyboards. The tape closes with the instrumental "Metamorphosis".

The tape was critically well-received and set Mentaur off on a heavy schedule of London gigs (and a tour of Cornwall). It would have been difficult for any London-based prog fan to miss them as they supported and headlined all over the capital. In April 1992, they were first band on at the Astoria, where Pendragon were supported by Galahad, and Kerrang! voted them the best band of the night, which was not overly surprising as by now Mentaur had moved a long way into the hard rock arena with live versions of their material far harder than those available on tape. However, this turned out to be Dan's last gig with the band, and Carlton Evans replaced him in the June. Further gigging led them into the studio in October and November to record their latest tape, 'Time Being'.

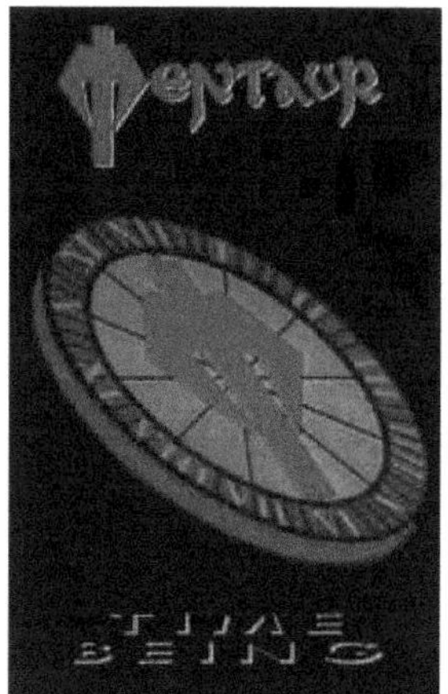

The tape has a far more professional look to it, with a glossy colour inlay and separate lyric sheet. Side One starts with "Far Cry", and Rob crunching some heavy riffs. It is then of some surprise that the song changes into a more keyboard-dominated ballad, but not to worry as Rob is soon back again. The changes in mood and style occur again and again throughout, and a riffing guitar and bass allows Tim to lay down a solo that builds into the guitar break: the song gets heavier as it progresses. Carlton's voice is slightly higher than that of Dan's, but does not seem to have the same power, which may well be down to lack of confidence behind the microphone, which will come in time. Second track is "Fugitive" (and not "Access Denied" as stated on the sleeve), which is introduced with a repeated bass riff from Nick. This song is typical Mentaur, with loads of guitar and soaring keyboards in a commercial rock setting: a rather unfair comparison is with some of Gillan's material. Carlton even has the chance to show what he can do in a rock setting with, at times, quite minimal backing. It works, and yet again puts Mentaur in the technical rock side as opposed to the straight prog field. "Forward Through The Past" is for the most part a ballad, which builds to a beautiful guitar solo, very restrained and in full keeping with the mood created by the keyboards. Final song on this side is "Access Denied", again a heavier number with guitar and keyboards combining to great effect. The whole of the second side is taken up with "Saviour Solution". Drummer Ed Lepper's lyrics are excellent, as always, but here he has excelled himself. The song is about a man developing computers to the extent that he decides that they are better placed to make decisions than him, so he gives over all control. Only one person realises what is happening, a programmer. "Your Lord requires freedom of action, and so you must relinquish yours, His decisions feed no fractions, He'll unlock all your closed doors, He takes all into account, when considering your case, in a fraction of a millisecond, He can end your human race". This epic, to my ears, really works. Carlton's singing on this is the best on the tape, and the whole band gels. Obviously, with a song of this length, there are many different styles and melodies, but they all work. Brilliantly.
#16, Dec 1992

MENTAUR
DARKNESS BEFORE DAWN

On a purely musical front, Mentaur were for a while one of the most interesting bands to come out of London in the early Nineties. The musical path they were following was not too different from that later taken by Shadowland, although they were more of a rock band. 'Darkness Before Dawn' is an attempt to take the best songs from their cassette albums and put them on CD. The choice of songs has been by the band themselves, they have been remixed, and the booklet contains copious notes as well as the lyrics. It is a long album, as would be expected, but I was extremely surprised by the omission of "Passive Resistance", which I always felt was one of the highlights of their live set, and there was also no room for "The Questing Beast". But, there is room for

"Days of Wrath", "Imperatrix" and a twenty-two-minute-long "The Last Battle". They may have worked their way through four vocalists, but this compilation is very consistent. In fact, it was very enjoyable to listen to these songs again, as it has been quite some time since I dug out the cassettes. Mentaur were one of the few Nineties prog bands not afraid to gig hard, and toured Cornwall, Scotland and points in-between. Musically they were a force to be reckoned with and although they are no more, this compilation shows what they managed to achieve.
#39, Jan 1997

MERCHANTS VICE
AMBER
The band released this debut album in 2003, but it has only just come to my attention. Apparently, Credo and Merchants Vice could well be touring together later this year and that is a move that makes total sense to me, as they are going to appeal to the same sort of audience, namely those who enjoyed the British Prog scene in the Eighties and wonder where it has all gone now. This is going to be termed 'neo-prog' by many, and that is probably the most accurate definition of the genre but as always that does not do justice to what is being performed. This is songs-based prog, yet only one falls under six minutes ("Dark Before Dawn" is under three minutes, which reminds me of Galahad's experiment of recording a prog song of that length). The album has a good sound and it is no surprise on reading the (very) small print that it was mixed and mastered by none other than Rob Aubrey, who is such a key component to IQ's sound. Bands such as Pendragon and Galahad have obviously been influences, while early Arena and possibly even some IQ have played their part. Les Wardle has a very clear voice and enunciation, so that even though he has a different vocal style to Geoff Mann he is also reminiscent of him. A very enjoyable album that anyone into the British prog scene will want to hear.
#83, Mar 2005

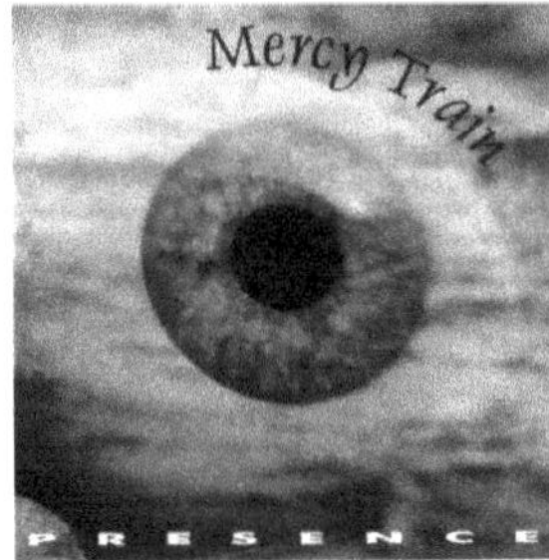

MERCY TRAIN
PRESENCE
Originally, Mercy Train were envisaged as being just a live outfit, being a project put together by vocalist Richard Burge and guitarist Karl Groom (Shadowland, Threshold, SOAT etc.): they were joined by Richard West (keyboards, ex-Shadowland) and Nick Harradence (drums, Shadowland). Mercy Train were completed with bassist Peter Gee (Pendragon) and have played many gigs, particularly in London, and managed an appearance last year at Greenbelt. This, their debut CD, sees Mercy Train being a heavy melodic rock band, with Karl very much in evidence. Obviously, Mercy Train are going to find themselves covered with a "prog" label by many because of the personnel involved, but nothing could be further from the truth. I mean, listen to "Prayers From The Electric Chair" then find a comparison with Pendragon, IQ or Galahad. It is impossible! There are going to be many progheads very disappointed with this CD, but

those of us who enjoy good melodic hard rock will find that virtually every track is a winner. Although not recorded at Thin Ice, the recording and production is spot on, which means that the CD can be cranked up to maximum, as it should be. From opener "Pure Emotion" to the closer "Loveless", which is the twelfth song, there is hardly a dull (or quiet) moment. I could find only one fault with the whole thing (apart from being too short at only 52 minutes), and that is that the bridge in "Big White Car" sounds uncannily like that contained in "Sympathy For The Devil". Anyone who enjoys Karl's work with Threshold, wants to hear Peter Gee play rock bass, or just enjoys their rock loud and proud yet melodic at the same time, should get this album immediately.
#21, Jan 1994

MERMAID KISS
MERMAID KISS

MERMAID KISS
SALT ON SKIN

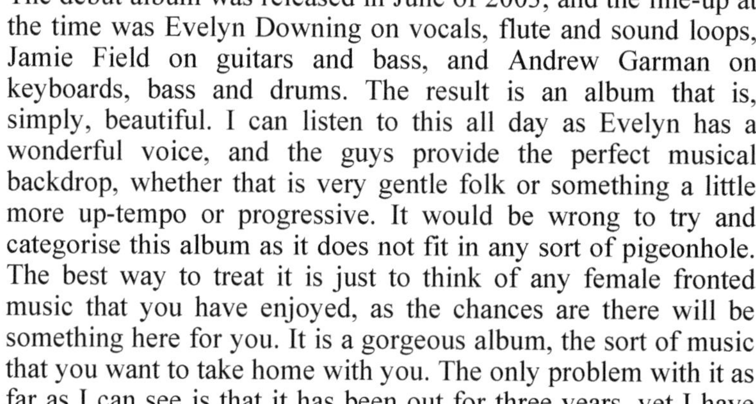

The debut album was released in June of 2003, and the line-up at the time was Evelyn Downing on vocals, flute and sound loops, Jamie Field on guitars and bass, and Andrew Garman on keyboards, bass and drums. The result is an album that is, simply, beautiful. I can listen to this all day as Evelyn has a wonderful voice, and the guys provide the perfect musical backdrop, whether that is very gentle folk or something a little more up-tempo or progressive. It would be wrong to try and categorise this album as it does not fit in any sort of pigeonhole. The best way to treat it is just to think of any female fronted music that you have enjoyed, as the chances are there will be something here for you. It is a gorgeous album, the sort of music that you want to take home with you. The only problem with it as far as I can see is that it has been out for three years, yet I have only just come across it!

'Salt On Skin' is the new release, a seven-track mini-album that bridges the gap between the debut and the next album. Musically Nigel Hooton has joined Andrew and Jamie, but what is unusual with this release are the singers. Evelyn has left the band to concentrate on her studies but has contributed to two of the songs, her replacement Kate Belcher sang on two more while her replacement and current singer Kate Emerson sang on the other three. Again, there is a diversity of styles, with the band moving from prog into more gentle areas. Possibly the most interesting of all is the delicate "I Go To Sleep" which closes the album. This is one of Kate's vocals and was recorded at her audition! No pressure then. I have enjoyed listening to these albums – like a breath of fresh air on a sultry day, and I am looking forward to the next full-length album. These albums are for those who enjoy good music, whatever the genre or style.
#88, Jun 2006

METAGAIA
PHONOGENIX

Metagaia was a project by Haruhiko Tsuda, who was previously guitarist in the well-known Japanese prog act Shingetsu. This was recorded in the latter half of the Nineties and most of the music is played by Haruhiko himself although he does use other musicians (including fellow Shingetsu member, keyboard player Akira Hanamoto on "Water Harp"). In some ways, this album is reminiscent of Kitaro, as it combines many different styles including electronic, ambient and possibly even jazz. The feeling is that of very much a New Age album, something to be relaxed to at the end of a day, or just played gently in the background while doing something else. This is not one to be studied, but rather is far more incidental in nature. It is never in your face but is pleasant, and I found it very enjoyable while at the same time feeling that I was being lulled as opposed to being preached to. *#86, Feb 2006*

METAMORPHOSIS
THEN ALL WAS SILENT

The third album from Swiss band Metamorphosis is a concept piece, based around a storyline of cloned children being killing machines, only Kenny is different. Given the subject matter it probably is not too much of a surprise that the album is not all filled with brightness and light, but there is a deftness of touch so that the lyrics do not overpower the music too much. The words are very strong indeed and, in that respect, it reminds me somewhat of the debut album by Tr3nity, but this contains a musical basis in Pink Floyd while the more restrained moments of Pendragon are also in evidence. I have not heard the other albums but would be interested to see if they follow the same musical themes as this, because I would say that the words came first which obviously affected the musical style. I have not heard a great deal of Swiss prog, or Swiss music in general coming to think of it, but if it is all this standard then I have been missing out. The arrangements are very strong with the keyboards playing the main focal point but the rest all very much having their part to play and some of the Gilmour/Barrett guitar lines are superb. Overall, this may not be an album to keep playing continuously, but one to return to and certainly, on that basis this is a definite goody with much to offer *#84, July 2005*

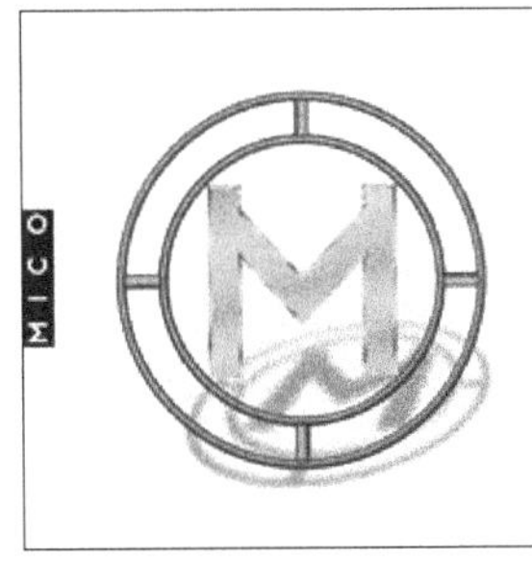

MICO
MICO

Mico is a group that features guitarist and keyboard player Fred LeDuc. Fred and I first were in contact over his progressive release under the name Deluc, and when I e-mailed him recently to discover what he was up to he asked if I would be interested in another project with which he was involved. I am extremely glad that he then sent me this CD, as this is superb, although it is much more of a pop album, with leanings towards jazz and soul.

The production is top quality and the overall impression is very much of a major label release as opposed to an independent. There is even a video track. Although Mico are a four piece (Fred guitar and keyboards, Anthony Scaffidi drums, Bernard Pascal vocals and Andy Watson bass), they have brought in extra musicians to fill out the sound, most notably four backing singers. This means that Bernard has female vocals to pitch against, and the music sounds better for it. Fred is happy to use classical acoustic (as on "Havana Moon"), or electric as the mood suits, and Andy is using a fretless bass, which adds to the warmth. The opening song, "Best Intentions" is upbeat and if released as a single with some backing would do serious damage to the charts. But, and this is a big "but", this album has been released by the band in Australia, and as it hasn't got a barcode I am assuming that they have yet to secure distribution. If this album fails due to lack of support, it would be nothing short of criminal as it is one I have deeply enjoyed and hope it will be picked up for a major release. *#57, Mar 2000*

MILLENIUM
REINCARNATIONS

'Reincarnations' is Millenium's third album and is the follow-up to 'Vocanda' which was released in November 2000. Although the band are Polish, and it has been released on a Polish label, the lyrics to the songs are in English (and printed both in English and Polish in the booklet) which makes it very accessible to the casual listener. This is progressive music of a dreamy relaxing nature, which lulls the listener in and has been done very well indeed. Vocalist Łukasz Gałęziowski has a very melodic voice, and while the range is kept to a minimum he sings with great power and emotion. Keyboard player Ryszard Kramarski provides the backdrop and the harshness and bite comes from guitarist Piotr Płonka. This album has been influenced by American AOR and based only on hearing the album that would be where people would imagine that the band hailed from. "Higher Than Me" manages to combine Emerson Lake & Palmer with Asia and Styx and comes out as a joyful rocker. Easy to listen to, but with lots of styles that mean that there is always more to get out of the album each time it is played. This is not in your face innovative progressive rock music, but rather music that can be enjoyed by any lover of that genre. *#68, Jun 2002*

MILLENIUM
DÉJÀ VU

MILLENIUM
INTERDEAD

It has been a while since I last heard anything by one of my favourite Polish prog bands and here I now have two albums to listen to. The first of these, 'Déjà Vu' was released in 2004 and was the follow-up to 'Reincarnations' which came out in 2002 and I reviewed some time ago. What is so good about this band is that they are just so easy to listen to; it is prog that is not too demanding, in the sense that the music is compelling yet immediate. The band wants you to enjoy listening to what they are performing as opposed to ramming something complex down the throat that is hard to get into. The vocals are softly sung with nice harmonies, and all the lyrics are in English, which makes the whole thing accessible. This is an album of songs, and although none of them are exceptionally long, they all display the maturity that only comes with a band being totally comfortable in what they are doing. Accessible easy to listen to prog with just a hint of bite as it covers both Gabriel and Floyd territory yet sounding nothing at all like either.

'Interdead' is quite a different album, as not only is it a concept album with a spoken passage at the beginning and end, but musically it shows that the band have again moved on. The line-up has changed slightly, and the new guitarist has added an extra touch with an edge that is rockier than before, with more attack. This is again very accessible, and contains more variety than 'Déjà Vu', and works better. With very fluid guitar lines it has let the rest of the band spread out a bit more, as they bring the rock back into their prog and while some sections could be thought of as Floyd there are times when IQ influences can clearly be heard. There is even a sax used at times and the male/female duets are particularly effective. This is the fourth Millenium album that I have been lucky enough to hear, and to my ears this is the best to date. *#84, July 2005*

MINDFLOWERS
IMPROGRESSIVE

This is the debut album from instrumental Hungarian four-piece Mindflowers. They comprise Balázs Szendőfi (bass, stick), Zoltán Szentpál (guitar), Gergely Gáspár (drums) and Zsolt Nagy (keyboards) and seem to be happily straddling the fields of progressive rock and jazz-rock. However, while complex and complicated this does not go into freefall as some jazz acts tend to, so the result is a very listenable and enjoyable album. It can be calm and collected, smooth and tranquil, or the total opposite, as the mood takes them. My initial feel was that it was as if Colosseum II had become mixed up with Jadis, but even then, that does not do the music justice. It is very fluid and melodic, and they go from out and out prog (as in "Red Spider") or bring in some folk influences (as on "Flo's Kisses") where they utilise a guest violinist. Although the two lead instruments of keyboards and guitar have struck up a dynamic interplay, which carries most of the melody, there is a great deal going on in the rhythm section. With a Chapman Stick being used on two of the songs, and Balázs determined to show that he can produce similar results on a normal bass guitar (well, a handmade seven string version), it gives the music a dynamic edge that is dense yet extremely light. There are lots of gaps and space within the music at times, yet at others it is just filled with notes and melodies. Easily one of the finest instrumental albums I have heard in recent years this is a joy throughout (although the insertion of a mobile phone text message notice going off at the end of one number did have me looking for my phone). #72, *Feb 2003*

MINDFLOWERS
NUANCES

This is the second album from instrumental progressive quartet Mindflowers, following on from their debut 'Improgressive', the title of which probably sums up their approach to music which is very jazz oriented and based on improvisation. That theme has been very much carried through to the second album, and it is bassist Balázs Szendől who is very much in control. He not only composes the bulk of the material, but he and his custom-built basses are very much at the heart of everything that is going on. He has a very deft touch and it is not unusual for him to be following the melody or taking the lead while the keyboards are providing support to himself and the guitars. There is the feeling that the songs are improvised, or at least not fully structured and arranged at the time of recording: while there is freedom and space within the framework, there is also that of a lack of direction at times. That they can play is never in doubt, but while this works very well as background music it does not function as well as it might in the foreground, although there are some nice touches and "nuances" as it were. *#88, Jun 2006*

MING FIGHTERS
HOMETOWN

MING FIGHTERS
TAKE ME TO BED

Ming Fighters are one of those rarest things in rock music, namely a trio. Hailing from Cumbria they comprise John Dunnery (guitar, vocals – John's father Barry has played guitar for Ozzy and Violinski, and his uncle Frank was in It Bites and is currently playing for Robert Plant), Iain Taylor (drums, backing vocals) and Wayne Wilkinson (bass, vocals). It is of no surprise that It Bites are a heavy influence on the band, and what we have here is a commercial rock act with good songs and musicianship: it is all the very highest quality. The 'Hometown' demo starts with (surprisingly) "Hometown", which turned out for the most part to be a medium-paced gentle rocker, although the (very) short guitar solo totally transforms the song with some riffing bass. One thing that always strikes me about trios is that if they are good, they are generally excellent, but if they are bad then they are dire. I am glad to be able to report that in the case of Ming Fighters it is a case of the former and not of the latter. Second up is "Ugly As Hell", which switches between acoustic and belting rock with seeming ease; the bridge features some great harmony vocals. The last track, "Don't Say", is an acoustic ballad, but the harder edge to the vocals brings added meaning to the lyrics: this last features just John accompanying himself. The other demo, 'Take Me To Bed', starts with the title song, which is another good commercial rock number with harmony vocals. "Granddad (Takes The Biscuit)" has a completely different type of riff, and I found this song reminding me of Ezra (although without the keyboards), while "Lovechild" is far heavier yet still very commercial. Here is a young rock band that play good commercial songs, and they could go all the way. *#20, Oct 1993*

MINIMUM VITAL

LA SOURCE, HUIT CHANTS DE LUMIERE

Minimum Vital are a French band comprising Thierry Payssan (keyboards), Jean-Luc Payssan (guitars, vocals), Eric Rebeyrol (bass) and Christope Godet (drums). For this their third CD (the other two being 'Les Saisons' and 'Sarabandes') they have two guest vocalists, Antoine Guerber and Jacki Whitren. For my sins, I get sent a lot of prog material and it is indeed unusual for a CD to strike me as different, accessible and wonderful on the very first listen. This one did all that and more. The lyrics, what there are, are all in French apart from the second track "La Villa Emo". However, the vocals and music blend so well together that I feel that it is a bonus that the mind is not distracted by words but rather just revels in the sound. Keyboards are very much to the fore, but the guitar is used to great effect when needed. A lot of thought has gone into this album and I defy anyone expect the hardened metalhead to fall in love with at first listen.

"Danse Des Voeux" is the first of the eight songs, and it kicks off proceedings with multi-layered vocals and almost jazzy keyboards. The overall impression is one of lightness and enjoyment: this is no heads down let's all play senseless solos band, but rather one that wants to have fun! There are a few guitar breaks to liven proceedings but it is the vocals and keyboards that draw the attention. "La Villa Emo" must be of high quality to follow this and it is just that. Keyboards and guitar interplay to such an extent that although the vocals do not enter the fray until after four minutes have gone by, it just does not matter. Apart from the vocal style (which must be said is more melodic than Gary Chandler's) this sounds like Jadis at their very best. And I mean at their <u>very</u> best. "Les Mondes De Miranda" shows a different side of the band as the bass hardens and they get down to business. But what is this? Suddenly the guitar is acoustic and is being riffed mercilessly while the keyboards provide the melody. The singing is again of the highest order and in this song takes a far more prominent part, being one of the few to contain "proper" lyrics. Halfway through the guitar changes to electric and the chords power out, transforming a great song into an even better one.

The album is full of differing styles, and a sound that is reminiscent of Jadis, but even they do not play a piece of church music that would not be out of place in an abbey ("Ce Qui Soustienne"), well it might be when all the band join in after the initial vocals. As Musea is a French label I tend to be sent quite a few French releases, but I have yet to hear another as composed, interesting and so damned enjoyable. In fact, it is so good that it caused me no end of problems because instead of listening to loads of different CDs I found myself coming back to this one repeatedly. One that I will be playing a great deal. If you enjoy good music with an emphasis on singing and musicianship, then I cannot commend this forty-seven-minute-long album enough to you. It is superb.

#19, Aug 1993

MINIMUM VITAL
SARABANDES

Since writing the previous review, I have now heard from Minimum Vital themselves, who along with an impressive collection of reviews (mostly in French I hasten to add) sent me a copy of this their second CD. I am now even more impressed than I was before. Why? Well, this one is just so different from 'La Source', yet they are consecutive albums. The term "progressive" is rather over-used these days, and sometimes gets put onto a rock band just because they use keyboards, but that is not the case with Minimum Vital. Working backwards through albums is never the best way of doing things, but this CD is influenced by very different elements from those that affected 'La Source'. True, the musicianship is still of the very highest quality, but lyrics here are at a real premium with the album being almost totally instrumental. But unlike most instrumental albums here is one comprised of just great songs! No meandering pointless solos here, rather very carefully thought out and well-constructed pieces. Yet again, we are graced with eight tracks, but of varying styles. There is the powerful dynamic "Sarabande No. 1" which has so much emotion during the rock passages and contrasts within itself the light delicate passages featuring jazz guitar. Then there is "Porte Sue l'Ete" which is a solo acoustic guitar piece, drawing heavily on classical themes. There is just so much in this CD that it is a joy to play, each time I listen to it there appears to be more to be discovered. For some reason I have yet to fathom, I have not seen a review of Minimum Vital in any of the UK prog zines I receive, and that is nothing short of criminal. Minimum Vital are major players in the French prog scene and I would love to see them play live over here. If they are half as good on stage as they are on CD, then it must be awesome. Of the two, I think I would pick 'La Source', but that may be only because I have played it more. They are both superb and well worth discovering.

#19, Aug 1993

MINIMUM VITAL
ATLAS

When I opened the envelope, and saw what was inside, a huge smile crept across my face. It has been years since I last heard a Minimum Vital album, and it took no time at all for the cogs to click into place and remember what an awesome album 'La Source' was. It made a huge impression on me at the time, but that was a long time ago (#19!), what would Minimum Vital of today sound like? I deliberately did not put it anywhere near a CD player until I had the time to devote myself to it – I did not want to play just part of it, but to be able to concentrate. Minimum Vital used to sing totally in French, and this CD had just one song that was partly in English, so it was all about getting a feel about what was going on. There are two lead singers (one male, one female), drums, guitar, mandolin, keyboards and bass, this is a band that is often on the lighter side of prog rock, but there is a joy within the music. During "Louez Son Nom" there is a section of vocal nonsense, where the singers are accompanied only by a glockenspiel, which gives way to the guitar solo. This is music to get lost in, with elements of bands as diverse as Tull or Gentle Giant, yet there is a sheer beauty and pleasure within it that is rarely heard. There is only one thing that can be done when this album has finished, put it on again! I found myself playing this so much that I had to ban it from myself so that I could get on with listening to other albums. A delight from start to finish: you do not need to understand the lyrics to enjoy a great album. *#79, May 2004*

MINOKE?
TANESHINA
This is a mini-album from Japan, only twenty-eight minutes long. I did look on their web site to see what I could find about them, but as there is no English version, I did not get very far. Four musicians (bass, drums, saxophone, keyboards), they are moving within different styles of jazz and while some of it is a bit too far out for my taste, there are times when they lock together and produce music that is very good indeed. There is a definite understanding of the concept of less being more, and it is not unusual to find sections of songs where only one or two are playing, while the others just wait their turn to make an impact. It is an interesting album but as to whether it is worth attempting to get this from Japan I am not sure, but if you enjoy jazz with strong melody from keyboards and sax, then this is worth looking out for. *#76, Oct 2003*

MIOSÓTIS
O MONSTRO E A SEREIA
This is the debut album from this Portuguese band and they are throwing in just about everything that they can think of, from prog through a lot of avant garde up to RIO. The result is something that to my ears is quite confusing. They can be blasting away in a total cacophony one moment, then quite abruptly they can be into something that is far more delicate and emotional. It is a hard album to listen to and with the vocals not being in English this creates an extra barrier in this instance. It is certainly experimental and 'out there', but while there are certain sections of some songs that are enjoyable and intriguing, this is far more outweighed by music that in some cases is virtually unlistenable. This is for those who do not want their music to make much sense and want to challenge normal listening forms. *#86, Feb 2006*

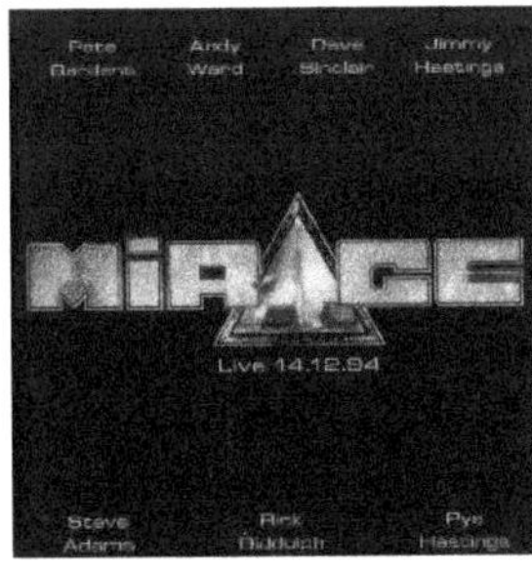

MIRAGE
LIVE 14:12:94
In 1992, Andy Ward watched Camel in concert, and while they were performing he realised that he missed playing music of which he had been an integral part. At the time, he had been working extensively with Richard Sinclair, and in live shows had included several Caravan songs, and then over the next eighteen months Andy started thinking about Peter Barden (also ex of

Camel) who now had a solo career in America. Andy's idea was to put together a band to play Camel, Caravan and Peter Barden material, and Peter readily agreed and brought in his guitarist Steve Adams. Andy enlisted bassist Rick Biddulph who he had worked with in Caravan of Dreams and the final pieces fell into place with ex-Caravan members Dave Sinclair and Jimmy and Pye Hastings. Their first ever gig was on 11th December 1994, and three nights later the show was recorded and is now available as a double CD. The album attempts to capture the very best of Camel and Caravan and works extremely well indeed. A dreamy and beautiful live performance has been captured as a band of consummate musicians goes through their paces. Anyone who is into either of the two bands, or just want to hear some wonderful songs being played brilliantly, must search this album out.
#31 Oct 1995

MR. GIL
ALONE
This is a band that has been put together by Collage guitarist Mirek Gil (the only other name I recognise is Collage bassist Piotr Mintay Witkowski). It certainly is a very different idea to what he has been pursuing before, as for the most part this is very laid back indeed. It is all very clever, but becomes rather bland, although "Set Me Free" livens up proceedings extremely well. It has a nicely put together booklet with lyrics in both English and Polish (they are sung in English), but I would expect nothing less from Ars Mundi. Whether it is worth pursuing this album from Poland for its music alone is another matter altogether.
#50, Aug 1998

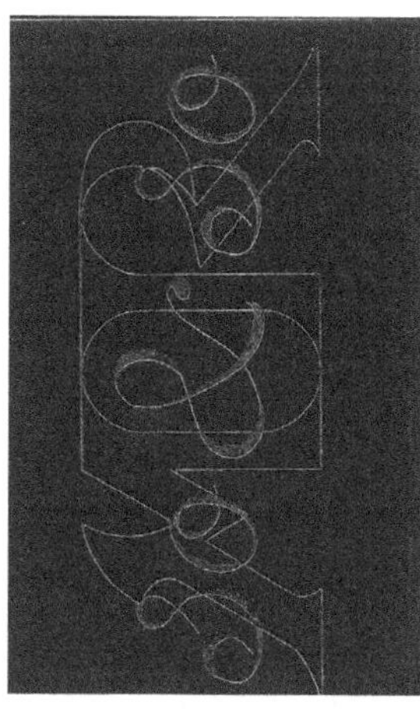

MR. SO & SO
THOUGHTS OF FEAR AND PRINCIPLE
Mr. So & So originate from St. Helens in Merseyside, and the guys all met up when attending Leigh College of Music in February 1991. The four-piece are Shaun McGowan (bass, vocals), Dave Foster (guitar), Kieran Twist (keyboards) and Leo Parr (percussion). Since their formation they have gigged extensively, particularly in the north west, and recorded this EP, which led to the interest of Pagan Media (home of Legend). Pagan signed them to record an album, which has just been completed, with mixing finished at the end of September and should be issued shortly. When that happens, this EP will be deleted, making it something of a collector's item. Not content with recording an album, they have returned to the studio and have recorded some songs that will hopefully see the light of day on a tape or flexi in the new year, combined with a song from the album. Apparently, the newer material is seeing a move to longer more epic-type pieces with a more Genesis or Yes feel than the material presently available, which is more Marillion or It Bites. So,

what about the EP I hear you ask? Well, it has already garnered some great reviews and it is not difficult to see why. It was produced and engineered by Steve Paine, and the sound is very good indeed. "But I'm Here" kicks off with some wonderful guitarwork laying the basis for a very commercial sound. Shaun has very clear vocals and still manages to play some very intricate bass. There is always the worry that the singer may only be a make-piece musician, but here all members work together at a very high level. Still you would expect that, as they have all been classically trained. "The Visitor" starts off with a far lighter feel, and the thought comes to mind again that the music is très commercial. It wouldn't be hard to imagine Mr. So & So making a dent in the mainstream charts: it is commercial enough for the normal pop lover who likes good songs well played, but at the same time intricate enough for the prog lover. All five songs are wonderful, but my favourite is probably "The Hypnotic" which is longer and features some great bass work. I am looking forward to 'Paraphernalia', which should be out by the time you read this: expect a full review next issue.
#15, Oct 1992

MR. SO & SO
PARAPHERNALIA
I was relieved when 'Paraphernalia' arrived last week. Steve had kindly sent me a preview tape some weeks ago, but as I have a CD player in the car I do most of my initial listening driving to and from work. Like the 'Thoughts of Fear And Principle' tape it is produced and engineered by Steve Paine, assisted by Jon Moreau (who of course also work together on Legend). Mr. So & So are a very young band, who have the musical ability and songwriting skills to go a long way. The album starts with "So Near So Far", which has very upfront bass and keyboards: indeed, Dave spends quite a long time waiting to bring his guitar into play. Shaun is a bassist of exceptional skill, and the upfront approach gives the band a completely different outlook and sound from any of the other prog bands around. Extremely accessible, even commercial, Mr. So & So's own peculiar blend of rock and prog work, brilliantly. "The Hypnotic" is one of the two songs that survives from the previous tape and is far harder than the previous song with a much more pronounced prog feel and not nearly as much commercialism. "Again" has a gentler style with acoustic guitars and soaring keyboards: gradually the song builds, layer upon layer, mellowing and soothing the soul. "Stand Tall" is back to a bass-led rock song that contains loads of keyboards. There is wonderfully restrained guitar from Dave, which exemplifies the group feel and sound. "The Sea" is the other survivor from the tape, again a slow number with loads of emotion and atmosphere. "It's Irrelevant" finally lets Dave out of the cage, as the song belts along, riding on the twin chargers of guitar and bass with the drums and keyboards hanging in there for all they are worth. "Mr. So & So" is the only instrumental on the album, with loads of emotion. The album closes with "Circus" which is the longest and by far the best song on the album, and apparently, this is most in keeping with what the band are writing at present. A song of parts, it starts with the keyboards giving way to some heavy guitar and Shaun straining to make his voice heard. The chorus has a great hook, which will be loved by all, that in turn leads to a stranger, certainly different, musical and lyrical passage. It is in total contrast to the

previous rock theme and does nothing to prepare the listener for the final rock passage to follow. There you have it, an album to be proud of. When I spoke to Dave he said that since the album had been released earlier in the week he hadn't stopped smiling, and I can't say I blame him.
#16, Dec 1992

MR. SO & SO
COMPENDIUM

Long-time readers of Feedback will already be familiar with some of the music of Mr. So & So care of the flexi that went out a while ago. An extremely technically impressive band, they originally met at Leigh College of Music and this is their second album. They are a four-piece, with bassist Shaun McGowan providing vocals, and it is probably his bass playing that sets the band apart from their contemporaries as it is very intricate and complex. This gives the band a different structure to many of the others as they are building songs around the bass as opposed to keyboards or guitar. That is not to say that the others are prepared to take a back seat, as Dave's brilliant guitarwork proves. He seems to have found a volume control for this album and is much more in your face. So, the guys are great musicians (Leon is currently studying for a degree in percussion while Kieran is no mean slouch when it comes to keyboards either), but what about the songs? There are eight here (one of which, "The Visitor" is from their debut tape 'Thoughts Of Fear and Principle') and they are all killers. Commercial they are, with great vocals and musical hooks. In fact, reviewing has been a nightmare as this CD has been hogging the player. Favourite track is "Tick-A-Box", which starts with some wonderful bass runs, and twists and turns in all manner of ways. It has some restrained parts that are in total contrast to the bedlam that also ensues. Mr. So & So and Cyclops have a real winner on their hands here. It is an album that appeals right across the board, not only to the progger but also to anyone who likes good rock music.
#28, Apr 1995

MR. SO & SO
THE OVERLAP

By my reckoning this album is at least a year overdue, but it is here now, at long last. It should have been out in time for the So & So's tour with Marillion last year, which went very well, but it was not to be. Those with long memories may remember a flexi being given away with Feedback some years ago featuring the lads, which was when they were signed to Pagan. They have since released an album on Cyclops before signing to Steve Rothery's Dorian Music label. In all that time, there has only been one change of personnel, the addition of Charlotte Evans on backing vocals – she does not sing on every song, but it gives the band an extra string to their bow. As always, the So & So's have a different sound to their music, as they are bass-driven as opposed to heading out from either the keyboards or guitar. That is not to say that they are backwards when it comes to riff mongering, just that they do it in as different fashion to anyone else. This has been one of their problems as they are not heavy enough to be a technical rock band, but they have too much guitar to be a prog band. Another problem is that they are too damn young! They are still in their early twenties, and here they are on their third album! More seasoned proggers have been heard to compliment the band on their technical ability through gritted teeth, as seeing them on stage makes them feel very old indeed.

Although this is a new release, in many ways it is like an old friend to me as I heard many of these songs from the demos that the band had sent me over the last couple of years. Favourite song is “Salamander”, which is also probably the heaviest song on the album. Take my word for it that it is track six, because there has been an almighty cock-up in the track listing which will be a pain in the ass for the newcomer to this music. If ever there was a weak point in the band it was probably Shaun’s vocals, but he seems to have gained a great deal in confidence and the addition of Charlotte enables him not to strain for the high notes that he was never going to reach. I must admit to missing Steve Paine’s touch at the production (which has been handled this time by Mike Stobbie), but hopefully this album will see the So & So’s making the breakthrough they so richly deserve. With Steve Rothery taking them under his wing and providing a bit of guitar here and there, it is possible that Marillion fans will search this out and I am sure that if you hear them you will love them. Nuff said.
#50, Aug 1998

MIST SEASON
MIST SEASON
Mist Season was formed in 2004, in Hämeenlinna (Finland) with a desire to play music that included “a spectrum of emotional and dynamic elements, bordering between progressive rock and fusion”. Even before putting the CD into the player I found that I was impressed, as this is a self-released instrumental album, but the booklet is twenty pages long, with each song represented by a photograph and a couple of lines saying what the music represents. The saxophone is as important an instrument as the guitar and keyboards, all either taking their solos or working together to drive the melodies forward. This is jazz combined with prog, but while this is a very easy album to listen to it could never be called easy listening. I think it would be fair in some ways to describe this as jazz lite, but that term never brings home the depth of melody and passion there is available within this album. It is something that can be enjoyed on first hearing, at least that was the case with me, but the more that it is played then the more the listener will get out of it. They liken their music to Camel, Phil Miller, Pekka Pohjola, Yellowjackets, Koinonia, Passport and Pat Metheny Group and while I must confess my ignorance of a couple of these I can understand why they mention Camel as although to my ears they sound nothing like them there is a very similar feel and styling to the music. If you go to the site, you can find more about the band and listen to some more of what is a very interesting album indeed.
#88, Jun 2006

MIZUKAGAMI
MIZUKAGAMI

This intriguing album from Japan has already been gaining many favourable reviews on the web. That Musea has released it in Europe, as well as Poseidon in their native Japan, means that it is relatively easy to get hold of. This is an important fact and although this album is sung in Japanese, it is something that all discerning progheads are going to want to have in their collection. Like many Japanese prog albums, there are some very dreamy and reflective passages, but what makes this album stand out are not only the clear pure (and very Japanese) vocals of female lead singer Tanaami Futaba, but also the way that they are attempting to bring together some traditional music with very Western prog. They also are not afraid to let rip and give the instruments a good workout, something that makes them stand out from many others. This is symphonic prog with a heavy use of synths, but while they may be looking to the Seventies and Jethro Tull, ELP and King Crimson, there are also elements of more modern bands such as IQ. The quiet and pleasant passages are more than offset by the complicated ones that follow, so that even though it is not possible to understand the words there is more than enough going on to make this an interesting and varied listen. *#78, Apr 2004*

MOLCA
SUPER ETHNIC FLAVOR

On the rear of this 2004 album they list the instruments used but when they get to thirty-four they just put 'etc.' For example, they use both Greek and Irish bouzoukis; I was not aware there was a difference! There are also many instruments that I have not heard of, such as erhu and charango, or a caxixi and a pandeiro. This Japanese band are trying to do exactly what they say on the album title, fuse together many different ethnic styles. However, within all this the musical thread has got lost, and there is the impression that whatever musical ideal was there at the beginning has been misplaced as they try to find more instruments to use. Bits of certain songs are quite good, but there are just so many differing styles being used that it all becomes just too much and instead of enjoying what they are doing, the listener (or at least me) can't take it all in and it jars. They may have achieved the goal of playing many instruments, but as for fusing music of different ethnic origins together that is another matter altogether. *#86, Feb 2006*

FRANCIS MONKMAN
21ST CENTURY BLUES

Francis Monkman first rose to fame as keyboard player and guitarist in Curved Air and was also in Sky as well as guesting on numerous albums. This is, I think, a new album but unfortunately, there is no information in the booklet at all, and although it is mentioned within the press release that Florian Pilkinton-Miksa (also of Curved Air) makes an appearance there is no indication of

that at all. Some of the music is okay, mixing prog with a rockier edge but the vocals have all been 'treated' and get very wearing after a very short period. Not one I will be playing again.
#65, Dec 2001

MONTEFELTRO
IL TEMPO DI FAR LA FANTASIA
Montefeltro are Piergiorgio Ambrosi (keyboards) and Attilio Virgilio (vocals, guitar), with assorted guest musicians, and as all the lyrics are Italian, and it was recorded in Rome, I have assumed that they are from Italy (although anyone with superior knowledge might be able to prove me wrong). The sound is quite different to anyone else; very light, but at the same time there is a lot of depth to it. At times, they sound like a mix of Yes and Floyd, certainly on the over-indulgent "Canto" which clocks in at over twenty-two minutes long. The music is very gentle and totally lacks aggression and energy, challenging the listener to just sit back and relax to the soothing sounds. Again, great musicianship, but a lot of it just swept right over me. For any Seventies prog lover, then you could do a lot worse than try this out.
#17, Mar 1993

MOON SAFARI
A DOORWAY TO SUMMER
There are those times, far too few and rare, that an album crosses my path that makes me want to grab everyone by the ear and say, "Listen to this! You must get it!" That is indeed the case with the debut album by Swedish band Moon Safari. They sent a rough demo to Tomas Bodin of The Flower Kings and he soon agreed to produce them, as he obviously heard the promise in what they were doing, as have I. This is progressive music that is far from the norm, a band that has mixed the best bits of Genesis and Barclay James Harvest with some more unlikely sources to create something that is accessible, lush and beautiful: in many ways, compelling and essential. The first thing that struck me when I put this on was not the Jadis style guitar or the wonderful tunes and musicianship, but the vocals. There are harmonies on here to die for, and I kept trying to think what it reminded me of. Not Yes, nor Gentle Giant, and certainly not Spock's Beard, and then suddenly the answer hit me: it was The Carpenters. It may be hard to believe but they have managed to produce layered and highly arranged vocals that are reminiscent of Karen and Richard and have moved them flawlessly into the prog environment. After I was over that shock I kept listening intently and realised that there were also elements of Elton John's arrangements from the Seventies – not to say that they sound like him, nothing could be further from the truth, but they do have similarities. If that is not enough to whet your appetite, then there is also a track that is more than twenty-four minutes long that does all that an epic should. This is an album I would use to get someone interested in prog who would normally stay well away from the genre, as it just has so much going for it. All the

songs are great, with plenty of hooks and catchy moments but there is still enough going on to more than satisfy the proghead. This is an incredible piece of work and one that I highly recommend indeed. I fell in love with it the first time I played it and the obsession has just grown and grown. Superb. The one thing I have yet to work out is why a major label hasn't picked this up yet!!??
#87, Apr 2006

MORIA FALLS
THE LONG GOODBYE

Moria Falls have been threatening this CD for some time now, and it has finally seen the light of the day on their own label, which they also hope to be able to use to highlight other UK talent. As one would expect from an album recorded at Thin Ice under the watchful ears of Messer's Nolan and Groom, the production is top notch while Clive also assists on backing vocals (and stands out a mile) while that nice keyboard player from IQ, Mr. Orford, adds some delicate flute. So, they are obviously liked by some of the most important musicians around (and not just because drummer Richard Jordan is one of those reprobates behind Silhobbit), but is it any good? At times, very atmospheric, almost dreamlike, it manages to bring keyboards and guitar together very well. The vocals are good and the melodies interesting and it would be a crime to say only that there is nothing bad about it. Yes, I enjoyed playing it and listening to it, but forking out for it might be another bet altogether. There is a lot of prog coming through at present, and while this is to be encouraged, it means that some is not as high quality as it might be. Moria Falls do not fall into the second-rate category but do not make it into the premier league either. A good CD, but I hope that the next will be better.
#33, Feb 1996

MORIA FALLS
EMBRACE

I must have upset someone, as though Moria Falls were more than happy enough to send me their debut album I heard no more after I wrote about it, so it is to Artur in Poland that I should thank for providing me with this. Yet again Clive Nolan and Karl Groom are heavily involved in the production side (with Clive also providing some backing vocals – he is not credited but can easily be heard). Of course, Clive owes a big favour to drummer Richard Jordan who in a previous incarnation was one of the brains behind Silhobbit and introduced Clive to Mick Pointer. The rest is history… So, not content with setting Arena on the world, Moria Falls are back with their second album, and is it any good? Um, yes, but with reservations. That they know what they are about is not in dispute here, nor the fact that they can write and play some good tunes, but rather that in many ways they appear to be looking for an identity that they can call their own. They open with "Tearing At The Heartstrings" which is damn fine but sounds as if it could have been released by Shadowland. "Crimes of Passion", although not sounding like Jadis, has some Chandler-

like guitar and I soon found myself playing the "Who does that sound like?" game. I think a proghead will find that there is plenty on here to enjoy, but it might help if they have little knowledge of the current underground scene as then they will probably like it better. Not a bad album by any means, but just not for me lads, sorry.
#49, May 1998

NEAL MORSE
NEAL MORSE
I know I keep saying this, but I truly and honestly believe that Spock's Beard are the best band to have come out of the States in the last ten years, and having seen them now play live, I am convinced that very soon they are going to be major players. So, having just released yet another album by the full band, lead singer (and multi-instrumentalist) Neal Morse is back with a more songs-based solo album. Apart from SB drummer (and harmony vocalist) Nick D'Virgilio who plays drums on all tracks (apart from opener "Living Out Loud" where Neal shows he can do that as well), Neal played all the instruments, sang all the vocals, wrote all the songs, and engineered and produced it. Not surprisingly, there are some very distinctive SB styles on show. Another way of saying that would be to say that as SB is a truly progressive band, mixing and melding all styles, why should the leader's album be any different? This is a masterpiece of song writing and storytelling; with Neal sometimes playing the role of the singer songwriter with just an acoustic guitar, while at others it is a full-blown band playing to the crowd. My own favourite (currently) is "Lost Cause" which twists and turns and displays more musical skill, style and hooks in five minutes than most bands achieve in a lifetime. Oh, shit, the whole album is just brilliant. It is a must purchase, one that you just must have. If you have ever heard Spock's Beard, then you are already fans. If you have yet to hear them, then get this, and then get all of theirs. I just can't say this enough times, this is brilliant!!!!!!!!!!!!!!!!!
#56, Jan 2000

NEAL MORSE
TESTIMONY
I may only be reviewing one album this issue, but what an album it is. When Neal made the decision that due to his religious beliefs he had to leave Spock's Beard there were many that were absolutely gutted at the decision, myself included. What did this mean both to the band that remained and to Neal himself? Spock's Beard have answered that with 'Feel Euphoria', which I have enjoyed immensely, but check out the live review to gauge some other thoughts. But what was Neal going to do? This is his third solo album, and while his second is still one that I play a great deal it is not one that I would overtly term 'progressive'. Then I discovered that the new album was going to be a double disc that was autobiographical in nature, telling Neal's story and how he found Christ and became a Christian. I was not sure how I was going to feel about being preached at for over two

hours, and musically how was this going to come across? Well, Spock's Beard may have become heavier without Neal, but Neal has not changed tack but rather has buried himself further into his influences. This is the logical musical follow-up to 'Snow', and any fan of that album (me sir!) will fall in love with this even more.

Neal has been joined by Mike Portnoy and Kerry Livgren and countless others to produce an album that is not only Spock's Beard through and through but is opening the music up to even more influences and experimentations. This album is more symphonic than previously, and even bombastic, with a large use of strings, and anyone that can put in a country song and have it make total sense within the overall concept must be doing something right. The move to using 'proper' strings instead of synthesised has given the music a more dynamic edge, and Neal is obviously happy with what he is producing, and the songs are packed full of emotion. This is his story, one that he lived through and is living again with the telling. The one moan I have with the promotional copy is that it does not contain the lyrics, and they have yet to be posted on Neal's site. Musically many themes are returned to, which gives the album shape and form, while the lyrics are pushing through the story and message. Yes, it is a testimony, yes, it is very much an overtly Christian album, and if you are anti-religious then I would say that you probably will not enjoy this very much. But if you have an open mind or are a Christian then this is an album for you. I used to listen to a great deal of White Metal and Christian music when I lived at home years ago, as my sister used to play it, but this is far removed from anything I used to listen to back then. Rock, jazz (with some blasting horns), country, classical, Beatles-style pop, this has had everything thrown into it and then some – Spock's Beard has been expanded.

Neal has exorcised the demons and has managed to convey a very personal message in an exciting and dramatic way that will leave all SB fans hungry for more. This is much more of a new beginning than a continuation of his previous solo career. He has taken his music into a new area, and with Spock's Beard moving in their own direction there are two kids on the block who are vying for attention. I have been an SB fan since I first heard 'The Light' and I am sure that I always will, but I for one will now always be looking primarily to see what Neal is doing. I have listened to literally hundreds of albums this year. This is my number one. Truly superb.
#77, Dec 2003

NEAL MORSE
ONE
Only a single CD this time (although it is also available with a bonus containing some covers), but the latest release from Neal Morse is again a concept album this time telling the story of the lost son. God and man were together, man left and then became unhappy until God sent his Son to lead mankind back to Him. Neal again played most of the instruments, although he was joined on the recording by Mike Portnoy and bassist Randy George (both of whom played with him on the 'Testimony' tour) and a string section. Musically this is following on from 'Testimony', as indeed that followed on from 'Snow'

so that anyone who wants to hear new music in a similar vein to that of classic Beard should turn to Neal as the solo artist as opposed to Spock's Beard who have taken a different direction. Although at one time I would never have imagined Neal working with a different drummer to Nick D'Virgilio, I now can't think of him being without Mike Portnoy. Nick is one of the best drummers in the business, but Mike is primarily a rock drummer (although very technical in his approach) and he adds an extra depth and power that previously was missing. When these guys want to blast out (just listen to the awesome introduction to "Author Of Confusion", which also features some of his multi-tracked vocals that he is known for) then they do so with impunity. Yet at the same time this is music that is picking up as many references from The Beatles as it is from Led Zeppelin and touching every prog base one can imagine from Genesis through to King Crimson.

I am not sure if it is better than 'Testimony', but it is quite a bit shorter (I mean, it's under eighty minutes long!), but I know that it is one of the best prog albums from the States that one is likely to hear this year, and I can't wait until he is back on tour. This is yet another album that is going to cement his reputation as an incredible songwriter and performer
#82, Jan 2005

NEAL MORSE
?
Neal is back with his third solo album since leaving Spock's Beard, and surprise surprise it is another concept. That makes four in a row including 'Snow', but it is a genre that seems very suited to his writing style. Three minutes just is not long enough to get his ideas across, which in this case is about the temple of the living god, and I for one am certainly not complaining. I love all that he has done to date, and this album is yet another in the 'must have' releases as he not only stretches himself, but also brings in more guests this time which adds to the album as a whole. Of course, Mike Portnoy and Randy George are here, but Neal no longer feels that he must provide all the rest of the main instrumentation himself so as well as having guests on cello, bagpipes (of course) etc. he has brought in some 'names'. Dream Theater keyboardist Jordan Rudess is helping, as is saxophonist Mark Leniger, and most interestingly three guitarists. It will be a welcome surprise to many to hear Steve Hackett, while the appearance of Roine Stolt from The Flower Kings is perhaps more expected given that they played together in Transatlantic. What must be the biggest surprise of all is the appearance of Neal's brother, Alan. When I played this for the first time I was convinced that I recognised his playing, but thought that it had to be someone copying the style and I was astounded to find out that it actually was him – this is the first time that a member of Spock's Beard has played with Neal since his departure, and when I interviewed Alan a while ago I said that if the Genesis analogy was right he would be the next one to leave. Is this the start?

Certainly, this is more exciting that what has been happening in the SB camp, with Neal appearing to have endless imagination when it comes to providing new types of songs

and the music ranges from almost lounge all the way to metal with every variation of rock possible in between. It has Neal stamped all over it, so if you do not like his other material you will hate this, but this is probably his most commercial yet with some great singalong choruses. Given the opportunity this would probably live on my player – it is awesome.
#85, Nov 2005

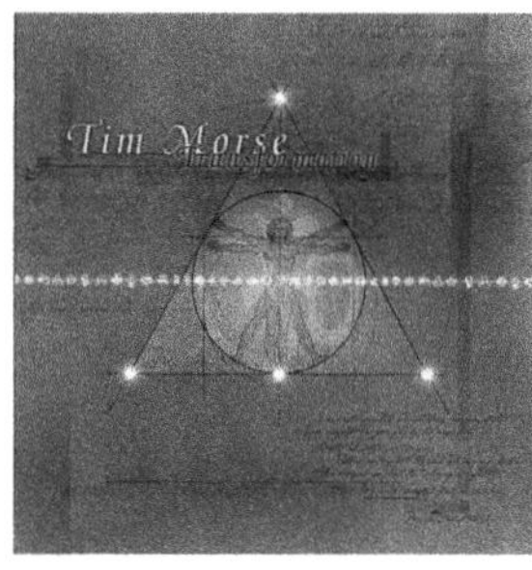

TIM MORSE
TRANSFORMATION
I do not believe that Tim is a relation to Neal, but again we have a Morse who is producing exciting and interesting prog music. Tim may be better known to some as an author of a best-selling book on Yes, so it is probably not surprising that there are a few Yes nods, but these are rare. This is all about the bringing together of Tim (mostly keyboards, plus some lead vocals and guitar) with Mark Dean (all other instruments) and then adding in the vocals of Richie Zeller. This is very much a prog album, with layers of keyboards and piano, but at the same time, it is also inherently a melodic rock album with plenty of guitar. It may be Tim's name above the door, but this is very much a group sound and not a keyboard workout. They have taken some Floyd, some Hackett, even some Kansas, that little bit of Yes, and thrown it all together and boy does it work. This is extremely polished, with enough time changes and little bits and pieces in the mix that brings a smile to the face. Richie appears to be approaching his vocals much more from a rock area than 'normal' prog (whatever that is), which gives the band a different flavour – it is reminiscent in some ways of the approach of Damian Wilson, but these vocals are much earthier, with more balls. This is one that progheads and even melodic rock lovers will not want to miss.
#86, Feb 2006

MORSOF
HEAP
Underneath the name on the album cover are the words Morning Machine And Soft Musume, so it is no surprise that this album is very, very much influenced by Soft Machine. They are a trio comprising Mikio Fukushima (guitars), Norifumi Uchida (bass) and Morihide Sawada (drums), but with lots of guests to keep the brass wailing and swirling. I like Soft Machine and tried hard to get on with this one but found that in many places although the guys at the front are trying to drive the music along, those at the back are so laid back that they are almost asleep, taking the audience with them. This is an album only for those into improvisational jazz. That they can all play is never in doubt. Whether anyone wants to listen to it is another matter altogether....
#78, Apr 2004

MOSCOW RILEY
EAT THE AMMUNITION

Although I did not think a lot of Summer Indoors' debut album, I was impressed with the follow-up 'Songs In The Key Of H', and thought it was a shame when I heard that they had split up. Then out of the blue comes the debut album from Moscow Riley, which features both Chris Dempsey (bass, vocals) and Andy Forest (keyboards) from that band. They are joined by Mark Starr (drums) and John Kirby (guitar), and despite the hype of the press release is still fun to listen to. It says here that this "is an album full of musical innovation and lyrical insight which will delight fans who are tired of the same old progressive clichés" and "it is a breath of fresh air, quite unlike any other progressive album ever released". I mean, I was out to destroy this even before I put it on! Well, while I may not fully agree with all the sentiments expressed above, I do have to say that this is a fun album with a helluva lot going for it. This is more rock progressive than progressive rock, and fair bounces along. Mike Starr is one, and he seems to give the band more depth by filling the sound which allows Chris to virtually provide a second lead at times, instead of having to keep the beat nailed down. The use of keyboard effects is done very well, but it is on the singing and melody front that Moscow Riley is winning the war. I mean, fancy calling an over the top powering number "Fluffy White Cloud"!!! If you like your prog to be fun, and your guitars to be big and meaty, then this is right up your alley. *#49, May 1998*

MOSTLY AUTUMN
FOR ALL WE SHARED..

MOSTLY AUTUMN
THE SPIRIT OF AUTUMN PAST

Cyclops label boss Malcolm Parker and I know that although we both enjoy progressive rock; we do not always share the same opinion as to what is good and what is not. It has been a long time since he started telling me that Mostly Autumn were one of the best bands around, but it took me ages to get any CDs out of him as they were doing so well. So, it was with some trepidation that I put their debut album on the player, and upon looking in the booklet noticed that there were eight people in the band! There are not many bands on Cyclops that boast a violinist and someone playing low and high whistles.

First up is "Nowhere To Hide (Close My Eyes)", which has an introduction of harmony vocals. This is followed by gentle instrumentation which leads into a rock number which sounds just like latter day Horslips, very definitely a good start. They use mostly twin harmony vocals, although Bryan's voice is more powerful than Heather's. Nevertheless, they are more than just a Celtic rock band. "The Last Climb" is nothing but pure Floyd, from 'Wish You Were Here' era, while "Folklore" shows that Bob Faulds would be quite prepared to have a battle with Ric Sanders: much of the music is a melting pot, as the band brings together many styles. Malcolm describes them as Celtic Rock meeting Pink

Floyd and that is probably as good a description as any, although it does not do them justice. What it does mean is that they have managed to capture a sound that is going to appeal to a great many listeners.

The 1998 album was followed a year later by the second (which must mean another is due soon). There was a slight line-up change in the meantime, with a new drummer and whistle player, but the music is as strong as ever. Heather's vocals are more to the fore this time, although the harmonies still play an important role. During opener "Winter Mountain", the mood changes dramatically and her voice shines high above Bryan's, very much like Maddy Prior. In "Evergreen", her vocals carry the song, as the accompaniment is minimal and atmospheric. This use of atmosphere is best demonstrated in closing number "The Gap Is Too Wide". The tension very slowly mounts with Heather's vocals giving way to a stunning chorus. As it mounts even further, Bryan provides a soaring Dave Gilmour style guitar solo. The impression on hearing it for the first time is that the song will fade out, but that is not the case as Iona musician Troy Donockley makes a guest appearance on Uileann Pipes to take over from Bryan. Two wonderful albums that are truly 'progressive' as they mix together many styles in a way to make them sounding fresh and vibrant. Essential purchases if you enjoy folk/prog/high quality music.

#59, July 2000

MOSTLY AUTUMN

THE LAST BRIGHT LIGHT

Already on their third album, Mostly Autumn are the brightest British light in Cyclops' firmament, and on the evidence of this there is no chance of it dimming at the moment. Mostly Autumn bring in Celtic elements and mix them with some progressive undertones, so that the songs stand very much in their own right. Add to that the strong vocals of Bryan Josh and Heather Findlay and this is a band to be much admired. Sometimes, such as "We Come and We Go" they sound almost Floydian yet on others (such as "The Dark Before The Dawn") they bring in the power of Horslips in full flight. By the way, the intro to that last number sounds very like Holst's "Mars" but is not credited.... It is an album that has beauty and delicacy ("Hollow"), or power and passion. They have been touring with Blackmore's Night and the added exposure can only do them good. This album will see them move on from being the Classic Rock Society's Best New Band; it has many layers that only become apparent when played many times, but even on first hearing it is an album to be savoured.

#62, May 2001

MOSTLY AUTUMN
PASSENGERS

'Passengers' is the first album that I have heard since they left Cyclops, and I was intrigued to see how they had changed in the intervening time. Anyone who reads the music press cannot have failed to see all the adverts proclaiming them as the new Pink Floyd, but that did not fit with my memory of the band. I recall them being much more folky than that and prior to putting this on I read the credits. Sure, each member of the band (there are seven of them) all play 'normal' rock instruments. But hang on, what is a bodhran doing there? Then I checked the guests and found that not only was there a guest cellist but also Troy Donockley was involved (low whistles, penny whistles, uileann pipes and bouzouki) as was Fairport's very own Chris Leslie on violin. Sounds a bit more folk than rock to me, and when I saw that Damian Wilson (Rick Wakeman, Threshold, Landmarq etc.) was providing backing vocals I was even more impressed. But what does it sound like? "Something In Between" has a piano introduction, then Bryan Josh and Heather Findlay lead the band in an almost Fleetwood Mac style number. Their voices work well together, and there is a real feeling of restraint as the shadows darken and the menace increases - this is not Floyd, but a very different beast altogether. "Pure White Light" is next up, and a solo riffing guitar does not give an indication of what is to follow. The first verse has Bryan almost growling the vocals, with just a drum beat to accompany the guitar – but when it comes to the bridge the Floyd comparisons all start to make sense, as for a few bars the listener has been transported back thirty-five years, then just as suddenly the bright and breezy chorus sweeps away all the has gone before. I defy any proghead to play the first two songs on this album and then not want to play the rest – this is a great start and the quality does not let up from here on in. Heather seems to have a more prominent role than I remember, and her voice works extremely well both solo and with Bryan's or Angela's, giving the band a strong 'focal' point. The music has great depth, and the band are equally adept playing music with a folk root or prog, even rock. For the introduction to the title number, it is just Heather and a piano with an acoustic guitar. As the song progresses it gets more and more powerful, not going over the top but building into something special. It may have been a long time since I last heard Mostly Autumn, but I am extremely glad that I have renewed my acquaintance – just superb.
#79, May 2004

MUSIC STATION
SHAPING

After hearing Nelko's album I just could not wait to start working my way through the extensive package of UBP artists that I had been sent. 'Shaping' is the debut album from yet another Bulgarian band, and the delicate piano introduction of the three-sectioned title track did make me wonder what was going to happen. The themes in this are repeated, discarded and then returned to and it is a lulling introduction into the album. As the band all come in for the prog metal take on the second section, the themes are repeated firstly on keyboards then on electric guitars. All in all, a

great way to start an album. They are not always as heavy as this, sometimes they are even more rocky as the introduction to "Home" shows that in many ways here is a frustrated hard rock band with the keyboards not making as much of an impact as they might. They can be more reflective, and little touches such as using a fretless bass and an acoustic guitar shows that they have thought about what they are doing, and it certainly does not come across as a debut album. All the lyrics are in English and Pavlin Manev has a strong and passionate voice that at times comes across as very like Michael Sadler. This is an interesting album that shows a lot of promise with some of the songs like "Past" being almost commercial, and more in the melodic rock mould that I would have imagined from hearing the first few numbers.
#84, July 2005

MUSICAL WITCHCRAFT
UTOPIA

This is the second album from Musical Witchcraft, but this time it is very much a group album whereas the first was basically a solo album from Kollár Attila who is flautist with Solaris. It is mostly instrumental, with vocals only on two numbers, and while it is being pushed as a prog album it has at least as much in common with folk, and sometimes getting quite close to New Age. The album initially started life as flute-acoustic guitar compositions and although the music has then been arranged and expanded upon, this is still the basis. The flute is often the lead instrument, as would be expected, and is constant throughout the album as the complete band does not play on every song, with the line-up changing as required. Sometimes the flute plays against a violin, and there is an interesting passage on one number where he is playing against a bassoon, which must be said does not happen very often in prog music. That is not to say that it is an acoustic album throughout and that the flute is always at the forefront, as there are times when the electric guitar takes control. Overall this is interesting, and while not as powerful as some, is still fun to listen to.
#72, Feb 2003

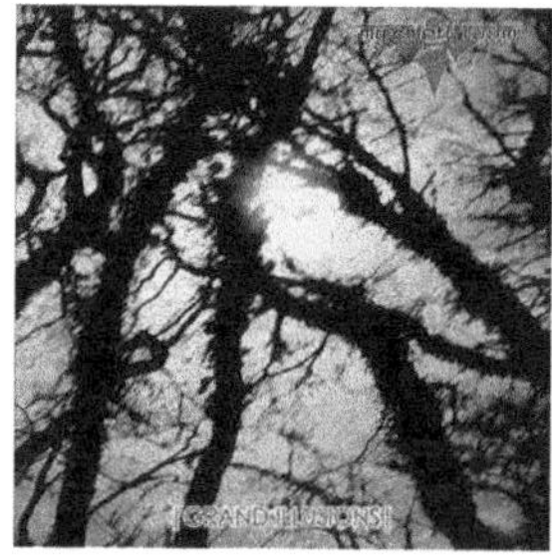

MY EMPTY ROOM
GRAND ILLUSIONS

My Empty Room are a Danish prog band, and this is their debut album. Only four songs, at just over forty minutes long, my initial reaction was that this is quite a short album until I put it into perspective and remembered that the reason that C90 cassette tapes sold so well was because you could fit an album on each side. The trio kick the album off with "Blind" which shows them almost in a prog metal light, but they are never that heavy although there are certain sections that do show the influences of Dream Theater and Chain among others. Niels Vejylt is a strong rock guitarist and although he can shred away, he does keep these speed influences under control for the most part. Jesper Nielsen (guitar, keyboards) has a good voice while Jakob Vand (drums, keyboards) keeps it

locked down. I am not sure how they perform live, but they come across well in the studio. This is music that at times reminds me of a heavy Galahad, with some elements of Pallas, but although they are a prog band, they are also a straight-ahead rock band as well and Queensrÿche also get a look in. For a self-produced debut this is a strong album, and with all the lyrics in English both words and music are very accessible. It may not be driving forward any progressive boundaries, but it is a fine listen.
#85, Nov 2005

MYSTER KAH
FRESQ
This is a concept album about the end of the world, but I do not know if this is a debut by Myster Kah or even which country they come from (although their currently under construction web site does have a French address). What I can say about the band is that they are a trio with Xavier Richard providing drums, Alec Hudson guitar, bass and backing vocals, and Yleah White on lead vocals, keyboards and whistles. The main influences appear to be Legend and IQ, although there are also some long instrumental passages which seem to owe more to Steve Vai. It is a very powerful album, and while it has quite a Seventies feel to the whole thing, there are some very strong passages that lift it out of the norm. The booklet contains cartoon-style artwork that goes with the storyline and is well-presented. I know that generally Malcolm is not keen on female vocalists so the very fact that he has signed the band is quite a statement about the album and it is one that I have enjoyed immensely. Most of the songs are between seven and eight minutes long which allows the band to build musical themes and in Yleah they have a very fine singer indeed.
#69, Aug 2002

MYSTERY
THEATRE OF THE MIND

MYSTERY
DESTINY?
Mystery is a Canadian Progressive band, one of the very few that I have heard over here, and the first of these albums is a reissue of their second, which was originally released in 1996. It is divided into two sections, "The Reality" and "The Dream", and the first of these commences with the title track, which is a rocky number. Vocalist Gary Savoie comes across in a similar fashion to Steve Perry from Journey, but overall the song probably sounds more like Styx. The next two numbers are ballads that are tastefully done, and there are quite a lot of slower more atmospheric numbers on the album than might have been imagined from the first song. The best song is "Black Roses", which moves from gentle acoustic melodies led by a flute to Kansas-style rock. Gary is a definite find, with the whole band working together to provide a very fluid sound. An interesting mix of gentle sweeping ballads and AOR with prog also making its' presence felt.

'Destiny?' is the newie and shows a band that has moved on from the previous record. While there is still large concentration on tuneful melodies and softer passages, they have also turned up the guitars quite a bit. While using electric guitars in a far more forceful manner they have also increased the use of fretless bass, which adds a different air to the proceedings. Gary is still in as good voice as before and there are two long songs in which he and the band can show off. The first, "Queen of Varja Space" starts off gently enough, but that is deceiving, while closing song "Shadow Of The Lake" (which is nearly fifteen minutes long) allows Michel to start with riffs and slow it down, instead of the other way around. Overall these are two high-class albums that will definitely appeal to all those interested in an AOR/Prog mix.
#50, Aug 1998

MYSTERY
AT THE DAWN OF A NEW MILLENNIUM

Mystery are one of the top progressive bands to come out of Canada, and with the departure of their vocalist Gary Savoie they have decided to release a retrospective. That is not to say that the band is calling it a day, as they have a new vocalist in Benoît David and will be releasing a new album before the end of the year. This is a closing of the first chapter and this album includes tracks from not only 'Theatre Of The Mind' and 'Destiny?' (both of which I have reviewed in the past), but also from their debut mini-CD 'Mystery' which I had not heard before. Mystery is very much the baby of guitarist, songwriter, producer Michel St-Père, and that these songs are played by three different line-ups with only Michel and Gary featuring on all tracks yet sounding as if they are from the same session, is a tribute to him. Sometimes a bit Floydian, sometimes a bit Kansas, this is a very polished progressive sound which will be of interest to all those into structured music whether they like this genre or not.
#58, May 2000

MYTHOLOGIC
STANDING IN STILLNESS

Mythologic came into being due to the desire of guitarist Steve Matustik (Andeavour) and drummer Brett Rodler (Leger De Main) to work together. Although initially they had problems meeting due to the success of their own bands, Chris Rodler finally succeeded in pushing them together. Of course, when they then decided that the ideal was working and that they needed someone to provide bass and extra guitar, who would they turn to but to Chris himself. They wrote plenty of music together, but they still needed a singer, and it was at this point that they turned to Leger De Main's Melissa Rodler: Mythologic were complete. With two guitarists and no keyboards the impression may be that this is a riff-hungry act that is more at home in the depths of hard rock rather than the more technical area for which these guys are known, but nothing could be further from the truth. The album opens with "Magic To Breathe" which is a short a capella number that demonstrates the beauty and control of Melissa's voice – imagine Alanis but with more depth and passion. Those who then think that this is going to be a laid-back affair are also going to be disappointed, as although we gradually drift, Rush-like, into "In Solitude" this is music that has rock as the heart and Melissa as the voice. It is deep, it is dark, it is simple, and it is gloriously complex with weird time signatures and Peart-like drumming. However, this is not a Rush clone, just one that attempts to walk through the same trees but taking a different path.

I have long been a fan of the Rodler brothers, more years than either of us probably like to recall, but when repeatedly they produce music of such consistently high calibre, I find myself yet again heartily recommending an album of theirs to you.
#76, Oct 2003

NAIKAKU
SHELL
This is the second album by Naikaku, a band that is built around the duo of Satoshi Kobayashi on bass and Kazumi Suzuki on flute. They then bring in support members and guest musicians, which gives them a full band. The bass has a very Chris Squire sound to it, and they obviously have a progressive approach to what they are trying to do, but they are also bringing in some strong hard rock elements with strident guitar and then over the top of the madness there is the clear sound of the flute. This is not used as much as one might imagine, and although there are some Tull influences, especially in opener "Crisis 051209", it is not too much. That all the guys involved in this can play is never in doubt, but there are times when they are just too complex for their own good and sometimes lose some of the musical thread. For me the best times are when they are rocking through and the whole band is in unison, such as on "Lethe" which is a hard rock instrumental with bags of promise. One to hear before purchase. *#87, Apr 2006*

NDV
KARMA
This is Nick D'Virgilio's debut solo album, and he has brought in help from many quarters, including from his day job with the Beard, and has also provided all the drums and vocals as well as some guitar and keyboards. One is never sure what a solo album from a drummer is going to sound like, even one that can sing, and the verdict is still out on this one. Some of the songs are very rhythmic; such as opener, "The River Is Wide" yet also contains good hooks, while others just are not strong enough for one reason or another to be on an album. Nick is one of the best drummers in the business, but he comes to the fore when playing other people's songs. This is probably for Spock's Beard devotees only. *#64, Oct 2001*

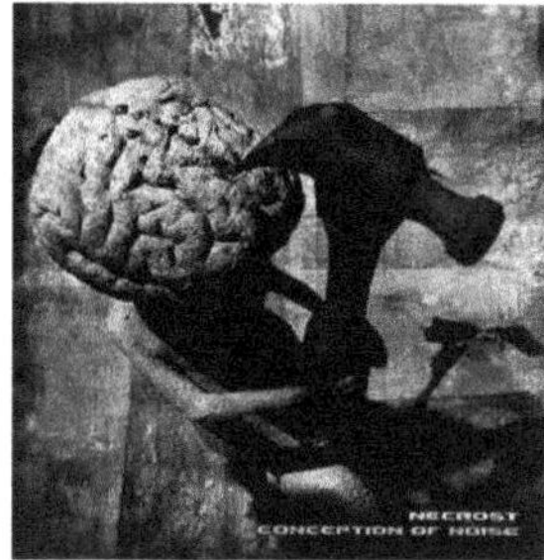

NECROST
CONCEPTION OF NOISE
This is quite unusual; the music a strange amalgam of progressive and death metal, plus this album was recorded at two distinctively different times. The first five songs being recorded towards the end of 2001 and the other five being recorded in 1999 (I think this latter may have been released as an EP in 2000). Looking at their site there have been some changes since this came out, as there is obviously a female singer on board, but as my Russian is worse than my Polish I stand no chance of knowing what has gone on. Musically this is quite strange, and they seem to fall between the two camps of prog and death – there are some extremely complex and interesting progressive passages that contain death growls, while to the deathhead this is far too complex. That they can play is never in doubt and I would be interested to hear how they have 'progressed' since then as there are some interesting ideas going on. *#85, Nov 2005*

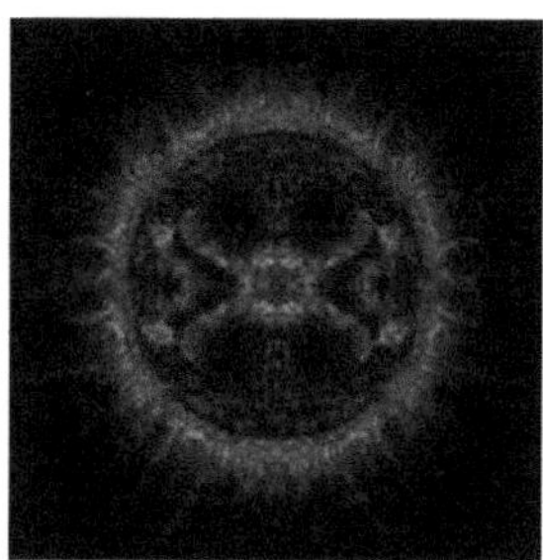

NEGATIVE ZONE
NEGATIVE ZONE
Negative Zone will not be the first band, or the last, to be likened to Pink Floyd in many respects, but what is particularly interesting here is that they have looked to 'Atom Heart Mother' and 'Meddle' as opposed to the later period. This is the debut album from this French quartet, but with all the lyrics in English this is going to appeal to quite a wide audience. They obviously know what they are doing, and the result is an album that is well constructed and polished, and it is hard to believe that they have not all been around for some time (although two of them were in Eclat). "Hold Out Your Hand" is so close, with everything coming together and a great Roger Waters style bass line, that one could almost think that this is a long-lost song from the great Floyd themselves. But although they have the sounds and the styles they are not just copying huge chunks of "Echoes", but instead using those songs as a musical starting point and then going off and creating their own music. There is no doubt that all fans of earlier Floyd will get a kick out of this, but although there is a sound from thirty years ago it is also quite different to anything else around. *#86, Feb 2006*

NEMO
IMMERSION PUBLIQUE – LIVE
Following on from three studio albums, French band Nemo have now released a live album, recorded 23rd April 2005: not resting on their laurels they already have another studio album planned for March. This quartet combine rock with prog as well as bringing in quite a lot of jazz, and the result is a very powerful sound indeed. All the guys are prepared to take a lead role, and the interplay between five string bass, guitar and keyboards can be quite stunning at times. Guitarist J P Louveton obviously has the passion and skill to

be a shredder if he wants to be, but uses his speed skills only when the music demands it, and this musical restraint is true of all the guys as they combine to produce some quite stunning music that can be full on and powering majestically through one second, and then stopping quite suddenly for some classical style piano. There are some vocals (unfortunately all in French), but these are gentle and atmospheric, adding to the overall mood. Still yet to be signed to a label (which surprises me as I would have thought that Musea would have snapped these guys up), they are going on their independent way and while this may not fit in with many people's views of prog it is a very good album indeed.
#86, Feb 2006

NEPENTHE
EVERYTHING WAS BEAUTIFUL...
The complete title of Nepenthe's second CD is 'Everything Was Beautiful and Nothing Hurt', a line taken from a Kurt Vonnegut novel. I ought to make mention here of the press pack that was sent to me from America as not only does it make my life easier but also gives the impression that here is a very professional band who are out to make a serious impact into the world of prog. The thing that immediately strikes you about the album is the way that the production has put the vocals at the very centre of attention, and that the music is designed to complement instead of distracting away from them. Yes, it is progressive music as this is primarily songs that can be categorised into that genre, instead of a deliberate attempt to recreate the sounds and styles of bands that have been before (hands up all prog bands guilty of that!). Some of the songs are very simple in structure, based around a basic piano, vocal or guitar, vocal melody that gradually becomes more complex as the song moves on. In "Beauty Is A Warm Mind" it is just vocal and piano: basic, yet compelling. This is not hard rock prog, but music that is gentle and, in many ways, can be said to be beautiful. The listener is rewarded by hidden pleasures in its' depths. I am concerned that they have parted company with singer Rosenfield as he plays a pivotal role in this album, but new singer Vince Ascoti is now well on board and the follow-up 'Thistle, Thorn and Ember' is already being recorded.
#52, Feb 1999

NERONIA
NEROTICA
Originally this band was called Ulysses, and had an album produced by Karl Groom and Clive Nolan some eleven years ago. Now they are back with a new line-up and name, but obviously have not forgotten their history. This is German progressive rock that is looking as far into the past as it is in to the future. Although they have been influenced by other German bands such as Everon, it is to Canada where they have been looking most as there are Saga-esque touches, as well as the much missed (well, by me anyway) London-based prog act Winter. The vocals of Falk Ullmann (ex-Tipsy Slut,

Waxmuseum) have a distinctive sound that moves them away from many of the modern prog bands; there is an edge, a real 'presence'. This debut album is one that I have found myself drifting into, for the proghead this is music that is floating yet for the areas where it meanders along there are others where there is real purpose and bite. The gentle sections just serve to emphasise the power of the guitar – for Neronia never forget that they are a rock band, although they are much more in the Pendragon area of music than Arena and light years removed from Threshold. It is an album that reminds me of the sort of material that SI were releasing, good solid prog, or even Marillion. It is not music that grabs the listener, but the more this album is played the more there is to be taken from it.
#79, May 2004

THE NEW GROVE PROJECT
FOOL'S JOURNEY
These songs were all originally recorded in 1984 (apart from the new song "Decision"), by Per Sundbom and Ingemar Hjertqvist in Sweden. Per provided keyboards, while Ingemar provided guitar, bass and vocals. Both musicians got married, and with the move of Ingemar to Switzerland in 1987 the whole thing seemed to be forgotten. However, by 1993 Ingemar felt that it was a shame that nothing had happened with the music and eventually managed to get a band together. He was joined by Roine Stolt (guitar), Andre Schornoz (bass) and Jode Leigh (drums, ex-England), while Per was only able to contribute to proceedings at the end, so Par Lindh took on most of the keyboard roles. With his addition, they could use Crimsonic's studio, and the album was recorded in September and October 1996. It is difficult to fathom that Roine had not been involved with these songs since their inception, since he has stamped his authority all over them: he has produced some of the most important European progressive albums of the last five years, and his trademark style is definitely in place. That is not to say that this comes across as a Flower Kings album, just that his contribution is exceptionally important. Of course, Par is also renowned as a recording artist and his keyboard sounds fit in with Roine perfectly.

Overall, the album is more rooted in the Seventies than the Nineties and has the classic timelessness of Roine's own work. Ingemar has a good melodic voice, singing more of the songs in a lower register than would be normally expected of a rock vocalist, and this sounds like the work of a mature outfit, with a lot of thought going into the arrangements and overall effect. They are diverse, with laid-back almost Floydian numbers sitting alongside those with blistering guitar attack. If you want to hear what good melodic rock prog can sound like in the hands of masters, then you need look no further.
#39, Jan 1997

NEW SUN
EXPECTATIONS
This is an extremely varied album, and while New Sun will be viewed as many as being 'progressive', they are much more about providing strong songs than conforming to any particular genre. The biggest thing to come out the album is a feeling of space, some of

which is due to the sometimes lengthy gaps between tracks, but also to the laid-back feel to many of the songs. It is music that is there to be listened to and enjoyed, but the guys feel no need to thrust it down your throat. While much more will be gained from sitting and listening to it quietly, this album also does very well from being played as background music. The first few times I played this I did so while doing something else, but found that songs that "Reflections", with strong vocal and lyrics but minimal backing always had a way of grabbing attention. Then the next song is much more rock based so that the listener is never quite sure what to expect. No lyrics in the booklet but they are obtainable from the web site; an interesting album.

#62, May 2001

NIADEM'S GHOST

IN SHELTERED WINDS

After IQ's 'The Wake' tour in 1985, singer Peter Nicholls left the band. In the July, he met up with old friend and guitarist Dave Bennett (who he had previously worked with in The Same Curtain) and they started writing songs together. Peter then joined Dave's band We Happy Few, to form Niadem's Ghost with bassist Dave Tompkins and drummer Brian Grantham, and their first gig was at The Manchester Gallery, supporting Geoff Mann. They independently released a self-financed album, 'In Sheltered Winds', in 1986 and in January of the following year Manchester's Piccadilly Radio broadcast three of their songs, one of which, "Endless Times", was repeated within a week because of so many requests. The band felt encouraged by this and released three songs on a tape, 'Thirst', in March 1987 but they did not manage to secure a deal and subsequently called it a day in October 1987.

Because of the involvement of Peter, these recordings have been fairly sought after by prog fans, although Niadem's Ghost were not a prog band at all. IQ's own label, GEP, have now released both recordings on one CD, together with complete lyrics and photographs, so that people can hear just what the band was like. The sound is far sparser and immediate than the band Peter had left behind: it is difficult to describe the music and magic they conjured up, as although they were a rock band they were not 'heavy' in any sense of the word. The vocals are very much to the fore and combined with distinctive guitarwork means that Niadem's Ghost had very much their own musical identity. My personal favourite must be "Wild Weather In Shallow Waters", which has some very gentle guitar at the beginning but as Peter turns up the power in his voice it is transformed into a storming and intense rock number. Great Stuff!

#17, Mar 1993

NICE BEAVER
ON DRY LAND

This is a great name for a band (apparently taken from a joke in 'Naked Gun'), and 'On Dry Land' is the debut album from the Dutch proggers. All the four-piece sing, and this is an album that is mixing together styles from bands such as Timothy Pure and Spock's Beard together with Rush and possibly even Kansas. "Culley on Bleeker Street" starts with the sounds of traffic in New York, and I was convinced that this album came from that side of the pond. There are sections within the songs that are stunningly intricate, while maintaining a very heavy edge, which shows that this band have real talent. Yep, there's a 'but' coming. Having heard the opener, I was convinced that I was hearing a great album, but that hope was dashed with "Oversight". There are large bits of this song that are wonderful, but the repetitive chorus just grates, and I found that my initial enthusiasm was waning. It was not brought back to life with "Wintersong", which I am sure was being deliberately depressing, and again I had problems with the chorus. The frustrating thing for me is that they can be very good indeed, and some of the songs are superb. They can combine emotion and musical ability with sensitivity and hooks that keep the tunes buoyant. "Hope You Don't Mind" has a lot going for it with strong vocals and guitars, and a brilliant break in the middle of the song with a total shift in direction. I know that other reviewers have given the album unqualified praise but for me it is "good, (sometimes great), but could be better".
#69, Aug 2002

NICE BEAVER
OREGON

Back in #69 I reviewed the debut album 'On Dry Land' from these Dutch proggers, and I said that I felt that the album had some great moments but that overall it could have been better as some parts just did not live up to expectations. That has been rectified with the follow-up, as this is a much more consistent piece of work. Any album that starts with a song more than twelve minutes long has something to say, and "Nights In Armour" is a great introduction. It starts slowly, gradually the drums take on a marching beat, and the keyboards and guitars make their entry almost as if Jadis or Camel had become an American marching band. The music builds, but it is so gradual at first that it just brings the listener in, holding them in thrall while the bass starts to give signs of what is going to happen next. Instead of the vocals coming in, there is an Andy Latimer-style lead guitar solo before the band start to rock it out some more. Mind you, they started the last album extremely positively and then fell away, but this time it is an album that brings a smile to the face from the first song to the last. This is a band that is as happy being instrumental as they are providing vocals, as happy playing prog as they are to crank out some riffs or even bring in some jazz. The result is one of the best albums to come out of Holland for quite a while, one that has won me over, and considering what I thought of their last album that is a job well done.
#82, Jan 2005

NIL

QUARANTE JOURS SUR LE SANAI

Originally released in 2002, this album has now been reissued by Unicorn due to the response that the band have had to their recent release on the label, 'Nil Novo Sub Sole'. As can be guessed from the title, this is a concept album, here comprising two tracks of more than thirty minutes long. All the lyrics are in French but there is a very good booklet, which provides lots of information in English. I have tried to get on with this album, but even though I have played it quite a few times, and am impressed with some of the instrumental sections, find that it is just too long and meandering. It never seems to be getting anywhere and although there is no doubting the skill of those involved there is the feeling that if they had stuck to shorter songs with more of a sense of direction then the result would have been much better. Not one to which I will readily be returning.

#89, Sep 2006

NOEKK

THE GRIMALKIN

Noekk are a duo comprising of Funghus Baldachin and F.F. Yugoth, and this is their second album under this banner. It is unusual to say the least, and it is probably best to let Funghus describe it himself where he says, "it is an exciting album for all fans of Prog Rock. We branch into vintage Hard Rock, get lost in folkloristic thickets, follow an invitation from Doom Metal and we will not refrain from slimy epic stuff either!" However, even that does not describe this album which is at times very heavy and others just downright strange. There is an epic feel to some passages, Gregorian to others, a feel of King Crimson here and a bit of over the top Sabbath there and the knowledge that these guys are going on a very twisted and torturous path to their goal, and even on arrival the listener still is not sure if he enjoyed the journey.

This is not music for the fainthearted – you must persevere with it and it even took me a few playings before I could get to the point where I was now starting to possibly enjoy what I was hearing. It is the sort of album that can easily be despatched to the cylindrical filing cabinet but having now listened to it a lot I am glad that I did so as this is music that is so outside of the mainstream as to be quite refreshing, once you get past all the melancholy that pervades the tracks. There are only three songs, but still comes in at a respectable 42 minutes long and while this is an album of atmosphere and foreboding full of the perils of being in a dark and frightening forest, I feel I did get something from it in the end.

#88, Jun 2006

TNR
THE CHESSBOARD
The Noisy Room are not a band, more of a project, as it began life as a home recording studio for Marco Olivetto's Ohm project. Nine albums were released on cassette before 1990, but none of them received any serious distribution. In January 1990, The Noisy Room moved to a dedicated apartment, and became a meeting point for musicians of every kind and style, mostly because it provided an eight-track studio at low cost. Fabrizio Daicampi (guitar) joined, as did Francesco and Lorenzo Graziola (sound engineer and manager). Two more cassettes were released, 'Rubber Walls' as Ohm and 'The Chessboard' as Ohm & The Fall band. This received a lot of interest from fans and other artists, such as Peter Hammill. In 1991 The Noisy Room became a record label, changed the studio to 24-track, and re-recorded 'The Chessboard' from scratch, while the band simplified their name to TNR. The album gained some new songs and features external musicians who were soon integrated into the band. It was released on CD in September 1992 and distributed by Musea and Progressive International, with the latter being so impressed that they signed the band to a worldwide deal. At the end of the year, they toured Italy supporting Peter Hammill. Marco sent me a copy of their newsletter, and if I had the room I would reproduce word for word what he says about every song, as it makes for fascinating reading. If only all bands provided this sort of information, my life would be an awful lot easier. Marco told me that he felt that the "progressive" label was restrictive, and on listening to this, I can understand what he means. Unlike many European releases, this CD is extremely listenable first time around, and the use of extra musicians has given Marco and Fabrizio the ability to spread out and create a real plethora of sounds and feelings. There is no doubting the musical ability of this band, and combined with their vision, here is a "debut" album that is a real masterpiece. The sound is distinctive, yet commercial, certainly unlike the other Italian releases I have heard. TNR have their own identity; they do not need to copy it from someone else. This superb album even has a UK release, from Oedipus Records. Lastly, I must mention their newsletter; as well as providing information for all TNR's activities, there are loads of American and European reviews, covering a very wide field of music.
#18, May 1993

CLIVE NOLAN & OLIVER WAKEMAN
JABBERWOCKY
This project is one that Clive and I discussed a few times before it finally came to fruition. It tickled him to think of recording an album which featured Rick Wakeman narrating instead of playing keyboards, and that featured Oliver but not his more well -known brother, Adam. This is a concept album loosely based around the famous Lewis Carroll poem of the same name, with Rick taking the part of The Narrator: Bob Catley plays the part of The Boy, with Tracy Hitchings as The Girl. The album is very much in the same theme as concept albums of the Seventies. In fact, it reminded me somewhat of Rick's own 'King Arthur'. This is due in no small part to the fact that Clive has successfully distanced his

writing from his previous albums, bands and projects, so this does not sound as if it is from Thin Ice. By using musicians who are not normally associated with him (such as Peter Banks and Tony Fernandez), Clive has also created further space. The keyboards are very dynamic, with strong interplay, and the long instrumental passages work very well in an orchestral fashion. The result is an album that must be listened to in its' entirety to get the full benefit, but it is worthwhile and very enjoyable. The booklet is well laid out and the use of Rodney Matthews as the cover artist hearkens back to another age and era. If you ever enjoyed listening to concepts in the Seventies (and who did not?), then this is an album that you will thoroughly enjoy.
#58, May 2000

CLIVE NOLAN & OLIVER WAKEMAN
THE HOUND OF THE BASKERVILLES

'The Hound of the Baskervilles' is the follow-up by Clive Nolan and Oliver Wakeman to their 1999 release 'Jabberwocky', but in truth this should be seen as the sequel to Jeff Wayne's 'War Of The Worlds'. Instead of Richard Burton we have Robert Powell as narrator, and he has the awesome presence and majesty that this album deserves. I have been playing this a lot in the car and Sara (who normally turns all my CDs off as a matter of course) has been listening to it and confessed in a moment of weakness that it is a good album. If they can get through to Sara, then this obviously has appeal for a much larger market than many of the Verglas releases. With different singers taking on roles (the usual suspects include Bob Catley, Tracy Hitchings and Ian 'Moon' Gould as well as others such as Ashley Holt from the Rick Wakeman Band), the idea behind the album is to turn the story into a concept album and to my ears they succeed brilliantly. While there is plenty of help on the musical front (Karl Groom, Peter Banks, John Jowitt, Peter Gee to name just a few), there are many keyboards on the album, which give it an orchestral feel, particularly in the long linking passages. However, the songs themselves are often full of passion and dynamics, such as the exciting "The Curse Of The Baskervilles". I have known Clive for many years and I think I have heard just about all that he has released in all his guises and can say honestly that this is the finest work with which he has been associated. The biggest problem he now has is getting this album out to those who need to hear it, because properly marketed this could be a huge commercial success. Get in before the rest and buy this superb concept album. *#66, Feb 2002*

NO-MAN
FLOWERMOUTH

No-man are essentially Tom Bowness (vocals) and Steve Wilson (guitars, keyboards) and since their formation in 1989 they have tried differing forms of music and have gained much critical recognition. They have worked with Mick Karn, Richard Barbieri and Steve Jansen from Rain Tree Crow, and the partnership with the latter two appears again on this their latest CD. Also involved are Robert Fripp, Lisa Gerard and jazz veterans Ian Carr and Mel Collins. The result is an album that already become quite a talking point among the prog scene. The music is hauntingly beautiful, simple yet extremely complex, ambient yet at times danceable. Tim has a lulling voice and listening to a song like "You Grow More Beautiful" it could be said that here is a very English version of INXS, although the guitars are not as raucous. This album has a way of getting inside your mind and staying there. It can't be played as background music as it sets up patterns and dreamscapes that demand attention. A single has been released from the album, "Watching Over Me", and this shows no-man at their art rock best. The drums gently draw you into the rhythmic, almost tribal, beat while the sparing guitar provides the minimal backing for the gently sung lyrics. Maybe this is not as accessible as some of the material around, but if you like Japan, INXS or art rock then I suggest you give it a try.*#24, Jul 1994*

NO-MAN
HEAVEN TASTE

NO-MAN
FLOWERMIX

It is nearly two years since no-man (Tim Bowness, vocals, and Steven Wilson, instruments) released their last album 'Flowermouth'. Since then they have parted company with One Little Indian and have set up their own label. 'Heaven Taste' is a selection of B-sides, rarities and outtakes recorded between 1991 and 1993. They fuse together many laid back styles of music, mixing ambient, New Age and jazz with dance and the result is an overlaying dreamscape in which to drift or move, as the mood takes you. As well as a reworking of Nick Drake's "Road", the highlight must be the twenty-one-minute-long title track that sees them working with Jansen, Barbieri and Karn, all of whom used to be in Japan. 'Flowermix', as the name implies, contains remixes of material from the last album. An additional player on this was guest Robert Fripp, as well as Mel Collins, and again dreamscapes play an important part in proceedings. Overall, these are enjoyable albums and they should both be available at a budget price through Voiceprint. Now is a good time to discover the joys of no-man. *#35, June 1996*

NO-MAN
TOGETHER WE'RE STRANGER

No-man are again a duo, with just a few guests, and there cannot be many bands that have been going fifteen years let alone recording while one of the members is also in a slightly more well-known outfit. Tim Bowness provides the vocals, while Steve Wilson provides all the instruments and if anyone thinks that this might just sound anything like Porcupine Tree they are very much mistaken. This album sees the band push Tim's vocals to the front, while the music swirls, moves and shifts behind. It is almost New Age at times but there is always a slight hint of menace that drives away the saccharine. It is timeless, ageless, modern yet hearkening back to the Seventies. There are Floydian touches, but no one could ever think that they are copyists. There can be just a gentle piano chord, followed by a line of sung melody: there are songs that are heart-achingly beautiful that if edited might even stand a chance in the charts. It is almost as if their previous albums have been leading up to this, as if Steven has managed to exorcise heavier demons with Porcupine Tree and here has come home to provide a stark view of what can be done. If these guys were designers then they would be minimalists, of that there is no doubt. This is not an album to jump into, you must be prepared to sit back and let it all wash over you (oh and do not turn up the volume at the end of "Things I Want To Tell You" like I did, otherwise you will jump out of your skin when the next song starts). Superb. *#73, Apr 2003*

NO-MAN
ALL THE BLUE CHANGES

Among my record collection, there is a double album of underground progressive music that was released in 1987 called 'Double Exposure'. Among such luminaries as Geoff Mann, Abel Ganz, Mazlyn Jones and Rog Patterson there is a band called No Man Is An Island Except The Isle Of Man with the song "Faith's Last Doubt". The band were behind the release of the album, with Tim Bowness also providing the sleeve design – but back then I can't imagine that he foresaw that in 2006 he would still be working with Steven Wilson and that they would be releasing a double CD retrospective of their work together from 1988 – 2003. The band's name was soon shortened to something far more workable and under that banner they have been producing music that is always refusing to conform, music that goes where they want to travel. If it is right for the violin to be at the front with the guitars crunching madly behind, or for the music to be delicate and wistful then it will be as it needs to be. Tim's vocals are at the heart of much what they do, with a breathy emotion and melancholy bringing it all together. No-man may not have been as commercially successful as Porcupine Tree which started life at the same time, but the quality of the music and songs has never been in doubt. Released as a digipak, there is a small essay on the band and then details of where every song was taken from plus who played on it etc. and is a great introduction to no-man. *#88, Jun 2006*

NO NAME
THE SECRET GARDEN

This is the second album by No Name, whose claim to fame is that they are from Luxembourg, which is not exactly renowned as being a hotbed of rock 'n' roll. Still, No Name quickly proves that they are damn fine musicians, based around the keyboards of Alex Rukavina. They have made the decision to mix melodic rock with as many different progressive sounds as they can find, which means that Marillion sits happily with Pink Floyd or Rush

while they are all friends of IQ. In fact, the very end of "Setpagone" sounds as if it has been lifted from "Garden Party", but it does not matter much as overall this is such a fun prog album. With so many different styles coming to the fore there is something for everyone and if you do not like what they are doing just hang on a minute and there will be something else. Still, the different sounds and styles knit happily together, and the album manages to succeed without ever sounding disjointed. It is not the best prog album I have ever heard, but it is in no way the worst either.
#34, Apr 1996

NOOM
NOOM

East German proggers Noom released this their debut album in 1994 and are currently in the studio hoping to have the follow-up ready for the end of the year. If it is as interesting as the first, then I look forward to it with anticipation. Many 'progressive' bands these days are very much 'regressive' in the sense that they follow a path already trodden by many others. Noom have managed to avoid that trap, as their major influence is not Genesis, but jazz. Rainer Ludwig has a very clear melodic voice (all lyrics are in English) while guitarist Oliver Schmidt has a very fluid touch. Keyboards are often used as a backdrop (but just listen to the complexity) while the rhythm section is spot on. The jazz element lightens proceedings but there are places where the music is dark and almost threatening. Highlight is the twenty-three-minute epic "To Be Founded On Questions" where the band shines. If you like class progressive rock that is a little out of the ordinary then contact the band in Germany, it's worth the effort.
#36, Aug 1996

ERIK NORLANDER
THRESHOLD

As well as working with Rocket Scientists, Erik Norlander has been working on his own project, aided and abetted by Don Schiff (bass) and Greg Ellis (drums). Erik is proud of the fact that there are no guitars on the album, and that the introduction to the booklet was written by Keith Emerson! Erik and Keith first met when Erik had just finished voicing a new synth; he not only programmed the Alesis QS8 synths that were used on the 1996 ELP tour but he was also one of their leading designers. On this album, he used these, as well as Mellotrons, MiniMoogs, an old Hammond Model D and the Emerson GX-I that was used on the 'Works' album. In his introduction Keith says, "new life flows through the veins, valves, oscillators and acoustic hammers of Erik's circuitry" and he sees to be quite a fan: on this showing it is easy to see why as Erik obviously took Emerson's work as a great influence and then moved onwards. The result is a keyboard album full of classical power and persuasion, bringing together many sounds in an imaginative and dynamic was. It is easy to forget that one is listening to an instrumental album, as these are songs and not just exercises in self-indulgence. If you have ever

purchased a keyboard album in the past and have wondered what it would sound like in the care of a real master, someone who can play instead of just relying on trickery and sequencers, then look no further.
#43, Aug 1997

ERIK NORLANDER
MUSIC MACHINE

ERIK NORLANDER
STARS RAIN DOWN

This 2003 double CD concept album saw Erik bring in many extra musicians including Kelly Keeling (MSG, Blue Murder, Heaven and Earth): vocals, Mark Boals (Yngwie, Ring of Fire): vocals, Scott Kail: vocals, Robert Soeterboek (Ayreon, Lana Lane): vocals, Donald "Buck Dharma" Roeser (Blue Öyster Cult): vocals, guitar, Peer Verschuren (Vengeance): guitars, Neil Citron (Lana Lane): guitars, Vinny Appice (Black Sabbath, Dio, Lana Lane): drums, Gregg Bissonette (David Lee Roth, Steve Vai, ELO, Joe Satriani, etc.): drums, Virgil Donati (Planet X, Ring of Fire, Steve Vai): drums, Tony Franklin (The Firm, Blue Murder, Whitesnake, Lana Lane): fretless bass, Don Schiff (Rocket Scientists, Lana Lane): NS/Stick. Here Erik has maintained a very heavy style to the music, and one of the highlights for me is "Heavy Metal Symphony", which crunches along and manages to maintain plenty of hooks and accessibility with the keyboards playing an important role with different sounds and structures while there is plenty of room for loads of guitars. In many ways, Erik does remind me of Rick Wakeman and I was not surprised to see that Rick puts his comments about this album at the end of the booklet. The booklet itself is also well worth mentioning as at thirty-two pages long there are comments from Erik, the concept story itself, plus all the lyrics and loads of artwork.

Unlike many concept albums, this is very accessible, and although Erik has brought in many musicians he has managed to maintain a band feel and if it is right musically then he is more than happy to place his keyboards into the background and letting others take the lead role. The music develops throughout and even though the complete album is more than 100 minutes long, it passes by very quickly indeed and is a delight throughout.

'Stars Rain Down' was recorded in Europe on tours spanning a period of three years, and while the result may not give the normal 'in concert' continuity feel of some live albums it manages to capture songs from throughout Erik's career. Within the booklet there are not only the lyrics to each song, but also when and where it was recorded and Erik's view on the piece. The band put together for the three tours was the same apart from the drummer, so some tracks feature Ernst Van Ee while others are Ed Warby. The rest of the guys are singers Kelly Keeling and Lana Lane (both of whom take leads as well as providing backing for the other), Peer Verschuren (guitar), and of course Don Schiff on NS/Stick where he can provide both bass and guitar at the same time if he feels the need! Listening to songs like "Beware The Vampires" there is such a hard rock feel that it is only the Wakeman style solos that give away that this is a band being led by the keyboard player. Kelly of course puts in a sterling performance while Lana is nothing short of her normal brilliant self, and here it is interesting to hear her sometimes take a backseat to Kelly. Not all the songs are vibrant rockers, there are more laid-back pieces within the set so there are plenty of dynamics and interest for all.

Erik approaches music from a different angle to many keyboard players, working hard to maintain a band feel so that even on a tour such as this he is not always centre stage. The music is very accessible due to this, and those interested in well-constructed melodic rock would also get a lot out of this as well as progheads, some of whom may find the music too guitar oriented and heavy for their tastes. It is many years since I last heard any of Erik's material, and I look forward to hearing more as these two albums are superb.
#87, Apr 2006

NOSOUND
SOL29
For NoSound read Giancarlo Erra, at least for his debut album as there is now a full band. This is music that is influenced very heavily indeed by the softer elements of Pink Floyd and Barclay James Harvest, as well as by no-man, and Tim Bowness of the latter has been working with NoSound recently, so it will be interesting to see what the collaboration brings forth. This is relaxing music, something that works well in the background or if the listener wants to just drift away gently. Due to the very nature of the music, there is a certain lack of dynamism and it is possible to switch off altogether, but this is something that can be truly beautiful and is worth persevering with. It will not be to everyone's taste, but this psychedelic swirling prog contains some great passages and is worthy of investigation.
#88, Jun 2006

NOVACT
TALES FROM THE SOUL
This is the debut album from Dutch prog metal act Novact, although they had previously released an EP under the name Morgana-X. Those four songs have now been re-recorded and added to another six to create a debut album that already has some reviewers talking about it as possibly being 'Album of the year', in March! What has excited so many people is that although it is undoubtedly prog metal, it also touches many other bases, so it is going to be enjoyed by more than just those interested in that genre. Technical rock, melodic rock, even straightforward hard rock can all be heard here. The linchpin is the soulful controlled passion of singer Eddy Borremans that carries above the maelstrom, yet is never bland and invites the listener in, to get more involved with what is going on. One of the major plus points from the music is that while

it is complex, it comes across in a fashion that understates the point. Major 'look how clever I am' sections are not high on their list of priorities yet listen intently and you will find that there is a great deal going on. The quality of the songs and the melodies combine to create music that on one level is easy to listen to and enjoy, being totally accessible, but on many other levels is complicated music that needs to be listened to many times to gain the greatest benefit from it. The production has made the album powerfully intense, so that the listener is dragged right in – there is no escape, and it must be played loud to get the most out of it. If you do not normally listen to prog metal but do enjoy melodic hard rock, then you should investigate this further.
#83, Mar 2005

NOVEMBER
FIRST OF NOVEMBER

November are a Dutch band, formed by Ronald Brautigum (guitar, bass) and Michael van Wassem (keyboards), both of whom used to be in the cult outfit Plackband. The line-up is completed by Ed Wernke (drums, ex-For Absent Friends) and Karel Messemaker (vocals). Some people have been raving about this album, and I was intrigued to find out what all the fuss was about. Anyway, I must admit to being more than a little disappointed: yes, the album is very melodic and atmospheric and contains some interesting songs, but all the time I could not help thinking that I was listening to a Peter Gabriel solo album. Karel's voice is a dead ringer for Gabriel's, and the songs are like what Peter was doing around the time of his fourth solo. In the end, I felt that by far the best song on the album was actually the instrumental "Return to '81". Some people will love it, but I am afraid this is not one to which I will often be returning.
#27, Feb 1995

NOW
SPHERES

This Belgian band have just released their third album, 'Deep', so I suppose it is a good time to review their second album, which came out in 1991. The line-up is Vincent Fis (vocals, guitar), Herve Borde (keyboards, vocals), Jean-Pierre Nelles (drums, vocals) and Veronique Duidaerts (bass, vocals). The fifty-three-minute-long album starts with the sound of gentle running water, and as the listener relaxes into a false sense of serenity and security, heavily distorted guitars crash into the ears. The gentle keyboard passage that follows is a good introduction to the rest of the album. The next song starts with Fis singing the title "Children of a Dying World" totally unaccompanied and then plays the riff. This use of a clear voice, followed by a dynamic guitar, is effective and leads the way to an Asia-style commercial number complete with harmony vocals: this song is so good that it could easily have been on Asia's debut album. It develops with acoustic guitars and finishes in a way I have not heard before; the lead voice gradually fades, followed by the instruments, leaving just the harmony backing

vocals loud and proud until that is all that is left. If the rest of the album had lived up to the promise of that song, then I would be running around screaming about the undiscovered album of the Nineties. As it is, the rest of the album is excellent in every way, with great vocals and musicianship, but I found myself just a tad disappointed as the other songs did not live up to my expectations. Still, it is an album to be rightfully proud of, and would sit very happily in any rock lovers' collection, especially if that person liked prog such as Asia, Yes or Rush, with some great guitar.
#17, Mar 1993

GARY NUMAN
PURE

Anyone my age will have little difficulty remembering seeing Gary Numan on TOTP, but they may not be aware that he has released twenty-five albums which have made the Top 75, which is quite some achievement. While his vocals are distinctive, his music has taken a much harder, darker, sound, and listening to the title cut of the album it is amazing just how much menace the man who once said that he had no one to love, can put into a few short minutes. I was listening to The Prodigy's "Breathe" earlier and it is surprising just how much the two songs have in common. Obviously, this album is a little removed from what I would expect. Not all the songs are as bleak, yet none of them were what could be termed 'pop' numbers. Gary has moved on from that now, as can be seen from his endorsement by Marilyn Manson, who joined him on stage to sing "Down In The Park", while he has also been working with Trent Reznor of Nine Inch Nails. There is a passion and power with Gary, that few keyboard-based musicians can ever match. Possibly, it is because Gary still uses a band, and plays guitar – he does not rely on keyboards to the nth degree. An album that I enjoyed playing.
#61, Feb 2001

NÛS
ALL THE VERTICAL ANGELS

Nûs have been in existence since September 1993, and 'All The Vertical Angels' is their debut release. They specialise in what they term ambient, but with vocals, and the result is a very strange mix indeed. When I first played it, I was not sure if I liked it, just because it sounds so unusual. That is not to say that it is overtly experimental or without distinct melodies, but rather that the swirling dreamscape created by the guitar, bass and keyboards is dominated by complex (live) drum patterns. The real strength is in the vocals of Percy Howard, who has a fifteen-year background of classical singing, punctuated by light opera and German lieder. As one would expect with that history, Percy has a wonderful technique and emotional range. He comes across as a slightly deeper, more emotional Seal, and the result when combined with the dreamscapes is outstanding. There is so much here for the listener, and progheads will fall over themselves to get it I am sure, but it is not restricted to that field of fans by any means.

Yes, it can be classed as ambient, but the vocals take it to a new label. Earlier I said that I was not sure if I liked it. I know now that I love it!
#35, June 1996

NYL
NYL
This Russian album was released in 2002 but has only now come to my attention, sent to me by my friends at Starless Records. As this is not one of their releases they have not given me any info about the band, and sadly the label site only appears to be in Russian which is not a language that I can deal with (i.e. it is not in English). So, it is just down to the music itself then. All the lyrics are in English, and musically they seem to be covering many bases with a touch of Saga here, some jazz fusion there, and some poppy moments when it suits them. This may not sound like an enjoyable album but this is something that is easy to listen to while never being easy listening. There are some delicate piano and vocal passages that work very well and apart from the accent there is little that one would point to, to think that this was not a European piece of work. It may not be innovative, and is certainly not essential, but it is an album that can be played and enjoyed by anyone who wants some solid neo-prog, that is not too heavy or hard in the guitar stakes.
#85, Nov 2005

OCTOBER EQUUS
OCTOBER EQUUS
October Equus are an instrumental quartet from Madrid, and following on from their demo 'Hydra', which was released last year, they have now released their debut full-length album on Ma.Ra.Cash. This is not music that is easy to listen to – it is extremely complex and complicated and while they have obviously been listening to classical avant-garde composers there is also plenty of RIO as well as some of the more unusual elements of bands such as VDGG and King Crimson, and possibly even Hatfield & The North. This is progressive music at its most challenging, and even I have found this hard to listen to. I can admire it and see how intricate and clever the musicianship is but when it comes to enjoying and listening to it for pleasure then that is another matter altogether. Treat with care.
#87, Apr 2006

ODYSSICE
IMPRESSION
Ah good, an instrumental prog band from Holland. So, I sighed, put it on, and then woke up. Odyssice have obviously been playing close attention to Jadis and Camel and have put together an album that may not have vocals but is no less for that. If I had to pick

fault it would have to be with the version of "Flower Of Scotland" (which I notice Malcolm pointedly avoids in the press release). Although the highlight for me and for many will be the guitar playing of Bastiaan Peeters, special mention must be made of the keyboard playing of Jeroen van der Wiel who provides the perfect melodic counterpoint. While much of this is restrained, there are some powerful moments to be heard and the result is an album that is most pleasing to the ear. If this style of prog is appealing, then this is a band worth discovering.

#62, May 2001

ODYSSICE
MOONDRIVE PLUS

Odyssice's first album, 'Moondrive', was originally released in 1996, comprising a thirty-minute suite divided into five songs. This has now been remastered and reissued by Cyclops, along with bonus songs and some CD-ROM elements which comprises live videos, biogs etc. (hence the 'Plus' of the title). Odyssice are an instrumental quartet and while drummer Menno Boomsa and bassist Pascal van de Pol keep it all together, there is no doubt that the melody stakes belong to keyboardist Jeroen van der Wiel and guitarist Bastiaan Peeters. While Jeroen trades licks with Bastiaan, he also does a fine job of providing a curtain of keyboards as a backdrop so that Bastiaan can provide Andy Latimer, David Gilmour, Gary Chandler-style lead lines against them. Although there are no vocals, they are not missed just because there is no room. This is extremely polished, with each musician knowing their place and working together to produce an album that is quite beautiful in some respects, and very interesting and enjoyable throughout. This is not an album that is hard to listen to, the music flows and ebbs, always with plenty of melody and a simple complexity. This is not about playing music at the speed of light or showing off as to how quickly things can be done but instead playing the music that suits the mood and the piece. This is an album for progheads who do not always want to be blown away or must work at their listening pleasure. *#78, Apr 2004*

O.S.I.
FREE

Office of Strategic Influence is Jim Matheos of Fates Warning on guitar, keyboards, and Kevin Moore (ex-Dream Theater, Chroma Key) on vocals and keyboards. This time around they have returned to their old bands for assistance, so the rhythm section is the mighty Mike Portnoy (Dream Theater, Neal Morse) on drums and Joey Vera (Fates Warning) on bass. To say that this is prog metal is somewhat missing the point, as these guys are coming across quite unlike any of the other prog metal acts around, as the amount of intensity is overpowering at times. The vocals are lower in the register, and are important, but it is the interaction of the guitars and keyboards that make this what it is, combined with the ferocity of the rhythm section. But, this is not all about bombast and being over the top, but also having lighter moments that work very much on their own merit which also mean that the heavier sections do come across very powerfully indeed. There are elements that could be thought of as Gary Numan and Kraftwerk while others contain keyboard sounds mixed with guitar that are way out of left field. Then just when you are getting to the end of the album and are thinking that you may just have a handle on what is going on they close with "Our Town" which is led by acoustic guitar!

There are elements of Floyd here as well, but OSI are making a prog metal sound very much of their own making and the album is all the better for it. This is something that fans of the genre are going to want to have - the mix of Dream Theater and Fates Warning is very much alive and kicking like a good 'un.
#88, Jun 2006

RYO OKUMOTO
COMING THROUGH
So, following on from Neal and Nick's solo works, Ryo has now decided that it is time for his new album. His solo recording career goes back as far as 1980, and this album is an attempt to revisit some of the songs that he has written over the last twenty years. While Ryo alone wrote three, four were composed with Neal Morse and Nick wrote the last. As well as employing the services of these two as vocalists (and Nick as drummer along with Simon Phillips and his own son, Sage) Ryo has also used the services of Glenn Hughes, Bobby Kimball and his wife Linda Green-Okumoto. Bass was provided by Dave Meros (he only needed Alan Morse to get the complete set) and Kenny Wild (who Ryo has been working with as part of Natalie Cole's band), while Steve Lukather, Michael Landau and Jun Sumida provided guitar.

This is not an album that would initially be recognised by anyone as being by Spock's Beard, although he has enough nerve to start the album with an eight-minute instrumental and includes a nineteen-minute piece with Neal singing. Songs such as the pop rock of "The Farther He Goes, The Farther He Falls" and the initial menace of "Slipping Down" shows that Ryo has a strong understanding of melodic rock, with a Floydian edge. Strong Hammond style organ is featured on "Highway Roller" and the distinctive vocals of Glenn Hughes fit in so well that this song would not sound out of place on any of Glenn's solo albums. Overall this album is there to be enjoyed, just do not expect a Spock's Beard outing. There again Ryo has little input to the writing of that material so possibly that should be expected.
#70, Oct 2002

OLYAM
CRISTAL RÊVEUR
Olyam is a multi-instrumentalist, and this is his fourth solo album. Although there are some guests, he provides most of the music himself, mostly on keyboards but sometimes on guitar. Yep, we are deep in the fields of Vangelis and Oldfield here, yet not quite as interesting. It's an okay album, yet that is all as it spends too much time in New Age areas and not enough in 'proper' prog. Consequently, the album has been used by me as background music at which level it works well. But, as for sitting and listening to it then I would have to be in a very mellow mood and wanting to just drift away. *#72, Feb 2003*

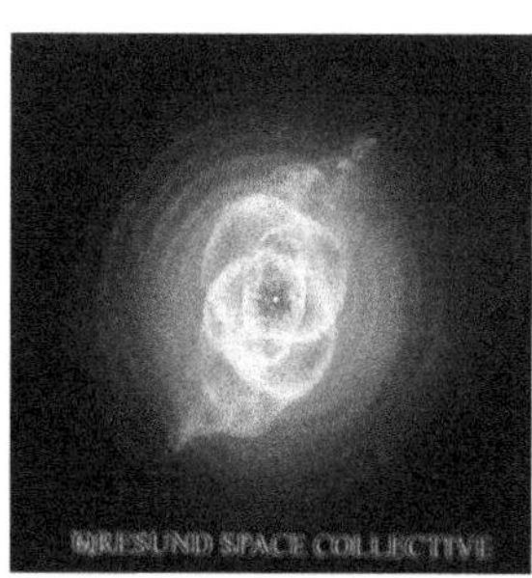

ØRESUND SPACE COLLECTIVE
ØRESUND SPACE COLLECTIVE
You may well be able to work out from the name what style of music these guys play – yes, space rock, with no vocals. The main core of the band are guys from Mantric Muse, Gas Giant and Bland Bladen, but others may turn up to join the improvised sessions that are at the heart of what this is about. They record all their sessions with the aim of making the music freely available through the web as mp3 downloads. This is a studio album, so am not sure if this has been taking from tapes of the sessions, if they improvised live in the studio, or if they have re-recorded something that they have previously developed. However it came about, this is a limited-edition release, and is very good if you like the genre. It is music to play late at night looking at the stars, letting yourself just drift into the universe of their creation. *#86, Feb 2006*

MARTIN ORFORD
CLASSICAL MUSIC AND POPULAR SONGS
It has been far too long in coming, but since Widge is in one or two bands, and does the odd bit of touring along with running a record label I suppose he has an excuse. Seriously, this is a solo album that many progheads have been looking forward to. No lyrics in the booklet, but a bit about each song and the players. Martin has gathered around him musicians he has been playing with for years, so Dave Kilminster and John Wetton join him from, um, John Wetton, while the rest of Jadis are here and the rest of IQ, but only the final song has a 'complete' band line-up as Jadis play out with an instrumental. While Martin provides most of the vocals, John guests on one while Peter Nicholls guests on another. The album opens with long held-down keyboard chords, with some lilting flute over the top, then some mandolin touches (all played by Martin) leading us gently into "The Field Of Fallen Angels". This soon goes into some Rush-style runs (with some great bass from JJ), then into a bombastic Jadis-style number. Martin is a great vocalist in his own right, as anybody who has caught him on a solo show will know, and it is wonderful to hear him on CD not just providing backing vocals. The song develops into a much

more intricate keyboard-driven piece without ever losing the central theme before switching tracks altogether into a more acoustic piece. By the end I knew this album was a winner. Up next was "A Part Of Me", which Martin co-wrote with John Wetton who provides the vocals. A laid-back beginning with repeated piano motif gave no hint of what was to come. It turns into a song that Asia would have been proud of, layered vocals, and Gary Chandler and Dave Kilminster locking horns on guitar. A speeding keyboard and guitar harmony show how well these players understand each other. This song is enough to make me want to grab each of you and force you to buy this superb album. There is the superb solo instrumental of "Quilmes" which Martin performs as a solo piece when on tour with John Wetton, or "Tatras" which is Martin's classical number. There is "Fusion" which used to feature in gigs by The Lens so lead guitarist on this is Michael Holmes. This is a fun up-tempo number with some great guitar leads. Oh shit, I could write about this album forever. I love it. If I have just time to mention one more song, then it ought to be "The Overload" which Martin co-wrote with Peter Nicholls who guests on vocals and is the closest thing to an IQ-style song on the CD. A great album from one of the nicest guys in the business. *#60, Oct 2000*

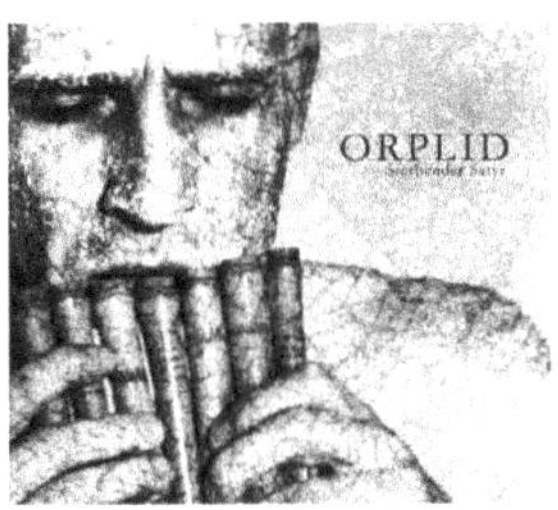

ORPLID
STERBENDER SATYR

'Sterbender Satyr' is the third album from Frank Machau and Uwe Nolte, and is a bringing together of cinematic images, using both acoustic music and vocals to create a world that seems very long ago, but also right up to date. It is compelling and unusual, containing a simple beauty and I am pleased that the album is sung in German as I think this adds to the mystery of the piece. They brought in singer Sandra Fink to take the lead role on their adaptation of Oda Schaefer's poem "Die Seherin" and the result is quite inspiring. This is an album that is all about soundscapes, creating pictures for the mind and at times it can be quite unsettling, but this is music that should have close attention paid to it always, as it is not something that can be put on in the background and forgotten. It certainly will not be to everyone's tastes, but I know that I found it interesting and give it time then you may do so as well. *#87, Apr 2006*

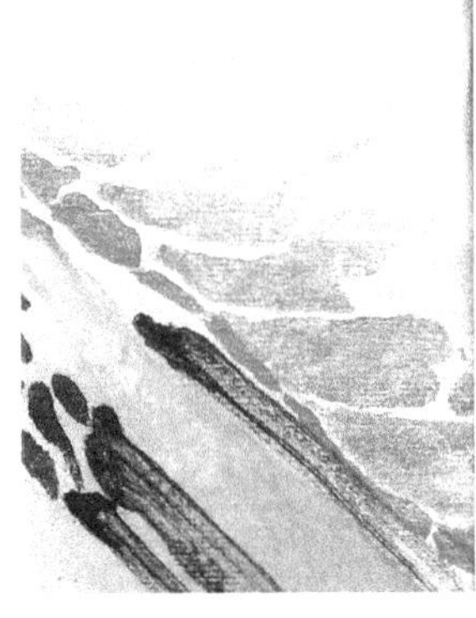

CLIFF ORSI
INNER LANDSCAPES

This was originally conceived by Cliff as an accompaniment to his visual work and is subtitled 'an exhibition for the ears'. In the booklet, Cliff says "Imagine your stereo as a gallery, each track an exhibit. What do you make of it? What is the work about? What does it provoke, evoke and/or inspire? How does it look?" Although we all recognise Cliff as an artist it is worth remembering that he came to prominence as the bassist on the first Arena album, 'Songs From The Lion's Cage'. This is not an album of bass music, but one where guitar and keyboards are often laid against each other, with simple themes explored and

repeated. I found the album very relaxing, and it made me think often of a stream, babbling over stones, but the music is very open to individual interpretation. While it would be possible to classify it as New Age I think it has a lot more going for it than that.
#58, May 2000

OUT OF ABBFINOOSTY
COMES THE STORM

Out of Abbfinoosty is Asif, who used to be in that band, but a clever marketing ploy has found himself with a new moniker. It wouldn't have anything to do with the fact that no one would have a clue who Asif was, but might recognise the name Abbfinoosty? No, I thought not. Asif provides all guitars, keyboards and vocals, although others help him out at times. I am also glad to report that he has used a 'live' drummer instead of one of those cursed drum machines. I am not quite sure what market Asif is aiming at as although there are some very good songs on here, there are also some that are extremely self-indulgent. Some rock, while others just drift along (stand up "Hell or High Water"). I am reminded of those albums from the early-mid Seventies, which were alright, but never seemed to fulfil the potential of one or two songs. Opener "When The Sun Explodes" has real promise, although feeling rather dated in approach. Overall, Asif may be Out of Abbfinoosty, but I preferred it when they were one entity. Bring back "The Wizard".
#37, Oct 1996

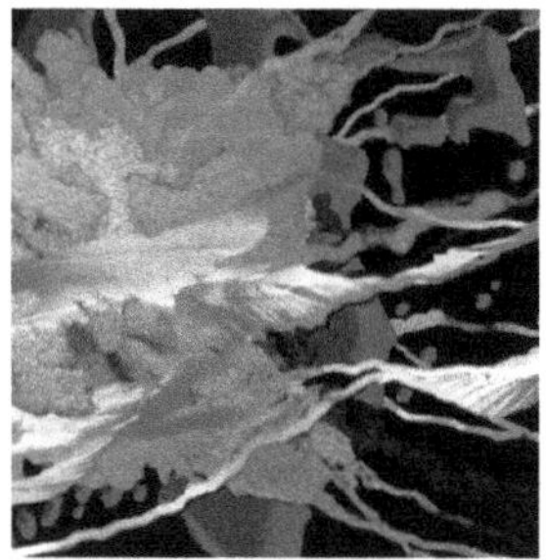

OZONE QUARTET
FRESH BLOOD

In many ways, this is a strange album, from a strange line-up. Ozone Quartet is a four-piece (as you would expect) and comprise Hollis Brown on electric violin, Francois Dyer (drums), G-Man (guitar) and Wayne Leechford (Chapman Stick). Yep, you have spotted the initial mistake: no vocals and the instrumentation itself is also unusual. When you take these four instruments and take them into a musical setting then I expected to hear something more jazz-like or improvisational, but this is primarily a rock album with structure. Yes, the violin does take the lead for the most part, providing the 'voice', but that is not always the case. It is not an album for the faint-hearted, or those who like their music presented to them on a silver platter. You need to work at this album, and you will be more than amply rewarded for your endeavours. Music sweeps and glides, moving through emotions and styles with great efficiency.

The mere fact that it is an instrumental album will put many people off even trying it, which would be a great shame. This is yet another act that I contacted thanks to Peter Renfro of ProgDay, and they went down well when they played there. If you enjoy music a little out of the ordinary, then you will find much to like here.
#53, May 1999

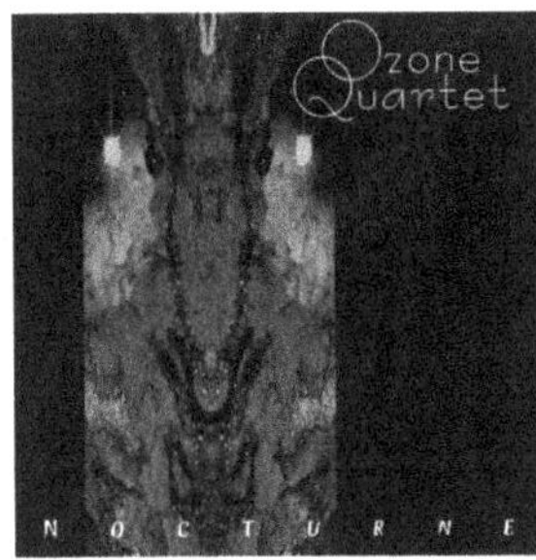

OZONE QUARTET
NOCTURNE

This is the second album by instrumental outfit Ozone Quartet who have a sound that is totally unique. This is a progressive band that is determined to produce music that is challenging and complex, bringing comparisons with bands as diverse as The Nice, ELP, King Crimson, Dixie Dregs and VDGG. While the violin playing of Hollis Brown provides much of the 'vocals' for the music, the whole band have major roles to play, swapping between styles and nuances. Francis Dyer utilises a wide variety of percussive instruments as well as standard drums, and Wayne Leechford provides an extra edge by being a master of the Chapman Stick instead of "just" a normal bass. The line-up is completed with guitarist Kenny Thompson who can be restrained, jazzy, or out and out rock as the music requires. This is not an easy album to listen to, in the sense that there is a lot going on and I found it necessary to pay close attention to get the most out of it. For those who want to get a lot out of their music, instead of a quick fix, then this is of great interest.*#56, Jan 2000*

OZONE QUARTET
LIVE AT LOCAL 506

Ozone Quartet reformed last year after a three-year hiatus and one of their first tasks was to release this recording, which took place at one of their last gigs in 2000. Ozone Quartet are a prog rock, jazz fusion act with an unusual line-up from North Carolina. On drums is Fran Dyer who can sometimes find himself on his own when providing stability, as Wayne Leechford plays Chapman Stick, which he can use a melody instrument in its' own right. Jeremy Shaw provides the rock muscle with electric guitar while Hollis Brown fights off all comers to take centre stage on electric violin. They played many gigs, as well as recording two albums, and they are all aware of what each person is doing onstage. Some of the interplay particularly between Hollis and Jeremy is quite breath-taking, while the others show they are no slouches either. This is music that is played and lived at pace, with each one willing to go up front or stay just behind as the mood and style demands. It is music that is intense and deserves to have a lot of attention paid to it – not something that can be played in the background. This is jazz with balls that can be threatening when it is needed, or full of fusion and smoothness. *#78, Apr 2004*

OZRIC TENTACLES
WATERFALL CITIES

One of the few bands that defy musical definition, the Ozrics are back with another instrumental extravaganza. Of course, I could attempt to follow the last sentence by saying that they sound like X crossed with Y, but it just does not work like that. If you have ever heard an Ozrics album then you will be pleased to know that this is one of their best (favourite is the opener "Coily"), and if you have not what are you waiting for? I

played this the first time with the lights out, laying in a hot bath, and the music just blasting. Maybe I should just let the band speak for themselves. "So here you go... Seven more windows into colourful worlds for all to wrap around the harmonic sensors! Instrumental pathways spiralling off into realms not often encountered but conducive to free mind travel. A blending of natural and not so natural sounds to create places in which to dwell momentarily in a state of blissful otherness! To trade these astral strands often feels a little precarious... but we like it! The journey continues." Possibly one of the very few bands that can truly call themselves 'progressive', they break down all musical barriers. Without the Ozrics, no musical education is complete. *#55, Sept 1999*

OZRIC TENTACLES
PYRAMID

There are indeed very few bands that have a sound that is unique, one that captures images and styles, transcending all attempts at pigeon holing. The Ozrics are one such band, and in the sixteen years since their first release, they have confounded all their critics and have managed to sell nearly a million albums in the meantime. A totally instrumental band is a rarity these days, and for one to have succeeded to the level that the Ozrics have is virtually unheard of. This mini-album comprises one brand new song, and four that were captured at The Boardwalk last year and are their first live songs to be released since 1992's 'Underslunky' album. Even though it is a mini album, it still manages to clock in at forty minutes long. The bass and drums underpin the music, allowing the flutes, keyboards and guitars to create the spell, the magic that is Ozric Tentacles. If you have ever heard and loved the band, then you will need no urging to find this album; if you have managed to miss them then your musical knowledge is sadly lacking and now is the time to make amends. Heartily recommended. *#63, Jul 2001*

OZRIC TENTACLES
ETERNAL WHEEL

If you have yet to hear the mighty Ozrics then a) why not? and b) this is the best way of finding out about one of the UK's finest underground bands. This is just a lovely tactile release to hold, as it is a double digipak that folds out, and contains a booklet. There are photos and their great artwork, but this is all about the music and any album that starts with "Jurassic Shift" is going to be all right with me. Ozrics are an instrumental band that does not sound like anyone else. Some people may say that they use some 'spacey' sounds a la Hawkwind, but these guys are not nearly as heavy although guitars do play an important part in their music. The keyboards, guitar and woodwind all seem to meld in a way that means that the music takes on a force very much of its own. The bonus CD also includes a video track taken from their wonderful 'Pongmaster's Ball'

DVD and the collection contains songs going back as far as 1990. It is a good way to discover a band that have entranced many fans and festival goers over the years, but somehow have managed to maintain their cult identity and never breaking through into the big time. Superb. *#80, Jul 2004*

MURAT ÖZTÜRK TRIO
SÖYLE

Although the album I am playing appears to have been released by Hemiola (whose web site will not come up), according to the Musea web site it is one of Musea's releases although it is on the Great Winds label. It does not take much to confuse me and I am rapidly getting a headache! What you all need to know is that it is piano based instrumental jazz, with the trio being assisted at times by guest sax and accordion and the result is an album that is always interesting albeit rarely too experimental, although they do get quite carried away on "Going To Off Mode". Only for those who enjoy jazz as opposed to dabbling in the genre. *#70, Oct 2002*

PAATOS
KALLOCAIN

It is always a safe bet that if a band namechecks Can as a reference point, they are not going to be playing music that is part of the recognised rock mainstream. I have not heard their debut album, but if it is as uncompromising and bleak as the second, then that would be some achievement. Lead vocalist Petronella Nettermalm has quite a warm and clear voice, at times reminding me of the almost naïve quality of Björk, as there is no struggle to get the vocals across, no real passion. The use of cello gives the music a different approach, but it is sheer starkness of the music that comes across, even though there is plenty going on with a Mellotron. It is music that in some ways is quite hard to listen to, just because there is a sense of emptiness through much (although not all) of it. This is an album that must be treated carefully, and I am not sure how many progheads will want to investigate. Certainly, quite a different band to be on Inside Out. *#80, Jul 2004*

PAATOS
TIMELOSS

I reviewed the band's second album 'Kallocain' in #80, and now Inside Out have reissued the band's debut 2002 album 'Timeloss' (with an additional fifteen-minute video clip). In the initial review, I said that one reference point was Björk and that is also true of the debut. This is music that is sparse and well-constructed; there is a real use of space, which is as important to the music as the actual notes. There is the feeling that the music

has a very different source to that of most prog, and the use of Nordic folk and jazz cannot be underestimated. It is timeless, it could have been recorded in the early 70's instead of the 21st century and is music that takes a lot of work. This is not something that is accessible, and consequently only a few progheads will be interested but if Can is your thing then why not give this a try?
#82, Jan 2005

PAATOS
SILENCE OF ANOTHER KIND
So Paatos are back with their third album, and yet again they show that they are not being influenced by much else within the progressive scene but instead are resolute on following their own path. In 2004 they toured with TheGathering and that has obviously had an impact on the music that they themselves are producing. While there is still the starkness and the beauty that one has come to expect, as well as the jazz and numerous other elements that make up the overall sound, they have noticeably now got heavier as well. This is not crunching rock throughout, but there are times when they do turn it up to good effect. There are not many bands where the lead singer also adds cello, yet this is an important part of the overall feel although it is for her voice that vocalist Petronella Nettermalm is most renowned. She has a very clear sound, yet also manages to bring in Björk stylings to provide an edge. This music can be fractured and clear, gentle and restrained with an improvised dangerous feel to it, or it can be far heavier and darker – whatever fits the mood. This may not be the most accessible prog music around, but it is some of the most exciting and in many ways invigorating. Yet again, Paatos have produced a very strong album indeed and while this does take time to get into, it is worth the effort.
#88, Jun 2006

PAIN OF SALVATION
ONE HOUR BY CONCRETE LAKE
The second album from Sweden's Pain of Salvation is again a concept, like the debut album 'Entropia'. In this case, it deals with a defragmented view of nature, humanity underworld at the end of a depraved century through the eyes of one man. It is quite a dark album, with a sense of menace. During "Inside" Daniel Gildenlöw says, "since 1990 there have been 93 wars in 70 states around the world with 5.5 million people dead. 75% of these people were civilians, one million of them were children!" Although primarily this will be thought of as a progressive metal album, it brings in more influences and textures than most. There are Georgian choral elements, and deep dark metal as well as more jazz-like styles. It is truly progressive and while they have been touring with Threshold and Eldritch this year, they are probably more truly progressive than either of them. 'One Hour By Concrete Lake' is a hard album to listen to just because there is so much going on, and is best taken in small doses, like all good

medicine. If you like your prog metal but thought that the genre was getting too hooked up on wannabe heavy metal bands then this is what you have been waiting for.
#55, Sept 1999

PAIN OF SALVATION
THE PERFECT ELEMENT

This is another concept album by Swedish outfit Pain Of Salvation and is only part 1! I enjoyed their last album 'One Hour By The Concrete Lake' so I was intrigued to hear this. While they have always been part of the progressive metal movement, this album sees them make some real strides in both parts of that genre. There are times when they are playing as heavy as any of the hard rock bands coming out of the States, yet they temper it by going through so many different musical styles and ideas. The gentle lilting vocals, accompanied by a delicate fretless bass can give way suddenly to brutality, while there is often a feeling of melancholy. It is the sort of album that can be enjoyed on first hearing, but it has great depth – and I wish that I had the lyrics so that I could study them. This album will only see their reputation grow.
#61, Feb 2001

PAIN OF SALVATION
REMEDY LANE

This is the fourth album by Swedish prog metallers Pain Of Salvation and although it is again a concept album, it is not a follow-up to 'The Perfect Element Part 1'. The band has decided not to work on a sequel just yet, although that is in place for the future. POS have been working with the usual suspects in the past, having toured with both Threshold and Arena while band leader Daniel Gildenlöw also found himself playing with Transatlantic. They have also confirmed dates with Dream Theater soon. Daniel describes the album himself as follows "If you're looking for a band that sounds like your favourite group, forget about us. But if you happen to be looking for a band that lets you forget your favourite group, take a few walks down Remedy Lane and you'll find that you're not the same person that you were before". The album is about failed relationships and the role of a person's past when entering a relationship. At times the music is very heavy, at others very light, but there is a constant tension between the two, so that the listener is never quite sure what is going to happen next. The vocals also take on an important aspect as they move between rock screams and almost spoken passages, while always maintaining a certain menace. While there are no long tracks (closer "Beyond The Pale" is the longest at less than ten minutes), the proghead cannot feel hard done by as there is plenty of complexity and intricacy to get their head into. Again, this is an intriguing album from Pain Of Salvation that may be too heavy for the proghead, while being too complex for those into metal, but it is rewarding for those who follow the path to the end.
#67, Apr 2002

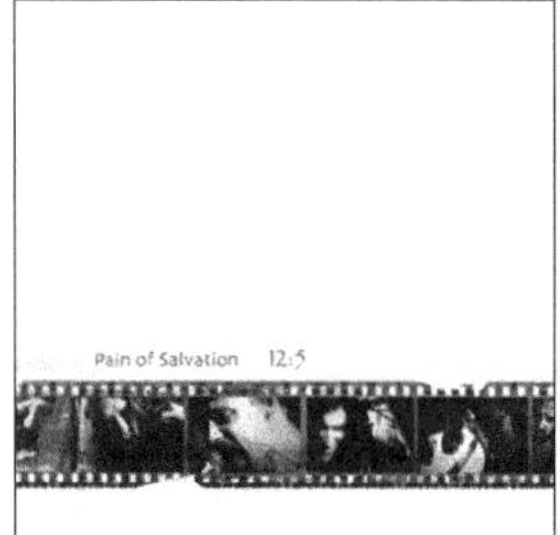

PAIN OF SALVATION
12:5

There is quite an unusual concept behind this album. Band leader Daniel Gildenlöw was asked if Pain Of Salvation were interested in recording a special radio show for Swedish radio. This resulted in this acoustic album being recorded in front of eighty invited guests, and with no extra instrumentation added, if you were there that night this is what you would have heard. The album is divided into three books, as is usual with POS, as there is an underlying story (titled "Brickworks) but most of the songs have previously been available on their studio albums. The difference now of course is back then they were powering prog metal and now this is in an acoustic setting. The band comprises Daniel Gildenlöw (vocals and guitar), Johan Hallgren (guitar and vocals), Johan Langell (drums and vocals), Kristoffer Gildenlöw (bass and vocals) and Fredrik Hermansson (keyboards). While the band is playing acoustically there is never any doubt that this is a rock band. On "Winning The War" there is the feeling that the passion is just going to take over the band. There may be no amps involved, but they seem intent on killing those acoustic guitars. It shows how well the songs are structured in that they can easily be switched from full on prog metallic mayhem to this environment. A fascinating album, which while obviously of more interest to fans of the band, will also have appeal to those coming to them for the first time. Just do not expect any of their other albums to sound quite like this. *#78, Apr 2004*

PAIN OF SALVATION
BE

I saw Daniel Gildenlöw onstage at Rotherham last Saturday when he was wearing a dress (!) and seemingly enjoying himself playing the part of multi-instrumentalist and singer in The Flower Kings. Now I am listening to his own band, Pain Of Salvation, who are quite a different musical kettle of fish. POS are normally thought of as inhabiting the prog metal arena but for this concept album they have made it even heavier in places, as well as bringing in elements of classical music, folk and gospel. As well as the band themselves, this also features a nine-piece 'Orchestra Of Eternity' who seem to hold the key to the whole thing. This album moves from one musical style to another, often blending them in together, but while many progheads will enjoy the interaction and the changes there are times when these guys cut loose just to remind us all that they are a metal band at heart. Or are they? The way that they move so effortlessly between the styles beggars the question as to where they see their roots: maybe the reason they seem to at home whatever they play is that this is their place. This is music that must be listened to, lyrics that must be studied. Yes, this is 'clever' music but what is wrong with that? Daniel thinks that to understand the band performing this album that you should see it at least four times, something that schoolchildren in their home town could do as the band have been road testing it in front of them at special concerts. I like this album, and the more I play it the more I feel at ease with it and the more I get out of it. Well worth investigating. *#81, Dec 2004*

PALEY'S WATCH
NOVEMBER

Paley's Watch comprise Marc Catley (more renowned for his work with Geoff Mann), Duncan Parsons and Marianne Velvart, and although this is their first release as Paley's Watch they have previously worked on albums together before. The album is about six characters from Bury in the 80's, and the title track is not even on the album but is only available on Tape Two of David Robinson's excellent Audio Directory. Lead vocals are mostly by Marianne, although both the others contribute, and she has a voice reminiscent of Maddy Prior. This is quite unlike anything else coming out of the UK prog scene, with a very heavy reliance on guitar playing long and complex lead lines. There is a feeling of freshness and light more associated with jazz than rock, and a good mix of electric and acoustic instruments while the vocals are pure and clear with good harmonies. Some people may find 'November' too laid back for their tastes, but the strong lyrical and musical talents on show will win Paley's Watch many friends. If you are interested in the highly melodic side of 'rock' then this will be one for you.

#26, Dec 1994

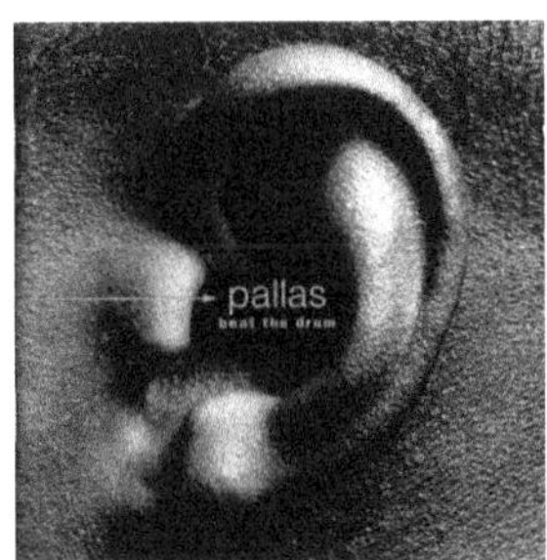

PALLAS
BEAT THE DRUM

Once upon a time, Pallas were certainly the hottest prog band to come out of Scotland, and the early albums showed such promise that it was no surprise that they were mentioned in the same breath as Marillion and IQ as the bands most expected to do well. But, that was a very long time ago and they have been quiet for many a moon. Part of the reason was simply geography with some of the band living in London and others in Scotland but finally they are back with a new album. The line-up is now Alan Reed (vocals), Graeme Murray (bass), Niall Matthewson (guitars), Ronnie Brown (keyboards) and Colin Fraser (drums). Graeme's bass is an important part of the band's overall sound, just as Chris Squire's is for Yes, heavy and clunky and gives the music a base to build from. Alan's vocals are as good as ever, but in all honesty, there is little here to get excited about. Although when they decide to give it some welly they prove that they still have what it takes. "Man Of Principle" is a case in point as it is the seventh song on the album but puts all the songs that preceded it firmly in the shade. Most of the album appears to be "safe" songs, plenty of keyboards and some strong vocals but little to give it that extra spark of brilliance that they used to have. It is when the guitars are put more to the fore that they sound more like the old days; they transform "Ghosts" when they come into play. But to my ears the guitars throughout the album are not utilised nearly as much as they should be. Overall, I was disappointed, but maybe that was because I remember the early Eighties so well. I even have a concert tape of theirs from 1986 at Southampton University and should confess that I would rather play that.

#51, Jan 1999

PALLAS
ARRIVE ALIVE

If you are a prog fan then you probably own a tape copy of this album, but it has now been made available on CD, with some extra tracks. Yes, the recording quality is mostly naff, but back in 1981 Pallas was the Scottish band most likely to challenge Marillion. It was this that saw them signed to EMI in 1983, when 'Arrive Alive' was reissued prior to their debut studio album for the label, 'The Sentinel', in 1984. I know I have already said that I am not a fan of the new album 'Beat The Drum' but when I put this on the player I realised once again just why Pallas are still as popular as they are. This captures a band at the beginning of their musical career (although in truth a version of the band had formed as long ago as 1974 and this line-up had been together since 1979) and while the production is poor, it is the songs that shine through. The title cut must be one of the most popular prog numbers of the Eighties and was re-recorded for 'The Sentinel' where it opened the album. I had not played it for a few years before putting on the CD but found that I still knew all the words and sang along very happily indeed! Songs such as "5 To 4" also shows the importance of guitarist Niall Matthewson and his interplay with keyboard player Ronnie Brown. If you have not already purchased this CD, and you are a proghead, then you must dash out and get this now, immediately. *#54, July 1999*

PALLAS
THE SENTINEL

PALLAS
THE WEDGE

Can there be any prog lover who does not have these two classic albums in their collection? 'The Sentinel' was the first album they released after they had a deal, but some of the songs such as "Arrive Alive" had already appeared in another form. From "Shock Treatment" to "Ark Of Infinity", here was a band determined to make their mark as the top prog band in Scotland (who said that was not too hard?). Even twenty years on the music and musicianship more than stand up to scrutiny. Euan Lawson was in fine voice, while Graeme Murray (bass, pedals, vocals etc.), Ronnie Brown (synths, vocals), Niall Matthewson (guitar, vocals) and Derek Forman (drums, vocals) proved that they could really cook. 'The Sentinel' is a concept album, based around the feelings the band had about the Berlin Wall and the arms race, but the ten songs all stand alone as well. 'The Wedge' had a different feel to it, partly as the songs were newer and fresher, but also because there was a new lead singer, ex-Abel Ganz vocalist Alan Reed. It opens with "Dance Through The Fire", surely one of the heaviest numbers they have ever done. There is another favourite of mine on here, "Rat Racing", which is one of their longer tracks. The album also contains three songs that originally came out on the 'Knightmoves' EP in 1985.

Nevertheless, while both albums have been re-mastered, and they have very good booklets with photos, it is for the enhanced tracks that many fans will head for first. 'The Sentinel' features a picture gallery, along with excerpts of Euan performing "Atlantis" at the Hammy O in 1982. This is thought to be the only footage of him with the band. 'The Wedge' also has a picture gallery, along with the video of the band performing "Win Or Lose". Two classic albums, which have been re-mastered, along with good booklets and some CD-ROM features. Who could possibly ask for more?
#60, Oct 2000

PALLAS
THE CROSS & THE CRUCIBLE
I admit it; I was not a fan of their last album. From a band that had produced such awe-inspiring albums in the past, I had expected much more. Therefore, it was with some degree of cynicism that I put this on the player. I expected to be disappointed. Now I have been wrong many times in the past, and will be again in the future, so I am very happy to report that I was way off the mark with this. It is a superb album, one that every proghead should put firmly in their collection. I saw Alan Reed the other night and I said to him that I was not sure how I yet rated this against 'The Sentinel' and he felt that it was very easy, this one is better. That is a bold statement given how progheads view both 'The Sentinel' and 'The Wedge', but one that he may well have grounds for. It has great vocals, great melodies, and sweeping passages that show that Pallas are still masters of orchestral thematic prog music. At times, they come across with hints of Pink Floyd, but for the most part, they are their own band, and for that their fans will be very pleased indeed. There are a few longer tracks for the band to get their teeth into and considering that three of the guys were in the original first stable line-up of 1979, the sound is fresh and inviting. Pallas are most definitely back.
#63, Jul 2001

PALLAS
THE RIVER SESSIONS 1

PALLAS
THE RIVER SESSIONS 2

PALLAS
DREAMS OF MEN
There is little doubt that when the prog scene started booming again in the late Seventies, early Eighties, there was one Scottish act that stood a long way apart from their countrymen, Pallas. They were one of the bands featured in the important Kerrang! feature on the new prog scene, and with Twelfth Night and some guys called Marillion played a famous gig in London. The first of the two sets find the guys at Glasgow Nightmoves on 29th March 1983 with original singer Euan

Lawson. The booklet contains some interesting photos, but it is for the album and the rarity value that fans will be flocking to this. The band were on fine form that night, but while they showed the power and emotion for which they were renowned, the production is not as good as it might be. There are only five songs, but with two of these being the classics "Arrive Alive" and "Crown Of Thorns" there is still plenty to savour. Perhaps more for the complete proghead than those who have yet to come across the band.

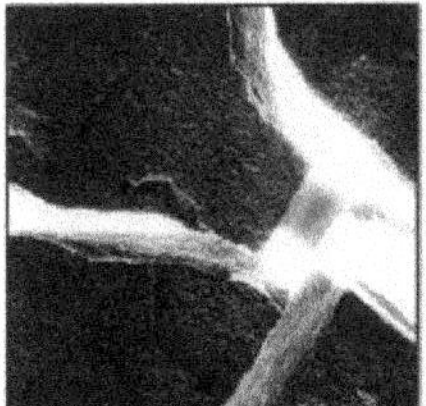

But there is a marked improvement in the sound for the second release, which showcases the band supporting Uriah Heep at one of the last gigs at Glasgow Apollo on 16th May 1985. By now Euan had left to be replaced by Abel Ganz singer Alan Reed. He had/has a different approach to the music and a smoother style that glossed over some of the backings and to my ears always produced a much more polished and classy sound. As they were a support act there was again only room for six songs, but the band were in their element and revelling that they were playing in front of a home crowd. Alan seems to have been taken by that aspect, while Niall Mathewson proves time and again that there is rock in prog as he rips into his guitar. The harmony vocals are also much more in evidence with the band being at the very top of their game. The one criticism is that it is just too short but given that this was the set that night one can't complain. If you enjoy your prog and somehow have never got around to 'The Sentinel' or 'The Wedge' then this is one for you, and if you have then you know you must get this.

Of course, after writing the above I was then sent the new Pallas album. What do they sound like twenty years on from the review above? Glorious, that's what. When it comes to intricate soaring prog with great vocals, melodies, crunching guitars and presence then it does not get any better than this. The majesty and power of opening song "Bringer Of Dreams" (just a shade under ten minutes long) is awesome. There is a maelstrom of prog noise and in the middle of all of it holding high court is Alan. He strides the music like a colossus even though Niall is doing his best to prove just how important the guitar is to progressive music, Scottish style. This is easily the best album they have produced for quite a while, one that is essential for all progheads. If you want your prog to be over the top with harmonies and intricate guitar and keyboard melodies, then this is indispensable.
#85, Nov 2005

CARL PALMER
WORKING LIVE - VOLUME 1
This is Carl Palmer leading his trio (Shaun Baxter, guitar and Dave Marks, bass) through some ELP classics and a drum solo, recorded live in Bilston on 19th July 2001. Given that there is nary a keyboard, let alone vocals, I was more than a little concerned as to how this album would pan out, but I must confess to being more than just a little pleasantly

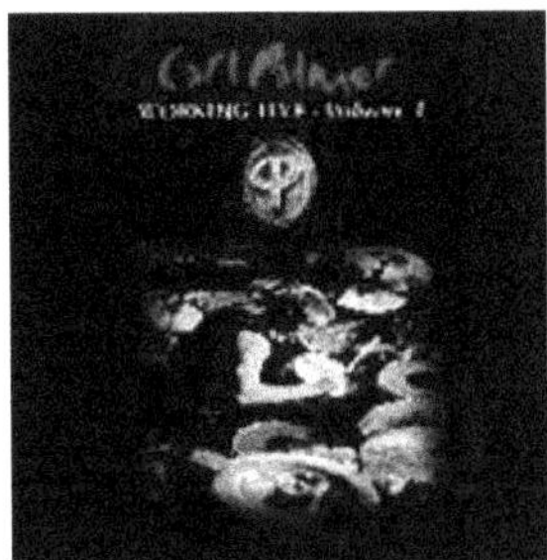

surprised. Looking at the songs I decided to play the sixth one first (yes, I know that I should not play a live album like that), as I was concerned to hear what they had done to "Toccata". It is one of my favourite ELP numbers, from the mighty 'Brain Salad Surgery' and I was intrigued/dismayed to hear what could be done by Carl without Keith or Greg by his side. But it transpired that there was no need for any concern as the guitar-led version on this album shows just how the music can be adapted (yes, I do realise that "Toccata" is in fact a piece by Ginastera that had been adapted by Emerson). My faith restored, I then played the album in the correct order, and thoroughly enjoyed "The Barbarian" etc.

Of course, it would have been too much to ask not to have a drum solo but given that this is the last song the listener can always turn it off early. This is an interesting album that any ELP fan will want to seek out – much better than I could have hoped.
#73, Apr 2003

PANGAEA
WELCOME TO THE THEATRE...
This is the second album from this Texas based outfit, both of which have been produced by Robert Berry. The fact that he has been involved from early in the band's recording history shows just how highly he rates their music. Although he was not involved in the songwriting process, it is possible to see the influence of Robert, as in many places this becomes a straightforward if enjoyable AOR melodic rock album. For example, listening to "The Fall of Rome" gives the impression of lightweight 80's rock, although that is not to say that the song is not worth hearing, as it really is rather good. But that can be contrasted dramatically with "The White Shaman" which has more of roots feel to it, due to the ethnic style drumming used throughout. This is a grower, the more I play it the more I have got out of it. While it may be a tad bland for some prog fans, if you like music like 80's Yes in some parts while more AOR in others then this is worth investigating.
#52, Feb 1999

PANGAEA
DEMO
This is a four track CD that has been sent to me by Andi Schenck. Apparently, they have finished recording a new album with Robert Berry and this is a sampler for that work. They are currently without a label and they are trying to sell the album at present, and on what I have heard here there shouldn't be a problem. Andi states that there has been personnel change, but as I had thought that the band had folded altogether, I was surprised to see this. "Myth" is a great number, with strong vocals and melodies while "The Panther" contains some tribal drumming. I hope that the new album will be taken up and released soon – best of luck guys. *#62, May 2001*

PETER PANKA'S JANE
LIVE 2002

Seeing as how Klaus Hess is not involved, and that Jane have acquired the 'Peter Panka' prefix I can only assume that there is either two versions of the band on the road, or that Klaus and Peter have had a dispute as to who owns the name. Certainly, when they were building the reputation of the band in the Seventies as one of the most important German rock bands they were the leaders with many hired hands, but now Peter is there with three others and Klaus not in sight. They have just been touring with Birth Control who is another mainstay from that genre. Recorded in Germany, there is no doubting the love that the crowd have for what the band are doing but as a live album it contains one of my pet dislikes, namely the way that it fades in and out. I know that it is rarely totally live, but I like to imagine that it is. As for the music itself, I should say that for the most part it is pretty ordinary and there is little here to get excited about. That it is well played and produced is never in doubt, and the crowd just lapped it up, but I doubt that they would have got the same reaction in the UK. This tour was to promote 'Genuine' which was also released on SPV earlier in the year but having heard this, that is not an album that I am going to rush out to discover. If you are a fan, then this will be indispensable but that is certainly not the case if you are not.

#71, Dec 2002

PANOPTICUM
REFLECTION

Panopticum released their debut album last April but it has only just come to my attention. That may be because this band is a rare beast indeed, a prog act that hail from Belgium – not a country normally associated with this style of music. They first came together in 1997 and they have spent the time since then wisely as this is a polished act, with obvious musical skills. This is music with a very firm foundation with strong drumming from Bjorn De Kock, and both Mattie Archie and Tim Coulembier like to riff as well as playing widdly-widdly (they both share guitar and bass). Dieter Cailliau is very important to the overall sound as he mixes and changes his keyboard sounds so that at times it sounds right up to date whereas at others it is very much rooted in the Seventies. Then to top it all they have the vocals of Shari Platteeuw, whose voice certainly contrasts well to the harder edge that they can portray: she has a good range and adds complex vocal melodies to the overall mix. In many ways, this is the sort of neo-prog album that I heard a lot of ten or fifteen years ago, but not so much these days so consequently this comes across as quite refreshing. There are elements of Galahad in what they are doing, and possibly even some IQ, but there is also room for areas that are more Marillion-esque. Overall, this is a fine debut album and I look forward to hearing more from the band as this shows plenty of promise and it can't be long before someone like Inside Out smiles kindly on them.

#86, Feb 2006

PARADOGS

FOUL PLAY AT THE EARTH LAB

Although this is mostly an instrumental space rock album, there is enough going on to make it interesting. Given the Hawkwind connection, numbers such as "Nile" (which is also on the 'Family Tree' album) are of little surprise, but there are also some more gentle numbers. They are all repetitive, but it made for interesting listening a few times. Whether I would play it a great deal is another matter altogether but at least for the Hawkfan here is an album that is worth having for musical content as well as just scarcity.

#62, May 2001

PARALLEL OR 90 DEGREES

THE TIME CAPSULE

Following on from 'Afterlifecycle', the new album from PO90 is based on the concept of time. Musically this is a very interesting album, with its' diversity being the main key to its' success. At times very laid-back Floyd, others like VDGG, while at others it is Porcupine Tree or Poisoned Electrick Head. The 'steal' at the beginning of "Fast >> Fwd" from a certain Floyd album (although the label assures me that this is the band's own work – is it bollocks) is a let-down as it demeans the album. A cheap gimmick for which there is no need as this album more than justifies itself. The title track itself is over twenty minutes long but comprises eight smaller pieces that allows the whole to be digested rather pleasantly. The first of these, "Belonging To Yesterday", starts life as a sweet gentle number which sounds even more so as it has just followed "The Single" which is a fast-paced rocker that could be just as its' title suggests. It is an album that does take a lot of listening to, as parts of it are far more immediate than others, but it is a rewarding experience. If you like your prog to sound as if it has a basis different to the Genesis or IQ bent flavoured by many that this is an album that you would do very well to discover. Not as out and out weird as some, but a real grower that is worth the effort.

#53, May 1999

PARALLEL OR 90 DEGREES

MORE EXOTIC WAYS TO DIE

As with many albums I listen to, the first playing of this was in the car. I had loaded the player with a few discs and initially did not realise that this was the sixth album by Parallel Or 90 Degrees. The reason is that for me they have made a step change with this release: it is the album that I never thought that they were truly capable of. In other words, this is a majestic leap into the annals of prog. This may be due to new guitarist Dan Watts who has given the music a much darker, far heavier edge. While they still maintain their

links with the style of VDGG there is much more also in the style of Porcupine Tree and even Radiohead. This is especially true for the eclectic almost hard rock "The Heavy Metal Guillotine Approach", or of course, there is "The One That Sounds Like Tangerine Dream" (okay, it is a filler link, but I had to get that title into the review somewhere). The booklet is also very comprehensive and by the time I had arrived home I was a convert. But, when I was looking at the album in a bit more detail I realised that this was an extended album, so I placed it into the computer and got quite a shock. As the album is not quite as long as usual efforts, they have included a compilation album, plus a completely printable CD cover, a complete album from 1989 plus other music. There is information about how the album was recorded plus an eight-minute video! It takes longer to go through all the music and information on the bonus than it does on the main album! I would recommend this album to all progheads if it did not contain the extras, so if you were ever in any doubt about this band then now is definitely the time to discover them.
#69, Aug 2002

MATTHEW PARMENTER
ASTRAY

Matthew is best-known for being vocalist and keyboard player with Discipline, an American prog band that I have raved over in the past. Here he is with his first solo album, which is very 'solo' indeed. Although he has been joined by Matthew Kennedy on bass, all it states on the CD is that he himself provides vocals 'et cetera'. Turn to his informative web site and you can see that as well as vocals he played the odd instrument including piano, guitar, drums, saxophone, violin, organ, synthesizers, and marimba, Theremin, and Mellotron sounds. The music itself is almost bleak at times, and often threatening. There is a real edge to this album which is quite different to much of the prog currently around. It brings in some of the menace that only IQ bring to the scene these days, throws in some elements of Gabriel and to my ears a liberal dose of Roy Harper. The guitar is not there that one would might expect with the last reference, but there is something about the whole feel, the way that the music and vocals hang together that make this analogy a good one. Matthew has always concentrated heavily on his lyrics, and no-one who has seen the rear of Discipline's 1999 live album 'Into The Dream' will forget his story about cutting his own eyeball with a sheet of paper. This album is more of the same and the more the listener studies the lyrics the more there is to be gained. I am also interested in the imagery of the cover – which is in black and white, what is that saying about what is within? There is a fairground behind the graveyard, and the two headstones at the front say 'mother' and 'father', what is the meaning? This is not an album that will be enjoyed by all progheads. This is not bubbly, fun music, but something that is far darker and brooding. It is an album that must be played repeatedly to get the most out of it, but those who persevere will be richly rewarded. Hopefully there will not be another eight years to wait for the next studio album as there has been since 'Unfolded Like Staircase', as this is an album of great depth and power.
#80, Jul 2004

ROG PATTERSON

FLIGHTLESS

This was Rog's debut full-length album; thinking about it, it is his only full-length album, but that is another story. It was recorded back in 1989, since when Rog has been involved in so many projects that he hasn't yet found time to record the follow-up, although he does keep promising (or threatening, depending on your viewpoint). I spent a pleasant few hours chatting with him on the way to a Credo gig a few months ago, and he is hoping to get more into the live field himself. Just before Christmas, he played a low-key gig in London, and in January, he was off to Norway to support Fairport Convention. The album features Rog on mostly acoustic guitar, and conjures up thoughts of Ian Anderson, Roy Harper and Jay Turner. Some people think that an acoustic guitar means no power or vitality, but they ought to listen to Rog belt his way through "Ergo Sum". A twelve-string guitar has never suffered so much punishment. He is an outstanding guitarist and can play in many styles, so "Ergo Sum" manages to convey many different passions and emotions, just with different styles of playing. Double tracking enables him to harmonise vocals with himself on "Party Piece" to good effect, but it is a shame that part of the music seems to have been "borrowed" from Jethro Tull's "Up To Me". However, this is nit-picking on an album that is quite superb. The second side of the record features just two songs, "Conclusion" and the title cut. The latter is more than twelve minutes long, and is lyrically the strongest, as Rog opens himself up for examination. For those who enjoy singer-songwriter material, or the acoustic side of Tull, then this album is a pleasure.
#22, Mar 1994

HENNING PAULY

13 DAYS

While working on Chain's album 'Chain.Exe' and at the same time writing the Babysteps rock opera Henning felt that he needed a break so of course the only thing to do was to write and record an album in under two weeks! He decided not to have any keyboards and brought in his brother Eddie Marvin to play drums while he provided the rest of the music. For the vocals, he relied on eleven friends to work on the thirteen songs. Of course, being Henning, this could never be a straightforward rock album, which may have been the original intention, as while that is very much the order of the day he can't resist having the music complex and not always in straightforward time signatures. With different singers working on songs in different styles this is a very varied album although it is always accessible. It is hard to pick out just one song but "I'd Like To" which is sung by Edward Heppenstall is one that is just superb. It has a real groove to it that at times almost comes across as Dan Reed Network as Henning moves from strummed chords to lead melody lines and back throughout. The chorus and bridge are particularly accessible and commercial; although Edward would probably have to lose the few swear words to get it played on the radio. Then there is "Six" where his Chain colleague Matt Cash suggests halfway through to turn the song into a ballad, so they do, but then he decides that is a bad idea, so it is back to the rock. This very enjoyable album certainly does not come across as a project that was conceived and completed in such a short space of time. Highly recommended. *#84, July 2005*

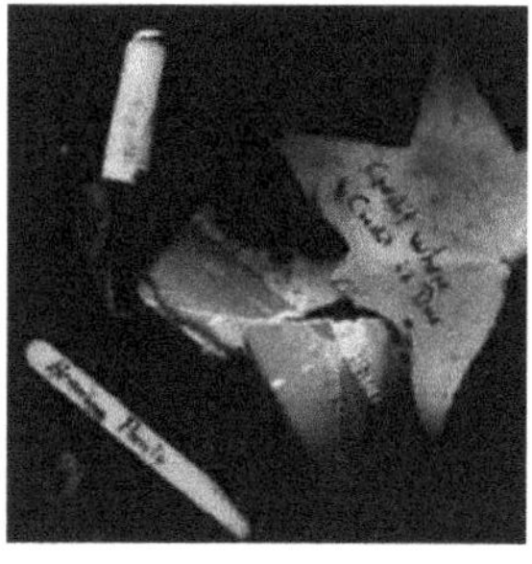

HENNING PAULY
CREDIT WHERE CREDIT IS DUE

When Henning Pauly decided he ought to plan his next solo album, he phoned his friend Juan Roos to see if he would be free to provide vocals. Juan said that he had two weeks free, in two weeks' time. At that moment, Henning hadn't written the music, and this meant that he had to have all the tracks written and recorded ready for the vocals in a fortnight. No worries. So of course, he has managed to produce an album that is just superb, in a very limited amount of time. Henning again plays all the instruments apart from drums, with Juan handling the vocals (although Matt Cash has helped here a little as well). This is one of the heaviest albums ever to be released where someone can include the word 'progressive' in the review somewhere. Henning has a great guitar sound, and when he plays a banjo alongside it, it somehow becomes even heavier. The main theme throughout this album, though, is humour. This is mentioned in the introduction of the booklet, but it is only by reading the lyrics that it all comes through. "Radio Sucks" is the story of some guys in a Volvo who run out of CDs and try to find something to listen to on the radio and it is so bad that they drive off the road instead. But when they get to heaven all the angels are singing Top 40 so are now in hell for eternity. Juan is German, and in "German Metalhead" he and Matt bounce off each other singing about the joys of hard rock even though "Prog still has its place, so practice every day". This does not sound like a rushed album at all, there are multi-layered vocals on "I Like My Video Games" and the guitar sound on "I Don't Wanna Be A Rock Star" is just awesome and I soon found myself singing along in the chorus. There is even a namecheck for label boss Shawn Gordon in "Copyright Conspiracy", and the album is a delight from start to end – if you enjoy your guitars very heavy and produced. I am a fan of everything I have heard from Henning and yet again, he has delivered the goods with this album that is awesome given the timeframe he was working to. It is a step removed from his work with both Chain and Frameshift but will appeal to fans of both; as well as to those who would not normally go anywhere near a 'prog' album. A wimp out this is not. (Nice also to see the Douglas Adams misquote on the tray card).
#86, Feb 2006

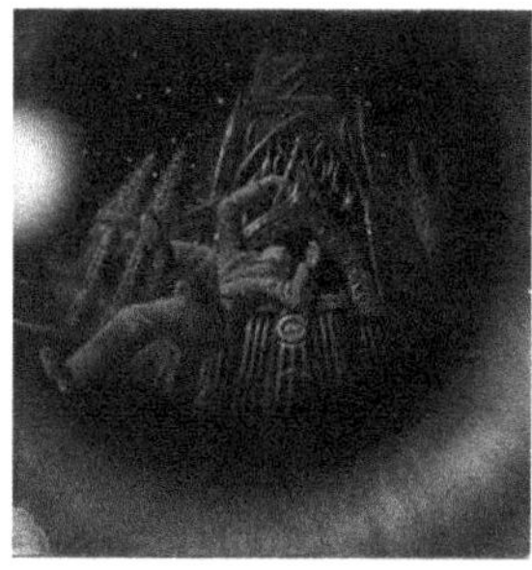

PAYNE'S GRAY
KADATH DECODED

This is the debut release by German proggers Payne's Gray, and it is a wonderful piece of work. When the album arrived I could not wait to get it on the player: the reason? The artwork for this album is amazing and the booklet folds out in to a poster that must be seen to be believed. All of this on a self-released CD! It shows up all the majors who can't be bothered with things like this anymore. The album is based on a novel by HP Lovecraft, called 'The Dream-Quest For Unknown Kadath'. Musically the band are certainly very driven, moving from almost metallic guitarwork (with some very strange time signatures) to acoustic guitar and piano at the drop of a hat. Also, they utilise two lead vocalists, a very rare thing, and their voices work extremely well together. The result is one of the best prog albums that I have had the pleasure to hear. If you like your prog rockier than most, but not up to the extreme of say Threshold, then this is right up your street. I have just heard that they will be supporting Psychotic Waltz among others and are out on the road during September and October. Remember, this is an unsigned band doing it all off their own back and they need all the support they can get – but I'm not asking you to buy this album out of charity, it's bloody excellent!

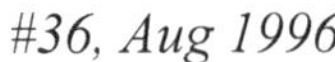
#36, Aug 1996

PENDRAGON
THE WORLD

Zeus Pendragon were formed in Gloucestershire in 1978 by guitarist and singer Nick Barrett and drummer Nigel Harris. Their ranks were swelled by bassist Robert Dalby and the later addition of John Barnfield on keyboards. Pendragon followed the route of many an aspiring rock band by playing anywhere and everywhere, and although they became well-known, they could not get themselves a record contract. Peter Gee joined the band as a second guitarist in 1981 but soon found himself switching to bass as Robert left the band. They released a three-track cassette, entitled 'Armageddon', on Sceptre Records and then along came Kerrang! The magazine ran a two-part feature on progressive rock from the Seventies and Eighties, and while the main feature was obviously on Marillion, who were just starting to break in a big way, there were also photographs and mini-articles on a host of others including Twelfth Night, Pendragon, Pallas, Solstice and Dagaband. It gave the band much-needed publicity and in 1983, they were asked to play at the Reading Festival in front of 30,000 people. Tony Wilson was so impressed that he asked the band to record a session for the Friday Rock Show. The subsequent set was broadcast in the November and repeated only six weeks later due to its popularity. Marillion's manager, John Arnison, offered the band the chance to record their debut mini-album for his label Elusive Records and 'Fly High, Fall Far' hit the shops at the same time they found themselves on a full tour of the UK with Marillion. The band decided to capitalise on the success of their debut by recording a full-length album, 'The Jewel', which was released again on Elusive Records in 1985. This gained Pendragon some major interest, and they were voted second best new band in Sounds and 'The Jewel' seventh best UK album.

They decided to start touring Europe, where they found themselves very much at home. In fact, more at home than home! Their first headline European gig was at the Paradiso in Amsterdam, where they played to more than a thousand people. They had two shows broadcast by Veronica Radio to more than a million listeners, sold out the 2500 capacity Locomotive Club in Paris, and were voted sixth best new band in France by 'Best'. It should be pointed out that at this time, no records had been released outside the UK. Returning to England the band played three consecutive nights at the Marquee, which were recorded for the album '9:15 Live' which was released on Awareness Records. This brilliant live set spawned the single "Red Shoes", and outsold 'The Jewel' within a few weeks. The line-up had now settled at Nick Barrett, Peter Gee, Clive Nolan (keyboards) and Fudge Smith (drums) and the band finished the year by headlining at The Astoria. The band set up their own label, Toff Records, named after Nick's penchant for wearing a top hat on stage. In 1988 their first release on the new label was released 'Kowtow' and was their most complete work to date. The title track is about Vietnam, where Nick believes he led a former life. Again, it was snapped up by those in the know, but ignored by the record-buying public at large. However, this has never deterred the band, who stayed on the live circuit, headlining a major festival at Jerez De La Frontera in autumn 1989. To date they have also headlined festivals in Holland, Italy and Germany. Europe has caught onto their music far quicker than the UK.

1991 saw their most ambitious project to date, 'The World'. Produced by Tony Taverner and with amazing artwork by Simon Williams (who recently did the covers for the EMI Classic Experiences releases), the album is immediately accessible and timeless. It captures all that is good about prog rock, great musicianship, wonderful lyrics and great melodies, yet does not fall into the trap of meaningless musical meanderings. Although Nick is the songwriter, singer and leader of Pendragon, he does not let his guitarwork override the rest of the band. The album displays the maturity of a band that have been played together for years and know exactly what they want to achieve and how to go about it. To put it simply, there are six songs on this nearly hour-long album and every one of them is a winner. Even the music press agrees, and Pendragon have been getting some rave reviews for the first time in years. To consolidate this success, they are just about to start another European tour, where they will be linking up with their old friends Marillion. It is strange to see how Marillion have fallen from grace over the last few years, but Pendragon now seem to be in the ascendance. They are arguably the leaders of the underground prog scene, which is about to break in a big way: when they discuss the Nineties prog scene then the name of Pendragon will be there at the very front. They have set up a very useful and informative newsletter, 'The Mob', and membership is only £5 a year, for which you not only get full details of what is going on, but also a free tape. All in all, Pendragon are a band that care very much for their fans, a factor sadly lacking from many these days.
#12, Feb 1992

PENDRAGON
THE VERY, VERY BOOTLEG

Pendragon is a name that should be familiar to many, if not all of you. Back in #12 I wrote a brief history of the band, and there was an interview with songwriter, vocalist, guitarist Nick Barrett. At that time, their most recent album was 'The World', and I hear through the grapevine that it has now sold a respectable 22,000 copies. Pendragon are one of the longest-lived of the underground prog bands, tracing their beginnings back to 1978. As well as Nick, Pendragon comprises Clive Nolan (keyboards), Peter Gee (bass, pedals, guitar) and Fudge Smith (drums). They are very active on the

live front, and run an excellent fan club called The Mob, whose members get the excellent Mob Mag, which keeps them up to date with all things Pendragon and Impy Imports (which Nick also runs), as well as information on gigs in their area. Every year there is a "freebie" which is available to Mob members and this year, for the first time, it is a CD (recorded last year at Lille, France). It was recorded straight onto two-track DAT by Benoit Caubian and mastered by Karl Groom (anyone noticed that the UK prog scene is incredibly incestuous?) who did the mix on the night. Because of the way it was recorded, there has been no opportunity to overdub or fiddle in any way, so if you were there this is exactly what you would have heard. A very refreshing and honest way to have a live release, as I am sure you will all agree. There are five songs on this forty-three -minute album, containing as it does the epic "Queen Of Hearts" from 'The World', which clocks in at nearly twenty-two minutes. The other tracks are the instrumental "Excalibur" which kicks off proceedings, "Total Recall", the haunting "And We'll Go Hunting Deer" and one of my personal favourites, "Solid Heart". For those of you who know and love Pendragon's music then here it is in all its soaring majesty. For those of you who may wonder what you are missing, it is prog of the highest order, by a band recognised as one of the top prog outfits in Europe. The only thing I could fault is that Peter's bass could do with being a little higher in the mix, especially for his solo in "Solid Heart". That being the last song of the set, the band leave during it one by one. First Nick, then Peter, then Clive, which leaves poor old Fudge to finish the song off by himself. The end of another great gig. If you enjoy prog then The Mob is worth joining as the cost is less than a CD anyway, which does not include all the other great benefits.
#17, Mar 1993

PENDRAGON
THE WINDOW OF LIFE

This is the first Pendragon album recorded at Nick's own studio, which has meant that he has could spend the time he wanted to on it. They have ended up with an album that is a logical progression from 'The World' and adds extra elements to the instantly recognisable Pendragon sound. One of these is the harder edge to Nick's guitar, which is aided and abetted by Mr. Groom at the controls. Opener "The Walls of Babylon" starts with some long held-down chords by Clive, which provide a backdrop for Nick to lay down some guitar lines a la Pink Floyd. This provides a very strong atmospheric start to the album, and a real sense of something getting ready to happen. It is the perfect introduction as it gently lulls you in: the guitar gently dies, the chords get a little more menacing, and then Fudge and Peter raise the tempo. It has taken more than four minutes for the song to start properly, but it is more than worth it as it drives along. It changes moods and style throughout the eleven minutes. "Ghosts" starts with a gentle piano introduction, to which is added gentle vocals and acoustic guitar. After a while, it moves into the area of late Seventies Genesis, but while there are definite nods to that, always it is Pendragon at the helm. The piano makes a very welcome return, with restrained guitarwork all providing the backdrop to some of Nick's best vocals. He says that finally he has a microphone he is happy with and it shows.

"Breaking The Spell" clocks in at more than nine minutes and is extremely powerful with some great guitar. There are some very long instrumental passages on this, which show Pendragon off in their best light. Fudge, Peter, Clive and Nick have been playing together for so long now that there is a real understanding between them. The guitar solo is extended but it is all part of the music, and the rest of the guys provide the perfect backdrop for Nick as they build up to the climax and the return of the vocals. "The Last Man On Earth" is my favourite on the album and is also the longest at nearly fifteen minutes. Still, it is divided into two parts, both of which are separate songs in their own right. "Skylight" is gentle and light, with the emphasis on the vocals with a minimal backing but gradually this becomes more of a rock number which dies into virtually nothing until "Paradise Road" comes blasting out. Lo and behold Nick is riffing the guitar, but as the chords come powering out attention is drawn to the amazing drumming of Fudge as he powers around the kit. Fudge plays the best on this album he has ever done, a result of being able to record 'live' for the first time. This song shows Pendragon at their most dominant and defies anyone not to fall in love with them; this song should be played at the max! "Nostradamus" begins gently, but rapidly becomes a bouncy Pendragon number that is easily the most commercial on the album. This is the sort of song that would be in the charts if there was any justice in the world. We close with "Am I Really Losing You?" which is more of a ballad. It gradually builds up but is faded out as it brings the album to its close. To my ears this is the best Pendragon album to date and would grace any CD collection.
#21, Jan 1994

PENDRAGON
FALLEN DREAMS & ANGELS

Here is 1994's release exclusive to members of Pendragon's fan club, The Mob. Last year it was a live CD but here we have four tracks of which three were especially recorded earlier this year. If you have not already sent away and have wondered what you get for your money, I can assure you that not only do you get the excellent Mob Mag but a tasty twenty-five-minute slice of Pendragon as well. "The Third World In The UK" is one of their songs that starts off quietly, but somewhere along the line it turns into a rock song of almost anthemic proportions. Clive takes the lead role for much of this, providing the sole backing for Nick's voice but the others are just waiting their chance to join in the mayhem. "Dune" is in a similar vein, although one repeated keyboard sound used within it, a harmonica, I found intensely distracting and was soon skipping the song. "Sister Bluebird" was back on the right track, with some powerful emotions conjured up by the restrained guitarwork of Nick. "Fallen Dreams and Angels" was recorded in 1991 and wouldn't have seemed out of place on 'The World' as Nick accompanies himself more on guitar and relies less on Clive to a certain extent. Extremely melodic, the double-tracked harmony vocals add to the overall effect. Not as rocky as they can be, but overall this is well worth having in your collection.
#24, Jul 1994

PENDRAGON
UTRECHT... THE FINAL FRONTIER

The mighty Pendragon fan club that is The Mob goes marching ever onwards with this year's release for members, a live CD recorded at Utrecht in Holland last year. Unlike 'The Very, Very Bootleg' from two years ago, no expense has been spared on recording and packaging: it is better presented than many full price albums and this is free with Mob membership! For anyone living in remotest Peru for the last fifteen years and does not have a clue who Pendragon are, they comprise vocalist, guitarist, songwriter Nick Barrett, ably assisted by Peter Gee (bass, bass pedals, guitar, keyboards, vocals, kitchen sink), Clive Nolan (keyboards, vocals) and Fudge Smith (drums). Together they produce prog of the very highest order, being extremely melodic and at times very complex, yet damned enjoyable and listenable. The seven tracks on here present a good cross-section of the band, with older numbers such as "Kowtow" standing up against newer ones like "Nostradamus". Ballads and rockers are both here, loud and proud. There is no better way of getting involved in the world of Pendragon than being in The Mob, and for the measly annual fee you get not only this CD but four issues of the Mob Mag with all the info on the band and all that is happening. I cannot recommend this club too highly.
#29, Jun 1995

PENDRAGON
THE MASQUERADE OVERTURE

Here is Pendragon's eagerly awaited tenth album, and the question that everyone is asking was whether they could surpass 'The Window Of Life'. Well, to my ears they have managed it with ease. They have built on the strengths displayed particularly on 'Window' and its predecessor 'The World' and have produced a masterpiece. There is a greater depth to the overall proceedings and I am sure that this is because of the time they could spend recording and honing. Nick's guitarwork has never been quite this fluid and when combined with Clive's keyboards the effect is glorious. Fudge and Peter have also relished the opportunity to shine, and together Pendragon show how a top band can gel to produce music of the very highest quality. Pendragon have been going since 1978 and have been at the forefront of the UK underground progressive scene for almost as long. It is a sad indictment of the music industry that this album will probably sell more than forty thousand, but if they had been called Pink Floyd or Genesis and produced an album nowhere near as good as this it would sell millions. It is a record to be savoured, like a rich red wine: just let the music take control and have the keyboards wrap around you while the guitars lift you up as you soar away. This is a brilliant masterpiece. Yes, there are nods towards the aforementioned Floyd and Genesis, but Pendragon have their own sound. If you get one of the initial fifteen thousand, then you will have another CD containing edit and extra tracks. Oh, and the artwork must be contender for cover of the year. What are you waiting for? Go and buy this. Now.
#34, Apr 1996

PENDRAGON
THE HISTORY: 1981 - 2000

Although Pendragon may have been relatively quiet of late, it is worth noting that Nick Barrett, Clive Nolan, Peter Gee and Fudge Smith have been responsible for some of the classiest prog music to come out of the UK in the Eighties and Nineties. This compilation is an attempt to lovingly put together a representative selection of their best songs, in a superb digipak with two 12-page booklets detailing the history of the band along with a discography. Why two booklets? Well, amazingly enough this has only been released in Poland so one booklet is in Polish (words by my good friend Artur Chachlowski) with the other being a translation. If you are a Pendragon fan then this is essential as not only is the packaging some of the best I have seen, but it also contains a video clip and two acoustic numbers ("The King Of The Castle" and "Paintbox") which have been recorded solely for this compilation. This is a great introduction to the band, a CD that anyone who enjoys Floyd style prog can purchase with extreme confidence.
#58, May 2000

PENDRAGON
ONCE UPON A TIME IN ENGLAND VOL 1

PENDRAGON
ONCE UPON A TIME IN ENGLAND VOL 2

These two albums are in a similar fashion to the Galahad 'Other Crimes & Misdemeanours' CDs. Each of them contains either songs which are unavailable elsewhere or are versions of songs that later appeared on albums (for example, there is a version of possibly their best-known song, "The Black Knight", which was recorded for a BBC session).

There is a very comprehensive biography of the band up to the point that Clive joined the band (the same in both booklets), but more importantly there are full recording details and some comment with each track. They do not appear to be in any order, as they jump from 1987 to 1981 then back as far as 1978, all on consecutive songs. There are also a few problems with the recording quality, as it can leave something to be desired. But hell, this is not state of the art, but rather an attempt to make available songs that fans have either never heard before or know of their existence solely from poor bootlegs. True, if someone was listening to Pendragon for the first time then "Catch Me If You Can" would not be seen as a class song. But it is important to the fan, as it is one of the few Pendragon numbers where Nick does not sing lead (it is provided by then drummer Nigel Harris). The care and attention to detail, which has gone into these releases, is plain, and while Pendragon fans are still awaiting the new album to follow on from the superb 'The Masquerade Overture' these are worth investigating.
#59, July 2000

PENDRAGON
NOT OF THIS WORLD

Can it really be five years since 'The Masquerade Overture'? In the intervening time, Nick has suffered personally, and some of this is brought home by the lyrics. There are some very bitter words at times, but the strongest message is probably on "If I Were The Wind (And You Were The Rain)" where Nick sings to his son. It is straight from the heart and I not only felt extremely moved when I read them for the first time, but also that I was intruding on a very private matter. Nick has bared his soul on this album, so that it is extremely personal and, hopefully for him, cathartic. OK, what of the music? In many ways, this album will appeal to followers of Floyd, Genesis and Camel, albeit with more majesty and grace. This line-up of Pendragon has been together now for about fifteen years, and although Clive has many projects of his own he enjoys playing with Nick as he bears no responsibility for song writing, and just has to play keyboards. Add Fudge Smith (now with short hair) and Peter Gee to the equation and here are four people who have total faith and trust in each other. It also means that the fans know exactly what they are going to get as well. This may not be innovative prog, but it is music that can be bought with confidence. To complete the package Nick has again retained the services of artist Simon Williams who works very closely with Nick to provide a visual interpretation of the lyrics. My family spent ages studying the booklet, long before we put it on to hear what it sounded like. Listen to the first part of the title cut to hear just how powerful and dramatic prog can be.
#62, May 2001

PENDRAGON
ACOUSTICALLY CHALLENGED

Over the last ten years or so there have been many 'unplugged' albums from hard rock bands, but this must be one of the first from a prog band. No extra musicians, such as on the Galahad Acoustic Quintet release a few years ago, just the normal guys strutting their stuff acoustically (in fact only three of the band feature, as there is no room for Fudge's drums). With Peter and Nick on acoustic guitars, and Clive on keyboards, this was recorded for a radio show in Poland, hence the release on the Polish label Metal Mind. The songs are taken from throughout their career and works well in conjunction with the DVD (see review elsewhere) as none of the numbers are duplicated. They even play a non-Pendragon song in "Unspoken Words", which is from Peter's solo album. They start with a dreamy version of "And We'll Go Hunting Deer", which is one of my favourite Pendragon numbers, and played in this manner it gives it an even more magical flavour than the original release. This album shows that prog music can be played in a simpler manner and still contain power and complexity (if that is not too much of a contradiction). Other songs of note are "Alaska" and "The Voyager", but while I wouldn't necessarily recommend this album to those who have yet to discover the joys of Pendragon, to those of us who have followed the band for years this is a delight. This digipak release contains a good booklet and photos, a multimedia section that

contains an interview with Nick and some live snippets, as well as extra information about this release.
#68, Jun 2002

PENDRAGON
LIVEOSITY

This DVD and CD combo brings together two releases that were previously only available in Poland where they were released by Metal Mind (although both have been reviewed in these pages before), namely the DVD 'Live At Last... And More' and the 'Acoustically Challenged' CD. The former finds the band on the 'Masquerade Overture' tour where they show yet again that when these guys kick off that they are one of the finest sights in British progressive rock. Okay, they have been doing it longer than most and this line-up is probably now the longest together of any of the UK's underground bands, but they know how to give the crowd what they want. Nick is obviously the focal point as he sings and throws himself into his guitar, but Peter and Fudge are one of the strongest rhythm sections around and there are few keyboard players who can match the presence of Clive Nolan. With songs as powerful as "Nostradamus" and "Paintbox", this is just a delight with "Leviathan" also going down well. Within the DVD there is also an interview plus the original video for "Saved By You".

Then of course there is the CD which finds Peter and Nick sat playing their acoustic guitars while Clive cheats somewhat by using modern keyboards instead of just piano. But any CD that starts with "And We'll Go Hunting Deer" will always find favour in my book as that has long been one of my favourite songs and in this setting, it is even more beautiful than before. Although I have had the opportunity to hear these over the last few years it is great to see that at long last they will be more easily available to those who want to hear some great prog music by one of our best bands. I mean, this is even available on Amazon!
#84, July 2005

PENDRAGON
THE JEWEL

PENDRAGON
BELIEVE

Twenty years ago, Pendragon released their first full-length album, 'The Jewel', which followed on from the four-track mini-album 'Fly High, Fall Far' which had been released the previous year. The line-up was the same as on that, namely Nick Barrett (guitar, vocals), Peter Gee (bass), Rik Carter (keyboards) and Nigel Harris (drums). It is hard to 'believe' that this album is now so old, as it still sounds fresh and inviting. It includes some of the band's most well-known tracks such as "Alaska", "The Black Knight" and of course "Leviathan". Any fans of UK progressive rock will know these songs well and with the remastering that has taken place they contain plenty of power. Take "Leviathan" for example, Nick's guitar just breaks out of the speakers as he plays that well-known riff and he is then joined by the keyboards as the band moves into the song itself. As if the original album was not enough, there are four bonus songs. The first two of these are taken from the mini-album, while the second two are brand new recordings from the current line-up of two songs from the days when they were playing The Marquee, "Armageddon" and "Insomnia". Given that this is available at a bargain price through Amazon now could not be a better time to find out about the band's past. But of course, now is also the time to find out about the brand-new album, 'Believe'.

It is seventeen years since Nick, Peter, Fudge Smith (drums) and Clive Nolan (keyboards) first released an album together ('Kowtow'), and since then the line-up has never wavered. Yes, some members of the band have been more prolific than others (okay, so Clive has been involved with more bands either performing, producing or writing than most of the rest of the scene put together), but when the call goes out that a new Pendragon album is due then they all respond. This is only the second Pendragon studio release in nine years, and shows the band moving in quite different directions. Nick has brought in many influences to his writing this time so that while it is music that will appeal to older fans of the band, this is also going to be bringing in those who have yet to be involved. "Wisdom Of Solomon" goes from reflective electric guitar in front of the whole band to an acoustic guitar piece where Nick plays both intricately and delicately while also riffing it like mad. When he starts singing the percussion is delicate and it gives the song a very different feel to what one would normally expect.

But as well as the reflection there are also times in this album where the band are playing probably at their heaviest that I have heard them, and it is this mix that in some ways makes it a more difficult album to get into. The first time I played it I found that I wondered what was going on, but by the third or fourth play it had grown on me so that now it is one of my favourite albums by the band. Just do not expect for this to sound like 'The World' as the band have changed a lot since then.
#85, Nov 2005

ALAIN PERNOT
BEYOND TIME AND SPACE
This is the debut album from multi-instrumentalist Canadian Alain Pernot. It may have taken him three years to record this album, but one can only hope that it does not take so long next time as this is so damn enjoyable. It is hard to decide where to categorise this, but I know that quite a few people mention Alan Parsons when they talk about Alain and I can see where that is coming from. This is based on songs and loads of strong melodies and hooks. Given that he has recorded this by himself,

there is a strong sense of self-control and the music is always working to emphasise the songs and the vocals instead of being extended solos just in their own right. The first time I played this I hit the repeat as soon as it had finished, and I have found myself returning to it quite often over the last month. Alain has a good voice, but knows his limitations so tends to sing in the mid-range and this works very well indeed. He has an interesting site where you can listen to snippets of material and this is an artist for fans of good music to discover.
#88, Jun 2006

PERSEPHONE'S DREAM
MOONSPELL

PERSEPHONE'S DREAM
OPPOSITION

Persephone's Dream are a female fronted progressive rock band hailing from America, and 'Moonspell' was their first album as a four-piece when Rowen Poole (guitars, keyboards) and Chris Siegle (bass, keyboards) were joined by Karin Nicely (vocals) and Ed Wiancko (drums). When I initially started playing the album, I was taken not only by how strong the vocals and instrumentation were, but in the care that had gone into the production and the atmospheric spoken introduction to the opening number, "Millennium Moon". I soon had the band's musical direction worked out, that they were a modern version of Renaissance, or did I? By the time I had finished playing the album all the way through for the first time I found that not only was I impressed but also quite confused. There are just so many different strands being brought together, both lyrically and musically. Take "Learning Curve" for example. It is starts off gently with plenty of acoustic guitar and folk influences, but the percussion on the first verse is quite at odds to the music and when the lyrics are listened to the realisation dawns that the song is dealing with the subject of date rape. As the songs progresses the electric guitar becomes much more important and the mood changes throughout the piece. Some of the songs are quite strange in their approach with "Earth Dreams" the longest on the album at over twelve minutes. It is quite a surreal instrumental, which has more than a hint of New Age, okay; it is full-blown New Age and, in many ways, is quite at odds with the rest. Overall, did I enjoy the album? A resounding "Yes". This is a prog band that is truly trying to be that, bringing together styles and music in a way quite dissimilar to others in the genre.

'Opposition' came out in 2001 and the band had grown to a musical six-piece with the inclusion of Kim Finney on keyboards and John Tallent on percussion. It is interesting in the booklet to see that Jonathan Fleischman (lighting and stage show design) and Audre (artwork and web design) are all credited as band members. I must mention the booklet design, as it is one of the finest you will see, with great artwork accompanying each set of lyrics. The booklet has also been printed on a different quality paper to normal so that it is not glossy, which gives it a tactile

sensation reminiscent of old album covers. Musically the band has decided to move into a darker and heavier sphere, with Karin's distinctive vocals rising over the top. While some songs tend to fit a bit more neatly into the neo-prog mould (although not completely by any stretch of the imagination), there are plenty of other influences such as Ozric Tentacles that clearly come through. Of the two I felt that in many ways this was the more complete album, one that makes more sense when listened to in its entirety, but in some ways, some of the sheer experimentalism and therefore 'difference' of the first album are missing. To that end it is hard to pick which of the two I favour, but they are both well worth hearing.
#70, Oct 2002

PERSONA NON GRATA
THE FINE ART OF LIVING
Although this may seem like a new band, what we have here is Bruce Soord and Neil Randall, although they are normally better known as Vulgar Unicorn. If this was a straightforward VU release then I would say that this is their fourth album, but should I instead say that this is their debut? Along with Bruce's other project, Pineapple Thief, Vulgar Unicorn have been producing some of the best truly progressive music to come out of the UK over recent years and Persona Non Grata have seen this being taken to a new level. While they are always undoubtedly a prog band, this is a band that is taking progressive music and moving it into different areas. If they are not too careful, they might find themselves being thought of as being 'commercial', and as a logical follow-up to Porcupine Tree or Radiohead and there are times when they could almost be just one place removed from Muse. But. there are also plenty of nods to 'traditional' prog influences such as Floyd, mixed with an extremely healthy mix of music that owes far more to the present than it does to the past. With each song being very different it is hard to pick a favourite, although I am a huge fan of "The Only Person I Hate More Than You, Is Me" which just blasts along with plenty of twists on the way. Go on, release an edited version as a single, and see what happens!

I can see this album causing plenty of problems in that many neo-prog lovers will feel that this is just too outside their box, but if only this could be brought to greater prominence, I am sure that Cyclops could have a major hit on their hands. It brings in so many different elements, including bands like Coldplay, that this needs to be heard by a much wider audience than the normal insular progheads. The initial pressing includes a bonus disc of rare and some previously unreleased VU recordings and is something that fans of good modern music should be investigating.
#82, Jan 2005

PETER ROOM
SUMIRE
There are not many times when I find myself totally lost for words when trying to review an album, but I think that out of the thousands I have listened to over the years this must

be one of the strangest. In fact, the only way to talk about it is by saying that it is downright weird. There may be gentle backing with a female singer doing very strange things with her voice which does not follow any melody that one can ascertain, or it may be just a full-on synth attack where the keyboard 'player' is moving the controls to get different frequencies of electronic sound – rather like a clean version of what Hawkwind was doing many years ago. The most positive thing that I can say about this album that after hearing it the next thing in the player sounds much better than it would otherwise. But what for me is even harder to understand is that all of this is very much deliberate and that the band want to sound like this – it's like RIO gone mad! This is only for those who want to find out something about strange Japanese experimental music.
#86, Feb 2006

PHIDEAUX
FIENDISH
Phideaux are a band led by Rich Hutchins and Phi Xavier, and 'Fiendish' is their latest release. They are so proud of it that they are offering it free to anyone who wants it! And take it from me; if you are interested in good music then this is an album worth paying for! Artur Chachlowski gave me a copy of this, and I am extremely glad that he did, as it is an album that I have been playing a great deal. I noticed that Neil Citron was involved on some of these songs, but this is nothing like Rocket Scientists or Lana Lane. It took me quite a while to work out who Phideaux remind me of, as this is a band that is approaching music from an acoustic angle, although many of them are rockers. Eventually it dawned on me that due more to the vocals than the music behind them, this band is very like Dulcimer, whose 'When A Child' CD is still a regular visitor to both home and car players. These are well-constructed songs, with great harmonies and lyrics, so much so that the music sometimes can be playing yet it is the vocals that are key. This is not a low budget CDR being given away, but a well-recorded album with a full band and a booklet containing all the lyrics and plenty of artwork etc. This is an album that I would be recommending for purchase, let alone when you can get it for free! The following is a quote from their web site. "It is said that we are space folk throwback concept rock - kinda like Pink Floyd or The Moody Blues. Some say we are Bowie-esque (or was that burlesque). We only make our songs because we love them. Check us out: You might not need those mind-altering substances once you have sampled our sounds." What else needs to be said? Go to the site, ask for the CD, then play it and really get into a superb selection of acoustically based progressive rock sounds.
#80, Jul 2004

PHIDEAUX
CHUPACABRAS
It has been quite some time since I last reviewed Phideaux, and 'Fiendish', but now multi

-instrumentalist Phideaux Xavier and drummer Rich Hutchins are back with their fourth album. It comes with a twenty-page booklet where not only does Phideaux state who plays what (there are a lot of guests), but also contains the lyrics, loads of artwork and comments about each song. It appears that many of these songs were originally intended for the last two albums (although at least one is many years older than that), and that he is using this as a way of clearing up old songs and putting them out into the public domain, although he seems to feel that just friends and family will be interested in these in which case he is doing himself a great disservice. What makes this album so interesting is that first and foremost it is an album of songs (although some of these are long, admittedly), and these have then been arranged and developed so that it is quite unlike much of the normal prog scene. In some ways, the depth and quality of the arrangements are reminiscent of Guy Manning, and he is not afraid to use a steel guitar or tin whistle or strings if that is what the music demands. When he describes it himself, he says that they "create a complex, humorous, pretentious type of overly artsy progressive psychedelic rock music" and that "with cellos, flutes, dobros and a host of nasty electric guitars and several singers, this spree is polyphonic and polytheistic." It certainly is all of that and it is music that the listener can lose himself inside, and with the booklet can see the songs that Phideaux Xavier has discovered for himself. This is a journey that is well worth taking, and by visiting the site you can find out more about the band, see plenty of comments from others as well as listening to some of the music.
#86, Feb 2006

PHIDEAUX
313
So, not having heard from Phideaux for some years before the last issue, I now have his brand-new album to review. It was written and conceived by March 13th, 2004 and the recording was completed on March 13th, 2005 so given the way that Americans write their dates I guess that is where the title comes from. Of course, it is only right and fitting that we have thirteen songs to listen to. Friends have yet again joined Phideaux Xavier and Rich Hutchins so there may be a different line-up for each song, but that is not important, as it is the lush arrangements that make these songs what they are. Phideaux may be singing about cats in a potting shed or asking, "Have You Hugged Your Robot?" but they all make perfect sense and are great fun to listen to as he mixes prog with psych but also brings it bang up to date so that even bands like The Flaming Lips could be considered as being influences. Many of the songs have a piano as the basis, but this moves onto other things. The songs are accessible, catchy, melodic and great fun, and shouldn't that be what music is all about? A special mention here must be made of Margi Schnibbe whose booklet cartoon style artwork adds to the overall feel of this project. If you want to listen to some of this man's music then go to his website where it is possible to download albums for free (yes, nada, zip), although not this one. This is a guy who loves what he is doing, and it shows. *#87, Apr 2006*

GARY PICKFORD-HOPKINS
GPH

One of the joys of being a Tull addict is searching out some of the projects that members have worked on either prior to or after leaving the band. So, it was when tracking down recordings featuring Glenn Cornick that I came across the band Wild Turkey. They released two albums and it was the second one that I heard first, 'Turkey'. Far from being just an album for the completist, this was an album that I wanted to play, as it was so good. I did not know any of the other musicians in the band, but the singer was Gary Pickford-Hopkins. The next time I heard his voice was when he was singing with Rick Wakeman on 'Journey' and 'King Arthur'. After that, there was a very long gap, although I did hear the Wild Turkey reunion album 'Stealer Of Years' in 1996. According to the discography in the booklet, he has been doing the odd recording, and now he is back with a brand-new album. A full band has aided him, including Ray 'Taff' Williams who he has played with for many years. This is a 'grown-up' album where the main concentration is on his melodious vocals, the songs being a vehicle for his talents. There is no pandering to fashion, just a man content in his art, accompanied by people who can rock a little or slow it down as the need arises. There are so many good songs on this album, but the favourite is probably "Loving You Means Leaving You" which is a duet with Bonnie Tyler. If his name were Rod Stewart this would be a monster smash. But there is a bonus song from 1986, which is superior to even that. This is "Why?" which was written about Peter Ham and Tommy Evans, both members of Badfinger, who were the authors of Nilsson's "Without You". Peter committed suicide in 1974 and Tommy in 1983. The song is here in two versions, one with explanatory narration over the top, and the other as it was when it was released as a single. It starts with just gentle piano and delicate vocals, but gradually the song builds and as the power starts to rise, Gary lifts until the chorus peaks. It is an amazing song with a powerful story to tell, and an incredible vocal performance. I find myself drawn back to this song repeatedly; the guitar break after the second chorus is full of emotion and is just right for the feel of the song. The music flows and ebbs, with strings playing an important part then it ends as it began. Incredible.
#74, Jun 2003

PICTORIAL WAND
A SLEEPER'S AWAKENING

For Pictorial Wand then you ought to read Mattis Sörum, who over three years managed to bring this project together. It is a concept album and Mattis describes it himself as this: "the story is about a person (any person) who wakes up after a long, deep look in the mirror and finally becomes aware of his mistakes and the bad and selfish way he has lived his life. This theme is set about the seven deadly sins and put in an abstract environment. The music itself goes from very heavy passages to lyrical acoustic themes and contains a lot of symphonic instruments and analogue synths. The songs are mostly long and there are many compositional relationships to bind it all together". Just looking at the booklet is enough to make any self-respecting proghead to place him or herself in a closed

environment (with a stereo of course) and to shun the outside world until the double CD has been played through at least once. This is an incredible piece of work, and to think that Mattis had to keep leaving the project to complete his education and then return is just amazing. This is 'proper' prog – music that is accessible but to get the most out of it the listener should pay close attention. I really wish that this was available as a record as I think that 12" would be a better way of going through the booklet than the standard 12 cm, but unfortunately that is not the case these days. The cello plays an important role in binding the music together, and while it may not be the heaviest piece of music around it is certainly very dynamic and full of passion. It is a mature album, one that has taken time to grow and if the listener if prepared to take the time to sit down to listen to this as an act instead of playing this in the background then they will be richly rewarded. Superb.
#88, Jun 2006

PINEAPPLE THIEF
ABDUCTING THE UNICORN
Pineapple Thief is a side project of Bruce Soord, guitarist with Vulgar Unicorn (hence the witty title). Apart from the fact that there are far too many programmed drums, this is a very interesting album. Vulgar Unicorn are seen by some as being one of the most 'progressive' bands around, but while the label wants to link these guys to Porcupine Tree, it should be said that Pineapple Thief are far removed from the prog scene. Of course, no one could consider them a chart singles band when they place a track at the end that is twenty-five minutes long ("Parted Forever"), but at times, these guys come across as a complex Travis. There are hints of VU, but that is to be expected, and it is only by knowing the band's history that they are looked for. Overall, this is a bright album, which while although contemplative at times, is both immediate and deep enough to warrant further listening. Worth investigating.
#59, July 2000

PINEAPPLE THIEF
137
'Abducting The Unicorn' was received so well that Bruce Soord decided to record another album by his side-project (he is of course a main member of Vulgar Unicorn), and I for one am very glad that he did. There has been a large use of classic keyboards, and this has added to the ambience, but this is very much an album that uses influences from the Nineties as opposed to the Seventies. While there are elements from Porcupine Tree and Radiohead, there are also more commercial touches. Imagine if you will, a song that takes elements from the above two bands and puts it together with Manic Street Preachers, and you may get some idea of what "Incubate" is like. The song is only 3½ minutes long: get this released as a single, it's great!! While very much a grower this album also has immediate appeal, and when the band brings Hendrix-style guitar together with Thom Yorke influences on "Doppler" the result is a song that will have many prog fans baying

for more. As in Bruce's work with VU this is an album that brings together many different styles in a way that is cognisant of them, but also very much in an area of their own. The debut album may have made 137 in the DPRP Chart of 2000, but I am sure that this one will finish far higher.
#69, Aug 2002

THE PINEAPPLE THIEF
10 STORIES DOWN
One of the mysteries of modern music is why The Pineapple Thief are not held in the same reverence as Coldplay, Radiohead or even Muse as band leader Bruce Soord has more than proved time and again that this band are at least equal to bands who gain far more recognition. That is the case again with '10 Stories Down' (preceded by an EP called '4 Stories Down' which contains two songs from this album plus two more), which is a new version of the limited '12 Stories Down' which came out last year. Want beautiful ballads? Got them. Want intricate music? Yep, that's here as well. Acoustic guitar? Violins? Wonderful Arrangements? That is all here in spades.

This is a band that probably more than any other on the Cyclops roster is veering straight into the mainstream yet without compromising their own musical integrity. This may not be a band that has shifted as many units as their hyped contemporaries but if you enjoy any of the above in a light reflective mood then you owe it to yourself to find out more about these guys as they are worth it.
#85, Nov 2005

MICHAEL PINNELLA
ENTER BY THE TWELFTH GATE
This is Michael's first solo album, although he has been recording with Symphony X for ten years and will undoubtedly be back with them when they go into the studio. But for now, he is showing his skills in best keyboard player fashion, and he has obviously been listening quite a lot to Rick Wakeman, while Keith Emerson has also been playing a part in his musical education. Although some of the music is modern sounding, there is plenty where he has been influenced by classical and baroque forms and has brought this into his own pieces (all are original apart from one arrangement). Some of the songs, such as the three-piece piano concerto, are very visual and while this may be too far removed for those who enjoy the prog metal of his normal band, anyone who enjoys listening to Wakeman will get a lot out of this.
#82, Jan 2005

PLANET X
UNIVERSE

Formed by ex-Dream Theater keyboard player Derek Sherinian (who has also played with Kiss and Alice Cooper), this instrumental band's line-up also features guitarist Tony MacAlpine (who to date has released eleven solo albums) and drummer Virgil Donati, (there is also a guest bassist, Tom Kennedy). It is somewhat surprising that there is only one longish track, with "King Of The Universe" just cracking eight minutes, but there is no disputing the note density. This hard rocking technically brilliant album is going to impress many people, but it is possible to dismiss this as an ego trip if the critic was so inclined: it can only be digested in small pieces; very much like a rich cake, they have over-egged it. There is little in the way of passion or soul, but if the listener wants to stand there with their mouth open in awe, then this may just be the one for them. It is sometimes reminiscent of Colosseum II when they delve slightly into jazz-rock, but by the end of it all I found that I was not only impressed but also bored. It is a CD which needs to be treated with care.

#59, July 2000

PLANET X
LIVE FROM OZ

PLANET X
MOONBABIES

'Live From Oz' is the second album from Planet X and contains material reaching back as far as Derek Sherinian's 1999 solo album (somewhat confusingly called 'Planet X') and forward to 'MoonBabies'. Recorded in Melbourne, on the final gig of the 2001 tour, the band were joined by Dave La Rue on bass (Dixie Dregs, Steve Morse). Planet X are an instrumental band comprising Derek Sherinian (keyboards, ex-Dream Theater, Alice Cooper etc.), Virgil Donati (drums, Steve Vai etc.) and Tony MacAlpine (guitar). This is all about music played in very strange time signatures, that is extremely intricate and always at risk of falling over due to sheer note density. It is not easy to listen to, and in many ways has more in common with jazz than it has with much of the progressive rock music that is around at present. That all the band are masters of their instruments is never in doubt but trying to follow the thread of the melody can be slightly more difficult. The fact that three of the fourteen tracks are solos for each of the band does also lay them open to the claim of being somewhat narcissistic and self-indulgent, but what saves them each time is that they are just so good at what they do. They are so tight that one cannot help but be impressed. The trick is to listen to this in a darkened room and just let the music sweep over you, particularly on the "Atlantis" suite which is seventeen minutes long.

'MoonBabies' was again produced by drumming legend Simon Phillips, who apparently is quite a fan. Utilising three guest bassists (Tom Kennedy, Jimmy Johnson and Billy Sheehan), this album took fifteen months to write and record and it is not a joke when Derek Sherinian states that their most exotic time signature is four/four. The band is trying to make music that no-one else can emulate, and with this album they must be close to achieving it. A completely instrumental album, sometimes it just drifts along while at others it is dramatically in your face. I kept trying to think if they remind me of anyone, but the closest I can come is Steve Vai crossed with Pat Metheny along with some awesome drumming and keyboards. Favourite cut is "The Noble Savage" where some noodlings give way to a music that is dark and dynamic, with a locked in style for Tony and Derek. This is music that is brings together progressive and jazz (while banging just lightly on the door of hard rock) in a way that is complex and complicated and in a fashion that can never be described as background. This is an acquired taste and will not be for all, but twenty years after punk the dinosaurs are stirring again. *#69, Aug 2002*

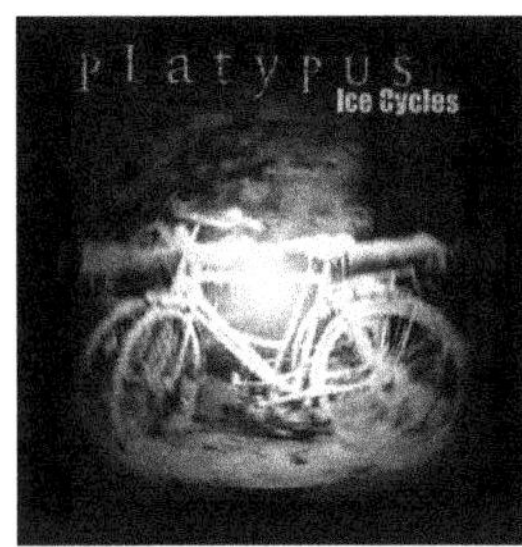

PLATYPUS
ICE CYCLES

I am a big fan of the debut, 'When Pus Comes To Shove', so was pleased indeed to receive the follow-up 'Ice Cycles'. Platypus was formed by bassist John Myung (Dream Theater), Kings X guitarist and vocalist Ty Tabor, keyboard player Derek Sherinian (Dream Theater, Alice Cooper, Kiss etc.) and drummer Rod Morgenstein (Dixie Dregs, Winger). While not as Beatlesque as the debut, this is an equally as impressive album with some great pop moments. Although these guys can all blast away or prog with the best of them, it is for pure pop combined with rock and great songs that they are renowned. Although as they prove in the closing instrumental "Partial To The Bean", which is over ten minutes long, they have not lost sight of their day jobs. By the way, that song is divided into seven parts, "Intro Pompatous", "Yoko Ono", "Yoko Two-No", "Yoko Three-No", "Platmosis", "Yoko Againo" and "Yoko Outro". That is not the only instrumental either with "25" showing that great rock numbers do not needs words as an instrument can quite easily carry the melody line. On "Cry" they can even make the listener believe that Tony Iommi is involved with the project as they kick off with some great "Iron Man"-style riffs. This is another great album, with plenty for the music lover. *#57, Mar 2000*

PODSDARAPOMUK
ON PASEWOLK AGAIN

PODSDARAPOMUK
ARKUNA VOULA TROOZO

I can't remember when I have been sent anything for review quite as experimental as this. Podsdarapomuk are a German band who have been residing in London since May last year, and if you want to catch them on the live circuit you should get your skates on as they return to Germany in April. They mix jazz with

rock, along with virtually every other influence you could name. On “A Fool’s Smile” for example, the drummer comes across as Keith Moon while the bridge sounds like an extremely warped blues! This is challenging stuff, with four tracks on the CD (‘On Pasewolk Again’) from 1995 and another four on the tape (from January this year), both collections clocking in at about sixteen minutes. Although challenging, it is music that is rewarding, coming across as a bastard child of Gentle Giant and VDGG with loads of other stuff thrown in for good measure. Bizarre? Certainly. Interesting? Definitely. If you are into music outside of normal definition, that ensures that you pay attention to what is happening (whatever Podsdarapomuk are, background they are not) then you need to hear this.
#40, Mar 1997

BILL POHL
SOLID EARTH

Bill Pohl used to be guitarist in Morning Thunder, a prog band from Fort Worth, Texas. The band weathered quite a few personnel changes, and became Crunchy Frog, but in 1991 found themselves without a bassist. At this point Kurt Rongey asked Bill to record an album for his Long Dark Music label. With John Livingstone (also from Crunchy Frog) on drums, and Tom Main guesting on keyboards for three of the tracks, Bill has produced an album of extremely complex and dynamic music. For the most part instrumental, here is an album by a guitarist of outstanding skill and ability. Indeed, I felt that although Bill can sing, this actually detracted from the album. It is difficult to think that for the most part there are only two musicians, as they manage to sound like a top-flight band. The songs are that, and not an excuse for speed of light masturbatory exercises that can so often be the case with albums of this type. There is plenty here for the guitar rock fan, as well as for the proghead as while this is first and foremost a rock album, the skill and style will also lend itself to the prog fan. Bill Pohl has been likened to both McLaughlin and Holdsworth, and it is not difficult to see why: this guy can play. This is a CD that benefits by being played repeatedly, as it just grows and grows. If you like jazz rock, prog rock, guitar rock or just plain old-fashioned top-flight musicianship then this is one for you. *#22, Mar 1994*

POISONED ELECTRICK HEAD
POISONED ELECTRICK HEAD

PEH were formed in 1986, since when they have gained quite a reputation. In 1988 and 1989 they took part in national band competitions, winning them both, and have now played more than 500 gigs in the company of bands such as Hawkwind, Ozrics, Cardiacs, Senser, Back To The Planet, Arthur Brown, Gong, Daevid Allen, Magic Mushroom Band etc. They have also performed at the Stonehenge, Glastonbury and Castle Morton festivals, as well as another thirty free festivals, organised events, and the odd megadog! The CD is unusual in that it does not list the band members, and I must confess that I'm not even sure how many there are! But does it matter? On the player now is their debut CD, which came out in June 1992, and the new one is due out in April. Their sound is a mixture of Twelfth Night, Ozrics, Cardiacs, Pink Floyd and Hawkwind (among others); a truly diverse sound well away from the rest of the UK scene. Traffic driving by and long held-down chords gradually introduce us to the world of PEH. Sequencers ascend and descend (reminiscent of HHGTTG) but gradually the sound becomes more staccato and guitars make their presence felt. "Unborn" brings in their own version of rock, but there is also room for the song to slow right down and take on new meaning, just before all hell breaks loose.

Lyrics are a very important part of the music, and they are certainly challenging – unlike most of today's. "Unborn" asks what right we have, to bring a child into the world, have we thought it out and what world are we leaving for it? For me the absolute highlight is "Twentieth Century Man", which is asking what is going to happen, and then we hear George Bush making a speech about Sadaam Hussein. This is against a backdrop of swirling guitars, but eventually the main musical theme returns, and the lyrics state the events leading to a nuclear holocaust. We all know about the horrors of nuclear war, but this is the first song I have heard that describes in detail what will happen to the individual. "Flying glass lacerates my face, my clothes melt, burn, stick to my skin, I have no body, all I feel is pain as my blood expands to burst my brain, sizzling heat licks my scream filled ears, so intense that it boils my fears, I will not even have time to go insane as my life evaporates". What I found quite horrifying, as well as the words, is that after the above description PEH play the theme from 'Mission Impossible'. A small musical phrase makes quite a statement all on its own. All in all, a thought provoking and very intense album. On a purely musical level it is very enjoyable, but when the lyrics are added to it, it shows just why Poisoned Electrick Head have such a reputation.
#22, Mar 1994

POISONED ELECTRICK HEAD
THE BIG EYE AM

POISONED ELECTRICK HEAD
OUT OF ORDER

Of all the bands I have heard for the first time this year, the one that I am most excited about is Poisoned Electrick head. PEH have a sound that is totally identifiable and recognisably unique: a statement that can't be placed at the door of many bands these days. Sure, it is possible to say that they reminiscent of other bands, like Hawkwind, but really PEH are out there on their own. Is it the vocal style, or the way that the sax is so important? I must confess that I can't put my finger on it, but I do know that I love it intensely. Having reviewed their debut only last issue, I am pleased that I can review their follow-up in this one. They are now signed up to Abstract who released a single, "Out Of Order", to promote the album. The artwork and booklet carry on from where the debut left off, giving them an artistic identity as well as a musical one.

I still do not know how many members there are in the band or who does what, but hopefully I will rectify that when I eventually manage to see them live. Kerrang! said that they "have a found a sound which is wholly their own: trippy, danceable, for psychos. John Barnes could not match these frontmen for energy if he overdosed on Isotonic Lucozade". High praise indeed. There are eight tracks on the CD (in fact there are nine, with the bonus not credited on the sleeve). They are all PEH, running on high octane fuelled with the guitar and keyboards driving the vocals along. This CD just cannot be played without movement from the listener. It is impossible to listen to "Mr Weasel" without bouncing. Hell, I would love to see this live because I can imagine the audience being one big sweaty mass of dancers. I loved the debut, but I love this one more. In fact, from the time I received it I have had a problem playing anything else to listen to and review because this is just brilliant!

The single that was released, "Out Of Order", is a definite must purchase as it contains three songs that have long been deleted. If I could drag each and every one of you into a record shop and force you to buy this I would, because your ears would love me forever. Get it, buy it, freefall in to the world of PEH
#23, May 1994

POISONED ELECTRICK HEAD
THE HANGED MAN
It has been way, way too long since the last PEH album, the wonderful 'The Big Eye Am'. Personnel problems and record contracts have been stumbling blocks, but now things appear to be settled in the PEH camp. Blueprint also now have the rights to 'Poisoned Electrick Head' and 'Unmistakeably Rainbow Trout', and they will be re-released later this year. 'The Hanged Man' is a more diverse album than before, although again totally recognisable as being PEH; there are not many bands as distinctive. There are fifteen songs, although some of these are just small connecting pieces. They are masters of tongue in cheek humour, both musical and lyrical, and at the same time cutting through and making a point with power. "Can You See What I See?" is the most scathing attack on the chart music industry I have ever had the pleasure to read. I bet it does not get any airplay! "Tied Up In Nots" and "I Drink Therefore I Am" are also candidates for top track, and yet again PEH have produced an album they can rightly be proud of. Not many bands find themselves compared to Gong and Alien Sex Fiend, as well as Devo, Cardiacs etc. However, Poisoned Electrick Head succeed just because they do not sound like anybody else. Now could not be a better time to discover what they are about.
#39, Jan 1997

JON POOLE
WHAT'S THE UGLIEST PART OF YOUR BODY?

Jon Poole is guitarist in famed UK underground outfit Cardiacs, and back in 1994, he decided to spend the summer recording an album all on his own that was to be a tribute to Frank Zappa and the Mothers Of Invention. The album was called 'What's The Ugliest Part Of Your Body' and contained sixteen numbers that were originally recorded by Frank between 1965 and 1969. The album sold well on tape and it has now been made available on CD by Org Records, an offshoot of the legendary Organ fanzine. Sean, Marina et al care passionately about music and never pander to fashion – discover the bands that they are trying to promote. Next issue of Organ available February 3rd – but I digress. Jon recorded the album using equipment that was out of date even then, which given the complexity of the music was something of a trial. Even now, he cannot explain why he persevered but I for one am extremely glad that he did. It is an album that can be enjoyed very much for its' own sake, yet at the same time makes the listener wonder just what the original sounded like and maybe it is time to investigate Zappa after all. In other words, as a tribute album it works on both levels. It is hard to believe that this is all the work of one man, and even harder to pick out a favourite, I love them all!!
#72, Feb 2003

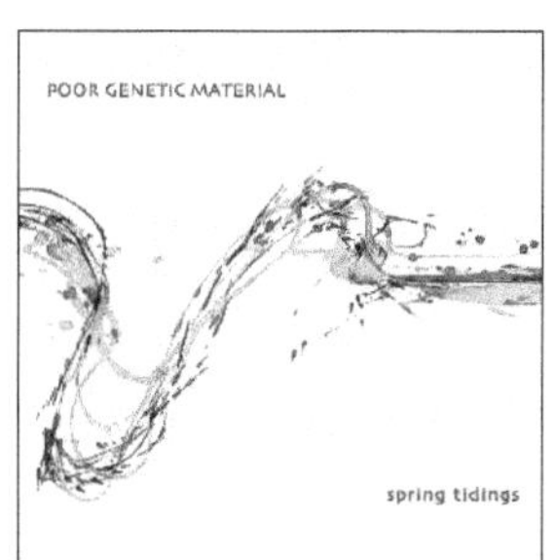

POOR GENETIC MATERIAL
SPRING TIDINGS

PGM are a band new to me, but this is the fourth of their seasonally titled albums and they have been around the German progressive scene for a few years now. Phil Griffiths is an outstanding singer who can also be found in Alias Eye, and is very reminiscent of Michael Sadler of Saga, but musically this is bringing together the very best of neo prog with some more melodic rock influences. They are not afraid to use a staccato approach to some of the music, while the keyboards and guitars mix, meld and flow. Listen carefully and you will find some very complex patterns going through the music underneath the main melody, and it all works very well indeed, with guitarist Stefan Glomb and keyboard player Philipp Jaehne swapping lead roles throughout. Dennis Sturm has a clear and solid bass sound while new drummer Dominik Steainbacher makes his presence felt as much by what he does not play (there are passages with no percussion) as much as by what he does. There is a real dynamic going on with this music, as they move easily from gentle and lulling to something that is far more in the face. It can be delicate or strident and commanding as the need arises and the mood changes. I kept being reminded of Saga the more I played it, (especially on the superb "April") but I think that is due mainly to the vocals, as in many ways PGM are more powerful and with a broader musical palette.

Overall an enjoyable album that already has me wondering what the others are like.
#87, Apr 2006

POPOL VUH
FUTURE SOUND EXPERIENCE
This was Popol Vuh's twenty-seventh album, and their third for Mystic. Originally released in a limited fashion in 1993, some new links were added to this to make it one flowing piece of music. This is mostly electronica, with some added musical instruments, but one that contains a certain harsh edge that takes away from the New Age feel. For me the songs containing mostly acoustic and electric guitars are the ones that work best, but the choral sections are quite strange. It should be said that Popol Vuh are an acquired taste, one that I have never understood, but during their career they released over thirty albums since their debut in 1970. The bandleader was Florian Fricke, the one constant in the career of the band, who sadly passed away on December 29th, 2001, following a stroke he suffered before Christmas. An album for those into Kraut Rock.
#66, Feb 2002

PORCUPINE TREE
SIGNIFY
Porcupine Tree has managed to break out of the underground progressive rock scene and gain critical acclaim: their last album, 'The Sky Moved Sideways', sold more than twenty thousand, and heavy touring and increased presence in the music papers has set the stage for them to become very big indeed. They were formed in 1985 when it was the work of one man, Steven Wilson (who also records with Tim Bowness under the no-man moniker). By December 1993 it had become a live unit with the addition of Colin Edwin (bass), Chris Maitland (percussion) and Richard Barbieri (ex-Japan, keyboards). 'Signify' is available as either a CD or double vinyl album (which contains an extra track) and manages to defy categorisation (except that it is truly progressive in the fact that they do not sound like anyone else) as it mixes ambient, hard rock, instrumentals and spacey themes. There are some very strong songs such as "Waiting" (which was an indie hit earlier in the year) and "Sever". However, there are other times when the music moves and hangs together, before drifting away. It is a wonderful album, which can only build on their previous success. You will be hearing a lot about these guys in the next few months – you have been warned. *#37, Oct 1996*

PORCUPINE TREE
STAIRCASE INFINITIES
During the sessions for the 'Up The Downstair' CD, more music was recorded than made it onto the album, along with two songs that were completed too late to be considered for inclusion. This CD EP includes three out-takes, plus the other two songs. PT says that it should be considered as the missing songs from the originally intended double CD that would also have included an edit of the first two phases of "Voyage 34". Over the last few

years Porcupine Tree have been coming to the fore as the most accepted of the new wave of progressive rock bands. When their latest album, 'Signify', hit the racks it seemed as if they could do no wrong and it is a truly an impressive piece of work. But these songs are earlier and more atmospheric, more instrumental, and in some ways, more self-indulgent and I question if these would be viewed in a positive light by critics who love the newer album. That may sound as if I am coming over negatively but that is not the case at all. These are very keyboard and mood oriented as opposed to rock and dynamic. Floydian? Yes, but in an early Seventies Floydian way. I wouldn't suggest this as a starting point for Porcupine Tree, but once you have got your teeth into them then search this out.
#42, July 1997

PORCUPINE TREE
COMA DIVINE
Porcupine Tree has found themselves in the rather unusual position of being a prog band that is liked by the critics. Having released albums that were well received, but not as commercially profitable as they could have been, they broke through in a big way with 'Signify' last year and are now back with a live album. The very short intro is torn apart by the immense riffing of Steven Wilson, who also provides lead vocals, and as a four piece there is room for long instrumental passages that allow them to demonstrate just how powerful a band can be within this genre. These are rockers first and foremost, and proggers second. That is not to say that keyboard player Richard Barbieri is a bit player, far from it, just that keyboards can be a cutting-edge rock instrument as well as a pacifier. Colin Edwin (bass) and Chris Maitland (drums) provide the platform on which to build, and they do, brilliantly. Within the same song they can come across as Pink Floyd, or Hawkwind, Genesis, or even Be Bop Deluxe! There is power, yet also restraint, and room to move inside the music. At times, it is the simplicity, such as at the beginning of "Waiting Phase One" which is beautiful, while at others it is the breathtaking complexity. Three songs break the ten-minute barrier while "Radioactive Toy" comes in at a monstrous fifteen plus. The crowd in Rome certainly enjoyed themselves and, on this showing, it is not difficult to see why. *#45, Nov 1997*

PORCUPINE TREE
LIGHTBULB SUN
Porcupine Tree is a rarity indeed, a prog band that dares to be fashionable. The line-up is also extremely stable, having been the same for seven years. Steve Wilson provides vocals and guitar (as well as other instruments, and most of the songs), Richard Barbieri is on keyboards, Colin Edwin on bass and Chris Maitland on drums. Porcupine Tree are truly progressive in the sense that they bring together many musical styles and are not content to stay in any one musical area for too long. They are not copyists or wannabes; they are very much in control of their own musical destiny. The opening song, "Lightbulb Sun", is a case in point. It starts life as a gentle acoustic guitar

number, with some delicate piano. Apart from the vocals, it could be classic Tull tinged with The Beatles. This suddenly becomes a rock number, and then as the rhythm section finally makes an appearance, it is a more upbeat indie number, yet all the time continuing the initial melodic theme. The next number, "How Is Your Life Today?" reminds me of Godley & Creme, with no rhythm section but mostly piano. From there, of course it is just one step to the psychedelic "Four Chords That Made A Million", while "Shemovedon" of course bears no musical relation to the songs that have preceded it whatsoever. When I had listened to this album all the way through for the first time, I immediately played it again. It is just a superb piece of work, one that easily surpasses the last studio album of theirs that I heard, 'Signify'. With this release, Porcupine Tree have come of age. If you love progressive music, have ever thought that it would be great if the bands of the Seventies were still cutting it in the Zeroes (well what else can you call them, the Noughties?), then look no further. *#59, July 2000*

POVERTY'S NO CRIME
SLAVE TO THE MIND

This is the third album by German Progressive Metal band Poverty's No Crime, all by the founding line-up. Having toured with bands such as Waltari, Virgin Steele and Angra they have a very high profile in Germany and Japan with their most recent album, 'Symbiosis', doing very well for them. However, they have now split from Noise who released the first two, and this is their debut for Inside Out. A great booklet gives the impression that this band is going to go places, but maybe this is contradicted slightly by the music. They play well together and have some good ideas, but there is no spark, no originality. Having recently been playing Threshold's debut again I was struck by the fact that although both bands supposedly play the same type of music there is a great gulf between them. Threshold come out with in your face riffs and great hooks and ideas while Poverty's No Crime do not play the hard rock card as much as they should, and the impression is a band that does not quite cut it. It is a shame as they are all fine musicians, but they need to take a step back and decide what they are trying to achieve. *#55, Sept 1999*

POVERTY'S NO CRIME
ONE IN A MILLION

The fourth album by German prog metallers Poverty's No Crime shows them in fine form. The summer sees them on the road with Spock's Beard, Threshold, Pain Of Salvation, Symphony X, Flower Kings and Devin Townsend so they are certainly being kept busy. But while the press release states how much heavier the band have become; it is an effect that is glossed over just a little too much in the production. The impression is that here is a band that can play, and has some great ideas, but will be totally different in the concert arena where the sound will be much rawer. On the plus side, there is a great version of Rush's "Distant Early Warning", another band that also suffered at times from too much

fiddling in the studio (it is easily one of the best Rush covers I have ever heard). I did enjoy the album but will probably be turning to label-mates Threshold for this type of music.
#63, Jul 2001

POVERTY'S NO CRIME
THE CHEMICAL CHAOS
Back with their fifth album, Poverty's No Crime show no signs of slowing down with yet another hard rocking set. While some of these songs probably come under the prog metal banner, there are others which are much more straightforward melodic hard rock. Opener "Walk Into Nowhere" is a good snapshot of the whole of the album – there are times when it is riffing hard, times when it is soft and gentle, sometimes all the band rocking hard and at others it is just vocals and acoustic guitar. All the time it is keeping to a strong melody so that even though the music is flowing and changing it is very easy to listen to. This would be a great gig opener, as it would pump up the crowd. But what makes this song for me is the small gap where a few finger-popped bass notes make their appearance felt and linger – it is small nuances that can really make a song.

Each song flows into the next, and the band is happy blasting along or just playing gently, but this never lasts for too long. On "Every Kind Of life" the guitars are blasting out while the keyboards gently follow the vocal melody, simple stuff but it works. Strong production helps the music to be captured at its' best, and the result is an album that is full of powerful songs and rocking guitars that anybody who enjoys prog metal should have in their collection. Superb.
#78, Apr 2004

PRESENT
HIGH INFIDELITY
This mostly instrumental album is challenging, to say the least. It is very much a jazz album, with the ten-man line-up including brass (a flugelhorn!) and cellos. The music cascades and sweeps, and while often strident and harsh is never anything less than powerful. This is not easy listening, but rather music that must be worked at to be enjoyed. It may not be an album to listen to often, even for those who enjoy jazz more than I do, but there is something in it that is strangely compelling. Themes move, disappear, and then come back again later. There are only three tracks, but the shortest is more than nine minutes in length while the longest is more than twenty-seven. A friend I have lent it to is enjoying playing this at very loud volume, and is a big fan of the horns, but for many this will be an acquired taste. Not for the fainthearted.
#66, Feb 2002

PRESENT
A GREAT INHUMANE ADVENTURE

Belgian Roger Trigaux first became well-known with Univers Zero, the band he formed with Daniel Denis in 1974. He left after two albums in 1979 to form Present although they then disbanded in the mid-Eighties. He later formed a duo with his son Reginald which later became a full band with the name Present. This album was recorded on their 1998 American tour, on the final date. The band had been gigging for five weeks so by this time they were extremely tight, which is certainly a great help when playing music like this. This is prog rock Jim, but not as many know it. Here we have challenging music that brings in jazz and improvisation and takes the term 'Avant Garde' to the max. Even some progheads will find that they cannot deal with music such as this, but for those who are willing to open their minds then this is quite a trip. If I want to clear a room then this is an album that I would put on, but if I want to savour in something that is extraordinary in the truest sense of the world then this is the same. There are only five songs, ranging in length from ten minutes to twenty-three, but somehow, they manage to encompass the world. Reginald and Roger have a wonderful understanding and there are some great guitar lines while at times Pierre Chevalier seems to be repeating the same piano chord sequences for minutes at a time to allow the guys out front to go off at extremes and bounce off each other. I have enjoyed playing this, in many ways it is an incredible piece of work. If you enjoy free form jazz but have never felt inspired to look to prog then you should investigate this, as should fans of Magma or King Crimson.

#86, Feb 2006

MARK PRICE
DOMAIN

Mark first became interested in music at a young age and started taking piano lessons at the age of eight. Over a period, his interest in the wider world of keyboards developed and he looked to musicians such as Tony Banks, Keith Emerson and Rick Wakeman for influences. During school and college years he tried to form or join various melodic rock bands, but most seemed to be playing punk or heavy metal and keyboards were not required. After various projects, he joined a heavy rock band with hints of Hawkwind, in 1985. This band was Channel 8, which in turn became Final Conflict. As well as various EP's, Mark recorded three albums with them, namely 'Channel 8', 'The Time Has Arrived' and 'Redress The Balance'. The last of these was released on CD to great approval, but Mark had left during the recording sessions with drummer Arny Wheatley. He then joined The Method, with whom he recorded one album, 'Moonchanges' (which is still unreleased), then again joined forces with Arny to form another progressive rock band, Framework. Mark stayed with them from their formation in January 1991 until this year, during which time they released 'Ninth In An Ocean of Time' and 'A Slice of Life' on cassette and 'Picture Glass Theatre' on CD. During the recording of their latest album, 'Confidential

Whispers', Mark was asked by Grace if he knew of any keyboard players looking for a gig to replace John Davies who had to leave for personal reasons, and he is now installed as the keyboard player for Grace, adding new insights to old songs.

Mark has certainly been active on the recording front, as apart from his activities with bands he has also recorded two other albums with Phil Meeks and ten solo works. The first of these was 'A Lake Full of Smiling Fish' back in 1984, and 'Domain' is the newest, which was recorded last year. Mark has never tried to push himself or his music, and it is only since joining Grace that he has started selling tapes in any number. Indeed, this piece is the first time that anything has been written about him. He does have a self-deprecating sense of humour and when he sent me 'Domain' he told me that it was a great album for recording over. He does himself a real injustice as the tape is great listening. I must confess that I rarely listen to keyboard albums (although Paul Ward's CD seems to find its way onto my player with regularity), but I have been playing this a great deal. Unlike some keyboard works, 'Domain' is very tuneful and enjoyable, with a style not unlike Jarre, and is an album for those who want to just sit back and let some relaxing sounds wash over them.

Varying in length from two minutes to nine, the twelve songs all give an insight into Grace's newest member. If you are wondering what keyboard players get up to in their holidays or are just interested in some melodic music which does not require you to suffer head damage while listening to it, then this is for you.
#18, May 1993

PRIME MOVER
ALIAS DRIVKRAFT

I admire the guys in Prime Mover as they are from the part of Finland where the population speak Swedish, and instead of taking the easy route and releasing an album in English (which apparently, they used to perform in) they have instead released it in Swedish. So, that means that 94% of the people in their own country will not have the language this is being sung in as their first language – it takes balls if nothing else. Mind you, with this prog album bringing in elements of Floyd and IQ and maintaining very strong melodies, as well as being influenced by metal, folk, jazz and pop, this is an album that goes beyond simple language difficulties. They had some guests add violin and trumpet which does give an extra flavour, but it is the way that they move from one style to another that makes this so interesting. They have decided that they want to make music on their terms, something that they enjoy and want to listen to themselves and this refusal to conform and to produce what people expect from Finnish prog has resulted in a progressive album that fans of Vulgar Unicorn and suchlike would do well to investigate.
#84, July 2005

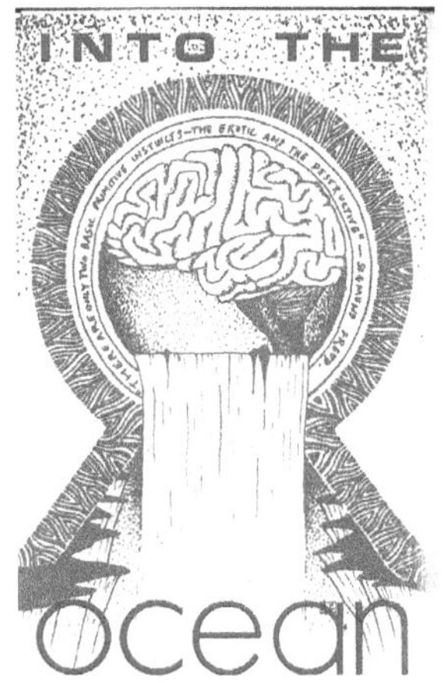

PRIMITIVE INSTINCT
INTO THE OCEAN

P.I. (as they are known to their friends) have been around for over six years now. At present, I have their latest tape on the deck, and almost unbelievably, this is the first time I have heard any of their material. They are regulars on the London gig circuit, and this tape shows why they have managed to build up quite a following. On first hearing one would have to say that the sound is very Pendragon, Marillion (Hogarth era) with more than a smattering of Big Big Train thrown in for good measure. The songs are extremely commercial and enjoyable with a heavy emphasis on held-down keyboard chords providing the backdrop for the rest of the band. Anyone looking for material in the Marillion genre could do far worse than search this band out. This tape is currently available, but when it is has sold out there will not be any more as it is forming the basis of the new CD. Material has been re-recorded and new songs added.
#21, Jan 1994

PRIMITIVE INSTINCT
FLOATING TANGIBILITY

P.I. were formed in 1987 by Nick Sheridan (guitar, vocals) and Andy Quinnell (keyboards) with Billy Geddes (bass), Rich Culham (drums) and Nick Brown (guitar). The first demo was recorded in '88 and the second in '89, which was also the year they headlined the Maidstone Rock Festival which was attended by more than seven thousand people. Later the same year Billy left to be replaced by Richard Chater who was in turn was replaced by Pic in 1990. In 1992, after numerous gigs (including supporting Ark on a national tour) and more tapes, Nick Brown decided to quit. P.I. stayed as a four-piece and recorded the 'Into The Ocean' demo which I reviewed in an earlier issue. This tape forms the basis of the CD, as these songs along with four more can be found here. Overall, it is very enjoyable, with good songs that work well. Nick has a good clear voice, and it fits well with the music.

Similarities? Well, there are at times hints of Pink Floyd and Barclay James Harvest, and this is certainly true of the guitar which mostly seems to be part of the overall background while not stamping any authority on the sound as a whole. This is not meant as a criticism, but rather that P.I. seem to be treading a slightly different path to many of the current scene, as there seems to be a move towards more rock prog than prog rock. The songs are commercial, very enjoyable, with current favourite being the catchy "One Way Man", which manages to incorporate loads of different styles and moods. I will be looking forward to the next part of the 'Voyage of Discovery' trilogy.
#23, May 1994

PRKLZ
DEUCE
This album may well be on Music Is Intelligence, but whatever it is, it is not prog in the normal recognised sense. There is quite a lot going on in between the driving riffs, but I got the impression that the band do not actually know what they want to achieve and therefore bridge many styles without being very good at any of them (although the frantic speed rock of "Tip Toe" does show promise). Consequently, I can't see how they will be able to keep an audience as there are so many different styles being tried, without any thought to continuity. An album that will appeal more to the metalhead than the progger, but even they may find this is a little too much to take as it moves from one area to another.
#31, Oct 1995

PRODUCT
AIRE
One thing about listening to so much new music is that even as the album starts I find myself starting to work out what I am going to say. Normally within the first few minutes of an album I can gauge if I am going to like it. By now, you would have thought that I would know better. I first played this album while I was decorating which gave me the opportunity to play a lot of albums back to back very loudly to see what I felt about them. If I hadn't had a paintbrush in my hand, there is a good chance that I would have turned this off after the first few minutes as it sounded as if here was another laid back almost New Age album. But the gentle beginning gives no impression of the guitars that are going to break through, then gently drift out again. I soon found that I was spending more time concentrating on the music than I was on the walls.

Product are a new band to me, and are a duo of Arman Christoff Boyles (songs, vocals, guitars, keyboards) and Scott Rader (drums, bass) with some guest musicians. The comparison that one soon starts to make is with Pink Floyd, although there is much more going on in the way of guitars. It is bleak and dark, but also intriguing and compelling. The vocals are there but are mixed so that they often take a back seat to what is going on, which gives the band a sound that is quite different to many. This is music that is restrained, even when the band are crunching as they do on "Age Of Reason" and is an album that works well on all levels. It certainly made my decorating go a lot better, but it is also an album to be enjoyed in a darkened room, listening intently and drifting into their world. It was only on visiting their web site that I discovered that this is a concept album based on the life of Galileo, and although this is only their second album they have been working together since 1990. Well worth investigation by progheads.
#78, Apr 2004

PRODUCT
THE FIRE

'The Fire' is the third album by Product and is a concept album based on the life of Nero. They are a duo comprising Arman Christoff Boyles (words and music, vocals, guitars, keyboards) and Scott Rader (drums, bass, vocals) with two guest vocalists helping on effects. In many ways, this is a sparse album, one with lots of space and emptiness, so although there are times when they come across as fairly Floydian this is not really indicative of the whole sound. There are some passages that are quite like classic Bowie, and these move and evolve, but overall, I felt that this was a more disjointed work than their previous album 'Aire'. It takes a lot to get into, and certainly is not as immediate as much of the prog that has come out recently. This is one to be heard prior to purchase and is not something to which I will be regularly be returning. *#85, Nov 2005*

PROJECT CREATION
THE FLOATING WORLD

This is the latest album from multi-instrumentalist Hugo Flores (Sonic Pulsar), and he has brought in some extra musicians to help him put forward this concept album about the development of life on a dead planet. This is a crunching work with the emphasis as much on the rock as it is on prog, and the mastering by Henning Pauly has managed to capture all the elements so that it can be played at the correct volume, loud! This is not prog metal, but it is very much a rock album and there are times when the intensity is almost like a wall of sound. The drums are being hit very hard, while the keyboards, guitar and bass at times all seem to be vying to be in the same space in the listener's ears, but instead of sounding confused it all sounds so very right indeed. It is a very accessible album and I can guarantee that even from the first note of the title song that you will find yourself nodding along with a smile on your face. Well that's what I did anyway... But there is more to this than just brashness, there is depth and with guests adding touches like cello and sax and two extra singers there is the feeling of a space and breadth. The booklet contains some superb artwork as well as the lyrics, and the result is an album that while not strictly prog in much of the sense is firmly straddling the line between prog and melodic hard rock and is something that I have thoroughly enjoyed listening to. *#87, Apr 2006*

PRONG
SCORPIO RISING

It has been seven years since the last Prong studio album but given that most people thought that the band had gone forever, maybe that is not too long to wait. Only singer and guitarist Tommy Victor is still there from the old days, but he is determined that this album is going to be seen as the follow-up to 'Rude Awakenings' and not a new entity altogether. The band came from hardcore roots, and "Regal" shows that those days

have not been totally forgotten, but for the most part this album is much more about down tuned guitars allowed to provide plenty of darkness and heaviness. It is a very heavy album, and there are some interesting songs within it, but for some reason this hasn't captured my imagination and there are plenty of other albums around that I will be listening to instead of this one.
#76, Oct 2003

PROTO-KAW
BEFORE BECAME AFTER
I have been a Kansas fan for many years, but it was only last year that I became aware of something unusual in that band's past, namely that prior to Kansas there was a totally different band with the same name, the only link being that of songwriter, guitarist and keyboard player Kerry Livgren. Amazingly some old recordings of the original Kansas had survived, and Cuneiform wanted to release them. Kerry agreed and contacted the guys and they decided to get back together again. The result is a brand-new album, with virtually the original band (second keyboard player Don Montre passed away at the age of 39, and bassist Rod Mikinski only had time to record one song and has been replaced by Craig Kew). Five of the songs are from the original period, with five new ones, hence the title. The band could not use the name 'Kansas' again but instead settled on Proto-Kaw as "Proto" means "Pre" and "Kaw" is most likely the original, Indian, name of the territory where Kansas is currently located. Given that Kerry Livgren composed these songs, as well as most of those of the later Kansas there is little surprise that there are some similarities. However, one major difference is that in the original Kansas there was no violin, as instead John Bolton provided saxophones and flute. This gives the music a very different feel, something that is described in the press release as "progressive jazz psychedelia". It is quite an unusual album to listen to in that it is so similar at times to the style of music I have loved for so long, but just different enough so that when I first played it I found that at times it strangely grated. But the twists and turns combined with Kerry's great song writing and Lynn Meredith's great vocals (apart from a small amount of work with Plastique, Lynn has not been singing for thirty years – incredible) have made an album that is an essential purchase for progheads. Although this will be picked up by many due to the Kansas connections, this is an album that should be heard in its' own right and is one I will often be returning to. *#79, May 2004*

PROTO-KAW
EARLY RECORDINGS…
The full story of this album is given away in the title, 'Early Recordings From Kansas 1971-1973'. When this album was released by Cuneiform there was far more interest than anyone ever imagined, which led to Kerry getting his old bandmates out of retirement and back into the recording studio. 'Before Became After' is certainly far more polished, but this more than stands up in its' own right and is a joy to listen to.

The songs on this CD are mostly demos with a few live cuts and were recorded by Kansas II. The biggest difference between Kansas II and Kansas III in a musical sense is that the former was far more 'proggy' and used saxophones instead of a violin, yet in many ways they are quite similar which probably is not too surprising given that Kerry wrote all the material. This is music with a real passion, possibly the reason that they were not successful is that it was just too progressive for the market in America at the time, but it would have been lapped up over here. Llyn has a great voice, and the musicianship is spot on.

Of special interest to the Kansas fan is that there are two songs on here which the later version of the band made far more well-known in "Belexes" and "Incomudro". This is a joy from start to finish, and any proghead will get a great deal from this.
#82, Jan 2005

PROTO-KAW
THE WAIT OF GLORY

So, Proto-Kaw are now back with their second 'proper' album. I wonder what Kerry's old Kansas bandmates are making of this situation, as their last studio album was 2000, whereas he has found time to now write two albums for the band that existed as Kansas before they did. The last album saw the band coming to terms that with the release of their demos on Cuneiform they were back in the limelight once again – the only one who has stayed in music was Kerry himself, and in some instances, they did not even have instruments anymore. That album was awesome in many ways (if you have not heard it then you should), but this time the band has tasted success not only with that album but also in a live environment for the first time in more than thirty years. This album was always going to be different, as although Kerry again has written all the songs, this time around the guys knew what they were doing to a far greater degree, and how to work again as a unit.

This is not as immediate as 'Before Became After', but 'The Wait Of Glory' is an even more interesting album. The last Proto-Kaw sounded what Kansas would have been like with some different musicians and instruments (if that makes sense); while here they are moving very much in their own direction. On songs such as "Relics Of The Tempest", there are similarities with Kansas, but given that Kerry wrote all the material that must be expected, but here it is much more in the feel and nuances as opposed to the whole song. At times, very dark, at times very dramatic indeed in the way that the woodwind combines with the guitars and keyboards, and at other times lifted by the power of Llyn Meredith's great vocals.

Yet again this is an album that is to be savoured and enjoyed and fans of good melodic music as well as all Kansas lovers should hear this.
#86, Feb 2006

PSYMBIENCE
IS

The debut album from this quintet was released last year, and for a self-release is nicely packaged with good artwork in a digipak. The music is also well produced which is a bonus, as here is some of the most complex prog that you are likely to come across for some time. The band are bringing together music from lots of different areas (think Tool, early King Crimson, Sigur Ros, Poisoned Electrick Head just to name a few I spotted) and then putting it together to make some musical sense. That this is not always clear is probably down more to failings on the listeners' part rather than that of the players. There is quite a lot of jazz improvisation going on in the background, but that is being torn apart from the cutting edge of music that they are trampling all over. This is not music for the faint hearted because it will take so much out of you just by playing it and trying to work out not only what is going on, but where the journey is going to take you. Vocals are strong and powerful yet for me the most important aspect is probably the fretless bass playing of Brian which holds this all together, underpinning melodies and either providing support or going off on tangents all his own. This truly is progressive music and because of that will not be to everyone's tastes (not even all progheads), but if you want something that is most definitely very well executed and so far out of left field as to be not on the map, then you will enjoy this.

#88, Jun 2006

PTS
TIDES

PTS originally formed in Holland in 1987 as a covers band and released their first demo 'Camera Life' in 1990. A second cassette 'Welcome To The Real World' followed in 1991, and their debut CD 'Nightlines' in 1992. It was after this release that they were signed by SI and 'Tides' is the result. Produced by Rinus Hollenberg (Timelock and Ywis), it immediately conjures up images of Marillion as Marco de Haan does sound very similar to Steve Hogarth, the songs are melodic, with the guitar restrained a lot of the time, but Ron van Kruistum does let loose with some searing solos. The keyboards tend to provide a curtain of sound for the others to work with, and for the most part it succeeds very well. It seems strange that this is another Dutch band where the drummer is also the vocalist (Wheels of Steels is another): a rarity indeed. "The Spy" is one of the better songs on the album, being just vocals with piano for the most part, although the use of a saxophone solo is very effective. At nearly eight and a half minutes, the title track is the longest and starts off peacefully, but is transformed using some powerchords, PTS can belt along when they want to and that is when they are at their best. The use of harmony vocals makes a great song ever better! There seem to be quite a few Dutch bands bearing this type of melodic progressive AOR style of rock, and PTS are probably one of the better around. One to get if you like this style of music, as the songs are enjoyable, melodic, well-crafted and well played.

#24, Jul 1994

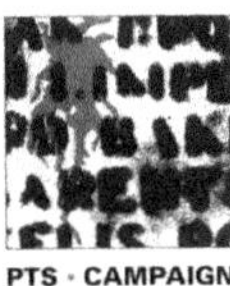
PTS · CAMPAIGN

PTS
CAMPAIGN

PTS were one of many bands left without a deal with the demise of Dutch label SI. I remember reviewing their last album 'Tides' and can't think of anything else about it apart from the fact that it is not nearly as good as this. With their third album, PTS appear to have matured into a very professional progressive rock band with melodic and AOR overtones that will find favour with all listeners of tuneful rock. Although they are only a four-piece, they have wisely added some backing vocalists and a saxophonist to give added scope and breadth to their sound. The sax adds a jazz influence in places, but it is the Floydian style backing vocals that enhance the music the most. That is not to say that PTS are relying solely on outsiders, but it does give the music a more polished accomplished edge. They do come across as Floyd at times, but also like Marillion, and it is one all fans of that band should search out immediately. In truth, there is nothing bad that can be said about this, and 'Campaign' is one of those rare things, namely an album from Holland that deserves its' press release.

#41, Apr 1997

PULSE ENGINE
POLARISED

Pulse Engine are a duo of Nick Cottam (bass, vocals) and Andrew Booker (drums, vocals). For those of you with long memories, you may just remember me reviewing Andrew's solo album 'Ahead' some seven years ago. This is an interesting release, in that it shows just what can be done with quite limited instrumentation. The guys have produced an album that they are probably able to play live, without the use of backing tapes etc. To many the idea of a bass and drum combo may seem either self -indulgent or boring or (probably) both. But although there are the odd noodlings along the way, that is allowable in the context of an album that is not only easy to listen to but is also enjoyable as well. I thought that I was going to either face a 'drum and bass' onslaught, or some jazz meanderings, but actually this album has its' heart much more firmly within the progressive world. There are times during "Inner Second" where they come quite firmly across as Yes, while at others it is Camel that is the main influence. I am not sure if it is the fact that Nick has a bass sound that can be used as a tightrope, a la Chris Squire, or the vocals, but more probably it is just the overall feel of the whole piece.

I found that throughout the album I had to keep reminding myself that it was only two guys producing this and per their web site they are very proud that they do not have to rely on tapes to get their musical ideas across. An interesting concept that deserves support.

#76, Oct 2003

PUPPET SHOW
TRAUMATIZED

This is a progressive band as regressive as they come: The Nineties have not taken place, nor the Eighties, and come to think of it neither has punk! By using keyboard sounds favoured by Genesis and Kansas many aeons ago, they have managed to come up with a sound that is a hybrid of the two (although without the violin). Three of the tracks break twelve minutes, and the shortest song (not including the pipe organ introduction) is still seven minutes in length. But this is not long pieces just for the sake of being long, but rather they need to be that long to allow for the development of the music and melodies. This is very mature prog and belies the fact that this is their debut album. Many bands have been around for years and have never managed music as good as this. In "Ring of Truth" there is real power and conviction with the voice of Sean Frazier. There is so much good music coming out of America at present, and with Puppet Show and Ad Infinitum, Kinesis have captured two of the best. If you enjoy prog that is tinged with good guitars and enjoy classic Kansas and mid Seventies Genesis, then you need to search this one out. Another goody.

#50, Aug 1998

PURSUIT
QUEST

The prog scene itself is not that big, but Pursuit are part of a growing sub-genre which hopefully will enable them to not only tap into the prog market but also into the Christian music scene, as this has a lot going for it. I get the impression that they had to go through a great deal to be able to complete this album, but this AOR/metal-edged prog has been worth the wait. With influences such as Rush readily apparent, this is music that can be complex and complicated, but often feels more straightforward due to the amount of melodies and hooks within the music. There is interesting pianowork with a varied use of keyboard sounds, while Dan Wolfe is obviously a frustrated rocker at heart. There is a message to be heard here, obviously, but even those who are non-Christian will be able to get a lot out of this. They switch and turn, always keeping the interest, with sometimes delicate and sometimes powering vocals from Andrew Zuchlke. This combined with the different musical styles means that theproghead always feels involved as the band moves forwards. This is an impressive debut, and hopefully the next one will not be too far away. For more details on the band then visit their site – but at least this indie release has been picked up and made more easily available over here.

#85, Nov 2005

QANGO
LIVE IN THE HOOD

Take a dash of Asia, add in ELP and you will have a good idea of what this album is like. Dave Kilminster and John Young join John Wetton and Carl Palmer for this enjoyable

romp through classic numbers from both bands. Of the ten songs, two are solos, and of the other eight three are by ELP (including a much more rockified version of "Fanfare"), and three are from the debut Asia album. Given that John and Carl have been playing together on and off for years, and that Dave is a member of John's touring band, then it is little surprise that these guys play well together, and although the major glory days are behind them, songs as good as these still deserve to be heard. I am not sure if they plan to tour again, or record together, so if you want to be able to hear yet again how they sounded on tour in 1999 then I suggest you get this now. Although it has been released on ELP's old Manticore label, I see that this is now available through Voiceprint.
#61, Feb 2001

QOPH
KALEJDOSKOPISKA AKTIVITETER
This was the band's debut album, originally released in 1998, and now available on CD through Record Heaven. They released a follow-up last year, but whereas that has vocals in English, this is fully Swedish. The line-up at the time included two guitarists, bassist, drummer and vocalist but even though there are some guests on sax and violin it is interesting to note that there are no keyboards. This seems strange as the band are performing music that has one foot firmly in progressive rock while the other is strongly rooted in psychedelia. The one band that they did remind me of is King Crimson, especially on "Vansinnet", the opener, which is the only one to feature violin. I am not sure why it took six years to produce a follow-up as this seems to be full of ideas and the album works very well indeed. There is also a single available, "Än Lyser Månen", which contains two songs not available on this recording. Try this out as you will be well rewarded with some great end of the Sixties style psych prog.
#85, Nov 2005

QUARKSPACE
SPACEFOLDS 6
This is the latest album from the American space rockers who originally started life as Quark! back in 1984. After some line-up changes and some dormant periods, the first album was not released until 1996, and this one follows on from 'Spacefolds 5' and 'The Hidden Moon' which both featured in the Global Progressive Rock Network's Top 100 CDs of 1999 (the only other band to do that was Djam Karet). This is an album of improvised space rock, and that it manages to succeed must be down to the relationship they have with each other, built up over many years. The music moves and twists, similar at times to Hawkwind, with possibly a few touches of VDGG here and there as well. Nice to see one of the tracks called "Guy Evans" as a nod to

VDGG's drummer. The songs vary in length from four minutes to over thirteen, and some parts are very dark indeed. They have played with Hawkwind, as well as at all four Strange Daze Festivals, and this space rock experience is one to share.
#61, Feb 2001

QUARKSPACE
SPACEFOLDS 7
Twelve songs of improvised instrumental progressive jazz space rock. Not as bad as it may seem, with some very good musicianship but there are a few times when they seem to lose the thread a little. Even with a great title such as "Jay The Prog Boy", it is an album that would only ever make it to background for my ears, although others may feel differently.
#64, Oct 2001

QUASAR
THE LORELI
Quasar were formed in the winter of 1980 by bassist Keith Turner, and after a while the line-up settled down with Cyrus Khajavi on guitar, Dillon Tonkin on keyboards, Paul Vigress on vocals and David Cairns on drums. In 1983 they released their debut album, 'Fire In The Sky", which heralded the departure of Vigrass. He was replaced by Susan Robinson, who had just left Solstice, and over the next eighteen months they played some 270 gigs and were headlining venues like The Marquee. The next problem faced by the band was the decision of both Cairns and Khajavi to leave. They were replaced by Kevin Fitzgerald (guitar) and Dave Wagstaffe (drums) and managed to get a song included on the (now important) compilation album 'Fire In Harmony'. If the line-up hadn't suffered enough, the next person to leave was Tonkin who in turn was replaced by Steve Leigh (ex -Tamarisk). Another period of touring ensued and during this period vocalist Susan Robinson also decided to call it a day, but not to be dismayed the band found a great replacement with the fantastic singer Tracy Hitchings. Finally, Fitzgerald and Leigh also left and were replaced by Toshi Tauchyia on guitar who brought in new technology that enabled the band to perform as a four-piece (with computer keyboards, aided by Tracy).

This line-up managed to stay together long enough to record the excellent 'The Loreli', which Keith kindly sent me. Even before putting the CD onto the player I was extremely impressed as the front and rear covers are quite stunning, with some of the best artwork I have seen for some time. The album itself is quite short at under forty minutes and only five songs, but it is quality and not quantity that counts. Considering that the band does not have a recognised keyboard player it is surprising to find the sound so heavily keyboard based, but the most important factor here is the stunning vocals of Tracy Hitchings. She has a voice that many so-called singers would die for: sometimes whispering, at others crying or soaring like an angel and then coming down with a rough hard edge. At times, pure and clear, at others harsh and secretive, she has wonderful pitch and breath control. That is not to say that the others are bit players, but rather that they provide the perfect backdrop for her to sing her heart out. The opening title track displays all these aspects of her voice in just the one song, very impressive. "Seeing Stars Pt. 2 (The Dark Star)" is far more up-tempo and rock as the band drive along in a far more commercial manner. In stark contrast, "As You Fall Asleep" starts off with bass, guitar and keyboards combining to provide a low menacing backdrop to Tracy's harsh vocals. As the song breaks her voice soars with real power and vigour. There is some wonderful restrained guitar in this song that would probably become a lot heavier live. The song progresses into a ballad, with everything becoming laid back, and then climaxes with some soaring keyboards: at more than ten minutes in length this is a song of many parts but is a well-structured whole. "Logic?" is a return to the more up-tempo form, with some driving bass and keyboards while album closer "Power In Your Hands" is a far slower track that gently winds you down ready to play the album all over again.

Since the release of 'The Loreli' in 1989, the line-up has changed significantly with Tracy Hitchings going solo (one album to her credit to date, which I have yet to hear), and Dave Wagstaffe now in Landmarq. Although I do not have the current details, Quasar are still a functioning outfit, but even if that was not the case, they can be justly proud of this album they have left behind. The vocals make this album stand head and shoulders above many other similar works and is well worth discovering.
#15, Oct 1992

QUEENSRŸCHE
TRIBE

I have long been an admirer of the vocal talents of Geoff Tate, and when he is surrounded by this band the results are often superb and are sometimes incredible. But it is a long time since 'Operation Mindcrime' and I must admit that the first time I played this I was bitterly disappointed, as it appeared to me that they had lost the spark of genius and I was going to be writing my first ever Queensrÿche review and slating them. But, it is never fair to review an album having only played it once and I persevered, and I am extremely glad that I did. It may not have the out and out brilliance of some of their albums of the past, but this is a grower. Somewhere along the line the music and vocals started to gel and make sense, and the technical rock kings were back in business. Some of the music is majestic, while others just this bit heavier, but while they may not be as frenetic as they have in the past there is in place a maturity and almost solemnity about the task in front of them. The production is spot on, and while there are moments when the band seem to be restrained, when played at top volume it is incredible just how much passion can be released. If you are a fan then this is an album that you should get, and while it may not be the best introduction to the band it is certainly a fine listen.
#76, Oct 2003

QUEENSRŸCHE
THE ART OF LIVE

It may not have been very long since their last live album but given that six of the fourteen tracks here on show were taken from last year's 'Tribe' then at least the set list has been adjusted more than a little. The six songs all appear within the first seven numbers with only "Sign Of The Times" to break the flow. Quite a brave approach from the band, and I'm not sure if it is one that totally works. They open with "Tribe" itself, with the bass line barely audible above the drums' introduction, as it is so low and dirty. The song seems to take time to get going, and I am not sure if this is well suited to the live environment. It does seem to be something of a strange choice as opening number, especially when "Open" is such a crunching song which comes across well. There are three songs treated acoustically, which do work well showcasing Geoff Tate's vocals, but it is probably the rising "Anybody Listening" and the closing "Best I Can" that shows that the band still can deliver the goods. At one time Queensrÿche were the leading technical-rock band around, but while there are some flashes of glory on this live album, they are somewhat rare. This is one for the fans, but if anyone wants to discover what this band are capable of then search out 'Operation Mindcrime'.

#80, Jul 2004

QUEST
OPPOSITE SIDES OF THE PICKET FENCE

I was sent this CD by Chris Rodler, guitarist with Drama in the States, as he has now set up a management company and he thought that I might like this, and boy was he right. Quest have been going since 1985 but it was only in 1993 with the arrival of a new vocalist that the impetus was given to recording this their debut. Musically brilliant, Quest are a five-piece utilising twin guitars with four of them doubling on keyboards as required (not often). Vocalist Allen McKenzie has a voice reminiscent both of Geddy Lee and Steve Walsh, and although Quest have obviously been influenced by bands such as Rush and Kansas it goes far further than that. Some of the songs are sensitive and balladic, while others are more complex and furious. Quest are not afraid to use space in their music, which means that the contrast between different parts of even the same song can be quite staggering. Acoustic guitar with gentle vocals can give way to thundering drums and powerful fretwork in the blink of an eye. Lyrically Quest are one of the strongest bands I have come across for a while. "Colorblind" is an extremely powerful anti-racism number while my favourite, "In The Name Of God", is about David Koresh and the Waco siege.

An American reviewer said, "If Kansas and Dream Theater mated, their illegitimate kids would be Quest". Quite a statement, more than quite a band.

#28, Apr 1995

THE QUEST
DO YOU BELIEVE?

The Quest were originally formed in 1986, but it was not until 1992 that the current line-up came into being. They comprise Shaun Owens (vocals), Graham Woodcock (keyboards), Andy Coffey (drums), Chris Dorman (guitar) and Pete Dunn (bass). Although former line-ups of the band had released various demos, this CD is the first release by The Quest as they are now. Initial reaction is the surprise that this is a British band at all, as their feet are firmly in the US pomp camp. They certainly have far more in common with bands such as Shooting Star than with IQ or Pendragon. The keyboards rise in majesty, with vocals soaring high, yet there are enough guts in the music to keep the rocker more than happy. They remind me of white metallers Stryper, although I can't think why. The songs are all unashamedly commercial, and enjoyable on first listen. One problem I can see for The Quest is that the mass media detest this type of rock with a vengeance, and the UK progger may also turn up his nose. This would be a great shame as this is a superb album, one that I will be playing a lot. My only quibble is that it contains eight tracks but is only just over thirty-seven minutes long. Maybe the next one will be of a more decent length, I look forward to it with anticipation.

#22, Mar 1994

THE QUEST
CHANGE

Two years on from the release of their debut 'Do You Believe?', The Quest are back with their new album. While The Quest could be labelled as a prog band, they have more in common with top AOR acts such as Journey: multi-layered harmony vocals, with just enough bite to the guitars to give the music a certain edge, combined with great hooks and melodies put The Quest way above a lot of music being produced in this field (I immediately think of Frederiksen/Phillips that was released by Now & Then a few months back). While they could not be described as a heavy band, they know how to rock just enough to keep the metalhead interested. Some of the songs have an extremely commercial catchy feel to them, such as the superb "Turn Away" which has American hit single written all over it. This is an album that will be appreciated by those into prog or American rock as there is great crossover appeal.

#31, Oct 1995

QUIDAM
SNY ANIOłÓW

Over the last couple of years Quidam have been making quite a reputation for themselves with their gentle melodic music, both inside and outside of their native Poland. I have just received this album and it is already a firm favourite as they mix gentle cello and flute with normal prog instrumentation and some beautiful female vocals. I enjoy listening to this, as it is relaxing, yet at no time does it become background muzak or New Age.

Bearing in mind this is a song and lyric album, with none of the words in English, that is quite an achievement. There is one epic, "Pod Powieką" which clocks in at fourteen minutes, but the rest of the songs are all about the five-minute mark, which seems about right for Quidam. While never being quite folk, some of these songs would not sound out of place on a religious album as Emila's vocals are pure and clear and almost sacred. The only word to describe "Prezebudzenie" is "beautiful" (I certainly could not tell you what it means). This is an album that most definitely deserves to be heard by a much wider audience than I afraid it is going to get.

#50, Aug 1998

QUIDAM

LIVE IN MEXICO '99

Currently one of the top, if not the top, Polish bands doing the rounds is Quidam, whose praises I have been singing from these pages before. Their fame has even reached the other side of the water, and they were asked to close the 1999 Baja Prog Festival in Mexico (where UK's Arena had also been playing). The Mexican crowd certainly gave them a warm reception, even though they performed most of their songs in Polish. It was also interesting to play "spot the tune" as one song included part of "Snow Goose" and another "Firth of Fifth". The most surprising thing for me was the choice of number with which to end, namely an extremely atmospheric laid-back version of "Child In Time" which found Emila straining (but managing to hit the notes). It shows how much a band can place their own sound on a song, even not one of their own: the use of flute managed to turn part of it into a totally different number. But, Quidam are a class act and this CD just emphasises what I have been saying, that this is a band that we in the UK should be looking out for. In many ways, this is harking back to the prog of the Seventies, but it also looks forward with a sound that is fresh and inviting. Give yourself a treat and mellow out to Quidam.

#56, Jan 2000

QUIDAM

THE TIME BENEATH THE SKY

Since the release of their debut album in 1996, Quidam have been building a reputation for themselves as one of the finest progressive rock bands from mainland Europe. Their last studio album ('Angel's Dreams') was so popular that they then recorded an English language version that was distributed worldwide by Musea. They were invited to play Baja Prog in 1999, and a recording of that gig was their last release. They have also toured with acts such as Colin Bass (with whom they have built a very close working relationship) and RPWL and have already been booked for the Rio Festival in Brazil later this year. Although the cover and booklet of this album are in English, the album is sung in Polish, and has been released in that country as 'Pod Niebem Czas'. I am not sure if there will be an English version of this album but the lack of understanding of the language in no way detracts from the album as the voice becomes another instrument. Emila Derkowska has wonderfully clear vocals and the whole band gels and shines together in a similar fashion to the way that Pink Floyd once did. With a flautist within the band (Jacek Zasada) it gives them the opportunity to move away from the (reasonably) standard five-person prog set up, and they have also used guests to fill out the sound even more (oboe, flugelhorn (!), mandolin, accordion).

This is a progressive album that really is, one that brings together different instruments and players in a way that makes it feel as if they belong together. The production is top quality, and care has been taken over the presentation with the CD itself in a slip sleeve. There is a cover on the album, a brilliant take on "No Quarter" that nearly breaks the twelve-minute mark, and the second half of the album is taken up with a complex piece which is thirty minutes long (although it can be subdivided into five songs). I have reviewed all Quidam's albums and this is by far the best, showing the majesty and grace that only a band at the height of their powers can achieve. This is an album that all progheads should have and love. *#68, Jun 2002*

QUIDAM
SURREVIVAL

When looking at the name of the album, it is shown as 'SurREvival', and I am sure that this is because this is two titles in one, 'Survival' and 'Revival'. It has been a while since I had last heard from the band but rate their last album 'The Time Beneath The Sky' as one of the finest Polish prog albums that has come my way. So, I was astonished to put this on and find a male singer! What had happened to Emila Derkowska?? Closer inspection of the booklet shows that the band has been through a few changes since their last release in 2002 as not only do they have a new singer in Bartek Kossowicz, but a new bassist in Mariusz Ziółkoswki and a new drummer in Maciek Wróblewski. Possibly this is why the band state 'Quidam are now' in the member listing as opposed to just putting the names.

I have followed the career of this band with interest, and even have a video of them in concert, but the change in singer and rhythm section has definitely had the biggest impact on their sound. It is almost possible to argue that this is a brand-new band as the sound is quite different to what they were doing before, in some ways more accessible and definitely far more Western – Bartek is a fine singer and there is no trace of accent in his English vocals so that they now come across far more as a UK act. The songs are top class, but the band appears to have taken something of a shift into a harder area and the flutes of Jacek Zasada are not as noticeable as previously. But the quality still shines through and I am sure that any proghead cannot fail to fall in love with this the first time they hear it – it is layered yet accessible, full of passion and hooks so that even though this is a new direction for the band they have embraced it and have made it their own.
#85, Nov 2005

QUIKION
HALLELUJAH!

This is subtitled 'Early Recordings Of', and most of the songs come from 1997 with one from 1995 and I can see from their web site that while they do not list this album, they do mention two much more recent releases on Trinity Records. With all the information in Japanese it is best to concentrate on the music, which I must admit to enjoying immensely. This is not one of the more straightforward line-ups, as they have a female vocalist who also provides concertina and rhythm machine, one guy on accordion and glockenspiel and the other on guitar. With all the vocals in Japanese this allows the mind just to wander along on the sound of the words instead of trying to gain the meaning from them and it is like sitting next to a gently babbling stream, while the light is dappled through the leaves of the trees. It is music that is restful yet evocative, very easy to listen to yet definitely not easy listening. It may only be the sort of album that will appeal to those who enjoy whimsical folk with a difference but those who dare to try and get this album will be richly rewarded indeed.

#71, Dec 2002

QUIKION
YORU NO HARP

This is the 2001 release by Quikion and its' style is extremely hard to define with a line-up that is unusual to say the least. The band is a trio with Totoki Yukiko (vocals, concertina, kantele), Oguma Eiji (guitar, bouzouki, ukulele) and Sasaki Emi (accordion, glockenspiel). It is an album that is reflective yet intense, dreamy yet passionate, modern yet timeless. Totoki sings in a very clear voice which would make the words easy to understand if they were not in Japanese, but this just adds to the mystique of the album as a whole. In some ways, she is closer to Kate Bush than Maddy Prior but somehow the clarity of her voice against the harshness of the accordion works extremely well. This is not music that will appeal to a vast market but those who can enjoy melodic music that is out of the ordinary will find much on here to enjoy – which will make it worth the effort to try and get this from Japan. I enjoyed it immensely.

#73, Apr 2003

QUIKION
RAMADAN

I have been lucky enough to have heard two other Quikion albums, and this is very much in the same vein as the others. They have an unusual line-up, Yukiko Totoki (vocals, concertina, kantele, psaltery, glockenspiel, toys, percussions), Eiji Oguma (guitar, bouzouki, ukulele) and Emi Sasaki (accordion, glockenspiel, psaltery, bells, drums, percussions, vocal), which in turn gives their music quite a different sound.

There are not many times I can listen to a piece of music which is basically acoustic guitar and accordion with gentle female vocals over the top and say that I really enjoy it: like the others, this album really is a delight. I have not a clue what Yukiko is singing about as all the lyrics are in Japanese, but this just adds to the overall feel of what is going on, the feeling that this is something that is quite special. The album is extremely atmospheric, the impression almost that these three are sat around a fire in the evening just playing and performing for their own pleasure. This may only appeal to those who listen to folk, as there is certainly nothing violent or loud about it in anyway, but those who investigate this further will be richly rewarded.
#86, Feb 2006

RADIOMÖBEL
GUDANG GARAM

This was the second album by Swedish band Radiomöbel which was released as a private pressing in 1978, and this is the first time that it has been made available on CD. This is symphonic psychedelic rock, with some interesting musicianship (especially some of the drumming), but it is rather let down by the female vocals. The production also is not all that it could have been but given the circumstances that probably is not too surprising. It is the instrumental passages where this album really shines with the keyboards and rhythm section laying down a gentle backdrop for some interesting guitar noodlings. Looking around on the web it appears that the debut is more highly favoured than this one, which has also now just been made available on CD by this label. For collectors only.
#85, Nov 2005

RAKOTH
PLANESHIFT

This album was recorded in 1999 and was originally released on the Italian Code666 label, but with the signing of the band to the Earache imprint Elitist for a four album deal the album has been re-mastered and has been reissued as a limited-edition digipak. The fact that the package has been so well put together means that the presentation comes some way to meeting the musical level set by this debut album by the Russian band. Rakoth have a somewhat unusual line-up as it features P. Noir on vocals, flute, Dy on guitars and Rustam on vocals, keyboards and programming. Needless to say, the music itself is also different to the norm, but I have found that it is weirdly compelling and extremely deep and thoughtful, almost contemplative at times. The label is advertising the band as "Tolkien-inspired black metal" but even that does not manage to convey what the band is trying to achieve. Parts of the album are folk-like, but with Gregorian style vocals, and I found that I could imagine a peasant collecting wood in the snow, battling against the cold. There are times when the music is slow, almost melancholic, but this can be lifted by an acoustic guitar and flute. What has this to do with metal you may ask, but when they open up, as on "The Dark Heart Of Uukrul", then the answer is obvious. Of course,

blistering full out attack does not mean that they must stop playing flute.... This is music that is different yet at the same time I found that for all its styles it fits together so well and demands to be played time and again. Truly an awesome album, with lyrics in English. Rakoth are working on 'Tiny Deaths' for release later this year and I for one am already looking forward to it.
#69, Aug 2002

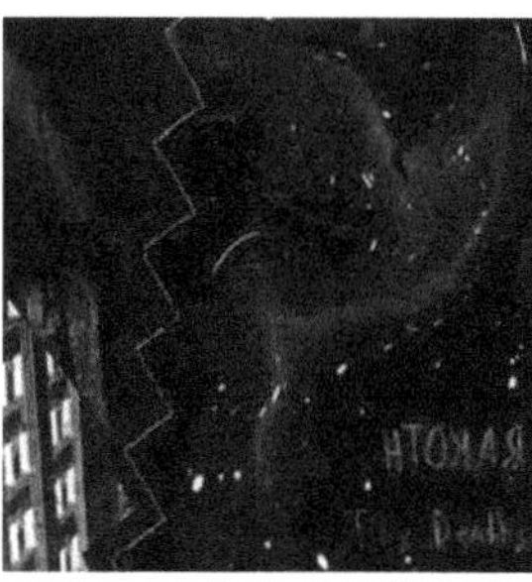

RAKOTH
TINY DEATHS

Back in #69 I raved about 'Planeshift', and how it was quite unlike any rock album that I had ever heard. That was a reissue on Elitist of the album that had appeared on Code666 in 2000, and with only a collection issued in between they have had plenty of time to come up with new ideas for this one. Yet again they have defied convention and have put together an album that basically avoids all attempts at description. This really is progressive music at the cutting edge, bringing together extreme rock with folky and surreal elements that must be heard to be believed. This album is just what I had hoped that it would be, namely a further pursuit of an unnamed musical ideal that we mortals can only get glimpses of. It is whatever it wants to be, and those who wish to travel into music that is so deep that there may be no end to the levels need go no further but to reach in and grasp what is on offer. Is it as good as 'Planeshift'? Not sure on that – I have played that album a great many times and this time I was expecting something out of the ordinary and last time it just blew me away. Not for the musically faint-hearted, this is music to be loved or loathed. You decide.
#76, Oct 2003

RAVANA
COMMON DAZE

This is the first album by Norwegian Ravana, and the only album to come out of Prognetik fanzine's record label. They have been paying attention to the Scandinavian progressive scene and while elements of Landberk can be detected, most of their influences appear to come from Anekdoten, who in turn were of course greatly influenced by early King Crimson. But they are far from being copyists and have included not only jazz but elements of heavy rock. That is not to say that this album is a blast from start to finish, but rather blistering guitar runs, or some grungy style riffing can offset the quiet, reflective passages. It all commences with some cello that immediately set me thinking of Anekdoten and comparing the two, which can be unfortunate. Seeing as how the cello is a "guest" and does not feature on all tracks then quite possibly another should have been the opener, possibly the dynamic "Wounded". 'Common Daze' shows promise and it will be interesting to see how they follow it up. Definitely different to the most UK bands (apart from very possibly Vulgar Unicorn), this is an album that rewards those who take the time to listen to it properly. *#41, Apr 1997*

RAY
SOMEWHERE IN THE UNIVERSE

When it says on the front cover "Dedicated to Ian Anderson and Jethro Tull", then there is a pretty good chance that this is not a technical album. What Ray Poehner and the others have done is pretty much plagiarise Tull to the nth degree and have only got away with it because they appear to be such huge fans. The trouble with any album like this is that while it can be enjoyed is that at times you find yourself thinking "would Ian have done it just like that" or "hang on, I recognise that lyric or hook etc." The album is rooted for the most part in the more acoustic side of Tull, covering the period roughly from 'Minstrel In The Gallery' through to 'Broadsword' and contains two covers, "Broadford Bazaar" and "Jackalynn", and the latter of these works particularly well. Why that song never appeared when it was originally recorded is something I will never understand, especially as it is now something of a live favourite. So, is it worth searching out from America? I think that if you are a die-hard Tull freak then this is an album that you ought to have, but if you're not, there is no need to put yourself out. While this is an album worth hearing, it is very much aimed at the Tull fan and if you do not like the object of Ray's obsession then there is no way that you will like this. I enjoyed it, but I do not know how many of you would say the same.
#43, Aug 1997

RAZOR WIRE SHRINE
GOING DEAF FOR A LIVING

Razor Wire Shrine is the name of an instrumental outfit that has been put together by the Rodler brothers, Chris and Brett. These guys seem to have an inexhaustible supply of ideas and musical ideas they want to explore, and this is the latest in a line of bands that stretch back as far as Drama and RH Factor and as recently as Mythologic. The work on this album commenced as long ago as 1997, but due to various problems (such as catastrophic hard drive failure which lost all the guitar parts) it has only recently been completed. On this project Chris provides rhythm and bass, Brett drums and Mike Ohm (also of Potato Battery) on lead guitar. Chris describes the album himself as "loud, complex, high-energy, rhythmically challenging, harmonically sophisticated, metal-coated, instrumental prog-rock with bad attitude". Not a bad way of looking at an album that while a shredder's paradise, has a lot going on. This is not an album that progheads will be deeming essential if they consider Genesis heavy, as this is primarily rock: seven songs that are extremely complex with incredible note density, and time signatures that are all over the place. With Chris providing bass for his own songs he has again been able to lock in tight with his brother, while also knowing exactly what the end product is going to be like. Mike is a graduate of the Guitar Institute of Technology in Los Angeles, and normally plays music with a more jazz slant and this has given a different edge to the music, as it is not being approached from just a hard rock or prog angle. It did take me a few plays to get into the album just because it is so incredibly intense, but the result was more than worth it as yet again the boys have delivered. *#80, Jul 2004*

RED JASPER
STING IN THE TALE

RED JASPER
ACTION REPLAY

Fed up the current wave of progressive rock and looking for something more raw and raucous, yet played with great skill and dexterity? If that is the case, then Red Jasper are the band for you. I asked Davey how he would describe the sound of Red Jasper to the unknowing and was told “Motörhead meets Jethro Tull”. Curious? Read on. Red Jasper were originally formed in 1987, but of the original line-up only two remain, Davey Dodds (vocals, mandolin, tin whistle) and Robin Harrison (guitars). Based in Wiltshire, they started an extensive gigging campaign to bring their brand of ‘Political Folk Rock’ to the masses, yet it is political more in the manner of Guy Fawkes than Karl Marx. The folk roots are there, but Red Jasper are far heavier and harder than Folk Rock and the songs tend to deal with social conflicts and the insanity of the current society. Environmentally Friendly Jasper: they describe it as English Ethnic Rock! Their first album, ‘England’s Green and Pleasant Land’ was self-financed, as was the follow-up LP, ‘Pull That Thumb Off The Top Of Your Head’. This sold well and attracted the attention of HTD Records who in 1990 duly signed the band. The resulting album, ‘Sting In The Tale’, attracted a lot of attention and manged to get reviews in both metal and folk magazines, surely an unusual accomplishment.

The album really is a mix of different styles, and at the time Red Jasper included a sax player in the line-up, and this was used to great effect. Kicking off with “Faceless People”, Davey’s very English singing style (sort of a rough Ian Anderson) features well in a song that starts slowly but gradually builds up into a climatic electric guitar finish. “Guy Fawkes” is just superb, with a sound very similar to that of Steve Taylor. It is a very catchy anti-political song with a great chorus, “Hey now let’s shout, Kick the politicians out, Let’s all raise a ringing cheer, Guy Fawkes had the right idea”. “Second Coming” has a great mandolin and powerful drumming introduction and the song itself is atmospheric with good use of tin whistle, while lyrically it tells how people have turned away from the Church to follow the false gods of greed and profit. “Secret Society” starts off with a powerful rock version of the James Bond theme, and is very rocky with strong lead guitarwork throughout. “Magpie” incorporates the old rhyme (“one for sorrow, two for joy...”) and starts and ends with harmony vocals. An electric song but with a folky feel, “I Can Hew” tells the story of a miner, with Davey’s voice totally unaccompanied for the first verse and chorus, and then joined by bass and drums for the second. Ric Sanders (Fairport Convention) guests on this number, and when he joins in it heralds a complex transformation for the song, as it turns into a manic jig with complex musical interplay between all the band. Absolutely brilliant. There are nine songs on the album, and I loved them all. It is totally different to anything else on the prog scene, so if you are at all interested in Jethro Tull or Fairport yet at the same time have a healthy regard for hard rock then you cannot fail to fall in love with this. Red Jasper’s strength is not only their musical and songwriting ability, but the fact that within each song they combine instruments and moods in a constructive yet interesting manner.

The current line-up of Davey Dodds, Robin, Dave Clifford (drums) and Jonathan Thornton (bass) have a live CD entitled 'Action Replay' coming out at the end of May. Recorded at the Bristol Bierkeller in January, it shows what the Jaspers are like in a live environment. What that is, is powerful, dynamic and tight, a real force to be reckoned with. Apparently, Dave Pegg hates this band and I can see why, as Fairport have as much in common with this type of music as many chart acts have with musical ability. The fifteen songs featured here are taken from the first two albums, as well as nine that are previously unrecorded, and shows Red Jasper in a far heavier light than from the studio work. Some of the highlights (although yet again every song is a winner) is the epic "England's Green and Pleasant land" which starts off with tin whistle accompanied by drums and is joined by the guitar as it gradually builds into an atmospheric number with Davey's vocals well to the fore. It picks up with the bass driving along and a great guitar break and returns to the gentle atmosphere only to rock out again. The three songs from 'Sting In The Tale' ("Second Coming", "Old Jack" and "Magpie") all transfer very well to the live environment and are far heavier than before. Indeed, there is a real battle in "Old Jack" for Davey to make his mandolin heard against some sterling guitarwork from Robin. "King of the Fairies" is a traditional Irish song that has been recorded in the past by bands such as Horslips, but it never sounded like this: there is some phenomenal guitar on this track that is just transformational. The album closes with "Cool To Be Crazy", yet another driving rock song with a great catchy chorus. There is a good chance that Red Jasper and Grace could be gigging together in the future, and that really would be a show not to miss – check them out!
#12, May 1992

RED JASPER
A MIDSUMMER NIGHT'S DREAM
It seems to have been quite a long time since the last studio album from Red Jasper, but the wait was well worth it. This is a concept album based on the themes derived from Shakespeare's play of the same name. The songs themselves "deal with the tension between illusion and reality, love and marriage and the supernatural". The CD is a complete package as not only are the lyrics included, but also the reasoning behind the album, and the intentions of the artist Timothy Harris, who designed the front and rear covers. Red Jasper are one of those bands who are totally at home either acoustically or at full rock power, and opener "Sonnet I" shows off the former with some wonderful guitars with overlaid tin whistles. "Virtual Reality", which follows, could not be more different with riffs in abundance. In fact, that is one of the great joys of this CD, as just when the listener feels they knows what to expect next, they discover that this could not be further from the truth. Third track, "Berkana", is extremely gentle and for the most part uses just sensitive keyboards and Davey's vocals, although Davey's mandolin makes an entrance towards the end which transforms the number into a more folky being altogether (apparently, this is a version of the Morris number "Lads A Bunchan", using dance as a

metaphor for life itself). The lyrics have had a great deal of time spent on them, as not only are they complex in style but have been written very deliberately in a Shakespearian style. The more time spent listening to the music and reading the well put together booklet, the more there is in it. As the listener gets more and more into Red Jasper's world, the more there is to discover. They have been performing the music complete with a slide show, and I am sure that this makes for compelling viewing. For any lover of complex music with very much an "English" feel, e.g. Jethro Tull, the rockier side of Fairport or Grace, then this is very much an album for you. They are touring in Europe with Shadowland next month and that is a show I would dearly love to see.
#21, Jan 1994

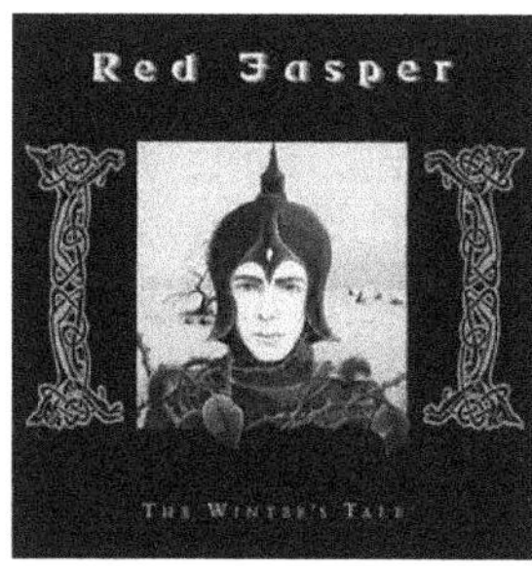

RED JASPER
THE WINTER'S TALE

Hot on the heels of last year's masterpiece 'A Midsummer Night's Dream', Red Jasper have now released the companion 'The Winter's Tale'. It explores the themes presented in Shakespeare's play in a musical context which links with the previous album, as well as exploring new avenues. Davey feels that this concludes this particular chapter in the band's history, and that for the future they will again be "progressing" into new fields hitherto unexplored. Red Jasper's great strengths are not only their songwriting and musical skills, but the fact that they sound like no-one else in the underground scene at present. They are always going to be compared with the harder side of Tull, as they bring mandolin and whistles into their performances, but they are by no means Tull clones. In fact, they sound nothing like them, which is a strange thing to say given that I have just compared them! Anyone who has heard the stunning 'Action Replay' or has had the opportunity of seeing Red Jasper in concert will know that they are very much a hard rock animal with far more to offer than blasting guitars. Indeed, 'The Winter's Tale' contains more threats of hard rock than the use of the medium itself. There is a lot of light and shade here, not just shade alone. Lyrically Red Jasper have few equals as can be seen within "The Shamen Song", "The Christian fathers feared me, took my festival and made it theirs, the birth of the sun – or the birth of a son, of their God at my solstice time".

The album is multi-layered in the sense that it is very enjoyable on first listen as it powers through, but there is so much to hear that it takes a few plays to fully recognise the majesty of the music. Highlight must be "The Scent of Something" which is about the feeling that there is something going on at the periphery of our senses, that we can't quite recognise. Musically it starts off with gentle interlinking acoustic guitars that then combine with keyboards and soft vocals which certainly provide no inkling that the song is going to turn into a riffing breathing hard rock number. Robin certainly shines, with some excellent lead guitarwork. I'll finish with the final words on the album, "If you have ears to listen and eyes to see, stay with me in the heart of the country". Nuff said.
#25, Oct 1994

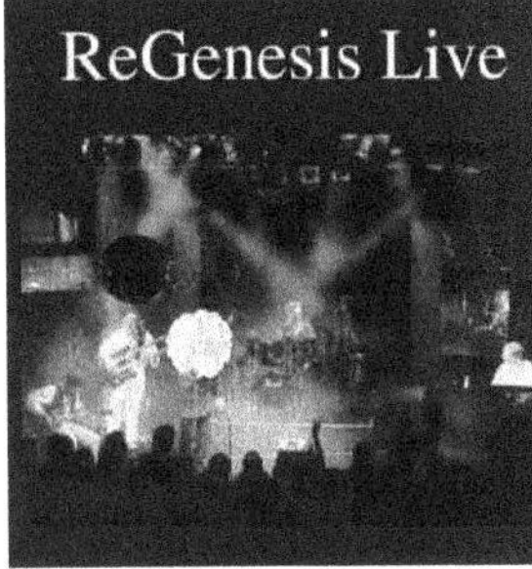

REGENESIS
LIVE
How on earth can I review this album? On one hand, it is brilliant, but on the other (just because of its brilliance) it is a total waste of time! I had better explain. I am probably not alone in bemoaning the explosion of 'tribute' bands that have taken place over the last few years. Yes, they can be a good night out, if only for a laugh, but these bands are taking up bookings at a time when live venues are closing. The result is that there are less and less good places for bands playing original material, and if these bands are being stifled at birth how are they going to progress? ReGenesis is a name well known certainly to those in the London area, and although I have not seen them I know that they are supposed to be excellent, and certainly this CD appears to reflect this (although there are one or two beautiful duff notes). They concentrate on Gabriel-era Genesis, even using costumes, but there's the rub. They are so good at what they do, attempting to faithfully reconstruct the Genesis sound, that this album defeats the object. Yes, the versions of "Supper's Ready" and "In The Cage", among others, are glorious. But if I wanted to hear them then I would turn to the original songs. It is not as if they are making the songs their own but playing note for note copies. The fact that there are two studio songs on here as well really compounds the error. So, the result is an album that succeeds very well indeed, but its own success is its downfall.
#40, Mar 1997

REGENESIS
LAMB FOR SUPPER
I must admit that I still do not know why people will buy ReGenesis albums, but as this is their third on Mystic someone must be. It is not that the music is not wonderful or that they manage to capture the original sound more than I would ever have imagined possible, but on a personal level I would rather listen to the original albums. This release features five songs from 'Lamb', along with "Supper's Ready" and a medley comprising "Dance On A Volcano" and "Los Endos". ReGenesis are very good at what they do, and when it comes to seeing them live then few Genesis fans could wish for more. When I saw them, I loved what they were doing, and I sang along with everyone else, but when it comes to playing a cover band's album time and again then somehow, I do not think I would. Recorded at the Genesis Fan Convention in Guildford earlier this year the crowd there lapped it up, and maybe you will as well.
#65, Dec 2001

RELAYER
A GRANDER VISION
I am indebted to Chris Rodler who passed my name to this Illinois based outfit, as Relayer's debut CD is impressive to say the least. Harmony vocals are again very important, combined with a harder American rock edge. Each of the five guys sing, and

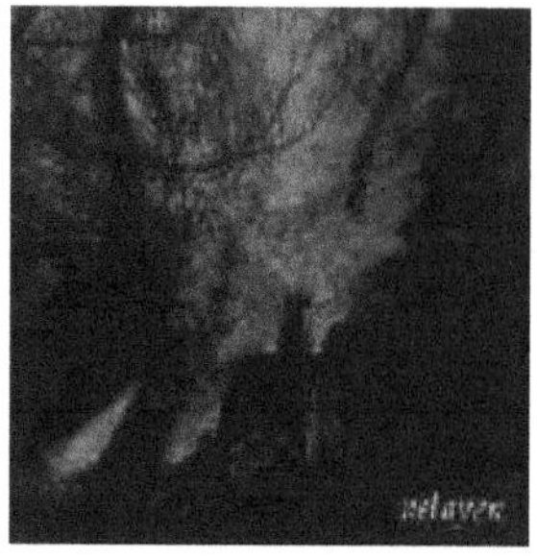

this places a different emphasis on the music to many. The guitarwork is hard and in your face, and on the opening number "Anyone" it provides a great commercial sound to the proceedings. "Grander Vision" is more than twenty minutes long, and this length allows the band to spread their musical wings, being far more keyboard led with Hackett-style guitars over the top. However, the sheer length of the piece allows plenty of room for dramatic changes with some great power chords and dynamic drumming. That is not to say that the piece is disjointed, as it is fluid and builds well. "The River" begins with acoustic guitar and gentle vocals, and although the rest of Relayer joins in, the impression is one of a lighter mood than previous pieces. This almost lethargic mood is wakened up with some dramatic keyboard and guitar interplay which heralds a soaring guitar solo, then it is back to harmony vocals and a gentle mood prevails. This CD only contains four songs, and clocks in at about forty minutes, but it is quality and not quantity that counts and the closing song, "Wire Mill Scars" again shows a different side to the band, being very much like IQ in style. Loads of widdly guitar gives way to a much harder edge. Relayer has obviously taken on board a lot of different influences (not just Yes) and although the other three songs show a very strong American influence, "Wire Mill Scars" could have come from the UK. These four songs show that here is an American outfit that are soon going to be making a name for themselves, and this is definitely one to look out for.
#30, Aug 1995

RELAYER
THE TEETHING FASHION
Many moons ago I heard from an American band, who sent me their four tracks debut CD, 'A Grander Vision', which was quite enjoyable. I heard no more until this arrived from Poland, of the same American band who are now signed to the German sub-division of a French label! At times, it seems a very small world indeed. This is intricate and at times frenetic prog/technical rock that puts the rock back into prog, while staying away from the hard rock genre. I get the impression that although this is heavy in places it is probably even more so in the live environment. Favourite song is "Madness" with some wonderful lyrics and highly complex interplay between all the band. At times, they go off into jazz territory with runs that are just breath-taking and while always in control the music can suddenly switch and turn from pace to peace, from mayhem to tranquillity. They have built on the debut and the result is an album that will be enjoyed by many.
#39, Jan 1997

RENAISSANCE
SONGS FROM RENAISSANCE DAYS
This is the first Renaissance album to feature Annie Haslam, Michael Dunford and Jon Camp in over a decade and is a collection of some released and previously unavailable

material dating as far back as 1979. There are quite a few guests, including Ian Mosley, Eddie Hardin and Geoff Harrison, but no indication as to who played on what. For completists then obviously, this is an important album as not only does it include studio versions of some songs that have been played in concert, but also some that were recorded in the Eighties and played on progressive rock stations supporting Annie's solo career. Sadly, as far as I am concerned, this includes a version of "Northern Lights" that just does not compare against the original. However, Annie can sing like an angel and overall this collection does her proud. I was fortunate to have two of these songs on cassette prior to release, and it found permanent residence in the car. There is something about "that" voice that captures and transports me away. All the songs are originals apart from Paul Simon's "America", which is changed into something more elegant and magical than the original, and I can see myself playing this album again and again. If you love great singing, then look no further than 'Renaissance Days'.

#42, July 1997

RENAISSANCE

OCEAN GYPSY

In 1994 Michael Dunford met vocalist Stephanie Adlington during workshops for his musical 'The Song of Scherazade'. With Stephanie, he then formed a band to record new arrangements of classic Renaissance tracks, resulting in 'The Other Woman', which was released in 1995. 'Ocean Gypsy' is a departure from that album, showing a return to the acoustic folk-rock style but here complemented with delicate woodwind and strings: the overall result is an album that will delight many. Stephanie has a wonderful voce and obviously is not fazed by having to follow in Annie Haslam's footsteps. The introduction to "Things I Don't Understand" is a wonderful example of breath control and pitch. It is an album that will certainly be enjoyed by fans of the band, as the new arrangements add something extra, while it will also gain new followers (strangely enough I found myself being reminded of Frank Dimino (Angel) during some of the vocalisations). This is a truly beautiful album that will be enjoyed by all.

#44, Sept 1997

RENAISSANCE

TUSCANY

Renaissance to many people mean just one song, the haunting "Northern Lights" but they were much more than just that, with many fans pointing to the album 'Scheherazade and Other Stories' as being the highlight of their career. Even though they were living on opposite sides of the Atlantic by 1998, Annie Haslam and guitarist Michael Dunford spent time discussing how to promote a stage version of that album. One thing led to

another, and drummer Terry Sullivan and keyboard player Jon Tout were encouraged back on board. However, Jon was unable to commit enough time for the project and a replacement was found in the very able Micky Simmonds (Fish etc.). With Roy Wood assisting on bass a new album has been recorded that captures all the majesty of the old days. Annie has a classical voice that many have tried to emulate but few have managed, and while it is her vocals that give the band their unique sound this is very much a joint effort with all the songs co-written by Annie and Michael. Songs such as "Dolphins Prayer" show what Enya has been trying to do for so long but has never managed to take it to this level. I have heard many Renaissance albums and am glad to be able to say that this is one of their best. Welcome back guys.
#65, Dec 2001

RENAISSANCE
IN THE LAND OF THE RISING SUN

This double CD captures Annie Haslam, Michael Dunford and Terence Sullivan joined by Rave Tesar, Mickey Simmonds and David Keyes. It was recorded on March 16th 2001 in Tokyo, in front of a very appreciative audience (although as usual for Japanese crowds they are deathly quiet while the songs are being performed). The use of two keyboard players means the band can stretch their musical wings, although with the amazing vocals of Annie it is rare that the band get to prove just what they are capable of. She has one of the most wonderful voices within modern popular music, with probably only Maddy Prior able to still command such a powerful range and clear tone for over thirty years. The band seem content to work together to provide the perfect backdrop, which allows Annie to let her voice soar. They perform their one 'hit' "Northern Lights" as well as a cover of "Moonlight Shadow" but such is the quality of the music that even someone who does not know any of the songs will enjoy it immensely the very first time. When Annie decides to sing high she really does, so that the listener just can't believe what they are hearing. The only way to describe some of this music is that if angels were on earth then they would sound like Annie. When the band get the chance to stretch as they do on the second CD they also prove that they have a great deal to offer and it is to their credit that they do not try to overpower Annie at any time. The production is top class, and this is an album of great beauty and majesty that I heartily recommend.
#71, Dec 2002

RETROHEADS
INTROSPECTIVE

This is the second album from Retroheads, and the first thing I did was to check among the seven members of the band to see if the lead singer was Damian Wilson (no its' not, it's Mike Mann). The vocals are a key part of this band, with the band not only having a wonderful singer in Mike but also in Ann-Kristin Bendixen and Deborah Girnius (the latter also providing flute) who give the sound a great degree of polish and power. The band

also uses 'old' keyboards such as Mellotrons and Mini Moogs, Hammond B3s etc. along with Taurus bass pedals. This gives the music a very retro feel while at the same time they are playing music that has obviously been influenced by bands like Spock's Beard, Floyd and IQ so they are providing a happy amalgam of 'classic' prog sounds along with some much newer ones. This gives the music a very warm and welcoming feel, it is all very approachable and enjoyable the very first time that you play it. This gives Mike a background where he can sing soft and gentle or rip up through the range as he is more than capable of doing, while the backing female vocals provide an extremely important supporting role. There may be seven musicians in this band, but the music never feels too over complicated or layered – the arrangements are very well done indeed. This is music for the proghead to lay back and settle into – it is warm and comfortable, and very well performed and produced indeed.
#89, Sep 2006

REVELATION
DEMO
Revelation were formed in June 1991 by Matthew Heinink (guitar, vocals) and Elliott Ware (keyboards), both of whom had recently been in Barcode. Revelation were completed by Spring 1993 with the addition of Mark John Aitken (drums), Fauzi (guitar) and Thom Bentley (bass – who has recently been replaced by Ashley Woods). The demo contains three tracks, "Addiction", "Witches & Wizards" and "Wicked Woman", all of which are certainly accessible and very enjoyable on first listen. "Addiction" gets things off to a fine start with a very up-tempo It Bites feel, "Witches & Wizards" is more laid back and is a controlled ballad which contrasts nicely with the more menacing and heavier "Wicked Woman", which turns into quite a belter. This song must be stunning live. All the numbers are very commercial, and I can see Revelation quickly making a name for themselves. Definitely one to look out for.
#22, Mar 1994

REVELATION
ADDICTED
I was very interested when I heard through the grapevine that Revelation had been in the studio, as I had previously booked them to support Credo at a charity gig last year. They are quite unlike any other prog band around, indeed they have stayed outside of the UK scene which has meant that their music has developed independently and have their own sound. The drums and bass drive along while Elliott Ware provides some sterling keyboard work: he reminds me a lot of Tony Banks, as his keyboard playing is approached very much from a piano point of view. Guitarwork is care of Fauzi, and after seeing them play again at the launch of the CD, I feel the production of the album is not as good as I had initially thought. Live, Fauzi is very much the rocker with added effects (another Genesis comparison here as some of the sounds he produces makes one think that they have come from keyboards), yet he has been muted on the CD. The line-up is completed by the emotionally wrought vocals of Matthew Heinink, who along with

Elliott writes all the material. There are quite a few musical comparisons to be made, from City Boy, Genesis and early IQ through to Uriah Heep. Diversity is the name of the game, with the Seventies very much a starting point. The songs are very structured and very different to each other, with even a jazz number ("Jack The Lad"). "Jack In The Box" starts off gently with atmospheric keyboards and flute but soon builds into a driving rocker while "Witches & Wizards" is acoustically based and is reminiscent in style of Uriah Heep's "Gypsy". Of the seven songs on the CD it must be "Freewheeling" that is the favourite as it rocks along, although not as much as it does in concert. All in all, this is a good debut, which will certainly garner interest within the UK prog scene. However, while the songs are strong enough, some more volume on the guitar would not have gone amiss.
#29, Jun 1995

REVOLVER
MIŁOŚĆ BEZZ GRANITZ

This is the second album from Polish band Revolver, but what will make people stand up and take notice is the fact that the opening song features none other than Nigel Kennedy. I was not aware that Nigel had been making forays outside of the classical field and why he would want to do so on an avant-garde piece that is instrumental apart from spoken vocals is quite beyond me. However, it does mean that there is a large sticker on the cover stating his presence, but it is only on the opening track which is quite at odds with the rest of the album. At over eight minutes it is also the longest by far, and I was certainly surprised to find that the rest of the album had a swirling psychedelic prog feel to it. It certainly is not one of the more accessible albums that I have come across, both musically and because the lyrics are in Polish, and some of the songs can be quite challenging to listen to while others sound twee in comparison. It is almost as if the band have not decided what musical style to follow so instead are throwing them all into the pot and see which one floats. Of course, one problem with doing this is that people may like some of what they do and not others, and I think that it is safe to say that this is the camp that I fall into. Not an album I would suggest searching for from Poland, unless you really want to know what Kennedy has been doing in his spare time.
#84, July 2005

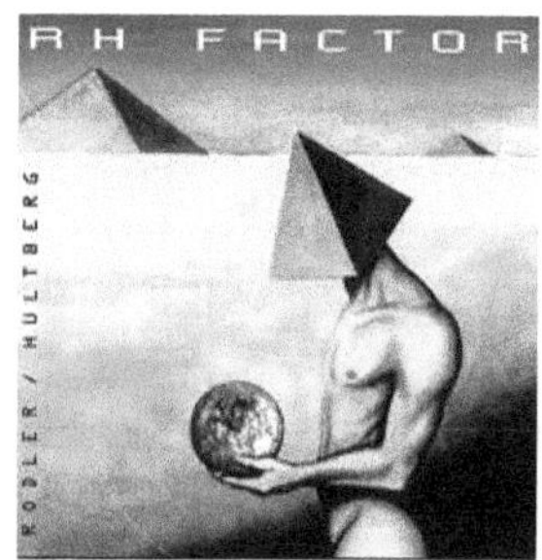

RH FACTOR
RH FACTOR

A long time ago I heard about a great American band called Drama who sent me a demo (which I raved over) and a work in progress tape containing three new songs. However, they went their separate ways with guitarist Chris Rodler and his drumming brother Brett forming Leger De Main with a new singer, taking a slightly different musical path. I do not know what happened to bassist and vocalist Kevin Hultberg back then, but I know what he has been doing recently as he is back together with the Rodler brothers to re-record/

remix and add some new songs that were not on the original tape. Now called RH Factor, and with a brighter and even more complex sound, these guys are back with a vengeance. The music is extremely complex, technical rock. When I heard the original tapes, I felt that it was very Rush oriented and while that is still one area of the sound there is much to it than 'just' that, with elements of Dream Theater or Queensrÿche. The introduction of "Extrinsic" wears me out just listening to it, let alone playing it. It is the harder, more complex, numbers that show the band at their best, as Kevin and Chris have a real understanding, so that they come across more as twin guitarists than as a guitarist and a bassist. The introduction to the instrumental "No Sale's Final" sounds as if it is the twin attack of Wishbone Ash at its best! Anybody who enjoys the more technical area of rock will fall in love with this straight away. It is complex enough for even the most hardened proggers, but at no time do they stray away from the fact that they are a rock band first and foremost. "Game of Chance" has such a commercial sound and great harmony hook that it could even be a hit on AOR Radio! Not much chance of that over here of course, seeing as how this is great music and that seems for the most part to stop it from having any chance of radio airplay or chart success.
#50, Aug 1998

RICOCHET
ZARAH – A TEARTOWN STORY
This is the second album from Ricochet, and is a concept telling the story of a young girl who was abused in childhood through to the murder of the perpetrator and then her suicide in jail. It is a very emotional album, but also one that takes huge chunks of Threshold attitude and mixes that with the likes of Arena as well as being reminiscent at times of Queensrÿche. The guys have been playing together for more than ten years and it shows in the way that the music can switch, and everyone stays together. Christian Heise has a very powerful rock voice and he really shines on this album which is very powerful indeed in places. It is prog metal but also stands firmly in the melodic, technical hard rock area as well. The story comes through and the more you play this album the more you will get out of it. Overall this is a very interesting and another solid release from the label.
#87, Apr 2006

RING OF FIRE
THE ORACLE
While great play in the press release is made of the reputation and previous bands of all the members of this new group (singer Mark Boals having just left Yngwie Malmsteen), what impressed me most about this album before placing it in the player is the name of the person who engineered and mixed it. Erik Norlander is a keyboard player and songwriter of some considerable skill for both his own band Rocket Scientists and for Lana Lane (co-engineer Neil Citron plays guitar for Lana). So even before playing it I was certain that this was going to be a keyboard led rock album of some kind, and I was not to be

disappointed. While Frontiers normally release AOR albums, and in fact are publicizing this as a neoclassical heavy metal work (whatever this is), I feel that if I must hang a label on this then it would be progressive. Sure, it is American (and not in the same prog area as Kopecky, Discipline or Salem Hill), and is much more rock based than most, but in many ways, this is Uriah Heep for the 21st Century. While Mark has a fine voice and probably sees this as his band, this is much more a vehicle for Vitalij Kuprij who is a very fine keyboard player. He also has a great understanding with guitarist George Bellas and their interplay at speed is reminiscent of Ken Hensley and Mick Box. A passionate album, and one that will appeal to both melodic rock fans and progheads, if they are prepared to accept that this music will bleed over into each area. I look forward to the next one with great interest.
#65, Dec 2001

RING OF MYTH
UNBOUND
'Unbound' is the first album by Californian trio Ring of Myth, who comprise Danny Flores (vocals, bass, keyboards), George Picado (acoustic and electric guitar) and Rick Striker (drums and backing vocals), and they have managed to produce an album that certainly does not sound like a debut! They come across as Rush crossed with Spock's Beard, not a bad mix I'm sure you'll agree. It is the harder edged songs that really make a difference, such as opener "Presence" which after a chaotic beginning fairly belts along. This is a great start to the album, with the interest captured and held immediately. Straight away the listener is impressed, held by the ears, with the jaw hanging down and the drool forming a pool on the floor. Of course, the song has to slow (loads of high harmony vocals here) just so that it can take off again. There is quite a high jazz element here as well, which they have used to their favour. "A Transforming" shows a different side to the band, although it is still hard hitting. "Thief Of Night" probably finds them at their most classic Yes-like, but they manage to make the sound their own just enough so that it is not a distraction. This was an album I enjoyed, and I hope to hear a lot more from them in the future.
#43, Aug 1997

RITUAL
RITUAL
This is a reissue of Ritual's 1995 debut album (which originally came out on Musea) and is certainly interesting, with some songs very different to other material within the current prog scene. Some of that is due to the line-up and instruments being used as while Patrik Lundström (vocals, electric, acoustic guitars) is fairly straightforward (although it must be mentioned that among his many sins is fronting the pop trio Blond at the Eurovision Song Contest in Dublin in 1997), the rest of the band are Fredrik Lindqvist (bass, bouzouki, mandola, mandolin, hammered dulcimer, recorders, tin

whistles, vocals), Johan Nodrgen (drums, percussion, mallets, jew's harp, vocals) and Jon Gamble (keyboards, harmonica, vocals). This does mean that the listener is not at all sure what the songs are going to be like, one to the next. Add a guest violinist among others and here is a band that really does want to be taken as being 'progressive', not 'regressive'. Some of the songs are much closer to folk than anything else, while others just belt along and of course some do both. Patrik's vocals are very clear, and he is as much at home singing gently in "The Way Of Things" or stretching out when the need is required. That song is a million miles away from "Typhoons Decide" which is far more complex and dynamic, with lots of movement between different styles: an album that progheads would do well to seek out. They are very different to the rest of the 'neo-prog' crowd, and it is always good to hear a band that are trying to take prog into new directions.

#78, Apr 2004

RITUAL

LIVE

There are not many bands that state that they play 'Swedish progressive folk', but Patrik Lundström, Fredrik Lindqvist, Johan Nordgren and Jon Gamble do just that. Patrik is also singer with Kaipa, but here he can really put himself to the test as he produces falsettos, screams, and vocal acrobatics while also playing the guitar. This really is prog at the cutting edge, as not only do they use many different keyboards sounds, but bassist Fredrik also provides bouzouki, mandolin and tin whistles as well as providing backing vocals. Add to that the style of music that they are playing, and it is obvious that they have as much in common with Gentle Giant as they do with folk. When they rock then these guys blast it out, but they can be very quiet and gentle as well when the need arises. This is complex prog, that brings in loads of different styles and makes a sound that is very much their own and quite unlike anything else around. But one of the joys of this music is that Patrik's vocals and melody lines means that even when it is very complicated indeed, this is something that can be enjoyed at a top level without really delving into the depths. This is an impressive double CD that certainly has a lot going for it.

#86, Feb 2006

RIVERSIDE

OUT OF MYSELF

This is *the* album that is creating noise in Poland at the present time. Originally released on a small label it was then picked up by Sony and the band have since signed with Laser's Edge for a worldwide release. This is one of those prog albums that goes into the head and stays there: think Porcupine Tree, Radiohead, Pink Floyd and darker bands such as Anathema then you may have some idea of just how good this is. It is not prog metal, but when the guitars come in they kick really hard. With the lyrics in English this is an album

that is accessible yet at the same time is darkly complex: there is a passion and presence that is sadly missing from many prog bands. This is not music that has been created to be listened to in a sterile environment, this is prog designed to be taken out on the road and performed in front of a sweaty baying audience. It is prog that mixes and melds, never forgetting that rock is a key element of what they are doing. Yes, there is room for acoustic guitars, but there is also room for Marshalls turned up to twelve, but even when this is happening it is not about bludgeoning the audience into submission (okay, part of it may be), but rather using it as part of another dramatic effect. Simply, this is one of the most enjoyable albums I have heard in the prog field for some time and yet again Poland are proving that they have some top acts.
#80, Jul 2004

RIVERSIDE
VOICES IN MY HEAD

This EP has been released to satisfy the demand of those who can't wait until Riverside's second album 'Second Life Syndrome' is released on Inside Out in November. That release is eagerly awaited, as there is no doubt that Riverside have become one of the most important Polish progressive bands in a very short period. So, this is just to keep us going until then, and I do not believe that any of these songs will be on the new album. The first five are new songs recorded at the beginning of the year, while the last three show them in front of a very appreciative audience in Warsaw in 2004. The large use of acoustic guitar with almost reflective keyboards gives their music quite a laid-back stance, one that can be reminiscent of Camel but without the Andy Latimer-style guitar. The vocals blend together almost like a male Corrs, with the result that it is possible just to drift into their world, and a wonderful place it is. It is strange to think that they have yet to release their follow-up album as this is just full of maturity, and the impression is that they have been around for many years and not that they are new to the scene. There hasn't been a great deal said about them over here yet, but there will be. The website is available in English (luckily), and if you enjoy your progressive music then this is a band that you really should be looking out for.
#84, July 2005

RIVERSIDE
SECOND LIFE SYNDROME

Polish act Riverside are back with the 'difficult' second album, but they do not appear to have had any difficulty at all as this is far more complex and, in many ways, darker than the debut. Those who picked up the extended EP 'Voices In My Head' will be pleased to note that none of the five tracks (recorded only last Jan-March) feature here. This starts in a very complex, low key, manner, but when they kick into "Volte-Face" the guitars are very much to the fore and although there is room for some Gary Chandler-like noodlings this is much more about a dramatic prog rock song with strong riffs. When the vocals start, they are accompanied just by keyboards and drums, and as with all good music it is the control of contrast and dynamics that really makes this special. Riverside have quickly built a reputation of being one of the finest prog bands to come out of Poland and it is richly deserved. This is music that switches and shifts so that while it does contain elements and styles of progressive music of the past, they also take a lot from the more dramatic sides of hard rock so that when the growls come punching through they are doubly dramatic, yet in the same song they can contrast that with gently played piano and feedback laden guitar. With this album being made widely available in Europe I am sure that these guys are only going to go from strength to strength. Progheads need to find out more

#86, Feb 2006

ROCKET SCIENTISTS

BRUTAL ARCHITECTURE

This is the second album from Rocket Scientists, following on from their successful debut 'Earthbound'. They are led by producer and keyboard player Erik Norlander with guitarist and vocalist Mark McCrite, and the line-up is completed with Stick player Don Schiff (who has not only played with Elvis but also with Raquel Welch!) and drummer Tommy Amato. To say that these guys know what they are doing is something of an insult! It is like listening to the very best British progressive rock of the last twenty or thirty years, with King Crimson crossing swords with Emerson Lake & Palmer, while it is also possible to find elements of Pink Floyd, Yes and Alan Parsons Project. Although it hearkens back to the great bands of the past, Rocket Scientists have also managed to capture a sound that is all their own. This is due in no small way to the use of a Stick throughout the album, which Don plays with great skill. They all know how to play off each other and they have so much confidence in their own abilities that there is no need to show off all their skills. The result is an album that is technically very complex, yet at the same time is not overpowering because it all fits together so naturally. This is not an album that attempts to rock out, but for the most part is at the softer end of the spectrum which is not a problem when the music is as interesting and complex and individualistic as this: one that needs further investigation.

#43, Aug 1997

ROCKET SCIENTISTS

EARTH BELOW AND SKY ABOVE

ROCKET SCIENTISTS

LIVE IN BRUSCHAL, GERMANY (VIDEO)

The video was recorded at the German Progressive Rock festival last year, while the CD is taken from that performance and another in America: I have played the video so much that it is surprising that it hasn't worn out. While I was working from home following my accident, I used to sit with my laptop and

have the video playing in the background, watching it while I was waiting for the computer to do something. Only one song appears on the CD which is not on the video, and vice versa. I must just point out that Lana Lane guests with the band for a few numbers and the song which is on the video but not on the CD, is her brilliant "Symphony of Angels", get the video for this song alone!!! Seriously for a minute, the video is of superb quality, matching the IQ 'Forever Live' set. Rocket Scientists are Mark McCrite (vocals, guitar), Erik Norlander (keyboards, vocals), Tommy Amato (drums) and Don Schiff (stick) and are one of the truly exciting progressive rock bands to be coming out of America. The music is incredibly complex and technical, but never so much that it loses the musical thread. This is amazing stuff, what a lot of progressive music aims to achieve but never reaches. I played the video to some friends and they could not believe what they were seeing or hearing. This is progressive rock at its very best.
#51, Jan 1999

KURT RONGEY
BOOK IN HAND
This is far more than just a CD of great keyboard music; it comes with a thirty-two-page A4 book containing drawings and handwritten lyrics to all the songs – literally a "book in hand" to study while playing the album. Everything is performed by Kurt himself (as well as producing and engineering), apart from the guest appearance on "Long, Dark Corridor" of Bill Pohl on electric guitar. Reminiscent at times of Seventies Genesis and Camel, it does not dwell in the past, but rather brings that style of music firmly into the Nineties. Gently layered melodies and softly sung vocals give way to more dynamic singing and powerful sweeping keyboards. At times the speed of the keyboard runs is devastating, yet at others just a few notes are used to great effect. Contrast and change are the order of the day, with songs very distinct from each other as different sounds and styles are utilised. Dissonance and dischord has its place as well, emphasising even more the harmony that prevails for much of the time. A great deal of thought and effort has gone into this album, as there is just so much here for the listener. Never boring, at times exciting and passionate, yet at others gentle and lulling, this really is an album that swings through a myriad of styles and moods. There is just so much here for any lover of progressive rock, as Kurt creates a sound unlike most of the other 'prog rock' currently being performed. It is so good, the fact there is virtually no guitar or bass is not noticed, yet at the same time 'Book In Hand' does not fall into the trap of being yet another synth album, there is far more to it than that. An album that must be really listened to it order to fully appreciate all that is here, I heartily commend it to any lover of keyboard-based progressive rock.
#22, Mar 1994

ROOK
JUDGE & JURY

Rook came together in the summer of '92 when John Boyes (guitar, ex-Freefall) and Julian Garner (keyboards, ex-Kick) started writing together. The middle of 1993 saw the band with a bassist (Steve Hart, ex-The Press) and a drummer (Carl Sampson, ex-Casual Affair) but with no vocalist. As Julian had been providing the vocals for song demos, the decision was made for him to be the vocalist and keyboard player which he does by using a remote MIDI controller to play all the keyboard parts. The whole band are heavily influenced by It Bites, and this comes through on the demo. They all sing, and this shows well on the best track of the six, "Far From Home".
#22, Mar 1994

ROOT
ILLUMINATION

Right, I must get my head around this. Root is a one-man project by David Kendall who obviously writes, performs and produces all the material. Oh, and he designs all the artwork as well. But the result is an album that certainly comes across as if it is a band production, and the only thing that gives it away that it is not released on a large label is that the paper in the booklet is not glossy, but there is artwork on every page with the lyrics. David obviously enjoys listening to Jadis and IQ, but interestingly they are not listed in his influences. Mind you, there are not many prog bands who would admit to being influenced by Starcastle (and probably quite a few who do not even know who they are). This is a songs-based album, one that is nice to listen to. It is not cutting edge, it is not overly dramatic, but what it is, is a strong collection of numbers that are entertaining, and while they are fairly mellow there is a restrained passion that do make them standout. Yet again this is an album that if you enjoy prog music then you ought to seek out *#84, July 2005*

ROUND HOUSE
JIN.ZO-NI.N.GEN

ROUND HOUSE
WINGS TO REST

ROUND HOUSE
LIVE @ 2001 IN OSAKA

I enjoy listening to bands that no-one else has ever heard of, and I particularly like hearing bands from overseas. So, I was very pleased to be sent these discs, but unfortunately, I have been able to find out very little about them on the web, and the sleeve notes to the CDs are of course in Japanese. Oh

well, better just listen to the music then. Round House are a five-piece instrumental progressive rock band, with roots firmly in Camel although they do use twin guitar interplay to fine effect and even manage to come across as Wishbone Ash at times. The debut album (which I think translates to 'The Facsimile Edition') was originally released at the end of 1978, with the first three tracks recorded in a studio and the other two recorded 'live' (for this reissue there is one more track from the same period). The sound quality does vary somewhat and is not as good as it could be at times (the bass is particularly low in the mix throughout), but when they are blasting out as on "Tour Of The Deep Ocean" then this is very fine indeed. The mix between prog, jazz, and more straight-ahead guitar interplay shows that this band could cut it inside either genre, and if all the songs had the recording quality of the first three then this would be extremely highly recommended. As it is, this is still an album well worth hearing. I think 'Wings To Rest' was released after the band had already broken up and is a collection of previously unavailable material that had been recorded in 1978 and 1979, which shows the band in a much more jazz fusion vein. The twin guitars are still very much to the fore, and any fan of good guitar will love the opener "A Red Rose And Whisper Of A Devil". Unfortunately, the sound inconsistencies that bedevil the first album also come back here somewhat, so that at times the impression is of listening to a second-generation tape instead of a CD taken from the masters. But what can't be hidden is that these are fine musicians with a strong understanding of each other and the impression again is that they have been recorded 'live'.

Three of the original five members got back together at the turn of the century and the result is a revisiting of their previously available recordings. I presume that this was recorded basically 'live' in the studio as there is hardly any audience sound (although the band are introduced at one point), and the overall sound quality is much better. Given that the two new boys are the keyboard player and one of the guitarists, they have fitted in extremely well and the result is an album that certainly stands up against the other two and as the sound quality is more consistent is the one that I would plump for. Round House are/were a fine band in the prog jazz-fusion mould and I have enjoyed listening to these immensely.
#71, Dec 2002

ROUND HOUSE
3-D

Some four years after 'Wings To Rest', Round House are back with their new album and it appears that there have been quite some changes in the camp. Masayuki Kato is still there on guitar (plus now programming as well), bassist Yoshiaki Uemura is still present, but there is a new keyboard player in Soura Ishikawa while both the second guitarist and the drummer have now left. However, the music does not seem to have suffered as what we

have here is a very professional sounding symphonic prog act that are bringing in lots of different styles, so that while there may be rock guitar going on in the background it could well be some wonderfully dated keyboard sounds taking the lead in the front. There are some strong structures and arrangements and the result is something that is accessible on first hearing and is an album that will appeal to both progheads and to those interested in instrumental music as this is quite fun.
#88, Jun 2006

ROUSSEAU
AT THE CINEMA
Rousseau is a German outfit that released three albums in the Eighties (all of which are available on Musea), and after fourteen years with nothing have released an album of all new material. I have to say that this quite a strange album to play, as it is virtually an instrumental followed by a song, followed by an instrumental, all the way through which is certainly uncommon. The album commences with a piano-led instrumental, which although quite short and pleasant did make me think that I would be listening to an album of laid-back classical instrumentals and nothing else. But, the songs themselves are quite different, and are sung in English so they are easy to understand. This is music that is very heavily influenced by Camel, and nothing wrong with that I hear you say. Jörg Schwarz has a voice that is sometimes reminiscent of Nick Barrett and if another band could be looked for within Rousseau's music than it would be Pendragon, particularly when it is uplifting and full of pomp. I would have preferred to hear an album that was not quite so formulaic in its outlook, and contained less instrumentals, but overall this is a pleasant listen while not ground-breaking or earth shattering.
#71, Dec 2002

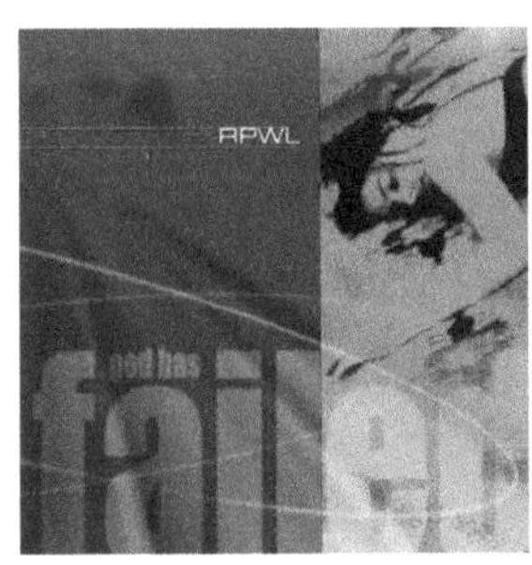

RPWL
GOD HAS FAILED
The first I had heard of both of this band and label was when I received an e-mail from Artur in Poland raving over it. I was soon in contact with label boss Dirk Jacob, and the debut album from RPWL is now on the player. Although this is their first, they have risen out of the ashes of another band, Violet District, which I have reviewed in these pages before. Digging through the files, I see that it was Artur who put me onto them originally as well, some four years ago. With three of the four members of the band having played together since 1992, it is no surprise that they have a good rapport with each other. The music is quite dreamy and reflective, yet always with lots of melody and ideas: it is easy to see why Artur was so impressed. Sometimes there are elements of late Seventies Genesis, while at others it is Pink Floyd or even The Beatles. Most of the music slowly builds, as opposing to impressing with intricate speed runs up and down scales. This is music that can be enjoyed without hesitation, music that is direct and allow the listener to enjoy it for its' own sake. One to cherish. *#60, Oct 2000*

RPWL
TRYING TO KISS THE SUN

RPWL's debut release, 'God Has Failed' created quite a storm when it was released eighteen months ago, gaining votes in many prog polls. So, the pressure was on when the band came to record their second album, and a desire to move away from many of the Floyd influences that pervaded the debut. But as they have only been together for five years, and initially started life as a Floyd tribute band it is perhaps not surprising that they are still a major influence on the sound. What has happened on this album is that the band have become more commercially aware and have concentrated on the arrangements. They sound nothing like Jadis but have managed to capture some of the Phil Spector-style prog wall of sound that can be found sometimes with their music. Listening to "I Don't Know (What It's Like)" made me feel that this would be a great single (okay, not for the UK market, but Germany itself perhaps?) with its' repetitive chorus and great hooks. Contrast that to the almost blues-oriented "Sugar For The Ape" which is much harder with the guitar at the forefront, although there is a Sixties psych section that just serves to drive home the dynamic contrast. This shows that RPWL are breaking through the musical barriers they found themselves constrained with on the debut. They created a stir in the prog world with their debut release and this is better. They have already been playing festivals in the States this year, as well as touring Europe and are soon back on the road with co-headliner John Wetton, so this could well be the year when they hit the prog big time.

#68, Jun 2002

RPWL
WORLD THROUGH MY EYES

RPWL have quietly been making quite a name for themselves as one of the top symphonic prog bands around, and in 'World Through My Eyes' have produced their most accomplished album so far. This is music that owes a great deal to Pink Floyd, and both Genesis and Steve Hillage have also had their impact on the sound. The Genesis link is taken a bit further as they decided that they were not vocally doing justice to the song "Roses", so asked Ray Wilson if he would step up to the plate and he manages to take the song to another level. But this is much more than an album to be purchased by the Genesis completist, as there is a lot going on from opener "Sleep" (which starts with mystic sitar and percussion before moving into something that is extremely powerful) through to the title cut which is only ten minutes long, but twists and provides dramatic elements often found in songs much longer. If you enjoy classic Floyd with extra influences as well, then this is for you.

#82, Jan 2005

RPWL
START THE FIRE

RPWL have been creating quite a storm with their studio albums, so the time was deemed right for a 'live' release. My version came with a sticker proudly declaring that it features Ray Wilson, which it does, but he only sings on two numbers. These are both found on the first disc which has been taken from the Rockpalast show earlier this year. RPWL are one of those prog bands who have strongly brought in the influences of classic Genesis and Floyd and then taken them into the new millennium with a heavy dose of Pendragon. I am still not sure if the songs here are superior to the studio versions, and when Ray walks onstage to join them on "Roses" he gets a huge cheer, and he then stays to perform "Not About Us". Yogi Lang has a fine voice and I am not sure if they benefit from the guest vocals, or if these are just a smokescreen, as they are mighty fine on their own. The second disc shows the band having fun, as there are some covers included here as they show just how indebted they are to Floyd with some careful selections including an extremely powerful "Welcome To The Machine". Comparing this to the SB live album reviewed later, then to my long-suffering ears it is obvious that this is the superior, with some strong performances from a band that is prepared to acknowledge their influences yet also want to make this music their own. *#85, Nov 2005*

RSC
CZAS WODNIKA

RSC used to be seen as the Polish answer to Kansas and were popular in the mid-Eighties but split up after just one album. However, ten years down the line they have reformed and recorded 'Czas Wodnika'. Not being very good with Polish, I think the album was recorded with a nine-piece line-up with three guitarists, plus the vocalist also plays guitar! (Luckily Polish for guitar is "gitary" while "organy hammonda" speaks for itself!). Although the use of violin means they will always be compared with Kansas, I feel RSC have less of an AOR feel, although during "Zbemoj" they do come very close. The heavy use of Hammond as opposed to synths (which are also used) also gives quite a distinctive sound, as do the guitar solos, which tend to have a different feel to what one might expect from a Western band. *#40, Mar 1997*

RUNAWAY TOTEM
ANDROMEDA

This album has the quietest beginning of any that I have ever heard; I had to turn the volume up to make sure that there was something going on! Dreamy layered keyboards then gave way to a much more Hawkwind style space rock attack, but that also did not last for long. This is an album that refuses to stick to any particular style, and there are hints of Magma, King Crimson and VDGG as well as an unusual singing style from Roberto

Goddardi. This is the third album from the Italians, who were formed in 1988, and is music that is challenging, and often defies description; just when I think that I understand what is going on, they change tack totally. The result is an album that is going to alienate all but the most devoted progressive fan. That is not a bad thing; especially as so many progressive bands these days are nothing of the sort. This hearkens back to the days of the early Seventies when the word 'progressive' really did mean that. It may not be easy listening, but I got a lot out of it.
#60, Oct 2000

SAD MINSTREL
THE FLIGHT OF THE PHOENIX
This may seem to be a band, but Sad Minstrel is actually a solo project by Malombra keyboard player Fabio Casanova. Only one of the songs is sung in Italian, with the rest in English, although lyrics to all are provided in the booklet in both languages. It is an album that is extremely deep, full of layers that belongs to a time long ago, the sort of album that was favoured in the Seventies, with lots of acoustic guitar and flute intermingling with dramatic vocals and keyboards. Electric guitars also play their part but often these are in the background, providing emphasis as opposed to cranking out the riffs, and sometimes a mandolin is the lead. Although Fabio did much of the programming and pre-production at home, it seems almost inconceivable that he managed to record the whole album in less than eighty hours. It is not all quiet reflection as the title cut itself shows, which contains many elements more normally associated with rock. It is music that will be of great interest to those that want their music to be both approachable and accessible yet at the same time to be different to the norm; an intriguing album that brings the listener in to a world of Fabio's creating.
#74, Jun 2003

SAENS
ESCAPING FROM THE HANDS OF GOD
This is the follow-up to 1999's 'Les Regrets d'Isidore D' that was released on Mellow Records when the band were called Sens. I have not heard that album, but if it is of the same quality as this one then I do need to search it out. This is a combination of instrumentals and songs, with five of them at more than eleven minutes in length. It is a truly progressive album; one that those who feel that the neo-prog movement is too constrained will fall in love with immediately. I can see why label boss Malcolm Parker is hailing this as the album of the year, and while I will not go that far (we long ago agreed that our personal tastes differ), I will say that it is an album that does need to be heard by progheads. It did take a few listens to get into, as is sometimes the case with prog, but that is not altogether a bad thing. The band are French, and they have little in common with much of the UK or American prog bands, although it could be argued that they have taken some influences from the Canterbury scene. Their influences for the most part are

much more in line with classical music and jazz, while bringing it altogether in a style that often takes a while to make sense of. The first time I heard the album I was not convinced at all, as it was going straight over me with just the few neo-prog passages connecting, but the more I played it the more I could understand what was going on. It is not prog that is immediate but those who persevere with this will be rewarded with one of the more truly progressive albums around.
#69, Aug 2002

SAENS
PROPHET IN A STATISTICAL WORLD
Sometimes it is possible to put on a progressive rock album and just revel in the way that the music seems to move effortlessly from one area to another, where musical complexity and ingenuity are taken as the norm and the album seems to be far too short, no matter what the length is. This is very much the case with the new album by Saens, which features two lengthy suites ("Dystopian Dream" and the title cut) which are further divided into five and seven songs respectively. They have been influenced by some classical literature, and I can see references to '1984' by George Orwell, 'Brave New World' by Aldous Huxley and 'The Time Machine' by H. G. Wells. What makes the album work so well is the way that they have decided that musically there are no boundaries, so pursue whatever musical ideal seems right at the time. This means that they can move from Twelfth Night into choral or even Saga without a pause for breath and is an album of incredible depth and density. It just is not possible to gauge the full merits of this album when playing it casually, this is an album that deserves to have time spent on it and the listener is richly rewarded. Easily one of the best albums ever to be released by Cyclops.
#80, Jul 2004

SAGA
FULL CIRCLE
I first came across Saga care of TV on the Radio, which led me to buying firstly the single "Careful Where You Step" and then the album 'Images At Twilight'. This was their second album and was the one that brought them to the attention of the rock fan in Europe. With a heavy emphasis on keyboards, although with the guitar never too far away, they soon were heralded as the kings of 'pomp rock' and in vocalist Michael Sadler they had one of the most recognisable singers in the rock arena. Seven million album sales later and they are back with a new album. Following on from a 'trial separation' in the late Eighties the original line-up reformed in 1993 and this is the fifth album since then and is class, sheer class: it oozes out of the plastic, dripping though every note. Songs such as "The One" show this off with riffs aplenty; swathes of keyboards, melodies and hooks to die for and Michael's vocals crowning the glory. Since I received this album it has taken a long time to get it off the player, much to the

detriment of the other albums I have been attempting to listen to. Their music hasn't moved with the times, as it has been timeless since their inception, and it is as if grunge or down tuning has never taken pace. This is music that is just wonderful. If you decided that you only want to buy one album from Canada this year, then this just must be the one. Superb.
#55, Sept 1999

SAGA
HOUSE OF CARDS
It is hard to believe that it is more than a year since I saw Saga at the LA2 promoting their last album 'Full Circle' yet here they are back again with a new album which is out in the UK on February 5th. Saga are one of the few prog/AOR bands around that have an instantly identifiable sound, with the distinctive vocals of Michael Sadler mixing and melding with the keyboard-driven rock. On songs like "The Runaway" I can close my eyes and picture myself back in my bedroom as a teenager listening to their second album 'Images At Twilight'; the music does not seem to have changed much at all. Yes, they bring in new influences, so that they do not sound as if they are trying to play the same song all the time, but this is Saga, and they do not follow the fickles of fashion but go their own way. They use acoustic guitars, and not all the songs are upbeat rockers, but it is on these that Saga excels. *#61, Feb 2001*

SAGA
MARATHON
There are not too many prog bands from Canada, certainly not with the history behind them like Saga who released their debut album some twenty-five years ago. Three of the current line-up played on that album, with lead keyboard player Jim Gilmour joining in 1981. While it is his links in with guitarist Ian Crichton and bassist/keyboard player Jim Crichton that provide the musical heart of the band, it is also singer and keyboard player Michael Sadler that gives the band their most distinctive sound. There are not many rock bands that utilise as many keyboard players as these guys, but strangely the focus is on providing good strong rock with melodic hooks, as opposed to an out and out keyboard blast. They can probably also lay claim to producing the longest ever concept album, in that 'Chapters' are still appearing as they did on the first album, although of course they are never in sequence: this album sees the appearance of chapters 14, 12 and 16. The opening title cut is a blast from start to finish, and it is only the tongue in cheek lyrics that let it down (pronouncing "Marathon" to rhyme with "Avalon"). They may drift a little on the slower numbers, but on songs such as "Hands Up" it sounds as if the Eighties have never been away, as they mix pomp and prog in a way that is undoubtedly their very own. They may be too keyboard oriented for melodic rockers, and possibly too AOR for progheads, but for those who can work past the labels and just enjoy the music there is plenty of strong stuff here to be heard. *#73, Apr 2003*

SAGA
NETWORK
Drummer Steve Negus may have asked for a sabbatical, but in many ways, nothing has changed; the Canadians have a very distinctive sound and it is as if time has managed to stand still. The guitar of Ian Crichton is still surprisingly to the fore (there seems to be more on this album than normal) while Jim Gilmour provides the layers of keyboards that makes Saga one of the top pomp rockers in the world. Of course, Saga could not be Saga without Michael Sadler and he certainly shows no sign at all of slowing down. The drum sound is also key to this album, and that is down not only to new drummer Christian Simpson (the line-up is completed by bassist Jim Crichton) but also because they record the drums in analogue while the rest of the music is recorded in digital: it gives them a warmer sound with more depth. This may not be a full-blown concept album but about half of the songs deal with the subject of TV as a medium and the effect that this can have on people. As always with a Saga album, it is one that fans will love and those who do not understand what all the fuss is about will happily ignore. When I saw them in concert a couple of years ago they said how nice it was to be back in the UK after a long absence and I see that they are playing the Mean Fiddler again on 31st October: shame that is the only date in the UK and on the tour they manage to fit in sixteen shows in Germany...This is Saga doing what they do best, and to my ears are a delight but if you have not enjoyed what they have done in the past then you will hate this. *#81, Dec 2004*

SAGA
THE CHAPTERS LIVE
From the very first album Saga have included 'Chapters' on the albums, never in the right order, but they have been there, and the fans have looked for them. Once, in 1986, they performed all the available Chapters back to back in the correct sequence for the first time. But back then there were only eight available, while now there are sixteen and again the band have performed them in front of an audience more than prepared to sing the words for Michael if he encourages them to do so, especially on songs such as "Don't Be Late" which together with "It's Time" are probably the highlights for me. Saga have always been viewed as a keyboards-based outfit, probably because there may be three of them on keyboards at some point, but they are also very much a rock band with some great crunching riffs. Michael has one of the most distinctive voices in rock and although it is now nearly thirty years since they were formed, he shows no signs at all of losing either the range or power. The only way until now to hear all these numbers in the correct sequence would be by burning tracks from different albums (even their debut album contained Chapters 5 and 6!), but here at last it is possible for the fan to hear them as they have been intended for all these years. The band is on form, and if you enjoy Saga then this is an essential purchase of that there is no doubt.
#85, Nov 2005

SAGA
TRUST
Back with their seventeenth album, the Canadians are showing no sign of slowing down and have instead produced an album that many fans are going to be heralding as one of their finest for quite a while. New drummer Brian Doerner sounds as if he has been there forever, while of course the rest of the guys have been, and here they have produced a sound that is probably more progressive than of late. Jim Gilmour may have not impressed me particularly with his solo album but here he is a revelation, linking in with Ian Crichton on guitar to bring forth the sound of Saga that is so huge and bombastic. Then of course at the front there is Michael Sadler who still has a great voice, and this album is so very fresh and inviting that it is hard to think that it is twenty-eight years since their debut release. 'Trust' is definitely going to satisfy those who have been fans for the length of the journey so far yet will also bring in new ones that have yet to discover the majesty of one of Canada's finest exports. The band are certainly not resting on their maple leaves but instead are still producing music that is exciting and relevant, and the result is something that fans of melodic rock and prog ought to rush out and buy immediately, if not sooner! *#88, Jun 2006*

SALEM HILL
THE ROBBERY OF MURDER
I first heard about this band from Artur in Poland, and a quick email to the States sent this winging to me. Checking the musicians involved I was surprised to see David Ragsdale from Kansas on violin, so obviously, Salem Hill are impressing more than just a few. This is a concept album, around the idea of murder being theft. In this instance the story is told of the father who is killed by a drunk driver, and the boy's reaction to it, first questioning when the father is going to arrive, and then deciding that when he is older, he will hunt down the perpetrator and exact his revenge. Although he finds the man, when he tried to kill him, he sees in the man's eyes the small boy reflected and remembering how he felt at the time he cannot go through with it. The whole subject is treated emotionally and carefully, without ever becoming depressing or tacky. The vocals are so strong, especially in the harmonies, that at times I felt myself thinking of The Carpenters, just because of the arrangements. That is not to say that this is a wimpish outfit, Salem Hill are very much a rock band. In the aftermath of the death of the father with "When", when the boy asks when his father is coming home and his mother attempts to deal with it for herself and for him as well, it is the delicate interplay that drives it all home. When the boy turns from grief to anger in "Someday", deciding to kill the perpetrator of the injustice, the music takes a much harder line, with distorted guitar making a welcome and justified presence on a song that musically wouldn't have sounded out of place on 'Lamb'.

This is one of the most enjoyable, and easy to listen to, concept albums I have ever had the pleasure of hearing. I am convinced that prog fans the world over are going to

welcome this band with open arms, and if you want great music with more than a hint of Kansas due to the violin interplay, and some very thought provoking and well written lyrics, then look no further than Salem Hill.
#51, Jan 1999

SALEM HILL
NOT EVERYBODY'S GOLD
If ever there was an album that I have eagerly been awaiting, it was this one. I gave Sara the booklet of their last album to read the lyrics, and she agreed with me that it was some of the most powerful and thought provoking she had ever seen. So how could they match 'The Robbery Of Murder'? Simple, don't. What they have done here is take the music in another direction without losing any of the power that was there before. David Ragsdale from Kansas has again graced proceedings, here playing on the thirty-minute epic "Sweet Hope Suite". Nevertheless, before getting to that, the last 'song' on the album, there is much more to enjoy. The opening instrumental gives no idea of the power of the following number "Riding The Fence" which has some very early Kansas sounds at times, particularly on the keyboards. It is with Kansas that musically they have the most in common, and that surely cannot be a bad thing. It is an album that is a joy from start to finish, with enough strange rhythms and counter melodies to please any proggers, often in the same song. "January" on its' own is enough evidence to buy this album, let alone the epic that is later. Spock's Beard, Salem Hill, Discipline and Kopecky are all very active prog bands from the States, and all deserve your support. Start here. *#62, May 2001*

SALEM HILL
CATATONIA
This is the third album from Salem Hill and was the album prior to 'Robbery Of Murder', which is the one that shot them into recognition in the UK. Their first two albums ('Salem Hill' and 'Different Worlds') have also been released by Cyclops in the UK as limited editions, but I have yet to hear these. Carl Groves re-recorded some of the keyboard lines that he was not happy with and this version has also been remixed and given new artwork. Salem Hill are one of the most exciting prog bands to come out of the States and this album proves it quite plainly. The songs are both simple and highly complex, the music is intricate yet accessible, the lyrics convoluted but easily understandable. They may be more rock based than many of their contemporaries, but they never cross the boundary into hard rock. While Carl Groves is very much the leader (vocals, guitar, keyboards, all the lyrics and most of the music) neither Pat Henry (bass) and Kevin Thomas (drums, vocals) are bit players and they are key to the overall sound. It may not have quite the immediate impact of 'Robbery Of Murder', but this is an album that I have already played many times and I am sure that I will be doing so again in the future. *#65, Dec 2001*

SALEM HILL
PUPPET SHOW

Salem Hill is definitely one of my favourite American prog rock outfits, and since first hearing 'The Robbery Of Murder', it has been a frequent visitor to my CD player. So, it was with some sense of anticipation that I looked forward to hearing this double live CD. Performances have been taken from a variety of shows over quite a long period of time, but it has been put together in a manner that means that this is not audibly noticeable. For the most part the band has a four-man line-up, with Carl Groves and Michael Dearing sharing lead and harmony vocals and both providing guitar. But there are times when one or both play keyboards, so it is possible to go from a guitar-oriented outfit to one containing no guitars at all. While Carl provides most of the songs, bassist Pat Henry also is no mean slouch in the song writing stakes while drummer Kevin Thomas completes the line-up. This is extremely melodic rock, that often reminds me of the mighty Kansas, and indeed ex-Kansas violinist David Ragsdale guests on "Brave New World", and the fact that it is an outstanding number by all concerned is incredible given that they were unable to rehearse together! The album starts with "Evil One" which has a delicate guitar and keyboards introduction, but the song has a harsh edge, which is played upon with Michael screaming the verse out through gritted teeth while Carl provides the more sympathetic vocals on the chorus. It is extremely hard to pick out a favourite, as the album is just so strong throughout. I suppose the five numbers taken from 'TROM' are hard to distinguish between just because I love that album so much, but they have picked songs from throughout their career and the result is an album that every prog or melodic rock fan should hasten out to purchase immediately, if not sooner. There is no doubt at all that this is one of the best albums that Cyclops has ever released.
#73, Apr 2003

SALEM HILL
MIMI'S MAGIC MOMENT

If I were asked to list my favourite ten progressive albums of the Nineties it would take me a long time to complete and I would probably disagree with myself at the end of it. But I know one album that would be guaranteed a place, and that would be 'The Robbery Of Murder' which these guys released back in 1998. That was their fourth studio album and now they are back with their seventh. I did not hear 'Be' from 2003, but I did really enjoy their awesome live album from the same year, 'Puppet Show', so I put this on the player with great interest. The four-man line-up is still the same as it has been since 'TROM', and yet again they have brought in David Ragsdale (ex-Kansas) to add his violin playing on a few tracks, and among the other guests is a certain Mr Neal Morse who adds his vocals to one song. They were originally going to record another concept album, but then decided not to go ahead with that but instead create some epic songs and tell a story in each, so there are only four songs on the whole album, but what an album it is. All the elements that one would expect from these guys is here in spades, whether it is complex and complicated musicianship or wonderfully

layered harmony vocals, all put together in an album that is immediately accessible and thoroughly enjoyable. I have often felt that Salem Hill have not garnered the recognition that they so richly deserve, and while I would still rather play 'TROM' this is an album that I will often be returning to as there is so much going for it.
#86, Feb 2006

SANDSTONE
LOOKING FOR MYSELF

Yet again we have another very strong prog band coming from Poland, and while Riverside may be the flavour of the month at the moment, this debut album is harder hitting with a style of Arena meeting Dream Theater. It verges on prog metal but at the same time is very melodic indeed, and there is plenty of light and shade to provide the right amount of variety to proceedings that maintains interest. It is hard to believe that this is their debut album as it is an extremely mature piece of work, and with six songs all over the seven-minute mark and a concept to boot (telling the story of the search of a young man through the world looking for love) it is very impressive. There is a tightness to this album, a feeling of a band really working together with a high level of intensity. Singer Marc Zmorynski has a strong voice yet is secure enough to let the band play for long passages while he quietly sits and lets them get on with it. The rhythm section is particularly strong with powerful bass lines, but it is the interplay between guitarist Jarek Niecikowski and keyboard player Grzegorz Marecik that really makes this album. They can play incredibly quick complex passages linked as one, or they can bounce off each other or even just be delicate and soothing. Grzegorz has a wonderful touch to the piano which also adds to the overall sound as so few keyboard players seem to know how to use this instrument in tandem with all the synths. I am very impressed indeed with this release and hopefully as it has been picked up by ProgRock this debut will get the publicity that it certainly deserves. All progheads need to hear this at the very least. *#88, Jun 2006*

SATELLITE
A STREET BETWEEN...

While Satellite may be a new name in the prog field, and 'A Street Between Sunrise And Sunset' their debut album, this is a band that have been formed out of one of Poland's most well-known and best-loved prog acts, Collage. Originally this was set to be a solo project by drummer and main Collage songwriter Wojtek Szadkowski, but he gradually brought in more and more musicians, many of whom he had performed with in Collage. They are signed to Metal Mind, the most important label of its type in Poland, and the artwork has been provided by Mark Wilkinson of Marillion and Fish fame. But what about the music? The band themselves have compared it most to 'Moonshine' era Collage but how about Western proggers who may have never heard that band? There is a lot going on, and while certain influences such as Genesis and Pendragon or Pink Floyd

can be picked out, it is easier to say that this is easy listening prog that is thoroughly enjoyable throughout. The album is sung in English and feels more like an American project and not a Polish one at all. The album starts with street noise and a snippet of a radio commentator, and the impression is a bustling American city. That is an intriguing way into the first song, "The Evening Wind", which at nearly thirteen minutes long is a great start. Of course, the guitar can't be hidden totally by the keyboards and there are some very powerful plays indeed. A favourite must be "No Disgrace" which is a belting prog rock number driven along by dynamic percussion and sizzling keyboard runs. This could easily be the most important album out of Poland this year, and the finest I have heard from that country since Quidam. Which one is the better? The jury is still out.
#73, Apr 2003

SATELLITE
EVENING GAMES
Satellite are back with their second album, following on from 'A Street Between Sunrise and Sunset' which was one of the best-received Polish progressive rock albums from recent years. The pressure does not seem to have got to the guys, as yet again they have produced a very well-structured and thought out album. It opens with the sound of barking dogs in the distance, and gradually the band introduce the title cut which is the longest song on the album at more than sixteen minutes. While there is always the impression that the guitars are going to break through, this track, and indeed the whole album, is very restrained – mixing elements of Genesis with Camel in a way that is never threatening and is somehow soothing. Of the more recent bands the nearest comparison would probably be with Jadis combined with Marillion, but that is not really right as the band move through various mood and styles but never really rocking as hard as they might have. There is a lot going on here, and there is some extremely complex music with great vocals which is very accessible. They just manage to stay the right side of being too bland, but I did feel that unless I was careful, I could lose concentration, and this could slip into background music. They could have done with more shade to go with the light but overall this is a very 'polished' (no pun intended) album that many progheads will enjoy. *#83, Mar 2005*

LEE SAUNDERS
A PROMISE OF PEACE
Lee used to be in Brighton band Crystal Void, and this is his first solo work, and what a work it is too. This is a concept album, which attempts to tell the story of the Second World War, using music and archive material containing speeches, radio and Pathé News broadcasts as well as dialogue from old war films. The amount of time and effort that must have gone into this is simply staggering. Musically it goes from gentle swirling keyboards, to out and out hard rock: Lee is a keyboard player and he has used other musicians to help him create the backdrop for his powerful lyrics and images. This

is not a celebration of war, but more a real remembrance that says we should not forget, because by doing that then we can all too easily let it happen again. "Those who do not learn from history are doomed to repeat it". The album it is most reminiscent of is 'The Wall', but I felt that it is more powerful than that. The guitars are louder, but it is the use of the snippets of speech that add a certain character to the whole proceedings. That most emotive of instruments, the sax, is used to great effect as it cries out in pain. Told in chronological order, it goes from the phoney war and the evacuation from Dunkirk through the Blitz and the turning of the tide that led in turn to Operation Overlord and eventually the return of some of the fathers. It asks how much people at home really knew what was going on, and whether they would have allowed their brothers, fathers and sons to go through it all. At times harrowing, it works both as a reminder of what has gone before as well as being extremely enjoyable. The album has been endorsed by The Royal British Legion, who get a donation from every copy sold, and there is a poppy attached to each CD case. This is an album that will provoke a lot of debate and may be too deep for those who want their music and subject matter to be light-hearted. Lee has produced an album to be rightly proud of.*#30 Aug 1995*

SCENES
CALL US AT THE NUMBER YOU PROVIDE

Over the years I have heard many reasons for the departure of a band member, but never has the reason for the lead singer leaving being because he has been doing so well in the German version of 'Pop Idol' that he has left to concentrate on his solo career! Neki had recorded some of the vocals that appear on this album, but they were completed by his replacement Alex Koch. Neki may live to regret his decision, as this album is going to be gaining a lot of attention in certain quarters. This is a very polished prog metal album which ticks all the right boxes with strong musicianship, good songs and melodies, great vocals and harmonies and of course possibly the most important of all, music that changes its' direction and can be simple or breathtakingly complex all within the same song. This is a very accessible work, although I did also find that the more I played it the more I enjoyed it. The cover on the album is very much out of the blue as the style is very different to the rest of the album, and Talk Talk is not a band that many think of covering, but "Such A Shame" works very well indeed. This is a fine debut from this German prog metal act. *#83, Mar 2005*

SCHLOSS ADLER
MUSIC FOR SURVIVAL HORROR

Schloss Adler is in fact Neil Randall of Vulgar Unicorn, although he is only credited as Schloss Adler throughout the album. This is an homage to the soundtrack of horror films and is quite different to much of his earlier work. There are fifteen 'songs' on the album, and the use of sound effects throughout certainly give it that 'horror' feel. But I found it quite difficult to listen to all of it in one sitting. Some, such as "Apparition" are extremely intense and emotive, and are also very visual, but there comes a point when the brain just can't take anymore. This is an album to be dipped into sparingly but an interesting idea all the same. *#65, Dec 2001*

DON SCHIFF
PEERING OVER CLOUDS
Don Schiff plays N/S Stick with Rocket Scientists, Lana Lane, and countless others and this 2005 album is just him and his instrument with Greg Ellis on percussion. For those who have yet to come across this particular instrument before here is a quote from the web "The NS/Stick™ is an 8-string stereo fretboard tapping instrument and the product of a collaboration between Emmett Chapman (creator of The Stick) and Ned Steinberger (creator of the Steinberger Bass and many other instruments). This instrument incorporates a number of ideas from both The Stick (the tapping fretboard) and the Steinberger Bass (the knee bar, headless design), as well as some completely new ideas as a guitarbass that can be tapped and plucked." Now you know what it is, try and forget all about it. This is an album of music, all new songs (apart from two) that were recorded very quickly, showing that Don has a wonderful understanding of fluid bass and guitar playing, all being combined in a new experience and it is hard to believe that this is just one man making these sounds on what is a string based instrument as opposed to also bringing in keyboards. This is music that is flying, beautiful and thrilling all at the same time. Probably my favourite song on the album is the one that I already know, "Under The Olive Tree", which is normally sung by Lana Lane, but here Don and Greg have turned it into something that is far more magical even than her version on 'Live In Japan'. There is an extra delicacy and restrained passion, with Don playing both behind the melody as well as providing the lead 'vocals'. Fellow Rocket Scientist and Lana Lane musician Erik Norlander was the person who asked Don to record this album, wanting progressive music just played on an N/S Stick and the result is something that is very enjoyable and listenable, while at the same time also managing to be quite different to what else is around. His one cover on here is a dramatic reworking of "A Whiter Shade Of Pale' which plays with the melody and is quite wonderful.
#87, Apr 2006

SECRET SAUCER
ELEMENT 115
Looking at the website this is the result of taking "members from the premiere US space rock bands and musicians who have toured with Hawkwind and Nik Turner, to a beautiful, remote location, locking them in a recording studio, and telling them to jam." Originally there was more than twelve hours of music but that has now been cut down to just twelve songs. Some have two synth players, some two guitarists, and it is not uncommon for guys to switch instruments either, but the result is very good indeed. This is improvised instrumental space rock, but the sound and quality of the

instruments is very good indeed and these guys are bouncing ideas off each other. In some ways, it reminds me of Quarkspace, and I was not surprised to see two members of that band involved in this project. This is music that shows just how good space rock can be when guys are improvising off each other, and with a superb production and editing by Paul Williams and Steve Hayes this is well worth further investigation if you enjoy the genre.
#87, Apr 2006

IL SEGNO DEL COMANDO
DER GOLEM
This is the second album by Il Segno Del Comando (Sign Of Rule) and is a project by Mercy and Diego Banchero of Malombra. They were inspired by a cult seventies film of the same name, and in 1996 released an album based on the plot. Since then the line-up has changed, and now contains four members of Malombra, (new boys being drummer Francesco La Rosa and keyboard player Franz Ekurn), along with guitarists Gabriele Grixoni and Livio Carusio. The film that originally inspired them may be dark and obscure, but in many ways, so is the music. This is prog with foreboding, huge gothic overtones and at times a sinister manner. It is sung completely in Italian, but that in no way detracts as it just seems right somehow. The press release seems to be at something of a loss to describe the album, and I am in complete sympathy as I have the same problem. It is dark and powerful, yet also atmospheric and ethereal. There is a feeling of a presence, something that is waiting for its' presence to be felt, and in many ways, would make powerful music for some dark film in its' own right. Fields Of The Nephilim go to church and get mugged by something dark and strange. Who wants to listen to an album like this, sung in a language that many in England do not understand? Well you all should – this is wonderful.
#69, Aug 2002

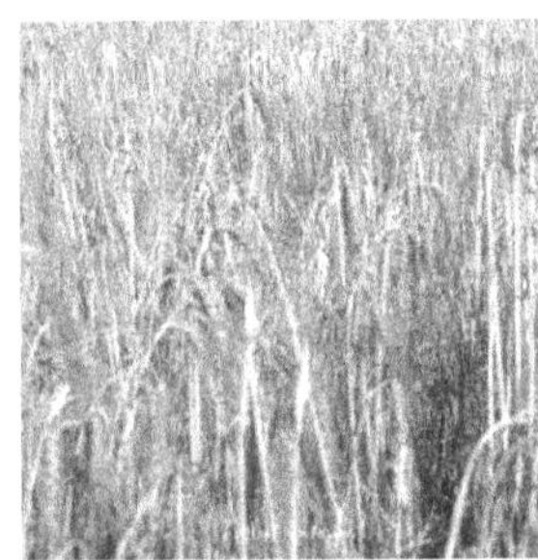

SENSES
FIELDS UNSOWN
This album has already been reviewed by Frank Blades in #41 but seeing as how I have now received a copy from the band it would be churlish not to mull over its' merits again. Frank said that the CD appears to fall between two stools of singer with backing band and a prog outfit. I feel that he has managed to capture the spirit of the album as Joan Morbee has a good voice and songs, and at times there is the impression that she wants this to be a one woman show while at others it is a group. The album commences with "Under The Weight Of The Rain", which has some delicate pianowork for the introduction, which soon picks up when the rest of the band join in. Vocally Joan reminds me somewhat of Sandy Denny combined with Grace Slick and to me there is very much a Jefferson Airplane feel to proceedings at times. There are only six songs on this rather short (thirty-five minutes) album, but they are all enjoyable, although at times this is

more of a middle of the road album than a proghead would expect. That is not to say that I have not enjoyed playing it, I have, but only investigate further if you want an album of songs that rely on you having an interest in high quality music as opposed to one particular genre.
#43, Aug 1997

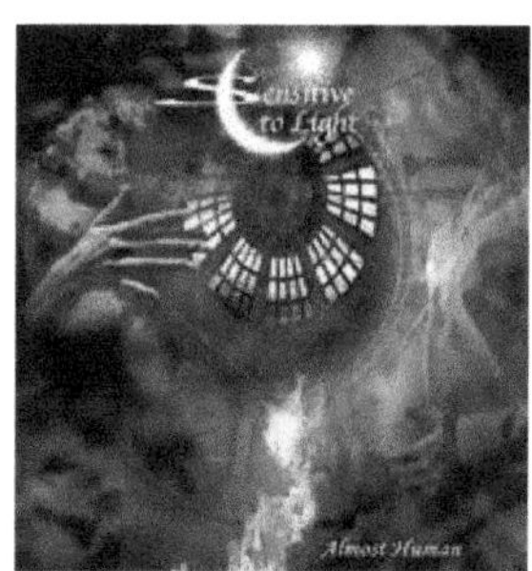

SENSITIVE TO LIGHT
ALMOST HUMAN
Sensitive To Light is a new project by Vynce Leff of Saens, and is a concept album telling the story of Pinocchio. What makes this album stand out though is not the undoubted musicianship of Vynce, but the vocals of Jenny Lewis. Jenny has come from a folk and Celtic background and sings in wonderfully controlled tones that makes one think of a trained choral singer as opposed to a 'rock' singer. She has incredible control within her range and it is her vocals linked in with the symphonic nature of Vynce's music that makes this CD work so very well indeed. It is laid back and thoughtful, and does not contain many pure rock elements, but instead brings in instruments as required, and the result is something that is truly beautiful. STL are not a duo; this is a band using live drums, bass etc. and hopefully that means that they will expand out of being a studio unit and will play live. It is a wonderfully layered and arranged album and is a joy to listen to. This is something that needs to be played and paid attention to, to get the most out of it, but with music as stirring and emotional as this that really is not a problem. In some ways like Karda Estra, yet also far removed, this is a classically church inspired album with incredible vocals that does warrant investigation from progheads.
#88, Jun 2006

SERAPHIQUE
CHRYSALIS
This independent release is going to polarise a lot of prog metal fans as the Dutch lads have taken the genre that much further and amid all the widdly-widdly and complex music one finds death metal grunts. They are not there all the time, but they do make a marked impact on the music itself. Listening to the instrumental sections one feels that the band have made a very deliberate decision to go down a path that few if any have dared to tread. Of course, the problem with this is that they can land between the cracks as it were and upset everyone who may like either one genre or another, then you get weirdos like me who like to hear something that little bit different and can be attracted to what they are doing. "A Barrier In Every Bridge" is quite different to the rest in that it almost sounds as if New Order are in the house with a lead melody from the bass and guitars backing it up, and the vocals being sung but the title track is up next, and it is all dandruff and long sweaty hair again. I was quite confused the first time I played this but gradually I got

used to what was going on and found that if I took every song on its' own merits then this is a very enjoyable album indeed. All I must do now is stop myself from turning it up all the time as it keeps upsetting the rest of the family.
#84, July 2005

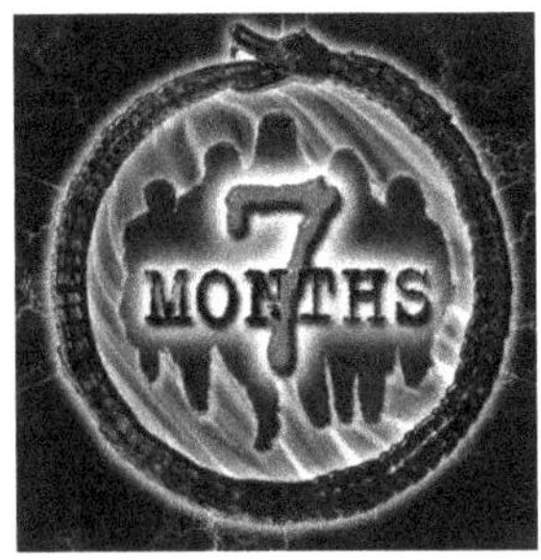

7 MONTHS
7 MONTHS

The press release states, "7 Months is an LA based band combining progressive time signatures, complex progressions with sellable commercial melodies designed to stand the test of time. The band members are all extremely talented with a knack for writing excellent songs but keeping the integrity and intricacies of well-designed music." That these guys can play is never in doubt, and Chris, Greg and Barry formed the band after they all met at Musicians Institute in LA where they were students. In fact, it could be argued that 7 Months are an Americanised version of the much-missed Mr So & So who also met at music college. They will never be viewed as being progressive by any followers of the UK prog scene as this contains far too many AOR influences, but for all that this is not a bad album. The press release likens them to Yes, Kansas, Rush, Saga and Dream Theater but to my ears I would argue that although they are different on the vocal front, I would have put them more with Journey and Styx, along with the aforementioned So & So's. It is an album that needs to be played a few times to gain the most from it, but it is also accessible first time around and there are some very strong songs. I particularly like the rocker "Stay" which contains not only good guitar riffing and keyboard overlays, but also plenty of melody and very strong vocals with a hook. It may not quite live up to the billing but is an interesting album all the same.
#70, Oct 2002

SHADOW GALLERY
SHADOW GALLERY

Shadow Gallery's debut came out in 1992, and shows highly developed prog of the American kind, i.e. tinged with a very heavy dose of AOR. One thing that does let this down quite badly is the production, which tends to fade in and out. They like using blistering runs to link to quieter passages, but these rockier parts are far too quiet. The impression is of Brendt Allman working his fingers to the bone while the producer (who is also the bassist) turns the volume down! This manages to diminish the enjoyment of the album for me, which is quite a shame as they are all brilliant musicians. The interplay is quite breath-taking at times; the note density must be amazing. But I found it a difficult album to listen to because of the production and if Steve Paine or Clive Nolan had been at the helm of this then the result would have been quite different.
#40, Mar 1997

SHADOW KEEP
CORRUPTION WITHIN

Shadow Keep is a British band (albeit with a Belgian vocalist), who have just released their debut album on German label Limb Music. They even attracted the attention of Thin Ice, with Karl producing the album and Clive playing keyboards on one song. The main selling point of this album are not the wonderful harmony guitar runs or blistering technical metal melodies, but rather the superb vocals of Rogue M, who has an extremely high range, coming across as a hybrid of Geoff Tate and Rob Halford and when vocals of this quality are placed against the attack of the rest of the band, then the result is an album that is going to impress. They have already played some shows with the likes of Dio and Dirty Deeds, and Brian Slagel of Metal Blade was so impressed with the band that he asked them to contribute to a Queensrÿche tribute album. That song, "Queen Of The Reich" is included here as a 'hidden' song. I have long that thought that Threshold were the holders of the technical prog metal crown in the UK but one of their founders has managed to produce an album that certainly sets Shadow Keep up as major challengers to that title. *#60, Oct 2000*

SHADOWLAND
RING OF ROSES

It is indeed unusual for any single album to capture the imagination of everyone, but that has happened with Shadowland's debut 'Ring of Roses'. To be honest, it was obvious from the beginning that there was going to be an album of great merit as this was very much Clive Nolan's baby, and with his trusty Thin Ice guitarmeister Karl Groom firmly by his side they were going to form a band and record an album to change the world!!! (I like it, a lot). For those of you who have managed to avoid reading anything I have written about prog over the last I do not know how many issues, Clive Nolan is keyboard player with the mighty Pendragon, and on top of that he runs Thin Ice Studio with Karl, and over the last year or so he has written for and produced Tracy Hitchings and Landmarq, and has organised and played on the Strangers On A Train and Casino projects. Karl is an outstanding guitarist who is also in Threshold, and for his sins he has been working extensively with Clive in many of his projects, not only keeping him sane and supplying him with bourbon but playing some brilliant music. Shadowland are completed by Ian Salmon (fretted and fretless bass, acoustic guitar), who has worked with Tracy Hitchings, Shout The Moon and Whistler's Mother, and Nick Harradence on drums (previously with NW10 and Mercy Train). It could easily have been assumed that 'Ring of Roses' would be an album very much in the vein of Pendragon seeing how long Clive has been with Nick Barrett, but nothing could be further from the truth. The album starts with "The Whistleblower", where Clive gently speaks over a held-down chord: any thoughts of gentleness and peace are soon shattered by Karl's guitar as the song bursts into life. It is obvious that as a singer Clive prefers to sing in a lower register than that favoured by others, such as young Mr Nicholson, but there is a great depth and emotion to his voice unmatched by many. Shadowland are very much a band, not an ego trip on anyone's part, so much so that the main instrument for the most part is not the keyboards but the brilliant guitarwork of Karl. It is also possible to say that the bass is the most important because of the wonderful effect created by using a fretless in a rock setting, or that the drumming is always right on. What comes across more than anything else is the restraint on the part of all players. Although not restricted by the parts they play, there is a time and place for everything. It would be easy for Nick to play double bass drum pedals all the way through the song, but by just doing this at the end it heightens the awareness and intensity that is felt throughout.

Next up is "Jigsaw", which starts with Clive accompanying himself with some delicate pianowork. This shows his voice off to good effect and provides a great contrast as the rest of the band delicately come in on the chorus. It is one of the two longer songs on the album, clocking in at more than eleven minutes. Because of its length, Shadowland can spread their wings and provide some wonderful moments of light and shade. Next up is my favourite song, "Scared Of The Dark", which has some real menace within it. The lyrics and music combine in a fashion that send shivers up the spine: there is real intensity to this song that leaves you feeling quite drained after listening to it. "Painting By Numbers" has the keyboards much more to the fore, with the bass taking the lead, which allows Karl to lay down some delicate melody lines over the top of it all. Harmony vocals and heavy chords from Karl finally lead the way for a screeching solo. "Hall of Mirrors" is the epic of the album, being somewhat over fourteen minutes in length. Both Nick and Ian felt that this was the hardest one to record, and it has so many parts and contrasts to it that it's not difficult to see why. Starting off with Clive singing over some gentle picking by Karl, it livens up as Ian provides some stirring fretless bass: soaring keyboards join as the song moves up-tempo, reverts to the previous style, and then allows Clive to play a small keyboard solo. All the time one gets the feeling that there is a definite aim in sight, and that all the musicians are working toward a common goal. There is a real sense of togetherness throughout the album, and none more so than on this song.

"The Kruhulick Syndrome" is the solitary instrumental on the album, and really allows Clive to finally spread his wings and show just what he can do with a piano and assorted other keyboards. Although not a solo piece, it does take a long time for the others to join in and what started off as a complicated piano recital becomes a rock number with some stunning guitar leads, although always retaining the original melody. The song climaxes and finishes in a way that is both dynamic and perfect. Album closer is the title song "Ring of Roses", and the slow start in no way prepares you for the joyful and light-hearted number, which is a great way to close. The chorus has an extremely strong hook, and forever etched in my mind will be the "Lurve Dance" that accompanies it, as demonstrated by Martin Orford and John Jowitt the other night at The Marquee. Some of you will have been lucky enough to catch Shadowland on their recent tour with Jadis. Live they are brilliant, and I must place them equal first on gig of the year (tying with Galahad at Whitchurch in July). As for the album, it screams in ahead of Jadis' 'More Than Meets the Eye' as my album of the year. As always, I am quite aware that I have not heard all the great albums that have been released, but it would have to be extremely mega to be better than this. 'Ring of Roses' is the fastest selling album on the SI label, and deservedly so.
#16, Dec 1992

SHADOWLAND
THROUGH THE LOOKING GLASS

Those of you who have known me for a while can imagine just how much I was looking forward to this album, having been up at Thin Ice when it was being recorded and discussing the reasoning behind every song with Clive even before the lyrics were completed. I just could not wait to get it on the player when it arrived from Holland so imagine my disappointment when I realised that the disc was faulty. However, I now have a replacement which unfortunately arrived too late for inclusion in #22, but it has been well worth the wait. I was worried that Clive may not be able to live up to the brilliance of their first CD, 'Ring of Roses', but those fears were totally unjustified. For those of you may not have heard of Shadowland, they are the brainchild of Clive Nolan, keyboard player with Pendragon. This band is the vehicle for his rock ideas and as well as playing keyboards (and even violin on this album) he also provides lead vocals. Joining him are his trusty guitarmeister Karl Groom, who works with Clive on many of his projects as well as running his own bands (including the mighty Threshold – their CD is a killer). The rhythm section is Nick Harradence (drums) and Ian Salmon (bass, fretless bass). Nick's contribution is far greater this time as he was able to play "live" drums, which was not possible on the debut. The emphasis with Shadowland is very much on high quality songs combined with top musicianship. Unlike many prog bands there are not any needless changes of time and styles, but rather everything is thought out and done with care. Clive is one of the top keyboard players in the field, and it is his playing that dominates proceedings without being overpowering. Karl's riffs provide the balance and this along with Clive's instantly recognisable vocals, which are sung in a slightly lower register than most, gives Shadowland a dark and heavy sound all their own. I love every track on here, whether it is the sequel to "Scared of the Dark" (from the first album), "Half Moon Street", or "When The World Turns To White" but I think top marks must go to the title cut. Clocking in at over eleven minutes in length, it shows all that is great about Shadowland. It commences with piano and fretless bass and gentle vocals, but the song changes into a more dynamic number as the rest of the band join in and Ian punches out the bass line. Gradually the song transforms into a many-headed animal with a very strong chorus that finds its way into the middle of your brain and stays there all day. This is a wonderful CD, and I for one cannot wait to hear it live later this year. If you liked the first or are just wondering what I am making so much fuss about, then buy it and find out why. *#23, May 1994*

SHADOWLAND
MAD AS A HATTER

Shadowland are a happy little band. They are no longer on SI but signed to Clive's own label, Verglas, the Thin Ice studio is now completed and fully functional in the new house, and the consequent pressures much reduced. Live keyboard player Mike Varty has also taken some of the strain from Clive by writing or co-writing music for three of the songs, and this is the first time that Clive has passed over the musical reins as it were. The result is a band having a ball, and you can hear it. The last album was recorded under a lot of pressure and although good, was more fragmented than it needed to be. However, there is a contentment that pervades this album and the result is that 'Mad As A Hatter' is even more powerful than the debut 'Ring of Roses'. Seeing as that is high on my all-time favourites list this is high praise indeed. Ian has again incorporated a fretless bass for certain passages and this really does give the overall sound a mellower feel, not so clinical. Karl also seems to have a freer approach than normal, and at times lets loose in a fashion far more in keeping with his Threshold activities: not that it sounds out of place, but again shows the vibe. Nick has at long last been able to record live drums in Thin Ice's own studio and has also been able to put in a better performance because of that. Yes indeed, Verglas has now released two albums, the debut by Arena and now the third by Shadowland. There are very few labels that can boast such high musical quality. If you like good melodic rock, prog, call it what you will, then 'Mad As A Hatter' is one you just must get. *#35, June 1996*

DEREK SHERINIAN
BLACK UTOPIA

Derek is of course keyboard player with Planet X, among others, but while this is a solo album of his, it sounds more as if a master guitarist has recorded it. When looking into the album a bit more closely the reason becomes apparent in that Derek has seen himself as composer, arranger and musical director and has then invited some guests such as Zakk Wylde and Yngwie J Malmsteen (among others) to come in and let rip. While Derek does provide some extremely complex melodies (aided and abetted by a rhythm section of Simon Phillips and Tony Franklin), it is the guitars that are centre stage. While there are places where the music calms down, and indeed there is room at times for some acoustic guitar, it is where the guitars are at their most ferocious that this album really flies. Derek has brought in guitarists with quite different styles and has used this to great effect. "Axis Of Evil" sees Zakk and Yngwie shredding and trying to outdo each other on a rock song that just blasts. The note density on this album must be phenomenal yet there are few times when it seems over-indulgent. Over the top, but it is music that makes the listener want more, not reach for the off switch. Derek may be a keyboard player but buy this not if you want to hear a Rick Wakeman sound-alike but if you want to hear guitarists going for it at top speed. *#73, Apr 2003*

DEREK SHERINIAN
MYTHOLOGY

As with Derek's last solo album, 'Black Utopia', one wouldn't really imagine that this is an album that has been put together by a keyboard player as it is packed full of riffs. Allan Holdsworth and Zakk Wylde trade licks on the opening, crunching "Day Of The Dead", and given that Allan normally plays music of a quite different nature he must have found this fairly interesting. But at the heart of it all is Derek who can provide swathes of keyboards for the guys to work against or can solo with as much speed as they can. In "God Of War" he pits himself against John Sykes and it is hard to say who comes out on top but there is no doubt the guys are having a blast. There may not be any vocals on this album, but it is so intense that there just is not any room. Other musicians featured are even more guitarists in Steve Lukather and Steve Stevens (bet Billy Idol never sounded like this), fretless bassist Tony Franklin, drummer Simon Phillips and violinist Jerry Goodman who duets with Derek to great effect in the powering "Trojan Horse". That song really must be heard to be believed, with Simon and Tony keeping up with Jerry in a way that defies description. This music must be described as progressive just because it is; touching on jazz and good old-fashioned hard rock this is an album where Derek has brought together some very different musicians and combined them in a manner that is wonderful to hear. *#82, Jan 2005*

DEREK SHERINIAN
BLOOD OF THE SNAKE

Derek Sherinian is back with another album, and yet again the keyboard player has allowed himself to be taken over by the guitarists for what is an interesting and varied hard rock album with progressive tendencies. Joining him for this outing are John Petrucci (guitar), Zakk Wylde (guitar), Yngwie Malmsteen (guitar), Simon Phillips (drums), Tony Franklin (bass), Brad Gillis (guitar), Brian Tichy (drums) along with special guests Billy Idol (vocals) and Slash (guitar) who help with the last number. Zakk provides vocals on "Man With No Name" as well as crunching guitar and it is sounds as if it comes from the Ozzy songbook, crunching and riffing with strong vocals and plenty of passion and rawness tempered by the keyboards. Zakk also duels with Yngwie on the title cut, which starts with some nifty fingerwork from Derek before it gets going into the song properly where the theme is then taken up by the guitars. Yngwie also appears on another song and as with Derek's previous work there is the feeling that he is happiest when working with strong guitarists. A special mention must be made of the last song on the album. Derek is currently Billy Idol's keyboard player, and during a soundcheck Billy started singing "In The Summertime", the rest of the band joined in and Derek knew that he had to put this on the album. I am not sure quite what Mungo Jerry would think of it, but this is very close to the original, apart from Slash's guitar line. Yet again Derek the keyboard player has put together an album, mixing instrumentals and vocal tracks, which is going to be beloved by guitar fans. Well worth hearing. *#89, Sep 2006*

SHINGETSU
LIVE

Recorded at the ABC Kaikan Hall in Tokyo over 25th and 26th July 1979, this captures Shingetsu just one month after the release of their debut album. What is obvious from the photos and from the vocals that this was a very theatrical band, bringing together the Japanese tradition with a love of progressive rock that was not only based heavily on Genesis, but also some more

rocky sections that would later become more prevalent in the work of bands like Twelfth Night. "She Can't Return Home" is a powerful rocker that many bands of today would be proud of with one of the two keyboard players following the guitar line and the other playing high and over the top. Drums are also an important part as they drive the band on from the rear. There is some exciting progressive rock to be heard on this album, with the only downside that the vocals could be higher in the mix and the overall sound is not as good as it might be, but it is a good solid introduction to the band that has made me want to hear some more. A joint release between the Japanese label Poseidon and Musea, this should be relatively easy to obtain for those who want to enjoy a 'new' prog act.
#81, Dec 2004

MICHAEL SHIPWAY
BENEATH FOLLY
This is just great: here is a keyboard player with a real rock mentality. The songs may well be instrumental and only using keyboards and their various effects, but the result is a CD brimming full of songs with real power and life. There is no room for lazing in the armchair and relaxing, as this music demands to be played at full volume. There are definite areas of light and shade, and some of the rhythms produced are different to the norm but work well. For example, "Caravan" starts off with an African feel, but the gentle keyboards swim in and out, almost lulling, yet in the previous number "The Folly" all hell had been breaking loose. All twelve songs are very different to each other and my favourite is closer "Return To Battle" – crank it right up and let the power of a really good rock keyboard player take you away. I would love to see this song performed live: if Michael can capture this onstage then it must be one helluva experience. All in all, this will appeal to those who like synth music in its' own right, or who enjoy keyboard playing within a rock framework. Simply outstanding.
#20, Oct 1993

SHIZUKA
SHO KA
There are certain albums where one tries really hard to like it, but only succeeds in just preventing the CD player from suffering serious damage in the effort to get it removed. When this started, I thought that it was a pleasant enough prog style, a bit lite, but then the vocals started. They are awful – if it is deliberately bad then someone ought to tell them that they achieved whatever it was they were trying to do. They very nearly succeeded in getting me to turn it off there and then, but I got through to the second track. Which was just as bad, if not worse, for very different reasons: in this case the lyrics were repeated over and over, so why did I bother getting as far as track three? Dedication I suppose. But what is this? A cracking rock song with good vocals – this can't be right. It is so far removed from the previous songs as if to belong to a different band altogether. After this it was downhill again, but at least I could now see that the

band were trying to do something out of the ordinary. They are experimenting and just have yet to decide on the musical form that they want to follow. To be treated with extreme caution.
#76, Oct 2003

SHOW-YEN
II
One can probably guess that this is the second album from this Osaka based instrumental trio, who were formed in 1998 by guitarist Yasuhiro Nishio. The line-up is completed by Hiroaki Fuji (bass) and Isao Moria, although the album does feel much more like a solo album with Yasuhiro just being supported by a very strong rhythm section. But this does mean that he has the opportunity to work in whatever style he wants, knowing that they are there to back him up. With the statement "Instrumental Progressive Hard Rock" emblazoned proudly inside the booklet as well as around the disc itself the guys are certainly making a statement to which they will either stand by or be shot down by, and this does contain many elements that are far more hard rock in style than fusion would normally allow so I guess the statement may well be correct. "A Thorny Path" shows a more delicate side but the last of the thirteen songs on the album does exactly what it says, with "(I Can) Rock 'n' Roll Again". This is not a shredders delight but instead something that has been together with care, and will be of interest to those who enjoy their instrumental music to be constructed and not just ripped through at 1000 mph.
#86, Feb 2006

SHUB-NIGGURATH
TESTAMENT
Gazul is a Musea imprint, and Musea had released some of this band's previous work. This album has now been made available, as one of the members has died, so it has been put out as homage. I have to say that even though my musical tastes are extremely wide and varied, this is not 'music' that I can get to grips with. It is extremely experimental and tries to create soundscapes of places that you would never want to visit. With a line-up of bass, drums, guitar and trombone that in itself is unusual. As it says in the press release "a band that definitely sounds like no one else!" but in this context, is it a good thing?
#74, Jun 2003

SIDE STEPS
STEPS ON EDGE
Side Steps are an instrumental jazz-rock band from Japan, who have so far released nine albums, and this is a reissue of their 1994 album 'Steps On Edge'. They are an

instrumental act and are all undoubtedly extremely strong musicians, but I did find myself thinking of them more jazz-lite than a band with real depth. This is unfair as there are some extremely fine passages – during "Triumphal Return" guitarist Atsunobo Tamura seems to play a solo at breakneck speed forever. He moves up and down the frets making musical sense of what is going on behind him, but this album must have seemed fairly dated when it came out ten years ago, let alone now. When they gel, they are quite some force to behold but a lot of the time I get the impression that these could be Americans with big cheesy smiles saying, "look at me – I'm clever". Very mean I know, sorry guys. I do have to confess that I did enjoy playing the album but whether I would return to it frequently then that is another matter altogether.

#78, Apr 2004

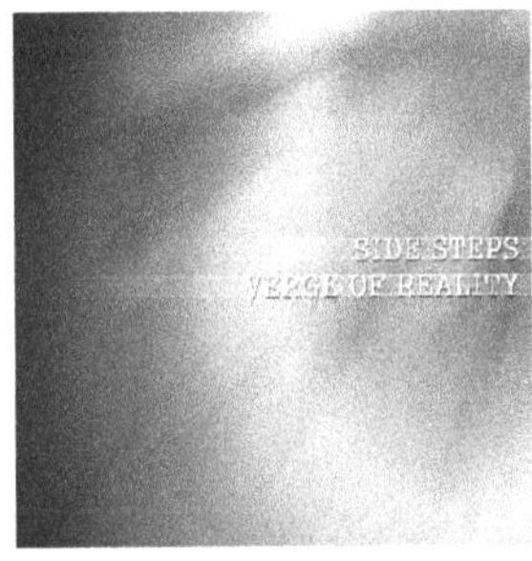

SIDE STEPS
VERGE OF REALITY

Instrumental jazz fusion is the order of the day with these seven songs, and while generally the rhythm section of Koichi Iwai (bass) and Ichiro Fukawa (drums) do not impose themselves too heavily, they do a good job of holding the fort so that guitarist Atsunobu Tamura and keyboard player Hiroaki Itoh can duet, or back each other up while the other solos quite fluently. This is very polished indeed, with a beck and call being well used, and the feeling is not that this is a new album from Japan, but rather this is an unearthed gem from the late Seventies when fusion was much more dominant. There is a moment at the beginning of "Edge Trigger" when I thought that Atsunobu was really going to rock it up, but it was only for the introduction and instead it turns into one of the best numbers on the album with great interplay from all, although the heavier guitar style does return again nearer the end. This is well worth looking out for if you enjoy this style of music.

#86, Feb 2006

SIEGES EVEN
THE ART OF NAVIGATING BY STARS

Eight years after their last, Sieges Even are back with their sixth studio album. That it is diverse is probably not a surprise given their influences, "Kansas, Metallica, Madonna, Iron Maiden, Pantera, Yes, Jaco Pastorius, King Crimson, Sarah McLachlan, Allan Holdsworth, Tool, Peter Gabriel, Julian Bream, a lot of Jazz, a lot of classical music". When they are heavy then the Metallica side shines out, and the complex time signatures that fluctuate and change within the material do a great job of hiding the fact that there is no keyboard player. This is somewhat unusual for a progressive rock band, but probably that is because in this instance the focus is as much on the latter as on the former. This is

complicated stuff, but the vocals are clear, and the harmonies work well even though musically the listener must 'expect the unexpected' as there is never a true indication of what is coming next. Apart from the introduction the shortest song is over five minutes long, while the longest of the seven is just over ten. That gives the band plenty of time to stretch their musical wings and there is certainly never the possibility of it getting boring as so many ideas, themes and musical styles are being tried. This is an unusual album, but is easy to listen to, and that probably has a great deal to do with the vocals, which are delicate yet powerful without being strained with the maelstrom going on below. This is an interesting album that Tool fans and rock oriented progheads ought to seek out.
#85, Nov 2005

SILENT EDGE
THE EYES OF THE SHADOW

I have only recently received this album but looking at the Dutch band's homepage it appears that it was released two years ago, so I am not sure what has been happening in between, but I am glad to have it in my paws now. This is prog metal with more than a hint of technical rock so bands such as Stratovarius immediately spring to mind, somewhat heavier than Dream Theater, but there are obvious aspirations. A lot of this music is very heavy indeed, and is played extremely quickly for the most part, which will mean that it is probably hard rock fans who will appreciate this more than the normalproghead. I mean, you could seriously lose your dandruff to sections of "Wasted Lands", mind you it would also means that you would need a neck brace as the keyboards and guitars seem to drive each other onwards, upwards and faster. This is a band that does know the meaning of light and shade, or at least of shade and darker shade, which means that they move the tempo and styles around, but when these guys are at full tilt, they are undoubtedly one of, if not the, quickest and probably heaviest prog metal band around. I only hope that the two-year delay has meant that there is a new album ready to go soon as this really rocks. *#84, July 2005*

SILVER LINING
THE INNER DRAGON

I have been writing for the French progzine Acid Dragon on and off for quite a few years, but I did not realise that Thierry Sportouche was involved with a band until recently. 'The Inner Dragon' is the first CD to be released by the Lyon-based Silver Lining, and Thierry provided all the lyrics and vocals. This is a quite an unusual album as the lyrics are telling the story of an English wood sprite but told in a French accent in the first person. There are also long instrumental passages and some of the lyrics are spoken as opposed to sung. Musically there is a great deal going on, with bands such as Pallas and IQ being obvious influences, as well as Camel and Arena. There are times when the music is almost basic, with plenty of complexity at others. The use of violin as lead instrument does give the music an extra edge, and with long instrumental passages the

band work hard at providing many different soundscapes. The first few times I played this I must confess that I found Thierry's spoken accent a little strange when supposedly listening to an English sprite, but then I got into it and anyway, having never heard a sprite speak before exactly what do they sound like? Nothing like Tull's "Jack In The Green" if this is anything to go by. What makes the album such a positive is that although there are musical references, this is quite different to any others around. It is not possible to play bits of this album; it must be listened to in its entirety.
#80, Jul 2004

RICHARD SINCLAIR
RSVP
Richard Sinclair surely needs no background history. A founding father of the Canterbury Scene, he formed The Wilde Flowers, was an original member of Caravan, formed Hatfield and the North, joined Camel, reformed Caravan, then in 1982 recorded an album of his own material as Richard Sinclair's Caravan of Dreams. Many gigs followed, and it is only now that his next album 'R.S.V.P.' has been released. Many familiar names can be found helping him out, including Hugh Hopper, Andy Ward and Pip Pyle. "What's Rattlin'" gets things under way, and as well as conjuring up thoughts of a jazz version of Fairport Convention at their most laid back, it contains some poignant lyrics, telling how they all feel. "I'm bored with Caravan, Fleetwood Mac and Uncle Sam, I'm sick of Tangerine Dream, Hatfield and Soft Machine, Radio Gnome and Henry Cow, we're not part of that now, One question we all dread "What's doing Mike Ratledge?", I'm tired of questions like "What is he doing, Mike?", "What's doing Robert Wyatt?", What's doing Kevin Ayres?", What's rattling Mike Doodladge?". The biggest plus of this album as far as I'm concerned is that even those not well versed in the Canterbury Scene, or into jazz, can find this album immensely enjoyable and listenable. Melodies and songs are very much the order of the day, and even though the songs can be complex with lots going on, there can also at the same time be an almost naïve simplicity which is immediate and compelling (the instrumental "My Sweet Darlin" being a fine example of this). For those looking for complicated and fluid jazz runs then you need look no further, but if what you want is an enjoyable album with soft lulling vocals then this is a real find. "Here we are – flying tunes like fireflies in the dark". Many years down the road, Richard Sinclair is still producing wonderful music. *#25, Oct 1994*

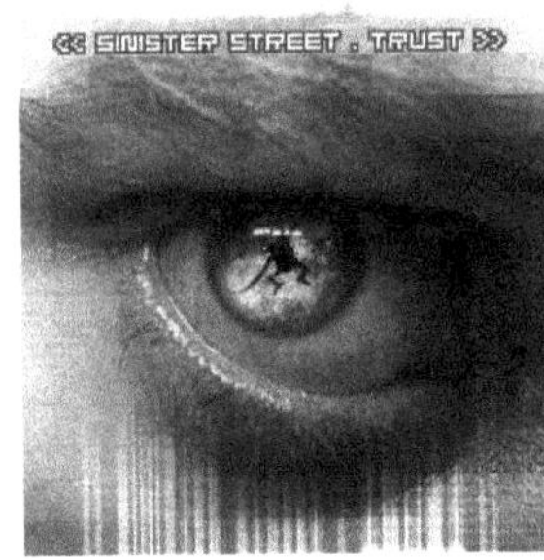

SINISTER STREET
TRUST
Sinister Street are a Dutch neo-progressive rock band that have been around since 1987 and 'Trust' is their second album, only ten years after the debut. Somewhat unsurprisingly the band has been through some major line-up changes since then but having not heard the debut I can't comment as to what effect that has had on the sound. What I can say is that this album is like going back in time and hearing again the burgeoning UK prog scene of

the early 90's. This album contains elements of many of those bands, most notably Galahad and Jadis, while also bringing in touches of Saga. This is very much an album that will appeal to those who may not normally look to Musea for prog rock of this calibre or style. It is exciting, vibrant, most definitely rock based and not in the least self-indulgent. Well, maybe it is just a little, but this is prog rock after all. There are strong melodies and keyboards, and neither allows one to overpower the other. The result is a nicely balanced album with the emphasis on songs and dynamics instead of overblown epics. Indeed, only a few of the numbers manage to break through eight minutes and the result is an album that is fresh and exciting. If the year was 1992 and not 2002 then this is the sort of album that would have most definitely have been released on SI and not Musea. Anyone who remotely enjoys neo-prog can safely purchase this album immediately if not sooner.
#69, Aug 2002

SINKADUS
AURUM NOSTRUM
Sinkadus will be viewed by many listeners as the most 'progressive' of bands, simply because they sound so much like early Genesis. Of course, there are many others who would say that they are not prog at all, but regression of the worst kind. Although the lyrics are in Swedish, the words are secondary for the most part to the music. Most of the vocals are harmony, care of Rickard Bistrom (bass) and Linda Johansson (flute), while the use of a cello (Lena Pettersson) gives the music a slightly different edge. I know that Cyclops boss Malcolm Parker rates this album extremely highly, but I feel that I can't do the same. Yes, there are interesting elements of early Genesis and ELP, and the instrumental passages work well, but there is nothing very exciting about proceedings. True, if you like your music more laid back then some then this will be of major interest, but if you like energy and vitality then you will have to look elsewhere. Sinkadus have been invited to this year's ProgFest in America, and I know that Cyclops will be providing the financial support to send them. I hope that they find a more receptive audience than yours truly.
#40, Mar 1997

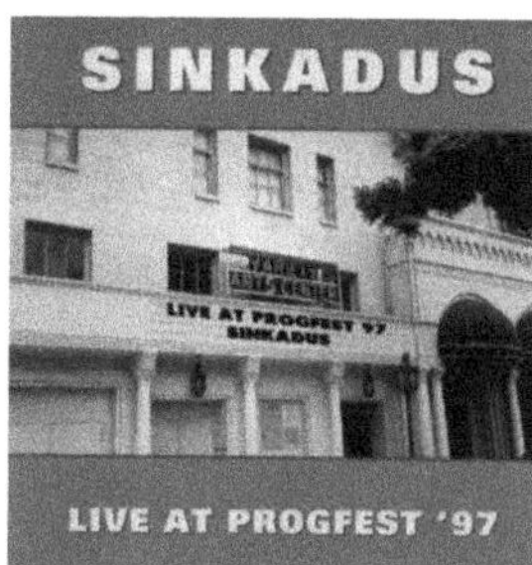

SINKADUS
LIVE AT PROGFEST '97
In 1997 Sinkadus released 'Aurum Nostrum' on the Cyclops label. This, their debut album, was so well received that only a few weeks after it became available they were invited to play at the prestigious ProgFest in Los Angeles. The live set they performed there was recorded straight onto ADAT and is here presented for our listening pleasure. If that was not enough, Cyclops are making this a limited edition which contains the original studio tracks that brought them to the attention of Malcolm Parker at the label. The songs were then reworked for the debut, so this is a

good value set to have. There is also a full translation of the lyrics in the booklet. However, in this case it would almost be a distraction for the band to be singing in English, as with Richard Linda singing in Swedish the ear then treats the vocals as yet another musical instrument. With roots firmly in the early Seventies, incorporating both flute and cello, this is an album that does take some listening to, to be fully appreciated. That is not to say that it is a difficult album, but rather one that must be given the attention it deserves. No, it is not immediate, but the more it is played the more there is to be discovered. This is music that really is honest to the original values of progressive music as it not only develops in classical forms but mixes and melds until its' identity is very much its' own and while it is possible to say that certain elements have been influenced by other bands, at the end of the day the sound is very much that of Sinkadus. The crowd gathered there certainly enjoyed the gig, and if you like progressive rock then you will love this too.
#47, Feb 1998

SINKADUS
CIRKUS

At times Sinkadus epitomises all that is good about Scandinavian progressive music, and at the risk of incurring the wrath of Malcolm Parker who thinks this is the best thing since the proverbial, this is not one of them. Oh, yes, there is all the right sort of music, long instrumentals etc., but it is all so dreary and um, boring. The only really positive thing I can say about it is that it is short for a modern prog album (only about 45 minutes). I have enjoyed their previous releases, but this is one that I can do without. It is good for background music, but nothing more. Liven up guys!
#53, May 1999

SIXNORTH
PRAYER

This is an album with a very clean sound, as if jazz rock fusion from the Seventies has now found its way to Japan. I am not denigrating the genre, or the album, it is just that this is what this sounds like. On opener "Magnetic Factor" the high vocals are used as an instrument, and somehow it reminds me of the Pearl & Dean music, but it is still enjoyable. When the band do go heavier as on "The Fourth Way" they show that they can be a powerful force, with room for the ideas to keep forcing their way through in a loose but constructed manner. Akihisa Tsuboy guests on one song, but the coup for the band must be the involvement of David Sinclair on "Richard", which is dedicated to his colleague Richard Sinclair. This contains a lot of clarity and simplicity with pure vocals, as well as some sections which are much more reminiscent of Matching Mole. Interesting and pleasant, but not essential.
#78, Apr 2004

JÓSEF SKRZEK
KONCERT ŚWIETOKRZYSKI

JÓSEF SKRZEK
U STÓP KRYŻA…

These two albums are quite different. They are both keyboard based, but here Jósef is combining church organs with synthesisers. The first was recorded in 1983 and he says in the booklet (which is in both Polish and English) how he felt safe playing music in churches. It is hard for us to ever imagine what it must been like in Poland at the beginning of the Eighties, but he says that although he had many offers to leave the country, he is glad he stayed there. The album is a recording of a concert he gave after the holy mass for Poland at Holy Cross Church in Warsaw and is a blend of religious style bombastic pipe organ pieces with something far more delicate from the synths, much more into the realm of Tangerine Dream.

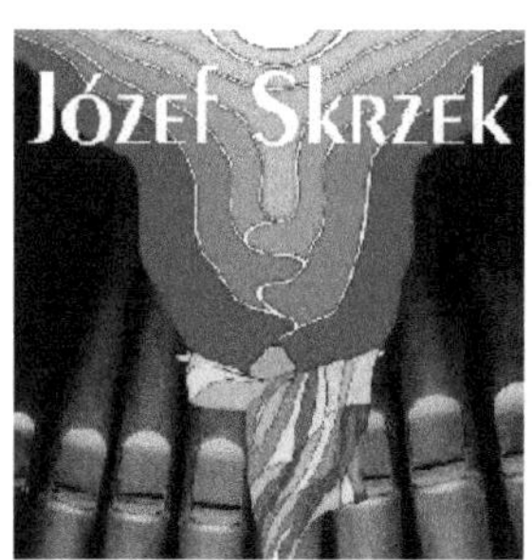

The second album was recorded some twenty years later, with some pieces again being recorded at The Holy Cross with others being recorded at the Jesus The King cathedral in Katowice. Having been brought up going to church regularly I have always enjoyed the power that can only come from a pipe organ being played by someone who really knows what they are doing, but even I am not sure how often I would be playing these. Although he does use Moogs and MiniMoogs the impression throughout that here is a classically trained musician using these as bolt-ons to his sounds and repertoire, just as both Wakeman and Emerson sometimes use pipe organs to supplement their synths. This is music that is going to appeal to someone who enjoys religious or classical music far more than the normal (if there is such a thing) keyboard fan, but a change is as good as a rest and if you are intrigued then contact the label.
#84, July 2005

JÓSEF SKRZEK FORMATION
WOJNA ŚWIATÓW – LIVE

This digipak release is a recording of the band performing a piece called 'War Of the Worlds' in Prague in 1981. It does state that it was recorded on amateur equipment, but the sound quality is quite good, having been remastered by guitarist Robert Golla in 2002. Some of the songs themselves are quite long, with one reaching twenty-two minutes. While Jósef himself provides keyboards, bass, and vocals it is the inclusion of both harmonica and saxophones that makes this sound a little out of the ordinary. They have obviously been influenced by VDGG and jazz but while this music probably sounded inspiring when it was being played in the concert there are long passages here where the band appear to be waiting for the next blast of inspiration. It gives the impression of containing quite a lot of improvisation and possibly the listener just had to

be there. It is very much of its time, and even in 1981 probably sounded a little dated so all these years on…
#84, July 2005

SKYRON ORCHESTRA
SKYRON ORCHESTRA
This is not an album that I expect to hear in 2005, at least not from a new release: if it was a reissue from thirty-five years ago then I could understand it, but this was recorded in 2003 and has just come to my attention. These Swedes have paid attention to Jefferson Airplane and then mixed those influences into prog so that they are creating music that sounds very different to anything else that is around. The guitar can rock when it is needed but the two primary sounds on the album are the very dated keyboard sounds of Anna Glans and the vocals of Veronica Lostjärna. There is something almost hypnotic about the album – the first time I put it on in the house I played it four times in succession. It is not the sort of music that I would say that I am desperately keen on, but this is just compelling listening. The keyboards are simple but direct, there is not anything flash about this, and the guitars are playing some strong riffs but usually it is kept underneath the organ. If you enjoy psych mixed with prog, then you are in for a treat.
#85, Nov 2005

THE SKYS
POST-MODERN GAME
I do not come across many bands from Lithuania, and at the moment I am hard pressed to think of any, but here we have The Skys with their third album, which was released in 2004. They are well known in their own country and with a song on the latest Melos Progcast they will probably gain a bit more attention from the West. This is prog music that is influenced both by early Pink Floyd and early ELP and sounds very much as if it has come out of the early Seventies. Part of that is due to the vocals of Jonas Ciurlionis who has a rough and raw almost bluesy approach to the music, with more than a hint of Tom Waits or Dan McCafferty. This does give the overall sound an edge that is often missing from some prog that can appear bland in comparison. This is hard hitting and emotive stuff and even though there are two guitarists it is not as heavy as one might expect. They do allow themselves to wander in different directions, and there are times when they bring in some acoustic guitars to provide balance and to allow the others to play off. Elements of The Doors, and The Nice and the result is something that may not be very accessible but that does reward those that are willing to make the effort.
#88, Jun 2006

SKYWALKERS
WALKING IN DREAMS

Skywalkers is the band formed by Mark Andrews, who was keyboard player with Galahad at the time of their brilliant debut CD 'Nothing Is Written'. Since then he has been keeping a low profile, although he did play on the Galahad Acoustic Quintet CD that came out earlier in the year. This tape is the band's first album, and Nik Butcher joins him on vocals and woodwind, plus fellow Galahad stalwarts Spencer Luckman (drums) and Neil Pepper (bass). The result is a mellow songs-oriented album, with woodwind providing much of the solo lines. Mark takes lead vocals himself on all but one song, and his good clear voice does justice to some very good songs. It veers more towards AOR/soft rock than prog, and although I feel that in places it would have been improved with some guitar, overall this is an enjoyable workout.
#30, Aug 1995

SLEEPING GIANT
PRIMATES

I was out with Jon Moreau (ex-sound engineer and producer for Pagan Studios) one night when he mentioned that he had heard from Dave Foster. Dave and I used to be in regular contact when Mr So & So had been performing and recording (long-time readers may even remember getting a flexi of that band in the distant past) but we had lost touch. A phone call later and we were discussing his new band, Sleeping Giant. As well as Dave on guitar it also features ex-So & So's Leon Parr (drums) and Charlotte Evans (lead vocals), along with James Rimmer (keyboards) and Simon Crumley (bass). My initial reaction was that I hadn't realised just what a powerful voice Charlotte had, as she had only previously provided backing vocals. Her voice can be emotional and powerful or frail like a flower, but always in keeping with the music.

This has moved quite a long way since the heady technical-prog-rock of the previous band, so far in fact that there is virtually no musical similarity (apart from a section in the opener "Everything Must Come To An End"). It is music that is thoughtful, almost reflective at times, and those who are looking for some of Dave's guitar solos will be in for something of a shock as this music just does not need it (okay, he just can't contain himself at the end of "The Longest Day", but it does not happen often). There are noodlings as he plays around the music, but this is all about being a vehicle for Charlotte's voice than allowing any of the band to spread their wings. This is a songs-based album that has prog elements and should appeal to anyone who enjoys good music. Highly recommended.
#69, Aug 2002

SLEEPY PEOPLE
TYPHOID & SWANS

I was sent a tape of a live performance in the studio, when Sleepy People were trying out the songs and attempting to get backing. I must confess that it received extremely heavy rotation in my car and I was very pleased indeed to get the new CD which has just been released on Edgy Records. At times, they come across as Poisoned Electrick Head with a heavy dose of Tull with just a smattering of Chumbawamba. It came as no surprise at all to me to find that they have been gigging with PEH. Although it is possible to pick up on a few musical references, what is refreshing about this album that in a similar fashion to PEH they are pursuing an area of music that will be called progressive, just because it is, but are not attempting to rehash old Genesis licks or being that (horror of horrors!!) neo-progressive. This is music that is enjoyable and exciting, while at the same time managing to be both challenging yet totally accessible. With roots in the early Seventies combined with late Eighties this album is a delight and although Sleepy People is not a name that is instantly recognisable to us Southerners, I am sure that this situation will soon change. A must purchase.

#46, Dec 1997

GILLI SMYTH.....
I AM YOUR EGG

This is the new album by Gilli Smyth, Daevid Allen and Orlando Allen. Originally this was intended as the follow-up for 'It's All A Dream', which had been released by Orlando and Gilli but when Orlando went to Europe Gilli took the songs already written and then added more to it, both by herself and Daevid. They also brought in some of the Gong family to help them out and this is the result. This is an extremely eclectic album, and it is strange to think that Daevid is still producing music that is both challenging and exciting given that he is 68 this year! Some of the songs mix Western and Eastern cultures in a way that works, while some are rockier and then there are others that somehow contain loads of hooks and are melodic. One of the most interesting and delicate is the beautiful instrumental "River Song". This features Daevid on his trademark glissando guitar and Harry Williamson joins him on twelve-string to create something that really is a wonderful blending of styles. The more one plays this album the more there is to find, from "Ship Of Fools" which is very reminiscent of Roy Harper to the ethnic "Midnight Sun". A fascinating album that reveals more each time I listen to it.

#87, Apr 2006

DOUG SNYDER & BOB THOMPSON
THE RULES OF PLAY

Doug and Bob have known each other for several years and played their first gig together as long ago as 1985: this was originally released in 1999 but has only just come to my attention. The focus of this album is the first of the three songs, which comes in at just

under 44 minutes long. This was recorded live in front of an audience (the other two songs were recorded live in the studio), with Doug providing MIDI guitar and Bob drums. It is difficult to describe the soundscape style that Doug uses, he is obviously influenced by Fripp, but it never sounds as if it is just one man providing all the melody as not only are there distinct lead melodies but there are also rhythm parts as well. Bob is not to be left behind in the skill stakes either as he is prepared to match Doug with complex and thundering drums parts. This is a very long piece of music, being performed just by two people, and of course there is always the fear that they are going to lapse into something mundane but although there are a few low points these are few and far between and they soon get themselves out of the spot. In some ways, this is quite reminiscent of Ozrics and if there were keyboards here as well, I am sure that the similarity would be even more obvious. This is trippy music that is inventive and interesting with a depth and honesty behind it. On the other two tracks (only nine and seven minutes long respectively) Doug puts down his guitar and instead uses keyboards but I am not sure if it is the change in instruments or the change in recording situation that makes these two songs seem far flatter. Overall this is worth investigation.

#87, Apr 2006

SOLAR

DARK PLACES

Solar is the band that has been put together by Arena vocalist Rob Sowden, who in this trio also provides guitar. He has been joined by Lawrence Jarvis on bass and Simon Bell on drums. There are various guests, including Arena guitarist John Mitchell who also produces the album, which was mastered by Rob Aubrey (IQ, Threshold, Arena etc.). Although there are prog references in abundance, this is music that is taking that categorisation and stretching it somewhat: there are times when they come across as Radiohead mixed with bands such as Coldplay. There is a depth and presence that Rob's vocals add to, as he sings in a generally warmer and more delicate tone to that which we are used to. This is rock, but it has space and a dreamy element not often associated with the genre. When the guitars kick in as they do on "Psycho", they are still in the background and behind the main thrust, as opposed to being right in your face. It is music that is reminiscent of the late Sixties yet being modern, almost with a Divine Comedy feel about it. If I had been asked what an album by the Arena vocalist would have sounded like, I would never have imagined this. It is an album that needs to be played a great deal as it certainly is a 'grower' but is worth the effort.

#78, Apr 2004

SOLARIS
BACK TO THE ROOTS

SOLARIS
NOAB

Along with After Crying, Solaris are one of the best-known Hungarian progressive rock bands – certainly one of the longest surviving. What we have here are the first two in a three CD series that are being released to show the different stages of the band and to provide fans with an insight. The first disc captures the earliest incarnation of the band, which existed from February 20th, 1980 until September 28th, 1980, with István Cziglán (guitars), Róbert Erdész (organ), Attila Kollár (flute), Attila Seres (bass) and Vilmos Tóth (drums). Most of the material is taken from the farewell gig of Attila Seres, who decided to leave, as he could not see a future for this type of music in Hungary at the time. It must be remembered that this was long before the political changes in Eastern Europe. The concert was recorded on a cassette player and I am very surprised indeed as the sound is excellent, and this shows the band playing great driving progressive rock music. The different instruments all have their part to play but it is the interaction between guitar and flute that are the most dramatic. Even today this is exciting and relevant and progheads, especially those into Anderson style flute, will get a lot from this.

Both first two in the archive series contain stacks of information and interviews with the band members but whereas the first booklet is in English unfortunately the second is currently only in Hungarian, which is a real shame as a lot of work has obviously gone into it. Because of this I am at a loss to say where the songs have come from, but I do know that fans of the band will be most interested in the inclusion of the title song, which is over twenty minutes long, and this is the first time that it has ever appeared in its entirety. However, even here the band has yet to be happy with a complete performance and this has been edited together from eleven different versions (apparently – although one would never guess from listening). The sound is improved from the first archive, and yet again we have a band performing flowing complex symphonic prog. This is really good stuff, instrumental prog with bite and flow. I do not know when the third archive is due, but there are plenty of other albums available and if you want to investigate in excellent Hungarian prog music then Solaris is the place to start. *#88, Jun 2006*

SOLSTICE
NEW LIFE

Solstice were one of the band's around at the beginning of the Eighties who were featured in Kerrang!!'s article on the new progressive scene (also included were Marillion, Pendragon, Twelfth Night and Dagaband). They were formed in 1980 by Marc Elton (violin, keyboards, backing vocals) and Andy Glass (guitar, who had previously played with Mick Pointer and Doug

Irvine, who later formed Silmarillion). They were joined by Mark Hawkins (bass) and Dave Harden (drums), who was replaced in 1981 by Martin Wright. This line-up recorded the 'First Light' demo and they were then joined by Susan Robinson on vocals in 1982, releasing 'Pathways' the same year. Susan was replaced by Shelly Platt in time for their first Marquee gigs, but tonsillitis forced her also to leave and she was replaced by Sandy Leigh in 1983. This line-up released 'The Peace Tape', appeared at the Reading Rock Festival and recorded a session for the Friday Rock Show. 1984 saw the band recording their debut album, but after nine months they were largely disillusioned with the whole affair, and 1985 saw the last tour of Solstice, with yet another vocalist. Although the band members went their own ways, both Marc and Andy stayed in the music business, albeit working in many different areas. 1992 saw 'Silent Dance' re-released on CD, and they were again inspired by what Solstice could have been, and a decision was taken to reform the band. As there had been problems deciding what tracks to put on the debut, it now seemed fitting to re-record their favourite songs from the same period, many of which had appeared on the demo tapes.

The new members were Pete Hensley (drums) and Craig Sutherland (bass), who had been working extensively with Andy over the previous four years, along with Heidi Kemp on vocals. The resulting CD, 'New Life', was recorded and produced by Andy at his studio, and released in June of this year. As anyone who has heard their early tapes or previous album will testify, Solstice had a unique sound in the early Eighties, and I am glad to say that this is still the case today. There are only six songs on the CD, with a running time of less than forty-two minutes, but it is just so good to have Solstice back up and running that this is forgiven. The CD opens with "Morning Light" (originally on the 'Pathways' demo), and the band sound quite restrained as the vocals take control. Soon, Andy cuts in with a powerful guitar solo that sweeps through the music and atmosphere like a knife. Indeed, 'Atmosphere' is probably the key word here as the music is very structured and multi-layered. Next up is "Guardian" which features beautiful vocals from Heidi, and some gorgeous violin from Marc. Solstice are not an in your face guitar-oriented prog band, but rather one that is prepared to create tapestries of sound, using each instrument as is fitting. There are times on the album, such as on "New Life", when the band belt along like a modern Curved Air with jazzy feels and just great vibes. When I play it in the car it is this track that has me bounding and singing along (much to Sara's amusement and consternation). In fact, in some ways it reminds me of Judie Tzuke. Six tracks of mastery and delight herald the return of Solstice to the UK prog scene, and we are all the better for it. Unfortunately, this CD has only been released in America, but it should be easily available on import. Solstice are currently in the studio working on a new album (working title 'Freedom') which will hopefully be available later in the year. I for one am really looking forward to it! *#20, Oct 1993*

SOLSTICE
SILENT DANCE
It is no word of a lie that 'Silent Dance' has gained a reputation of being one of the most significant 'underground' prog releases of the Eighties. Produced by Nigel Mazlyn Jones, this album was extremely important at the time, and it is great to now have it available on CD. Unlike many of their contemporaries, there was a great use of folk influences, mixed

with rock. The vocals of Sandy Leigh were compared with Jon Anderson, the rhythm section of Mark Hawkins (bass) and Mark Wright (drums) kept it all tight, and this allowed the interplay between Andy Glass (guitar, backing vocals) and Marc Elton (violin, backing vocals, keyboards). "Peace" drives along with soaring violin, harmony vocals, heavy-hitting bass and just so much quality: it soon changes into a more 'Peaceful' entity altogether, with expressive vocals and guitar. It is so very different to the 'prog' of today, and really can be seen to be 'progressive' as Solstice mixed many styles and created new ones of their own. Songs such as the instrumental "Return To Spring" can only be described as beautiful, as in this one the use of acoustic guitars allows the wonderful violin playing of Marc to shine as he takes the lead role. Keyboards are kept to a minimum throughout the album, and it proves that "prog rock" is not always the same as "keyboard dominated". "Cheyenne" starts with wonderful virtually unaccompanied vocals that add real depth to the songs, with the vocals kept high in the mix and a sparing use of other instrumentation meaning that the ear is extremely focussed. Gradually the band come in, but never spoiling the initial effect. To someone who has never heard this album, it is difficult to convey exactly how Solstice sounded and how important 'Silent Dance' was, it still sounds fresh and relevant today, and is as enjoyable as when it first came out. A classic in 1984, it is still the same ten years on. *#22, Mar 1994*

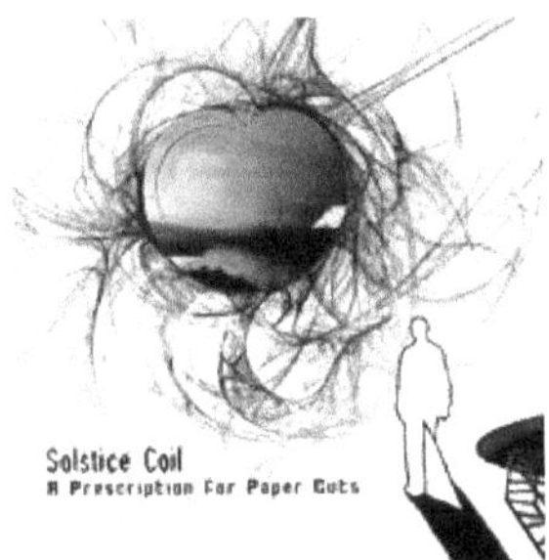

SOLSTICE COIL

A PRESCRIPTION FOR PAPER CUTS

I do not get much music sent to me from Israel, in fact in nearly sixteen years of writing I can honestly say that this is the first (although I have reviewed bands from Israel in the past, that has been sent to me by European labels). And if that was not enough, they are a prog act as well. Possibly because they are geographically so far removed from the main progressive centres the result is an album that is quite unlike any that I have heard recently. They themselves say that "Solstice Coil's music blends the powerful sound and emotional charge of alternative bands such as Radiohead, Muse, The Mars Volta and Porcupine Tree, with the precise compositions and arrangements of classic prog bands such as Genesis, King Crimson and Yes, as well as influenced by modern prog and prog-metal groups Dream Theater, The Flower Kings, Pain of Salvation and Anekdoten". So, there you have it. They are an amalgam of many styles and the music is extremely complex and complicated. This, combined with the vocals of Shir Deutch, where he often sings falsetto or with his voice seemingly at odds with what is going on, results in an album that at times is quite uncomfortable to listen to. This really is prog that is progressing as although there are times where it is all lovely and gentle with plenty of harmonies, there are just as many times when the music is strident and far more challenging. What makes this album work so well is the sheer diversity – this is not run of the mill 'normal' prog music. This is an independent release with a sixteen-page booklet featuring the lyrics as well as artwork and I know this is a band that we are going to be hearing more of. This really is an album for progheads to get. *#87, Apr 2006*

SONIC MUSIC
THE PRISONER

Sonic Music is a one-man band, Larry Benigno, who used to be in Radio Piece III. This is music that has been inspired by Gentle Giant and by late Seventies Genesis. Larry also has strong vocals, something not always the case with multi-instrumentalists and a very strong idea of what he wants to achieve. It is an album that although while obviously proggy also has some pop sensibilities as well as a great sense of humour (listen to the title cut to get what I mean). This is very accessible, very approachable and in many ways, is an album definitely out of time as it has none of the overbearing seriousness and 'cleverness' that can pervade some of today's bands. He is happy poking fun at himself with some pastiches such as in "Johnny The Waffle Man" but even when this is happening, he returns to the very melodic and very controlled vocals that do have a hint of Phil Collins about them, except not quite as whiney. The more you play this album the more you will get out of it, and while on some levels it could be considered almost lightweight when being considered as a prog album, I instead like the pop stylings and humour that make this so approachable and enjoyable.
#87, Apr 2006

SONIC PULSAR
OUT OF PLACE

This is the second album from Sonic Pulsar, a project put together by multi-instrumentalist Hugo Flores where he has been joined by Carlos Mateus (acoustic guitars) and Nuno Ferreira (bass). There are obviously live drums on the album, but I can't see it stated who played them, while Hugo provides everything else. This is an album that has been polished, honed, so that everything fits in place and while "Out Of Place" is reminiscent of classic Rush that is only because the production is so spot on, with complex melodies and bombastic drumming all combining with a powering solo to create something that is both intense and engaging all at once. While the guitars are a main point of focus, so are the keyboards, and Hugo obviously is at home on both. Themes are discarded, then returned to, so that the song seems to be sweeping around the listener and I soon felt that I had been gathered up and was being taken on a journey – one I was looking forward to. This is definitely prog, but with a feel that is quite unlike what normally thinks of the genre as Hugo stretches the limits. He is one of those guys who is happiest when producing music and this is not the only project that he is involved with, but this is his main aim and certainly this is an album that grabs in the listener. The only way to play this is quite loudly and let the rest of the world disappear as it is intense, yet creative, dynamic and thundering all at the same time. It is very modern and discards most of the 'normal' prog influences yet is prog through and through, with an emphasis on the rock side without ever turning into metal. There have been other releases, and one wonders how they stand up to this one, as this is quite wonderful.
#85, Nov 2005

SONUS UMBRA
SNAPSHOTS FROM LIMBO

Apart from knowing that Sonus Umbra used to be called Radio Silence, I know virtually nothing about this band. In the credits, they thank various bands, but the only name I recognise is Ilúvatar (if anybody knows anything about Kurgan's Band, Uncle Gut, Chaos Code, Mad Crusade or Kromlech then please let me know). I get the impression that they used to be based in Mexico but are now in the States, although I could be wrong. The bandleader is bassist Luis Nasser (who also provides keyboards and backing vocals) who wrote or co-wrote all the material, and he has put together an album which is much more in depth than one that I would normally expect to hear from many American bands. The emphasis is on music and melody, while not going down the neo-prog route favoured by many. There is much more in the way of songs than even Spock's Beard and the result is an album that moves from guitar-based to keyboard-based very fluidly and easily. Andres Aullet has a very warm voice, and he sings in a lower register, which complements the music. Drummer Jeff Laramee and guitarist Ricardo Gomez complete the line-up. Yet another very enjoyable album from the Moonchild stable.

#60, Oct 2000

SPACE AVENUE
VOICES FROM THE OTHER WORLDS

The debut album from Space Avenue is yet another example of how buoyant the scene is in Poland. Six songs, which come in at approx. 37 minutes long, with lyrics all in English, this is an album that mixes neo-prog with hard rock to create something that is both melodic and inventive. It is good and crunchy, with hard riffs and strong interplay between the guitar and keyboards while the rhythm section drives it along. But they can also go heavier, while not going into prog metal but more into hard rock as the introduction to "Dream" clearly displays, and for some reason this always reminds me of Nickelback mixed with Musc with possibly just a little Machine Head thrown in for good measure. However, the synth sounds are very dated and there are times that this sounds as if it could have come straight out of the Eighties scene. Now, this is self-produced and self-released (nice booklet), and it does suffer slightly on the sound side. It is obvious that this is not a major production but bearing that in mind this is still an interesting album indeed, and any band that dares to include a song that is more than fourteen minutes long will always get my vote.

#87, Apr 2006

SPACED OUT
SPACED OUT

This is an instrumental jazz/rock/prog album from Canada. No, please keep reading; it's actually very listenable and bloody enjoyable. Bassist Antoine Fafard wrote the whole album and possibly it is this that keeps the album so tight. While the guitarist can go off

and lead the melody within a loose structure, the rein is not allowed to go too slack, so he can't go off and do exactly what he wants. The first time I played it was in the car, and I listened to it fully without turning it off, not something that I manage even with hard rock albums. It is not hard to enjoy and is an album to mellow down to.
#62, May 2001

SPACED OUT
EPONYMOUS II
The second album by Spaced Out is much like the first in the sense that it is mostly an instrumental jazz-rock influenced progressive album which is bass-led. That is because bandleader and composer Antoine Fafard is a superb bassist and has put the band together to play his songs. This quartet is no mean slouches in the instrumental stakes, with guitarist Louis Côté in particularly fine form. Although the songs themselves are structured, the musicians improvised the solo passages yet managed just to keep the right side of total self-indulgence. I enjoyed playing the album, both when listening intently, or just relaxing with a good glass of red wine, and that is all I ever ask from jazz.
#64, Oct 2001

SPACED OUT
SLOW GIN
This is the third album from the Canadian instrumental jazz rockers, and while bassist and keyboard player Antoine Fafard is still very much the leader of the outfit, he is assisted this time not only by drummer Martin Maheux and pianist Éric St-Jean but also by new member, guitarist Mark Tremblay. This has added another layer to an already complex band and has given them even more room in which to explore. After an introduction, the next number up is the title track and it shows the band locked in and moving at incredible speed. The use of fretless bass allows Antoine to slide between notes and combined with the extra attack of Mark this has some extremely heavy moments indeed. For a musical reference, it would probably be best to compare them with Colosseum II, although always with more of an emphasis on the bass. The guy has immense skill, of that there is no doubt, but he never lets it get too overblown. There is always room for one of the others to come in and take over so that the music never has time enough to get boring, which it well might if the bass was the lead instrument all the time. This is an extremely enjoyable album that not only will be enjoyed by lovers of jazz-rock but also by those that like their prog to be a little more adventurous than may always be the norm, while extremely listenable and enjoyable. *#74, Jun 2003*

SPACED OUT
UNSTABLE MATTER
Spaced Out are back with their fourth studio album, although these days it is mostly Antoine Fafard as not only does he write all the material, provide bass and keyboards, but on this album, he has also provided guitar for the first time. He has been joined by drummer Martin Maheux and guitarist Mark Tremblay and the result is something that is a step change from what Spaced Out have been doing before. While the songs are often very much led by the bass there is now a higher keyboard content in the music, with a greater interaction between the players. While the band has previously been introducing some jazz into their work there has now been a move far more into 'straight' prog territory, but with a great deal of complexity. This is an instrumental album, but it just does not seem like it, as in many ways this is just an album without words – there just is not room within the musical structures for lyrics or voice. Easily their strongest and most complete work to date – this is Spaced Out showing that instrumental progressive rock can be extremely dynamic and vital, who needs vocals? If you enjoy prog, then you will get a lot out of this. *#89, Sep 2006*

SPACEHEAD
EXPLODE INTO SPACE
Think Hawkwind and you will be there with this the third album from Spacehead which is subtitled 'Inhalations 1998 – 2000'. Apparently, these guys did tour with Mr Brock and co in 1997, and I am sure that in a live environment they would come across very well indeed – if they had a half decent soundman. Unfortunately, it appears that the soundman went for a very extended tea break when the band were in the studio and consequently the volume levels are far too low on the disc but turn it up and it is still like listening to music with the speakers covered in cotton wool. Now, it may be that this is a deliberate ploy on their part, but if that is the case then it failed. It certainly sounds as if these guys know what they are doing within the genre, and these are proper songs as opposed to jam workouts, with lyrics and everything! But the sonic quality is far too poor to make this of interest except to diehard fans of the genre, which is a real shame, as what I can hear sounds promising. *#87, Apr 2006*

SPACE MIRRORS
THE DARKER SIDE OF ART
Space Mirrors is led and directed by Alisa Corals who provides synths and vocals, and Michael Blackman joins her on guitars. They also have two guests on the album, one of them being Arjen Anthony Lucassen who provides some guitar and narration. I certainly was not aware of his appearance as a guest, and he recorded his guitars at his studio in Holland while Michael recorded his guitar at his studio in Australia, and Alisa

did the rest of the work in Russia. Of course, the album has been released on a Scottish label, and the follow-up has been released on a Greek label. This is an international project if nothing else! Musically this is a swirling morass of space rock, but it is bringing in many different styles and thoughts – so much so that this album is very different to much that has been released within the genre and is all the better for it. There are times when the guitars come crunching through and the feeling is very much of Hawkwind, but there are often times when they are in the back seat and it becomes more like Tangerine Dream, and at others far more like Ozrics. There are not many vocals, the reliance is very much on the music and although there is the impression at times of free form improvisation it is far less prevalent than many others. The result is something that contains far more depth than many space rock albums that I have heard and is certainly worthy of investigation.
#87, Apr 2006

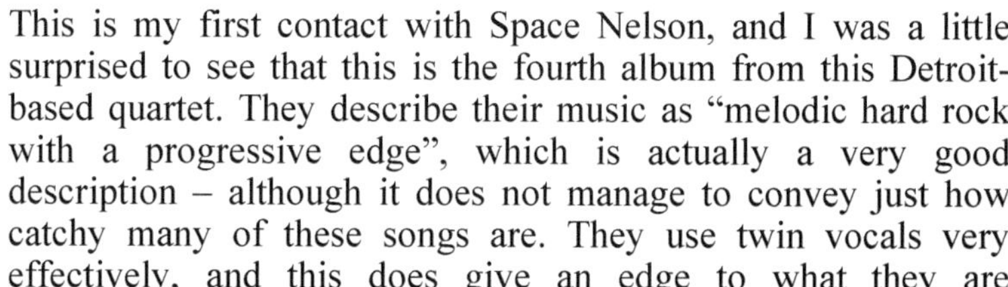

SPACE NELSON
DON'T PANIC

This is my first contact with Space Nelson, and I was a little surprised to see that this is the fourth album from this Detroit-based quartet. They describe their music as "melodic hard rock with a progressive edge", which is actually a very good description – although it does not manage to convey just how catchy many of these songs are. They use twin vocals very effectively, and this does give an edge to what they are performing, as do the strong choruses. Pete Hopesberger also uses a variety of different sounds on his keyboards, while the guitar sound is clean and crisp. Although there is a lot going on within the music there is also quite a feeling of space so that it does not feel at all intense or over the top, which makes the music very accessible and enjoyable to listen to. They have opened for King's X recently and one would have thought that with music like this their spiritual home would be on Inside Out as well, and I am surprised to see that they are currently unsigned. There are elements of this music that reminds me of their Detroit counterparts Tiles, with a sound that is very up to date and so catchy that it could almost be said to be 'poppy' at times with some Alex Lifeson-style guitar. This is a very strong album that mixes the genres of neo-prog and melodic rock extremely well indeed and I look forward to hearing more from these guys. *#86, Feb 2006*

SPACE RITUAL.NET
LIVE AT GLASTONBURY...

It is obvious from the name alone that there are some Hawkwind connections going on, but it is just a bit more than that and it is possible to argue that the origins of the band go back as far as Group X in 1969. Their first gig on August 29th, 1969, included Nik Turner, Mick Slattery and Terry Ollis and here they are all back onstage together again. Also involved is Thomas Crimble, who was Hawkwind bassist from July 1970 to April 1971.

Commander Jim Hawkman has also been playing with Space Ritual.Net and various other ex-Hawkwind luminaries have been involved, including Del Dettmar who joined them for the current tour. Even young Michael Moorcock has promised to put in appearance! This album was recorded at Glastonbury and Guildford last year, so what about the music? There are two drummers (Terry is joined by his son Sam) but to say that they come across as classic Hawkwind seems to be stating the obvious. They resist the temptation to play "Silver Machine" followed by "Brainstorm" and instead concentrate on their own material, but it sounds as if classic Hawkwind are back. One song that is a notable exception is their version of Coltrane's "Blue Train" which shows that they have more than one string to their sax. The only thing that spoils this is the abrupt ending or interruption as the album moves from track to track but that may be just from playing it on a PC. It is a fun album with good sound and if you are a Hawkfan then you will have to get this. *#72, Feb 2003*

SPECIAL EXPERIMENT
FORTUNE MEMORIES

Special Experiment is a project that has been put together by Dzidek Marcinkiewicz, and this is their debut album. It is instrumental, contains eight songs, and while Dzidek is a keyboard player this album does also contain very strong guitar lines. It is quite symphonic in sound and style, and with strong melodies and themes. It may not be as overtly rock as prog metal but certainly carries quite a lot of hard rock guitar. But the impression is given sometimes that the album was written with a singer in mind, and now the guitar takes the lead instead, so it is a case of wondering what it would have been like if a powerful voice had been brought in. This is a very enjoyable album in its' own right but if there had been a singer then it would have been even better. Although Dzidek is Polish he now lives in Germany where this album can be ordered from.
#73, Apr 2003

SPECIMEN 37
THE ENDLESS LOOPING GAME

The second album from Boston band Specimen 37 is a concept which "chronicles seven days in the life of the nameless "specimen," one man locked in an existential struggle to find meaning in everyday mundane acts. Sitting in traffic. Eating. Dating. Working. The specimen is antagonized by the world's myopic preoccupation with fame, religious conformity, war and material wealth. The specimen's debilitating fear is that he'll never find meaning in a world that seems to turn on an axis of meaninglessness, and in this chapter of the specimen's life, it's never clear whether or not he finds hope." As it started with layered keyboards and some weird sounds and clips, I was starting to wonder what on earth I was listening to. It was not Tangerine Dream or Pink Floyd, but there are definite similarities. But as the album progressed (good use of words here), I realised that this was an extremely complex world where rock and weird synths could sit happily side by side. This is prog music, but not the common or garden type and is all the better for it. Finally, it came to me who this band reminded me of, the mighty Poisoned Electrick Head (can it really be 11 years since 'The Big Eye Am'?). PEH were a band (past tense unfortunately) who took their love of all things unusual and blended it with space rock to create something new, and although Specimen 37 are in many ways very different they are also similar in others. The more I played this the more I liked it. The more I liked it the more I became convinced that Empathy, Gee-Roj, Mojonine, Ponder, Sketch Element and their guests have created a mighty album that should appreciate to fans of good music, whatever the genre. *#84, July 2005*

SPECIMEN 37
ADVERSE REACTION

In #84 I was very impressed with S37's new album 'The Endless Looping Game', so much so that I asked Empathy for an interview and he also sent along their debut album from 2000. This is quite a different piece of work to the follow-up but is again heavily influenced by Animals-era Floyd but putting on opening song "Magnascope" you may well wonder what I am talking about as it kicks off with hard rocking guitars and treated vocals. Just as one is getting into the groove it all stops and there is the feeling of delicate lounge lite as the band noodles along with some female vocals. But just as the listener settles into what is going on it is again time for a change as the music fades away into some jazz-style drumming and then the keyboards come in on a totally different tack. And so, the album 'progresses'. This really is progressive rock, with the rock coming from the guitars and hard-hitting drums and bass and the progressive part coming from the kitchen sink that has been used to mix all the musical ingredients. But unlike some other bands that try to bring in loads of different influences, this really works as a coherent whole. They use samples, noises, snippets of sound to bring out their ideas and the result is something that is both invigorating and exciting. I just can't believe that this has been out for five years and is the first that I have heard about it. Hopefully you will have found the interview with Empathy interesting, and that the reviews of the two albums will have you wanting to find out more *#85, Nov 2005*

SPEKTRUM
SPEKTRUM

Spektrum is a semi-supergroup in that it contains members of Galleon, Cross and Grand Stand as well as vocalist Lizette von Panajott. I was immediately taken by just how commercial sounding this album is as it comes across as a mix between It Bites and 'And Then There Were Three' era Genesis. Certainly, nothing that could be construed as being a bad thing. It has a definite Eighties feel and yet is also very fresh and quite different to much that is currently on the underground

progressive scene. There are not many bands that use similar musical references, and this is surely going to be an album that is going to make them many friends. This is music that is melodic, and often quite different from one song to the next. I really like "Land Of Longing" and can almost imagine that being released as a single while the following number "Now" moves from space and gentleness to some driving guitar. This is an album that has so much going for it yet at the same time is not only intricate yet is also so very listenable. The vocals are different to the norm, which gives the music an added edge. It is a debut album, yet given the background of the players it is of little surprise that this is of such high quality. A superb album that progheads need to search out.
#74, Jun 2003

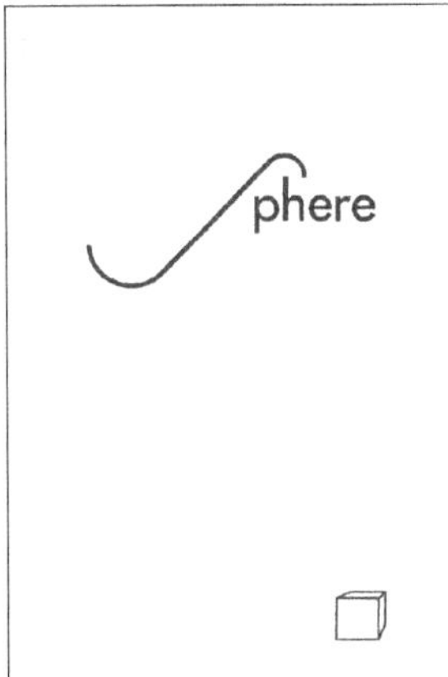

SPHERE
SPHERE
After the Jadis and Shadowland gig at the Marquee in December, I was given a demo tape by a band I hadn't previously heard of, Sphere. Since playing and liking the tape all attempts at contacting the band have met without success, which is a pity as the tape shows promise. Also, it seems that they may well have broken up, or at least are going through a period of change (another way of describing this would be to say that at least two musicians have left). So, what do we have? The five-song tape was recorded last year by Steve Anderson (guitar), Bill Burnett (bass, vocals), Neil Durant (keyboards), Frank Watson (drums) and John Duncan (lead vocals). It kicks off with "Lighthouse", which for the most part is an up-tempo straightforward rock instrumental with Steve and Neil trading licks. What was a little unusual was the very heavy use of distortion in the guitar. "Behind The Masques" shows a lot more promise, with far greater use of keyboards, but again that distorted guitar is used at times for effect. Sure, there are little hiccups apparent, with the voice fading here and there, but overall a gallant effort. The other songs, "Breezeblock?", "No Country" and "Undertow" are all also worth listening to. I get the impression that Sphere are/were a lot heavier in the live environment than in the studio, and this is borne out by the fact that they supported Mentaur at their first gig of 1993. The tape is interesting and hopefully a foretaste of things to come.
#17, Mar 1993

SPHERE
SIGNATURES
It has been a few years since I first heard of Sphere, and they have been plagued with bad luck, mostly concerning personnel. Indeed, even as I listen to this demo which was recorded last year, I know that they are again without a vocalist and are currently trying to gig as an instrumental outfit. However, they have now signed a deal with Cyclops and are looking for a singer. There are four songs here and it marks quite a step forward since the last demo I heard. At times, they are reminiscent of the quieter side of Genesis, and

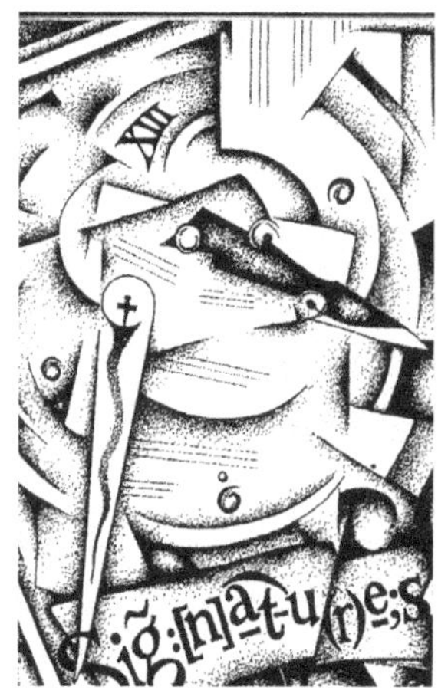

certainly veer more towards the more balladic and gentler side of prog, although there are elements which show they can rock if they put their minds to it. Neil Durant is the main player, being one of the brightest young keyboard talents around, and it is he who has kept the band on track after turning down the gig with Grey Lady Down. I look forward to hearing Sphere on CD later this year.
#29, Jun 1995

SPHERE³
COMEUPPANCE
I have been racking my brain and have had to give up. I honestly can't think of a CD I have been waiting for longer than the debut by Sphere³. Back when the guys were singular as opposed to a power I used to be in regular contact, especially with keyboard player Neil Durant. I started reviewing the band as long ago as #17 (March 1993) and every time I saw Neil at a gig, giving out one of their numerous flyers I would ask when the new album was coming out. When Malcolm told me that the album had actually been released, I told him that I wouldn't believe it until I saw a copy, as I have been waiting for this even longer than the second Credo album! The band is Neil (keyboards), Steve Anderson (guitars, who also played for a while with GLD), William Burnett (bass) and Jamie Fisher (drums). While Jamie only joined in 1996 the others have been playing with each other since 1991 or thereabouts so it is no surprise that by now, they know what they are doing. Yes, I am treating this review quite light heartedly but that fits in with the whole feel of a band that has always been self-deprecating and full of humour. Is it because the album is not much cop and I'm being kind? No, the reverse is definitely the case. It may have been an inordinate time in the making, but this must be one of the finest jazz-oriented albums that it has ever been my pleasure to hear.

Each of the four are master musicians, and they all have huge parts to play within each song so that if the listener concentrates on just one player then he will be surprised at just how much is going on. There are not any egos on show, each provides as little or as much as is required, so during the same song William can provide some stunning finger popping bass or just play a few delicate notes here and there while Neil plays gentle keyboards or lovingly strokes the ivories and tinkles with his piano. The biggest problem that Cyclops is going to have is how to get this out of the prog market and into jazz, as any fan of Weather Report, Return To Forever or Brand X will take this fusion album warmly into their bosom. I have seen one article where the reviewer says how much he is

looking forward to the follow up. All I can say to that is do not hold your breath and maybe, just maybe, within the next ten years we may get another album. I certainly hope so, as this is superb!
#73, Apr 2003

SPHERE OF SOULS
FROM THE ASHES….
This is the debut album from Sphere of Souls, a Dutch band that has been put together by ex-Sun Caged members André Vuurboom (vocals) and Joost van den Broek (keyboards). It is prog metal of the highest quality, with a sound that is both powerful and extremely heavy while also managing to maintain a clarity that is not always prevalent in this style. The line-up is completed by Kees Harrison (bass), Rob Cerrone (rhythm guitar), Anand Mahangoe (lead guitar) and Ruud van Diepen (drums). Given that André also provides guitars on the album (as well as writing virtually all the material) it is probably not surprising that guitars play such a key part, with Joost often content to play a supporting role. André also has a very powerful rock voice with loads of range and this gives the music a very forceful edge. Even though the music is often very heavy it never loses the prog edge and there are some strange time shifts and plenty of complexity to keep the proghead interested. This band shows a lot of promise and I am sure that we are going to be hearing a lot more about these guys in the future.
#87, Apr 2006

SPOCK'S BEARD
THE LIGHT
It is not often that everyone within the prog scene is discussing one band and album in particular. However, that is the case at the moment with American outfit Spock's Beard. All those who had heard it was telling me what an amazing album this was, and it was with eager anticipation that I finally whacked it onto the player. Imagine my delight when I realised that everything I had heard about it proved true, and then some. Imagine if you can a band that seems to take all the best elements of Yes, ELP, Kansas, Pink Floyd, Colosseum II and Gentle Giant and then throws in a dash of Alice Cooper along with a bit more jazz and hard rock for good measure, and you start getting some sort of idea of what this band is all about. 'The Light' is simply one of the most complete albums I have ever heard, and it is no surprise that these guys are getting such high praise. The four-piece are led by Neal Morse (lead vocals, Mellotron, Hammond Organ, keyboards, acoustic and electric guitar) and he is more than ably abetted by Alan Morse (lead electric guitar, cello, Mellotron, vocals), Dave Meros (bass and French horn) and Nick D'Virgilio (drums and vocals). Three of the four songs are over twelve minutes in length, with the superb "The Water" managing to make it to twenty-three! These guys mix many influences and make a sound that is wonderful to the ears. They have taken the

Seventies as a starting point and truly progressed from there into the Nineties with an album that should be hailed as a classic. If an American band ever deserves to break out of the underground and become a truly global success, then Spock's Beard are it. Great songs with glorious melodies and hooks and enough switches and turns to more than maintain interest, this album deserves to be huge. It will not be long until it is not just prog lovers talking about this amazing album, so get in on the act early and grab Spock's Beard with both hands.
#33, Feb 1996

SPOCK'S BEARD
BEWARE OF DARKNESS

By now I am sure that anyone remotely into prog will have purchased Spock's Beard's 'The Light', surely one of the most important debuts to come out of America in the Nineties, whatever the style of music. Of course, now there is the little difficulty of following it. When everyone without exception has been singing the praises then they must have been under a lot of pressure, but of course they do not show any of that with a second album that is certainly as good and may even be better! Starting off with a radical reworking of George Harrison's "Beware of Darkness" (from 'All Things Must Pass'), which shows a heavy Yes and jazz influence, we are into "Thoughts". This seven-minute number is one of the best prog songs I have ever heard, filled with vocal harmonies, melodies and hooks in abundance, it has "CLASSIC" stamped all over it in mile high letters.

Away from the 'new' feel of the last piece, "The Doorway" starts instead with a classical piano instrumental. A theme is developed on Chris Squire-style bass, which is then repeated on guitar as the song develops. Simple ideas such as singing a verse with riffing guitar and drums, with no bass or keyboards, is definitely effective. Acoustic guitar is used liberally for effect, dropping in and out of the song at some unexpected moments. I mean, there is so much happening that it is amazing that they managed to get it all into under twelve minutes! "Waste Away" typifies what they are about, starting with acoustic guitar and vocals, similar in some ways to some of Ian Anderson's solo pieces. It develops into a blasting rocker, but there is so much more than that as it builds, dips and weaves.

There are seven songs here, with only two breaking the ten-minute barrier (closer "Time Has Come" is more than sixteen minutes) and is an album that is a joy to listen to. It yells "class" from the first note to the very last and sets levels of excellence that many will aspire to but very few will ever attain. If you have ever listened to progressive rock or wonder what on earth I am prattling on about, then I seriously urge you to get one of the best albums of this genre that you are ever likely to hear.
#40, Mar 1997

SPOCK'S BEARD
THE OFFICIAL LIVE BOOTLEG

I have been singing the praises of this band, along with just about everybody else, ever since I heard their debut monster 'The Light'. The follow-up 'Beware of Darkness' was just as good, if not better, and while both have been released in the UK by Giant Electric Pea, this album is only available as an import (although GEP have still got some copies left so if you're quick you just may be able to pick this up). It was recorded at ProgFest in 1995 and demonstrates what a fantastic act this is. I cannot remember when I was so impressed by an American outfit: I mean, this is brilliant! For your money, you get not only the whole of the debut album, but also "Thoughts" from the second. That song alone is worth the purchase price. Harmony vocals? Yes. Musical accomplishment and dexterity? Yes. Tunes and melodies? Yes. Songs more than ten minutes? Oh yes indeedy. The overall result is an album that is breath-taking in what it has to offer. Playing this immediately after ELP's 'Live At The Royal Albert Hall' I was struck by the similarity in what they are both trying to achieve, and that in the Nineties Spock's Beard seem to be better at it than one of my all-time favourites. If you have ever enjoyed progressive rock at its' very best, then Spock's Beard is an act you should know.

#42, July 1997

SPOCK'S BEARD
THE KINDNESS OF STRANGERS

It is getting difficult to find new things to say about Spock's Beard. If you have had your head in a bucket for the last few years, then they are simply the best thing to come of America in the last decade. Genesis even "borrowed" drummer Nick D'Virgilio to play on 'Calling All Stations', but there was never any chance of him leaving the fold. Why? Because everyone knows that this band are going to be huge. It would not surprise me if this is the last album they release through Giant Electric Pea, who have the European rights, and that next time they go for a major. As well as Nick, Spock's Beard are still Neal Morse (lead vocals, piano, all synths, acoustic guitar and occasional electric guitar), Alan Morse (electric guitar, cello, Mellotron, backing vocals), Dave Meros (bass and vocals) and Ryo Okomuto (Hammond Organ and Mellotron). Oh, and Nick also provides backing vocals. The thing about this band is their ability not only to be technically brilliant but also to mix so many styles into a single song that it almost makes the mind reel, but the way they move through all the forms always makes sense. Whether it is going from a hard rock section straight into strings with no warning whatsoever, or putting in an acoustic guitar interlude, it always sounds right. Favourite song is "The Mouth Of Madness" which is just wonderful: riffs are followed by different players and those keyboards just blow you away. If you have ever wondered what progressive rock in the Nineties is all about then you can do far worse than pick up Spock's Beard, consider it an investment in the future of your musical tastes. I have not lived with this enough yet to be able to say that it is the best thing that they have ever

done, because their debut album 'The Light' came out of nowhere and melted everyone's minds while the follow-up and live album (which features all of the songs from the debut plus to my ears the best song from the second) are all still regular visitors to the deck. As is by now expected from these guys this album is brilliant. Get with confidence!
#47, Feb 1998

SPOCK'S BEARD
DAY FOR NIGHT
Consistently the best band to come out of the States in the Nineties, the guys are back with yet another album. Their output is prolific, and here they are with their first for Inside Out having left Giant Electric Pea. What is it that makes them so good? The first minute of "Gibberish" provides the answer as even the most hardened critic could not help but be swayed by the musical interplay and intricacies which gives way to a capella harmony vocals of the highest order. They still manage to get away with sounding like no one else but loads of people all at the same time. During this song, I kept thinking about Kansas, just because of the keyboard sound and style, but with no real evidence to back it up. Only one longish track on this album (shame, shame) and that is "Crack The Big Sky" which just fails to break the ten-minute barrier. It commences life as a soft jazz number, with some emotive fretless bass, but that does not last too long as crashing guitars and keyboards give way to handclaps! That is the beauty of this music; it is deeply intricate and often moves in unexpected directions. When the vocals stop, it is almost as a ballad, with gentle keyboard backing – then the keyboards finish and it is just the guitar, bass and drums, With Spock's Beard you are never sure what they are going to do, except that not only are they a great prog band but a wonderful pop act as well. The chorus is just great singalong sweeping pop music. America's top band are back, with more listening delights for your pleasure. If you have somehow managed to miss what I have been saying about this band ever since I heard the American release of their debut album, then read this now. They are the best at what they do from across the water, and indeed there are few over here that could touch them. Released through SPV this has widespread release through the UK so there is no excuse for not getting this. Just superb.
#53, May 1999

SPOCK'S BEARD
THE BEARD IS OUT THERE
You are probably all getting a bit fed up of me saying this by now, but Spock's Beard are the best band to come out of the States this decade. There are few that even come close to the standard of progressive rock that they are producing. After reviewing their latest studio album imagine my delight when Inside Out sent me this live one. It is an album that I have reviewed previously when (shock, horror) I had bought it. Back

then it was called 'Official Live Bootleg' and had only been released in the States. Now it is much more readily available and, even more importantly, it has an extra track missing from the original. Buy this and you get the whole of the most important debut album of recent years, plus the best song from the follow-up ("Thoughts") and the bonus song "Waste Away" (also taken from the second album) here put together with a raucous version of Hendrix's "Fire". I suppose that drummer Nick D'Virgilio is the most well-known having played on 'Calling All Stations', but these guys are all great musicians and (apart from keyboard player Ryo Okomuto) quite superb singers. You want harmony vocals? Just listen to "Thoughts" and marvel at what SB can provide in a totally live environment. No backing tapes for these guys or messing about in a studio afterwards, if you had been at ProgFest in '95 this is exactly what you would have heard.

But what is it that makes them so damn good at what they do? It is hard to put it in a simple fashion and probably the best thing to do would be to sit someone down, put on "The Water" and leave them to it. The longest song on the debut album (which only contained four songs and still clocked in at more than 55 minutes), it is reproduced here in all its' glory. From the gentle introduction, which builds to Neal Morse forcing out the words "I am the water" through the myriad twists and turns of one of the best pieces of modern music you are ever likely to hear, I could listen to this every day and never tire of it: twenty-three minutes of sheer magic. When the electronic vocals give way to 'normal' singing there is undoubted passion and fervour, especially during the hard rock section where Neal shouts "Fuck You!" Although many Spock's Beard fans will already have the original version of this, there is nothing to stop you all from rushing out and purchasing the reissue. A great band, and a great live album.
#54, July 1999

SPOCK'S BEARD
DON'T TRY THIS AT HOME
Recorded on the last tour in Holland, this CD is only marred by the fact that it is too short by far at under an hour, but I have been assured by the record company that this was due to a problem with the quality of the tapes. That aside, here is one of my very favourite bands on stage and as I play this, I can again see them in my mind's eye, as they were that wonderful night at the LA2. In fact, this CD could not possibly match up to that experience as it is only from being there that I realise that so much of their gig is missing from the CD. But, and it is a huge "but" indeed, what is contained on this CD is more than enough evidence that the Beard really are one of the best in the world at what they do. They are all superb musicians, and with great vocals and wonderful songs how can these guys do any wrong? Spock's Beard appears to be one of the very few modern 'prog' bands that have managed to find a place in the hearts of the traditionalists. I have been in love with their music since I first heard the original American release of their debut, and they just seem to be getting better and better. Many of the songs on this CD are from the latest album, but they also mix in some of the older stuff and change songs so that the original is only a basis for them to play around. Any one of these songs

will make most modern prog bands want to pack up and go home. "Gibberish" has some of the best multi-part vocals that will ever be attempted by a modern rock band, while "Day For Night" is a perfect opener with its' bombastic singalong style. This CD caused me a lot of problems in the sense that all the time I should have been listening to other material I kept justifying to myself that I ought to play it just one more time... If you want progressive melodic rock at its' very best, then it just can't get any better than this. At least, not until their next album...
#58, May 2000

SPOCK'S BEARD
V
I may have mentioned before, once or twice, that in my humble opinion Spock's Beard is the best band to ever come from over the pond. Their latest release does nothing at all to make me change that opinion. It took me a little while to get into this album, but once I did then I found that I had real problems trying to listen to anything else. There are a few long numbers, but also some shorter ones. I think that if I had to play one song to try to entice a new fan that it would be one of these, "Thoughts (Part II)". It starts life as a gentle acoustic guitar ballad, but at the end of the introduction Neal puts an edge on his voice as he sings "I thought it might be really great, to show you how I feel inside, but I think, maybe not". This heralds the introduction of the rest of the band, who repeat and then play around the musical motif. Gradually the pace picks up and gets more complex then stops dead as the band produce harmony vocals a la Barber Shop from out of nowhere. The song moves from one extreme to another, with the initial phrase returned to twice. It may not be very long, but it is superb. I am also a big fan of "All On A Sunday" which starts life as a Kansas sound-alike, but yet again initial musical perceptions can be misleading and in the case of Spock's Beard downright wrong. Spock's Beard may be the huge fish in a pond that seems to be getting smaller every day, but if the rest of the musical world cannot see what they are missing then that is their loss. This is yet another great album from the band who have managed to be prolific without losing quality.
#60, Oct 2000

SPOCK'S BEARD
SNOW
It has been a long time since I first heard 'The Light', and I think that it is safe to say that since then I have been a fan. They are the most exciting and dramatic progressive rock band around, driving the genre forward and in this album, they have come of age. This is THE album of the year; I cannot imagine anything else coming close. 'Snow' is the band's first concept album, and with 115 minutes of music they have allowed themselves to stretch in the way that they have been threatening in the past –

no stranger to epics, this is a whole new ball game. The double CD is about a young man who is blessed, and cursed, with the gift of healing and tells the story of the problems that he faces and how he overcomes them.

As Neal says "When it rocks, then it rocks more than before. When it's soft, then it's softer than before. And when we decide to play complex parts, then it's more over-the-top that it ever was". Some of the songs have extremely catchy hooks ("Devil's Got My Throat" being a case in point), while others are just breath-taking in their complexity, or just simple and commercial. I can't wait to see this played live as the guys are blasting away one second, then it is a capella vocals, or it comes from incredible note density to just simple work on an acoustic guitar. I listened to it in its entirety in the company of a VDGG fan who had never heard Spock's Beard previously and he was stunned. Here the band are bringing together all their rock and prog influences and moulding them into something truly new and exciting. There is nothing here to fault. The songs and musicianship are of the highest order, and the production top class. In fact, the only issue with the album that I have is that when I put it on just to play a few tracks I feel cheated if I am unable to listen to the whole thing again. The double CD is being released in the UK on August 26th (distributed by Koch) but there is also a limited edition available that contains the 2 CD digibook version with a 28-page booklet. It comes in a special box plus an extra bonus disc with a cover song, live acoustic versions, and some outtakes and dialogue. If you only buy one progressive rock album this year, it is this one.
#69, Aug 2002

SPOCK'S BEARD
FEEL EUPHORIA

Okay, let's get the Genesis comparisons out of the way at the beginning, shall we? A well-known band releases what is seen by many as a concept album masterpiece of great complexity, only for the singer to leave (in this case, even before a full tour is undertaken – at least Gabriel was Rael), who was then replaced in turn by the drummer as lead singer. The band continued in a different musical area than before, and released 'A Trick Of The Tail', um, sorry, 'Feel Euphoria'. Right. SB are not Genesis, and Nick D'Virgilio is not Phil Collins, and by the way, I really enjoyed 'Snow' and return to it often, playing all of it, which is not something that can be said about 'Lamb'. Like many SB fans I was extremely concerned when Neal left the band. This is because he was the main songwriter, the bandleader, and a multi-instrumentalist to boot. Just how were they going to replace him? I do not think that there was ever any doubt that Nick was going to take over as singer – he always sang the encore with Neal on drums, and he has a great voice. For the new album, the decision was eventually taken not to bring in a new musician, with Ryo taking over the entire keyboard playing, although the band did collaborate with some outside songwriters.

Without Neal, they have moved away from much of the overtly proggy material and more into a hard rock area, although in many ways they could argue that they are more progressive than before as they have now moved away from much of the Spock's Beard 'sound'. The album starts with "Onomatopoeia", which my dictionary defines as 'using words that imitate the sound they denote' and with hissing fires and ticking clocks they probably have it right. When I first played this, I could not believe what I was hearing, as this is a rock song first and foremost – blasting along, certainly for the first section. Where was the SB I loved? But, the more I played this the more I fell in love with it. I believe that the guys have placed this as the opener just to wake everybody up and demand to be met on their own ground. They are not the band they were when Neal was involved, they have evolved. Evolution means change, and this is something I now welcome, although it was hard the first time. There is a lot going on in this track, with gentle harmony vocals as well as crunching guitars.

From here on the band show that they have plenty of musical tricks, with Ryo demonstrating what a fine keyboard player he is. Simple ideas such as stopping the music so that Nick can sing unaccompanied works extremely well on "The Bottom Line", with harmony vocals abounding. They are trying new ideas, and the feeling here is of a band that has bonded together over time, and then been thrust together and have grown even more because of it. The title track is particularly dark and menacing, with a bleak verse contrasting against the more vibrant chorus. The highlight of the album is the lengthy "A Guy Named Sid" which shows just how Nick has changed as a songwriter. The second section, "Same Old Story" rocks and bounces, and even if in the future they drop the whole song from the set, this is going to be in there for years. In my mind's eye, I can see Nick strutting the stage as this is blasted out. The 'choir' is a bit contrived, as I cynically felt that it had been put there to show that Nick and Alan can sing fine on their own, thanks, but overall this is a masterpiece, moving through loads of different styles and rhythms. I may not have liked it as much as I could have when I first heard it, but now I am hooked. I love this album and I am sure that there are many out there who feel the same. Superb.
#76, Oct 2003

SPOCK'S BEARD
OCTANE

This is their eighth studio album, and second post Neal. Spock's Beard are always going to be viewed as having distinct breaks in their musical career, much like Genesis, and comparisons are always going to be made between music with Neal and music without. Not only was he the singer and voice of the band he was also the main songwriter. The last album saw the band produce a strong piece of work, but there was the feeling that it was a band in transition, a band looking for their own sound. With 'Octane' they have found it. Although Nick says that there are many progressive elements, 'Octane' owes far more to various rock influences than it does to prog. Listen to "I Wouldn't Let It Go" (part of the seven-song epic "A Flash Before My Eyes") and it is impossible not to hear the strong influence of Tom Petty – not something that would be expected from the band that recorded 'Snow' – and at one point they even come across as

Led Zeppelin! But the important thing to remember is that this is a very different band, even though all the musicians here played on 'Snow', the outlook has dramatically changed. Instead of being presented with songs and then arranging them and having some impact to their structure, they are writing all the material with some outside friends and 'Octane' shows the way that they are going to be heading.

Listen to "Surfing Down The Avalanche" and it is a powering rock number that any fan of melodic metal would definitely bang the noggin to, but there are also large areas on the album where Al's electric guitar is absent and instead he turns to acoustic. There is some prog, but for the most part it is a state of mind that they really can progress and find their own footing without having to always look backwards at what came before. The album is full of surprises, and not something that I would ever have imagined the band producing in the way that the music often follows a rockier trait, be it hard rock or AOR, yet it can still be incredibly complex or simple. In many ways, this could be considered the 'difficult' second album, but they have far surpassed the 'debut'. If you miss the 'old' Spock's Beard then you need to be following Neal, but if you are interested in hearing some great songs that are moving and twisting around from a band that knows where it is going then this is an album to savour.

The Beard is dead. Long live the Beard.
#82, Jan 2005

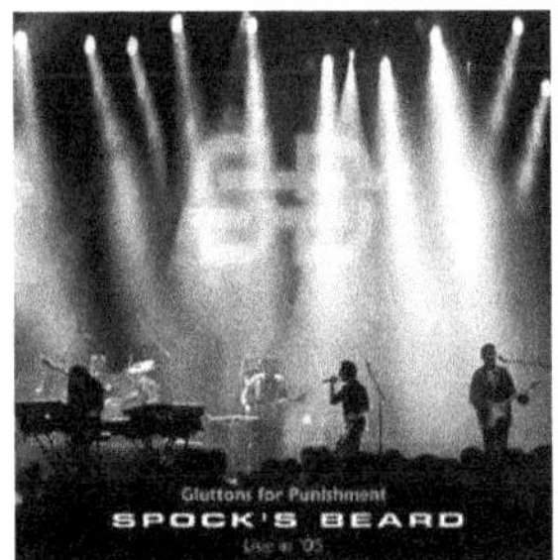

SPOCK'S BEARD
GLUTTONS FOR PUNISHMENT

This is by my reckoning the band's third official live album, following on from 'The Official Live Bootleg' (later reissued by Inside Out as 'The Beard Is Out There') and 'Don't Try This At Home'. But of course, the major difference with this one is that it is the first one with Nick out front and Jimmy Keegan on drums, i.e. the first live album without Neal. So, having now recorded two studio albums since his departure it is of no surprise that this set is based mostly around these, and most of 'Octave' has an airing. Nick had a great voice, and I always thought that he was more than capable of being a frontman as he proves here. Jimmy is also a fine drummer very much in the Nick mould, and he certainly fits in well.

What this boils down to is whether one likes the 'new' Beard compared with the 'old'. Unlike the Genesis loss of singer with which they will always be compared, there has been a major change in the musical emphasis and ability of the band. It means that Ryo has far more work to contend with, and the band is not as keyboard oriented as they were, although Nick being a guitarist in his own right as well does mean that they have not lost that aspect. The music now is far 'friendlier' and not as challenging as it was previously which means that they may well be gaining more fans from the mainstream, but they are probably going to be losing them from the prog arena. This is a strong album, as is 'Octave', with "Surfing Down The Avalanche" crunching out in fine fashion. But they are not the band they were, which means that the two 'old' numbers they perform just do not work for me. "At The End Of The Day" and especially "The Light" have Neal thrown all over it and Nick can't match the passion in the voice and Ryo just does not have enough hands and fingers. The result is a double album of the tour earlier this year that shows a band who are still cooking, but whether I would go and see them again is another matter altogether. I would much rather play one of the earlier live albums, but that is just my personal choice. *#85, Nov 2005*

STARLESS
CLEAR BLUE WATER

I must open with a quote from their press release: "If you believe that all rock bands should be under nineteen, photogenic, and sound like someone else then Starless are going to be a big disappointment to you. Put the tape in the bin now, because you will not be interested in us". Yeah, got me hooked straight away as well. Starless are a Swindon based band, and they have formed their own record label to get their product onto the market. They are correct when they say that they do not sound like anyone else, although starting points could well be Manitou or Jump with at times a smattering of Simple Minds thrown in for good measure. They are a reviewer's nightmare, just because they refuse to be categorised and shift musical styles with ease. They are definitely an English rock band (yes, I know Simple Minds are Scots), but although the guitars blast out at times, they are not HR. They do have progressive tendencies (there are cures) but they are not a progressive rock band as currently viewed. What they are is a song-based outfit that seemingly have come out of nowhere but are producing music of the highest order. I had never heard of them until the CD had popped through my letterbox and speaking to various others no one else has heard of them either. This is a real shame as this album is a gem, and it will appeal to anyone who refuses to listen to pigeonholed music but rather takes each album on its own merit. The sense of humour is obvious in the press release and shows in song titles such as "Wife & Two Veg". At times extremely powerful, at others gentle and melodic, this is an album that defies description apart from the simple fact that it is quite superb.
#30, Aug 1995

STAR ONE
SPACE METAL

Star One is the brainchild of Arjen Anthony Lucassen who provided not only the vision, all the songs, but also bass, guitars, Hammond, Mellotron and synths. He was joined by Ed Warby on drums and used four main vocalists in Damian Wilson (Threshold, Landmarq, La Salle etc.), Russell Allen (Symphony X), Dan Swano (Edge Of Sanity, Nightingale) and Floor Jansen (After Forever). He brought in some guest keyboard players such as Erik Norlander (Rocket Scientists) and even convinced Dave Brock to make an appearance on guest vocals! It has been released as a limited-edition double digipak and that is the version to get hold of. Arjen is best known for his albums as Ayreon, but his last CD was more of an atmospheric album under the name Ambeon. This is an attempt to bring out a hard rock space metal album for the 21st Century, and it succeeds brilliantly.

There is always the fear that a project of this kind will have a disjointed feel, especially when one musician plays so many instruments, but that is not the case here. Another factor which works very well is that the four vocalists are all very different so it is always possible to pick out exactly who is singing what. On "Set Your Controls" all the singers play a part, but they all still sound distinctive. The album was inspired by some of Arjen's favourite sci-fi films and the project itself is named after an episode of "Blake's Seven". While I do not want to take anything away from the main album, which is simply superb, I must just mention also the Hawkwind Medley that is a bonus. "Silver Machine", "Brainstorm", "Spirit Of The Age" and some others played as if they are new fresh songs yet always maintaining that Hawkwind element, given the distinctive and definite seal of approval by Dave Brock providing the vocals. Ten minutes is just not long enough. Already established as a personal favourite for waking up the office at 06:30, this is class from start to end.
#67, Apr 2002

STAR ONE
LIVE ON EARTH
Back in #67 I raved about the new project that had been put together by Arjen Anthony Lucassen, Star One. That concept album has since been taken on the road and he has brought with him many of the musicians that were initially involved. This means that there are five singers involved, all with a part to play, and on songs such as "Set Your Controls" when they are vying for position it is a sight to be heard. (yeah, I know, but you get the idea). Of course, one of the singers is Damian Wilson and I have never hidden my admiration for his vocal prowess, yet here he is fine company and fits in well instead of dominating the proceedings. This is technical hard rock, with just enough prog influences to keep fans of that genre interested but, in many ways, this is more complex than even Damian's old outfit Threshold, although not quite as heavy. This is a concept album being played live, although with some added songs that are not on the studio, but there are some spoken pieces to set the scene. It can be played as separate songs, although if possible it is best to sit and listen intently to the double CD in one sitting. This is the version that I have been sent, but I believe that it is also available as a double CD with a DVD, which must be worth seeing. If you want complicated hard rock with more than a touch of prog metal than this is it.
#73, Apr 2003

STEELWIND
THE KH PROJECT

Steelwind were formed by Kevin Humphrey in 1999, and although the band took a break after the release of their second album 'Jawhook' in 2002, he felt he had just too music inside, so went on recording. The result is a ten-track album where he plays all the instruments, as well as providing vocals. The feeling is one of a band instead of a solo project and it must have taken some time to get it all together. Although Kevin says he feels this is a progressive rock album, I would put this much more firmly into the AOR camp, as it comes across very strongly as Reo Speedwagon with some touches of Kansas. It is packed full of hooks and although it can appear a little lightweight at times it is an album that can be enjoyed very much on first hearing. What is also different to a lot of the music that I normally listen to is that this is a Christian album, so if you interested in that scene then this is certainly much better than Larry Norman or Cliff Richard, although not quite as heavy as Stryper. Kevin has a very clear high voice and he has layered the harmonies so that any of fan of classic AOR will want to hear this at least. *#84, July 2005*

SIMON STEENSLAND
THE ZOMBIE HUNTER

This is Simon's second CD, following on from 'The Simon Lonesome Combat Ensemble', which came out on Musea Parallel. Unusually for a solo progressive musician, Simon is a percussionist, although he plays some other instruments as well. This means that he approached the music from an unusual angle, and although he has used some guests he is primarily responsible for most of the sounds that we hear. This is one of those albums that you just know that you not going to like, but from the outset find yourself strangely compelled to listen to it all. I kept telling myself that I was not enjoying it yet found it impossible to turn it off. When it had finished, I had to play it again to check that I really hadn't enjoyed it. So, all in all Simon has produced an album that has a lot going on, certainly different to anything else I have heard, and owes more to modern classical music than it does to rock 'n' roll. Not an album to be played either as background music or for pleasant listening, but if you want an album that you must listen to and is a challenge then this is the one. *#32, Dec 1995*

STEREOSCOPE
STEREOSCOPE

Stereoscope are a project that has been put together by Jérémie Grima and Sébastien Bourdeix who are both in Black Noodle Project. They had some pieces that they felt would not fit within the overall feel of that band, so decided to record them under a new name and the result is something that is acoustic and in many ways minimalist. It is an album where space is as

important as sound, and the guitars and delicate piano combine with the vocals to create something that is a joy to listen to. This is relaxing music that somehow manages to convey an intensity while also being laid back and never in your face. This is not folk, it is something that is still more akin to prog, but is acoustic and glorious. All the songs are in English and this is a very accessible album that deserves to be heard by a wider public.
#86, Feb 2006

ROINE STOLT
THE FLOWER KING

Roine used to be guitarist with Swedish band Kaipa, whose albums have just been re-released by Musea (and reviewed in earlier Feedbacks). Here Roine provides not only guitar and bass, but also keyboards and most of the lead vocals (as well as designing the sleeve). I was not quite sure what to expect, but it certainly was not the best rock album to come out of mainland Europe in 1994. There is just so much here for the melodic rock lover. The opening cut, the title track, has flowing guitar lines and a style that is reminiscent of Jadis (with melodic low-key vocals): it is so emotional, and lifts and swells the heart.

The first time (of many) that I played it I just could not believe what I was hearing. However, this album is far more than just one song. Roine's guitar playing is strangely like Steve Vai at times, especially with some of the sounds that he manages to coax from it. At times, you think that you are listening to 'Passion & Warfare'! However, Roine is no young copyist as he is nearly forty years old and has been recording for many years, and it is this wealth of experience that has enabled him to cut such a brilliant album. "Humanizzimo" is over twenty minutes long, but to my ears it is the closer "Scanning The Greenhouse" that typifies the album with great guitar, along with clear vocals. It gradually works its way back to the original theme and repeats the chorus from the title. Originally unavailable in the UK, GFT have had so many requests that they are now stocking it. What an album!
#27, Feb 1995

ROINE STOLT
WALL STREET VOODOO

Those looking for yet another prog workout from the leader of The Flower Kings are going to be in for something of a surprise here, as Roine has released an album that is far more steeply based in the blues. Of course, being Roine this still has his trademarks all over it so instead of being a straight blues album in the manner of classic Fleetwood Mac or Eric Clapton, it still contains quite a few elements of both prog and psyche. The other thing that makes one realise straight away that this is an album by Roine is that it is so long! One thing he can never be accused of is not trying to provide value for money as yet again this double CD is nearly two hours in length. Generally, this time it does seem to work, but even so a little judicious editing wouldn't go amiss. Neal Morse in one of a few guest artists on the album, providing some lead vocals and even some Hammond Organ, revisiting his old Transatlantic buddy. One of the songs that is interesting is the one cover on the album which is not some hoary old blues number but instead is the Joni Mitchell number "Sex Kills" which here is rocked up and, in some ways, is one of the straighter songs.

It is interesting to see Roine revisit his roots and trying to capture the style of music that got him interested in the guitar in the first place, but as with all of his work it is never straightforward although even with the complexity and styles being used, it is in many ways one of his simplest albums since 'The Flower King' itself. It should interest fans not only of The Flower Kings but also bring some new people in as well.
#86, Feb 2006

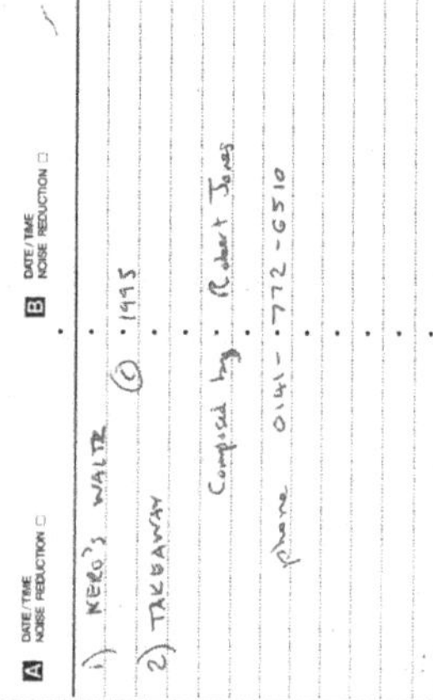

STRANGEBREW
DEMO
I have been sent two songs by Glaswegian band Strangebrew (actually they were called Eklexis when they sent them, but things change). What we have here are two dreamy numbers mixing together Pink Floyd and Jadis in a way that is quite good: I have certainly been sent far worse prog than this in the past. Of the two the second song "Takeaway" is the stronger and wouldn't sound out of place on a full-length CD. Strangebrew could have a lot to offer the prog set up in the UK, as they are coming at it from a slightly different angle to most of the bands, with more emphasis on dreaminess and moods. I will follow their future with interest.
#36, Aug 1996

STRANGEBREW
DEMO
I have heard again from Scots proggers Strangebrew, who appear to be developing at a very fast rate indeed. The three songs contained on the tape ("The Grind", "Baby" and "The Foxhunt") all show different aspects, with the first being a belting rocker, the second balladic, while the third is more prog. Mick Magic is going to release an 11-track cassette through Music & Elsewhere in January, while the guys are also looking at the possibility of a self-financed CD later in the year. With a 'live' drummer now on board, the future is looking very bright indeed.
#39, Jan 1997

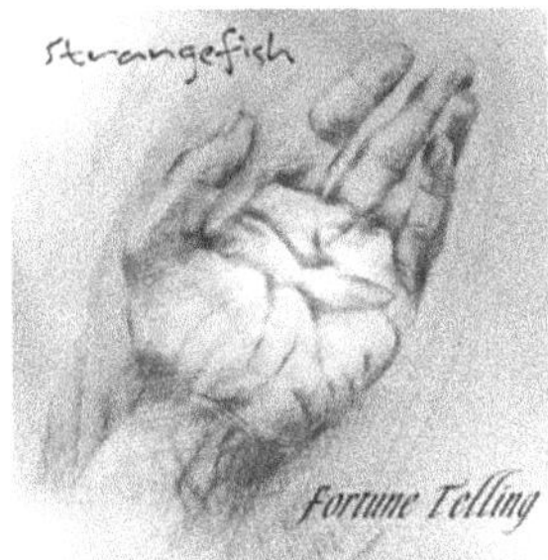

STRANGEFISH
FORTUNE TELLING

I must admit to being late in coming to Strangefish. I first came across them a few years ago when their debut album 'Full Scale' was released and CRS were going mad about them. However, it has taken until now for me to get in touch with the band so that I can see what all the fuss is about. This is a prog concept album with everything in it, from strong dynamics to gentle acoustic, from instrumental through softly sung passages and the result is something that is a pure delight from start to end. The basic story is about a person who wins instant riches on the lottery, but does it make him happy and how does he react to that realisation? Self-produced and released on their own label this is very much due to the band's own choice, as I am sure that there would be any number of record companies who would want to snap them up. There are times when there are glimpses of Genesis and at other more Floydian, but they are very much a band with their own sound and it is only the force of Steve Taylor's personality and his vocal talents that allow him to stay on top of the music. It is going to be hard pushed to find a better prog album coming out of the UK this year: these guys have put down a very firm line in the sand and progheads and lovers of good music really need to find out more about a great band.
#87, Apr 2006

STRANGERS ON A TRAIN
THE LABYRINTH

The colourful cover, care of Peter Nicholls (IQ), did not prepare me for the CD itself inside; make sure you have your dark glasses on when you open the box. It is only fitting that a CD of this stature has a well-presented booklet containing all the lyrics and yet more artwork. When this album is seen in the future as being a landmark release, it is only right that all aspects of the package are top grade. It really is a CD to get lost in, there is very limited use of drums or bass, relying at times just on stunning pianowork or gentle guitars providing the backing for two people singing like angels. There is just so much depth to the whole recording, it demands that you give it your full attention and pay it the respect it deserves. It is very unlike most other music around and is only like other Thin Ice material in the sense that it is top quality. It is strange to think that the album Karl recorded prior to this one was by Threshold and that could not be more different.

The periods of instrumentals are breath-taking, yet so are the vocals as Alan and Tracy sing as if they have shared a stage their whole lives. It is more like a classical piece divided into movements, than an album of songs, there is just so much to listen to and you must be prepared to do just that: once you start concentrating on the music the rest of the world seems to disappear. It is a soaring masterpiece that will be appreciated by lovers of all good music, going far beyond the normal boundaries of prog and sets a standard few can emulate. *#19, Aug 1993*

STRANGERS ON A TRAIN
THE KEY PART 1: THE PROPHECY

Well, here at last is the reissue of the very first SI release. For me the last SOAT album (part two of the trilogy) was one of my top five albums of 1993, so I have been eagerly awaiting the re-release, which features new artwork and some extra keyboards, as I hadn't heard the original. I was not disappointed. The line-up for the debut SOAT album was even more minimal than that for the second, with Tracy Hitchings on vocals, Clive Nolan providing keyboards, drum machine and backing vocals, and Karl Groom on guitars and basses. Like 'The Labyrinth', it is a unique mix of progressive rock and classical music in the firm control of someone who loves both. I have long been an admirer of Tracy's vocals, and when combined with the piano and orchestration of Clive and the fretwork of Karl the result is simply outstanding. There appears to be more instrumental passages on this album, probably because there was only one main vocalist, and it is not as rocky as the follow-up. Instead what we have is an album with lots of dynamic piano and the rest of the music interwoven around it. Classical? Certainly. Progressive? Definitely. It is an album that demands very careful listening to, and you will not go around whistling the tunes for a while, but is that so wrong? There are lighter passages, such as "Lightshow", where Clive takes a back seat to Tracy and Karl, but for me the highlight here is the piano work. There are few keyboard players around content to dispose of their computers and sequencers for the myriad of sounds at their disposal. Here Clive does it with ease, and as it is so rare it feels totally refreshing and new. So, if you enjoyed 'The Labyrinth' and have been awaiting the opportunity to get the first part of the trilogy then now is your chance. If instead you are wondering what all the fuss is about then now is the time to find out.

#22, Mar 1994

STREAM OF PASSION
EMBRACE THE STORM

Following on from his last Ayreon project, Arjen Lucassen decided to put a new band together using mostly unknown musicians; some of whom actually got an audition from contacting him through his website. In some ways Arjen took something of a back seat on the musical performance side as he only provides rhythm guitar, but he has created a band around the vocal talents of Marcela Bovio (who was herself an unknown before featuring on the last Ayreon work) which is dark and gothic yet is also light and powerful. At times this is dramatically heavy with the bass line often providing the foundation for the guitars, but Marcela's clear vocals go over the top or just cutting right through the music as they demand to be heard. In many ways, this is Arjen's most commercial project yet as the nearest comparison would probably be Evanescence, although it would probably be a bit harder to look for a hit single. This gothic style with strong female vocals does appear to be in fashion at present, and with this being a bloody good listen and fully enjoyable from first play, can only help it gaining attention. There

are times when it is overblown and over the top, just as it should be, while at others it is far more reflective but is always full of passion whilst containing myriad layers. The more this album is played then the more there is to hear, with some cracking guitar solos from Lori Linstruth contrasting well with delicate piano. Well worth hearing and worthy of investigation by anyone who enjoys strong rock numbers with a female singer.
#85, Nov 2005

THE STRING CHEESE INCIDENT
ONE STEP CLOSER

SCI should gain a medal for their name if nothing else. Apparently, they are part of the jam music scene in the States and they bring together loads of different styles from folk through bluegrass and jazz into melodic rock. What they remind me more of anything else is a version of The Band, but up to date. Then there is one more difference as well, the songs are not as good. When it works, and I think more important than anything else when the listener is in the right mood, then this is an album that is bringing together loads of different styles in a way that is quite different to much else around. When it does not work, or the listener is in the wrong frame of mind, then this is something that I thought had died thirty odd years ago, and with good reason. This is a group and album that will polarise opinion and is very different to other bands on the label. Producer Malcolm Burn (Bob Dylan, Emmylou Harris) has a strong pedigree so possibly he sees something here that I do not, but this is not something that I will be rushing to again. Of course, unless I am in the right frame of mind, in which case I may somehow find this indispensable.
#85, Nov 2005

ST 37
THE INSECT HOSPITAL

This 2003 release has only just come to my attention, and it is without doubt one of the strangest albums I have ever heard. It is dedicated to Rocky Erickson (Thirteenth Floor Elevators) and one of the four pages of the booklet is a photo of Rocky himself. Also, ST 37 covers his song "Cold Night For Alligators" along with Brian Eno's "Seven Deadly Finns". But what makes this album so strange is the sheer dichotomy between the lengthy instrumentals and the shorter songs. The opening song, "Solaris", is over thirteen minutes long, but the first five plus minutes of this is a looped piece of music with some strange effects added (the whole instrumental is thirteen minutes long). I could not make up my mind if they were trying to be early Pink Floyd but with far more menace and bleakness, or just something totally out of left field. What I can say with some certainty is that it is a very unsettling piece of music, which is hard to listen to, and is probably best described as being endured rather than enjoyed. Then "Land Of Treason", which comes across as a poorly recorded punk song from the Seventies, follows this. What on earth is going on?

By the time I listened to a track that was basically people talking over some backing music I was slowly losing the will to live but I decided that my masochistic tendencies were coming through and that I would listen to this album right to the end. But although Joy Division and Can (among others) appear as influences, this is not something that can be listened to when sober. There are two more lengthy instrumentals at the end, but they are no easier to listen to than anything else on the CD. I am sure that this will gain cult status among fans, but it is safe to say that I am not one of them.
#83, Mar 2005

SUBAUDITION
THE SCOPE
This is the debut album by the duo of Antti Korpinen (vocals, acoustic and electric guitars, piano) and Roope Niemelä (piano, electric guitars, bows, fretless bass, keyboards), and is extremely atmospheric. They have brought in a couple of musicians to help with woodwind, and the impression is of a music so delicate and fragile that it is like a spider's web – beautiful yet at any time something could come along and destroy it. When asked to describe their music Antti even manages to provide some confusion with the answer "Imagine a spring morning, how the mist intoxicates you as you walk towards the lake shore. The water surface is not covered but with a mere inch of ice. You think to yourself that any morning now the ice will be gone, the waters will be flowing boundlessly. As you inhale the cool spring air once again, you realise that the answer has been in plain sight all along - a moment of release". I know that this is delicately wondrous, and that if you are prepared to take the time to really listen to what you are hearing then you may get something quite magical out of this album. It is to be played at dusk, preferably outside, and then just let yourself drift away on the music and let you mind wander where it will. They have been compared to both Tenhi and Sigur Rós in the past, but for me I think that this is the sort of acoustic visual atmospheric music that rely does defy both comparison and description. Wonderful.
#88, Jun 2006

SUBSPACE RADIO
SUBSPACE RADIO
This is the debut album from Finnish band Subspace Radio and was released at the end of 2004 but has only just come to my attention. The band comprises Max Malin (drums), Juha Mattila (guitars, vocals), Teppo Nurminen (keyboards, vocals) and Jarkko Sarén (bass, lead vocals). They are mixing melodic rock with prog, and the music can be very layered at times with a lot going on. Although the guitar may be playing lines and blending in with the keyboards, it is not unusual for it to suddenly switch to power chords and the whole approach changes into something that is far rockier and attacking. The nearest I can think of describing it would be as if Rush were playing

something more along the lines of Spock's Beard but every so often Alex got fed up with what he was doing and started it crunching out. The result is music that is very powerful, and quite different to much of what is going on within the 'normal' prog scene. Jarkko has a pleasant enough voice and fits in well with the music. None of the tracks are very long, with all of them about six minutes long apart from closer "Home" which gets to just under nine. They describe the music themselves as "melodic, progressive influenced rock. Tight, and yet atmospheric and fluent, with respect for melodies and versatility, and with layered and cross-referencing structures". It is intense, with a wall of sound approach and the result is something that is both accessible and rocky and something that I have really enjoyed playing.
#87, Apr 2006

SUMMER INDOORS
THERE'S ORANGIE

I saw Summer Indoors at Whitchurch earlier in the year, and while they were okay, I did not think they were exceptional. I was quite surprised, as I was being led to believe that they were the greatest thing since sliced bread, and that they were going to fill the void left by the demise of It Bites. What we have here is the CD release of their second demo tape (with some extra material). It was heavily delayed for some reason and has now arrived some six months after it was due out. I have played this album a lot, trying to really get on with it. Summer Indoors utilise guitars a great deal, more than many of the bands currently covered by the "prog" banner, but not as heavy as Threshold, Freewill or Mentaur for example. The songs are commercial, but there seems to be something missing, and for the life of me I can't put my finger on it. What we have are ten songs, with a total running time of just over an hour. For the most part they are enjoyable (particularly the instrumental "Here It Is!"), but I do not honestly think it will set the world alight. Possibly too much guitar for the total proghead, and not enough for the rocker? Or is it the vocals? There again it may well be that I was not the right one to review this. All I know for certain is that there are many releases that will be getting more play on my deck than this.
#21, Jan 1994

SUMMER INDOORS
SONGS IN THE KEY OF H

Unlike many within the prog scene, I was not too keen on Summer Indoors' debut album 'There's Orangie'. I must confess that I am not sure whether this was due to the quality of the music or the fact that their appearance at Whitchurch, where they acted as if they were the only band worth considering and slagged off others, coloured my opinion. Certainly, I have not played their debut since I reviewed it but on the power of the new album, I may have to return to it and attempt to listen to it

with fresh ears. Summer Indoors are very much a guitar-oriented prog outfit, with overtones of It Bites and some of the songs are quite commercial, such as "Supersonic Hero", and work very well on all levels. True, the vocals of bassist Chris Dempsey are limited in range, but work well with the music. At the end of the album I found myself wondering if maybe they are not such bad chaps after all, and I had to play it again just to make sure. A few years ago, they were being talked about positively by many people, and after hearing 'Songs In The Key Of H' I must add my name to that number.
#30, Aug 1995

SUNSETH SPHERE
STORM BEFORE SILENCE
This powerful album demands to get close attention from progheads. The debut album from these Hungarians, signed to the Dutch Hammerheart label, which normally is associated to more extreme types of music, deserves wide exposure. They bring together many styles including Pink Floyd, The Gathering and Legend. In fact, when Kyrah is singing high and the music is racing on it is the closest I have ever heard anybody emulating Legend. The music can be almost melancholic and thoughtful, or frenetic and quick. It can wash over the listener or demand close attention. It is impossible to digest so many sounds and styles on just a few hearings; it must be played repeatedly to get the full benefit. It is not music just to play quietly; it must be listened to intently. It may suffer, as it is too proggy to gain many hard rock fans yet at the same time the rock element may be too much for the proghead, I hope not.
#64, Oct 2001

SVANN
GRANIA CZERNI I BIELI
This is an interesting album that I have been sent from Poland. The band site only appears to be working in Polish and I can't find anything out about either the band or album in a language that I can understand. So, at least that means that I do not have any preconceived ideas. There appear to be two female vocalists, who bounce off each other quite well, and the band move from a rock pop into almost prog metal at times. I think that it would be better if I could understand the lyrics, but here I should treat the vocals as an extra instrument. There are moments when the guitars kick off and the band starts to come alive yet at the same time, they can provide wonderfully emotive and carefully thought out moments of passion. I have no idea if this album is available in the UK but for those who want to listen to something that virtually no one else in the country has ever heard of, then visit the Rock Serwis site.
#74, Jun 2003

SYLVAN
X-RAYED
This is the fourth album from Sylvan but is the first that I have heard – if the others are anything like this one then I have been missing out. Here we have a band that while sitting within the progressive rock genre are one of those rare beasts, namely one that is trying to be progressive. Each song can be a journey through different styles within itself, let alone when comparing one to another. Radiohead are an obvious influence, but there is something more melodic about Sylvan although they have the space down to a tee. It is exciting music that also is very laid back, music that needs to be investigated and searched through, but the rewards are there to be heard. The more I played this album the more excited I became about it – there is just so much in here. Think Porcupine Tree, think IQ, even think Japan but most definitely think music that at times is quite different to anything else around. Listen to "Fearless" and one could imagine that this was the Chilli Peppers trying something different! The production is spot on, with each instrument clearly defined yet also part of an encompassing blanket of sound. When they want to rock, they can do so, but for the most part the guitars are held back. The result is one of the freshest and invigorating albums I have heard within the prog scene for some time. Progheads need to discover this.
#79, May 2004

SYLVAN
POSTHUMOUS SILENCE
Sylvan are back with their fifth album so date, their first concept. This is complex prog with many layers, and as one can guess from the title this is not going to be a bright bouncy piece of work. "It tells the story of a father, who discovers for the first time the life of his lost daughter through her diary. He gets to know the chains and fears, her search and the consequences of her actions. Those who let themselves drag deep into the story, will realise, that the life of the daughter is strongly correlated with our own fate and that the responsibility of the father is perhaps ours as well." This is one of those albums where it is a real shame that the promo is not a complete release as the only way to get the full strength and power of this album is by reading the lyrics and the stage descriptions saying what is happening, setting the scene. This is music that should be played repeatedly to get the most out of it and I can guarantee that any proghead who hears this will realise that Sylvan have outdone themselves this time and that this is even better than their last album 'X-Rayed'. Imagine some of the stylings of Muse mixed with Coldplay and then Floyd is brought into the mix with maybe some Jadis and a little bit of IQ with a larger dose of Marillion then you might, just might, get some idea of just what this album is about. But there again if you play this you will find that instead of being just a list of influences Sylvan are very much going their own way and creating new progressive music that is just that. Many critics are already calling this the album of the year. We are only halfway through, so I do believe that it is far too early

to comment like that, but I do know that this is a prog album of some importance that I am sure I am going to love more each time that I play it.
#88, Jun 2006

SYMPHONY X
V

No press release, but when an album is sub-titled 'The New Mythology Suite' there is a fair chance that it is a concept album. It is very ambitious with the use of orchestration, overpowering harmonies, complicated songs and melodies, and, um, I do not like it. Now if only I could put my finger on why that it is, then perhaps I would be in a better position to explain my feelings. In the end, all I can say is that the album makes me feel claustrophobic – it is all embracing, and I need a bit of spontaneity and freedom. Perhaps it is a mood thing but whenever I have tried to play it, I have felt the same way.
#61, Feb 2001

WITSEND
COSMOS AND CHAOS

SYZYGY
ALLEGORY OF LIGHT

Witsend were a band formed by three friends, Carl Baldasarre (guitar, mandolin, vocals), Sam Giunta (keyboards) and Paul Mihacevich (drums) who released their debut album in 1993. I do not think it made it to this side of the pond as I hadn't heard of it until recently, but it has just been reissued so is again available. Although Carl does sing on "Circadian Rhythm" (and a very pleasant voice he has too), this is an instrumental progressive rock band who are throwing everything into the mix. Sam provides bass on the keyboards with his left hand, so that is always basic, but the rest of the instruments are providing some extremely complex and powerful music. Focus on any of the three guys and the question should be asked as to why they are not more widely known – Paul's drumming is quite simply some of the best of any style that I have come across, and he provides a rhythmic background that is both stable and adventurous while Carl and Sam either interact or counterpoint what the other is doing. There just often is not any room for singing. This is music that any fans of 'traditional' prog such as ELP or Gentle Giant will be interested in, although there is very much a modern slab of bands like Jadis along with some guitar heroes such as Steve Vai.

Various questions should be asked about that album, such as why was not it more widely known and why on earth did it take them ten years to record the follow-up? (Okay, so they now have nine children between them, so they were probably busy with other things). When they came to release the new album, they found that another band were now called Witsend, and as they hadn't copyrighted the name had to pick another and they decided to be known as Syzygy. Of course, to add to the confusion the second album is called 'Allegory Of Light', while on the cover it states 'M.O.T.H.' which is the first part of the three-song cycle, "Allegory Of Light". Making sense?

It may be somewhat confusing, but this is an album that is certainly worth the effort of trying to work out what is going on. They may not have been recording in the intervening years, but they certainly have stayed practicing so that in many ways this album is even more complex than the debut. Again, the concentration is on instrumentals, but the vocals such as on "M.O.T.H." show a very different side to the band. They have a skill that allows them to pursue a style of music and be masters of it. Sam is more to the forefront on this album, but Carl's guitars still often lead the music while Paul's drumming is again a revelation. Any prog or instrumental music fans ought to seek this band out. As the last album was released in 2003 hopefully we should have a third inside the next eight years and I know that I will be awaiting that eagerly. As an aside, I also ought to compliment the band, as the press pack they sent was the best independent pack I have seen in many years.

Syzygy is certainly not a name on everyone's lips but if you are a proghead (and many of you are), then this is a 'new' band to discover.
#83, Mar 2005

Robert Newton Calvert: Born 9 March 1945, Died 14 August 1988 after suffering a heart attack. Contributed poetry, lyrics and vocals to legendary space rock band Hawkwind intermittently on five of their most critically acclaimed albums, including Space Ritual (1973), Quark, Strangeness & Charm (1977) and Hawklords (1978). He also recorded a number of solo albums in the mid 1970s. CENTIGRADE 232 was Robert Calvert's first collection of poems.

Hype 'And now, for all you speeding street smarties out there, the one you've all been waiting for, the one that'll pierce your laid back ears, decoke your sinuses, cut clean thru the schlock rock, MOR/crossover, techno flash mind mush. It's the new Number One with a bullet … with a bullet … It's Tom, Supernova, Mahler with a pan galactic biggie …' And the Hype goes on. And on. Hype, an amphetamine hit of a story by Hawkwind collaborator Robert Calvert. Who's been there and made it back again. The debriefing session starts here.

Rick Wakeman is the world's most unusual rock star, a genius who has pushed back the barriers of electronic rock. He has had some of the world's top orchestras perform his music, has owned eight Rolls Royces at one time, and has broken all the rules of composing and horrified his tutors at the Royal College of Music. Yet he has delighted his millions of fans. This frank book, authorised by Wakeman himself, tells the moving tale of his larger than life career.

There are nine Henrys, pur ported to be the world's first cloned cartoon charac ter. They live in a strange lo fi domestic surrealist world peopled by talking rock buns and elephants on wobbly stilts.

They mooch around in their minimalist universe suffer ing from an existential crisis with some genetically modified humour thrown in.

Marty Wilde on Terry Dene: "Whatever happened to Terry becomes a great deal more comprehensible as you read of the callous way in which he was treated by people who should have known better many of whom, frankly, will never know better of the sad little shadows of the past who eased themselves into Terry's life, took everything they could get and, when it seemed that all was lost, quietly left him ... Dan Wood ing's book tells it all."

Rick Wakeman: "There have always been certain 'careers' that have fascinated the public, newspapers, and the media in general. Such include musicians, actors, sportsmen, police, and not surprisingly, the people who give the police their employ ment: The criminal. For the man in the street, all these careers have one thing in common: they are seemingly beyond both his reach and, in many cases, understanding and as such, his only associ ation can be through the media of newspapers or tele vision. The police, however, will always require the ser vices of the grass, the squealer, the snitch, (call him what you will), in order to assist in their investiga tions and arrests; and amaz ingly, this is the area that seldom gets written about."

Bill Harkleroad joined Captain Beefheart's Magic Band at a time when they were changing from a straight ahead blues band into something completely different. Through the vision of Don Van Vliet (Captain Beefheart) they created a new form of music which many at the time considered atonal and difficult, but which over the years has continued to exert a powerful influence. Beefheart rechristened Harkleroad as Zoot Horn Rollo, and they embarked on recording one of the classic rock albums of all time Trout Mask Replica - a work of unequalled daring and inventiveness.

Politics, paganism and .... Vlad the Impaler. Selected stories from CJ Stone from 2003 to the present. Meet Ivor Coles, a British Tommy killed in action in September 1915, lost, and then found again. Visit Mothers Club in Erdington, the best psychedelic music club in the UK in the '60s. Celebrate Robin Hood's Day and find out what a huckleduckle is. Travel to Stonehenge at the Summer Solstice and carouse with the hippies. Find out what a Ranter is, and why CJ Stone thinks that he's one. Take LSD with Dr Lilly, the psychedelic scientist. Meet a headless soldier or the ghost of Elvis Presley in Gabalfa, Cardiff. Journey to Whitstable, to New York, to Malta and to Transylvania, and to many other places, real and imagined, political and spiritual, transcendent and mundane. As The Independent says, Chris is "The best guide to the underground since Charon ferried dead souls across the Styx."

This is is the first in the highly acclaimed vampire novels of the late Mick Farren. Victor Renquist, a surprisingly urbane and likable leader of a colony of vampires which has existed for centuries in New York is faced with both administrative and emotional problems. And when you are a vampire, administration is not a thing which one takes lightly.

"The person, be it gentleman or lady, who has not pleasure in a good novel, must be intolerably stupid."

Jane Austen

Lightning Source UK Ltd.
Milton Keynes UK
UKHW051535220722
406228UK00002B/12